O_h M_y G_{oat!}

Just how intelligent
are the animals we eat?

SHANE GEHLERT
Drawings and photos by the author

For my favourite animals: Crissy and Rachael
and for all the animals I was fortunate enough to call
friends and companions.

First published in 2025 by Capra Books
This Edition published in 2025 by Capra Books

Capra
Books

Contents

Introduction

The break looked ominous, the hoof dangling from the front leg of its hapless owner like a piece of limp spaghetti. The hoof in question belonged to Rosie, an 8-month-old mixed miniature goat, who inadvertently decided Friday afternoon would be an opportune time to break the said appendage. Livestock animals have impeccable timing, usually selecting the most inopportune occasions, like weekends or after vet hours, to fall ill, injure themselves or generally do stupid things. However, a call to our long-suffering vet offered some encouragement, agreeing to see her even though it was late in the day. X-rays revealed a clean break, which was reassuring as a compound fracture would likely mean a one-way trip to the forever pasture. The following day, the vet set a cast on the gammy limb, after which Rosie then became a very spoiled house goat, spending the next six weeks in a small enclosure next to our back door, fed on a steady diet of carrot treats until the cast was removed.

That evening, whilst cooking dinner (I'm the delegated cook in our house), a thought suddenly struck me. Staring down at the sizzling pork chops, crackling and popping in the frypan, I wondered why I felt nothing for the animal that died for my dinner, yet I felt compassion for the injured goat. Whilst shopping, did the thought ever cross my mind that this was once a living, breathing creature? Did I even consider how the pig was farmed? Did the animal spend its life in a stall or free range in a field and experience a good life? Tightly bound in glossy plastic and labelled as loin chops, the attractive packaging on the supermarket shelf obscured any evidence that it was once a living, breathing, highly social creature.

Ironically, the pork chops in question cost around ten dollars, but the goat trauma exercise ended up costing $600. Surely, pigs are more intelligent than goats?

Ruminating over these ruminants set the wheels in motion to explore just how intelligent the animals we often consider as food are. I know from my own personal experience around pets and farm animals that they possess high levels of intelligence, but that also makes me biased. Yet despite that knowledge, I continue to eat meat, enjoying lamb chops, steak and chicken, even though we raise our own chickens and goats. This forced me to examine not only my own beliefs and motivations, but also what influences other people's relationships to animals. For instance, why do we spend considerable amounts of money keeping pets, grooming, walking, photographing, showing them, making videos of their entertaining antics, yet rarely consider the cooked animals we stuff in our pie hole? And have no illusions, humans are very good at stuffing vast quantities of an array of cooked animals into our mouths!

As I began researching how much meat humans consume, I was gobsmacked by what I found. Homo sapiens collectively munch their way through millions of kilograms of meat each year, consuming vast amounts of poultry, fish, and red meat. Australians consumed an average of 134 kilograms of meat per person in 2021, with chicken representing the most popular meat at 49 kg. Most poultry birds have an average weight of 2kg, so that's roughly 24 whole chooks (Australian slang for chicken) per person per year! Not to be outdone, the USA came in at 149 kilograms per person, consuming a whopping 58 kilograms of chicken meat per person. [1] However, meat production and consumption on an industrial scale, sadly, is not limited solely to domesticated farm animals.

Eating the National Emblem

The Australian emu is a majestic giant flightless bird that stands around five feet tall and is iconically Australia's native chook, well, not actually a chook but a *ratite* of the order *Dromaius*. Together with the celebrated kangaroo, the emu adorns the national emblem, the Australian coat of arms. Both animals were selected for their iconic status and inability to walk backwards, symbolising a nation that continuously moves forward. Ironically, in Australia, we also eat our national emblem!

Emus were touted as the next big thing in farming in the early 1990s, and many farmers invested heavily in the giant birds, betting the farm on the high-quality meat, leather, oil and feathers from the birds. In 1996, there were around 500 emu farmers across Australia, some farms with thousands of emus, but the industry spectacularly collapsed, not living up to the hype espoused, and by 2018, only 12 emu farms were remaining. [2] Kangaroos have fared considerably worse, with the 'harvesting' of kangaroos an ongoing industry. Grazing practices, which often provide plentiful water supplies for livestock, also offer feed and water to kangaroo populations, meaning that populations can sometimes explode. What's seen as a solution is to selectively harvest kangaroos through an allocated quota system. The 2019 macropod (kangaroo) quotas and commercial harvest for NSW, QLD, SA and WA were 1.5 million. That's one and a half million kangaroos slaughtered for pet food, human consumption and pest reduction in a year.[3,4] It is an odd way to treat a country's national emblem.

Moral Jujitsu

What lies behind our ability to compartmentalise our beliefs, to celebrate two unique animals on a nation's emblem, yet treat them both so appallingly? As humans, we tend to be kind and benevolent to some animals, yet cold and indifferent to others, seeing them simply as food or a product. Aside from our coat of arms, kangaroos are one of Australia's most famous tourist drawcards, alongside the 'cute and cuddly' koala. Tourists pose for photos with kangaroos in enclosed zoos and nature reserves, where they can purchase kangaroo souvenirs and plush, cuddly toys as mementos. Many children's books and cartoons feature kangaroos as characters; one of Australian TV's most famous kangaroos was undoubtedly Skippy. A small eastern grey kangaroo, Skippy, possessed human-like powers of perception and often assisted her sidekick, Sonny, in foiling the bad guys and saving the day. The irony is not lost on the fact that several large Australian supermarket chains feature kangaroo sausages, steak, and mincemeat, with kangaroo meat being a popular pet food in Australia for dogs and cats. Heck, I was even in a big city tourist souvenir shop recently and saw a display stand of kangaroo paw backscratchers and kangaroo testicle bottle openers!

Therein lies another paradox: we import a mammal (sheep) into a continent that for millions of years contained only marsupials (kangaroos, wallabies, koalas, etc.), then cull the marsupials because they compete with the foreign animals and feed their carcasses to another pair of imported pests. As much as we love our dogs and cats, they have contributed significantly to the decline and extinction of many species in Australia, particularly due to the ruthless efficiency of the feral cat. Yet despite the toll that rogue moggies take on local birds and small mammals, we still place immense value on our fully imported pets, investing vast amounts of time, money, and affection in an animal we often consider part of the family. The pet business in Western countries is a multibillion-dollar industry, supplying every conceivable pet accessory imaginable to a vast array of diverse animals we consider pets.

Of course, this is nothing new; the desire to care for and interact with an intelligent and emotional being that is different from our own species has persisted since recorded and ancient history. Some of the earliest evidence of our bond with animals comes from mid-Neolithic burial sites, where dogs are interred with their masters, a common practice in Europe some 4,000 years ago, indicating a desire to share the afterlife with another non-human, sentient being.[5] Animals were also highly prized and respected in ancient Egypt, with the frequency and variety of animal depictions in art and hieroglyphics unrivalled anywhere in the world. The last millennium BC witnessed a proliferation of animal mummification in Egyptian society. Cats, dogs, monkeys, crocodiles, and fish were commonly wrapped, tarred, and interred both as eternal companions for the afterlife and as representations of deities.[6]

These ancient societies viewed animals as essential sources of food, a conduit to deities and spirits, and companionship. One could then argue that these early societies likely believed that animals possess the ability to experience pain or pleasure, that is, to be *sentient*. Most non-human animals exhibit evidence of sentience, experiencing pain and pleasure, and many demonstrate an extensive repertoire of emotions. There is also compelling evidence that many animals exhibit levels of consciousness, including the ability to think, reason, and be self-aware.

So profound is this evidence that in 2012, following a conference at Churchill College, University of Cambridge, a foremost group of international neuroscientists came together to write *The Cambridge Declaration on Consciousness in Non-Human Animals*, which declares:

> *"The absence of a neocortex does not appear to preclude an organism from experiencing affective states. Convergent evidence indicates that non-human animals have the neuroanatomical, neurochemical, and neurophysiological substrates of conscious states along with the capacity to exhibit intentional behaviours. Consequently, the weight of evidence indicates that humans are not unique in possessing the neurological substrates that generate consciousness. Non-human animals, including all mammals and birds, and many other creatures, in-*

cluding octopuses†, also possess these neurological substrates." [7]

In short, animals do not need a human-like neocortex in order to feel emotions or be conscious, possessing brain structures necessary for consciousness and intentional behaviour, much like humans. Often, the behaviour an animal exhibits can be so human-like that it leads to *anthropomorphism,* whereby we attribute human traits, often erroneously, to animals. The dog that looks 'guilty' for tearing up the pillow, the cat that shows disgust at the strange-smelling food or is plotting the demise of the dog and its owner. Dogs dressed up in outfits or sitting in strollers or prams are classic cases of anthropomorphising what is essentially a genetically modified wolf and transforming it into a 'fur kid'! Perhaps anthropomorphism explains why spending time around farm animals leads to noticing human-like traits in those animals, often wrongly anthropomorphising them.

Small farms or 'hobby farmers know how quickly livestock can cross the boundary of a food animal and transform into a pet. It is a common practice not to name a farm animal that you intend to eat one day! I gave up naming our laying hens after having to dispatch so many when they reach the end of their short, artificially selected lives. It would also seem that we are able to morally disengage from the idea that our beloved pets also escape and cause immense damage to native wildlife. We also disengage from the idea that an animal can be intelligent and sentient, transforming that creature into an 'essential' commodity called food.

De-farming Us

A disturbing poll conducted by the Australian National Farmers Federation (NFF) in 2017 found that 83% of Australians described their relationship with farms or farming as 'distant' or 'non-existent', alarming figures according to the President of the NFF, Fiona Simson.[8] Agriculture is essential to the meals on our plates and the fibre on our backs, and despite rapid urbanisation, should not be "out of sight, out of mind", explained Simson.

Fifty years ago, most Finns had friends or relatives on farms, with Finland's long history of farming dating back nearly 4000 years.[9] However, Finland followed the same process of transition to industrialised farming in the 1950s-1970s as many other Western countries. The number of farms declined significantly, resulting in a current generation of children who have little or no contact with farms and a somewhat naïve, romanticised image of farming practices.

America, too, followed this industrialised pathway, with the 'mom and pop' farms either swallowed up by large corporations or disappearing under new housing developments, explained David Robinson Simon.[10] Even as demand for dairy products grew exponentially between 1954 and 2007, the number of US dairy farms decreased from around 2.9 million to just 65,000, with 99% of animals raised in concrete and steel factories.

In Australia, the growth of cities, towns, and suburbs since the post-war boom period of the 1950s, coupled with the increasing industrialisation and automation of farms, has led to an unprecedented disconnect between people living in rural and urban areas. Amy Lawton and Nicky Morrison of Western Sydney University described that over the last decade, the world's population has become more urban than rural, which in Australia has led to rapid expansion into peri-urban areas.[11] Heavily driven by market forces and the insatiable desire for more housing, residential land has become a more valuable commodity than rural land, leading to a 66% loss in land classified as 'primary production' in the Greater Western Sydney area alone.

Dairy farms once dotted the landscape around Brisbane, a city with a population of approximately 2.8 million people. In 1910, there were 3,353 commercial dairies on the Darling Downs, an area west of Brisbane, with around 85,000 cows. The current population of cows is marginally less at 70,000; however, there are now only around 240 farms according to the Qld Farmers Federation. Greater distances between farms and urban and peri-urban areas mean that many children grow up with little or no contact with a farm or its animals, remaining oblivious to how milk is produced, how eggs are made, or where the lamb chops they enjoy come from.

The downsizing of the iconic 'quarter-acre block' (1,000 sq m), a relic of post-war Australia, has seen land sizes shrink incrementally over the last several decades as new land releases have dwindled and population growth has increased. This makes it nearly impossible for someone to grow vegetables, own an average-sized dog, or have a few backyard chickens, especially on a 200-square-metre block that consists mostly of a house.

Urban sprawl has intensified the disconnect between us and farming, as well as between us and nature, with land clearing often decimating populations of native creatures. This means that chance encounters with these animals are rare and sometimes terrifying for the uninitiated. My spouse and I are fortunate enough to live on the verge of native Australian bushland and have become accustomed to the comings and goings of native animals. Giant lace monitors (*Varanus varius*), commonly known as goannas, often invade our chook pen. They have never harmed the chooks; they are simply there for the eggs, which, if we are too slow to collect, end up as goanna breakfast. This is not a problem, just an animal we share our environment with, like the coastal carpet pythons that live in our roof. The pythons are non-venomous constrictors and mostly keep to themselves, whilst also keeping down the rodent population. One year, a rather large python, around 10 feet long, spent more time than usual hanging around the house. Turns out it was after the mother-in-law's small dog, whom we were pet-sitting! Increased contact with native animals that surround us reduces fears and false conceptions about these creatures, fostering a greater appreciation for the animals with which we coexist.

In the Netherlands, there is a Dutch term, *Koeknuffelen,* which literally means 'cow cuddling', where in a strange and heartwarming tradition, people travel from the cities to the countryside to spend time around farm animals. The Dutch have long known of the physiological and psychological benefits of *Koeknuffelen,* allowing people to de-stress and recalibrate emotionally.[12] Perhaps we could all do with a bit of *Koeknuffelen* from time to time!

The Meatropocene

Farming has also played a significant role in the transformation of the animals that now inhabit our planet. We live in a new epoch, dubbed the Anthropocene, formally known as the Holocene period (*from the Greek meaning 'whole' and 'new'*), which began 11,700 years ago with the end of the last ice age. What differentiates the Anthropocene from the Holocene is the dramatic effect humans have had on the planet's climate, environmental change and biodiversity loss.[13] The Anthropocene precipitated a large-scale shift from a hunter-gatherer culture to an agrarian culture, known as the Agricultural Revolution, which in turn led to a gradual but dramatic decline in the number of wild animals that now inhabit our planet. Yuval Noah Harari, in his book *Homo Deus*, goes so far as to say that a single species of ape, *Homo Sapiens*, has so fundamentally changed the global ecosystem in a mere 70,000 years that the impact may surpass that of the Chicxulub asteroid that annihilated the dinosaurs.[14] As of 2015, wild mammals (land and marine) comprised only 4% of the Earth's biomass. Humans comprised 34%, and which one took first prize? You guessed it... cows. Livestock make up a massive 62% of the total global biomass, with cows winning first place at 35%, closely followed by pigs (12%), buffalo (5%) and sheep and goats (3% each). Amazingly, the biomass of poultry (71%) far outweighs that of wild birds (29%). [15] In fact, if you took all the chickens in China and stacked them on top of each other, they would extend to the moon and back twice. (6 billion chickens, average height 25cm/ 384,400km to the moon = 1.5 billion chickens there and 1.5 back x twice). China's population in 2022 was 1.4 billion, and its chook population was 6 billion, around four chooks for every person (CPP), similar to both the USA (4.8 CPP) and Australia's (4.2 CPP). One wonders if aliens did visit Earth; they might be tempted to call it Planet Chook and ask to speak to the supreme rooster.

The staggering environmental cost of maintaining this bovine and poultry biomass is immense and largely unsustainable. Eleanor Slade and Paul Manning, in their TED.com animation, explain that each day, the animal kingdom generates enough poop to equal the water volume flowing over Victoria Falls. [16] They go on to explain how the humble dung beetle eats, tunnels and buries the poop into the soil, saving us from being knee-deep in dung!

Not only do cows produce the most poop of the domestic livestock, but beef also has the lowest protein conversion efficiency ratio at 3.8%, compared to eggs at 25%, requiring 25 kilograms of feed to produce just 1kg of beef and around 50-70 litres of water a day to thrive. [17] With animal production increasing exponentially over the last century and developing economies becoming wealthier, the demand for meat as a source of protein will likely continue unabated. Perhaps we should call this era the Meatropocene rather than the Anthropocene!

But how should we view domestic and 'livestock' animals? Merely by their utility, as a commodity, a necessity, or as sentient beings who think and have rich emotional lives? To give an insight into how our ancestors may have viewed animals and their intelligence and agency, traditional societies, such as hunter-gatherers, offer the best clues. Peter Sutton, who lived periodically with the traditional Wik people of Cape York, Australia, describes how the Wik people frowned upon treating resources carelessly. A freshly killed animal was spoken to with empathy, often accompanied by tones of regret and pity. Even the remains of eaten flying foxes are systematically laid out on bark and disposed of carefully. [18] However, numerous traditional societies display an ambivalence toward their prey, with little empathy displayed for prey animals killed for survival needs. In a study examining 28 ethnographic groups of hunter-gatherers, ranging from the Hadza of East Africa to the Tiwi of northern Australia, Barton Thompson of Albright College, Pennsylvania, found low levels of sympathy for prey animals in almost all these groups.[19] However, if the animal was perceived as having pseudo-spiritual associations or human-like traits or qualities, then the agency was attributed to that animal and greater respect, concern and sympathy were shown. Once again, the animal's utility comes to the fore, seen as both a food source and a connection to a spiritual realm.

Modern Western culture also tends to view animals, through their utility, as simple commodities: food animals are simply 'livestock', labour is provided by animals such as sniffer dogs, pack horses, and lab rats, while pets are companions and best friends. And yet we also anthropomorphise animals, attributing humanlike characteristics to their behaviour; we differentiate them based on cuteness and relegate them to levels of importance based on perceived intelligence. We battle cognitive dissonance and buffer our identities by 'virtue signalling' our good intentions on social media. It is a strange situation we have with the fellow creatures we share this planet with. Evidence from hunter-gatherer societies suggests that we are innately predisposed to be indifferent to animals; however, the question, albeit a moral and ethical one, is whether we should be indifferent.

It is not my intention to ask or attempt to answer difficult moral and ethical questions; my education is in psychology, not philosophy. Throughout the book, I will try to illustrate how humans have divided themselves from animals, what intelligence is, how it is measured in humans and animals, how goats, sheep, chickens, cows, and pigs fare in the brain department, and what it all means. Lastly, I will attempt to unravel why we eat animals, the stories we tell ourselves to justify it, and how industrial farming practices are affecting us and the planet, and why we should perhaps consider eating less meat.

I will conclude with some disturbing facts and figures that lend weight to the concept of the *Meatropocene*.

In 2021, the US Meat and Poultry industry produced 27.95 billion pounds (12.67 billion kilograms) of beef or the equivalent weight of 70,000 Boeing 747 aircraft![1]
Global meat production in 2023 amounted to 370 million tonnes. Poultry production totalled 50 billion pounds, or 22.7 billion kilograms, the equivalent weight of 16,667,000 cars or 125,000 blue whales![19]

Number of animals slaughtered each year worldwide

Chickens	1961- 6.6 *billion*	2023 - 76 *billion*
Cows	1961: 173 million	2023: 309 million
Pigs	1961: 376 million	2023: 1.51 *billion*
Goats	1961: 102 million	2023: 550 million

Number of Live Animals per Country 2023

Number of cattle in Australia	29 million
Number of chickens in Australia	109 million
Number of cattle in Brazil	238 million
Number of chickens in China	5.2 *billion*
Number of pigs in China	434 million

Source: Ourworldindata.org

Us and them

With his god-like intellect which has penetrated into the movements and constitution of the solar system—with all these exalted powers— Man still bears in his bodily frame the indelible stamp of his lowly origin.

Charles Darwin, *The Descent of Man*

In the Beginning

No one likes to be made a monkey of, which is made apparent by the considerable time and energy humans have spent throughout history separating ourselves from our mammalian ancestors as the 'superior' beings, dominating and controlling the wild beasts of the earth. This is made abundantly clear in the Biblical creation story.

> *God said unto them, be fruitful, and multiply, and replenish the earth, and subdue it: and have dominion over the fish of the sea, and over the fowl of the air, and over every living thing that moveth upon the earth", Genesis 1:28.* [1]

Subdue in the original Hebrew text is 'Kavash', a verb meaning to bring into bondage, in Aramaic: to tread down. 'Radah' (Hebrew) translates as 'have dominion, dominate or rule.'

Thomas Aquinas, in the *Summa Theologica*, 1265-1274, wrote:

Wherefore, as man, being made to the image of God, is above other animals, these are rightly subject to his government.

He further described

From this it follows that even the souls of brute animals are subsistent. But Aristotle held that of the operations of the soul, understanding alone is performed without a corporeal organ.

Subsistent being a soul that exists separately from the body, and as animals are 'sensitive' creatures bound only by bodily reactions, they are devoid of a soul. The reference to Aristotle aligns with the belief that only the 'intellectual soul' can operate without a corporeal organ (body), the thinking and reasoning of man subsistent, and the brutish animals purely reactionary. In fact, the Greek philosophical tradition was perhaps the earliest recorded attempt to describe the divide between 'us and them'.

The Philosophic Phaedo

The classical period in Greece marked the height of art, culture, philosophy, and science. The philosophical tradition attempted to make sense of the world through a lens of reason, as opposed to mythology, superstition, and magical thinking. No doubt Socrates (469 BCE) is the father of Western philosophy, renowned for the so-called Socratic paradoxes, such as 'virtue is knowledge', 'an unexamined life is not worth living', and 'harming another is more shameful and worse for the wrongdoer'.[2] Socrates never documented his teachings; most recorded wisdom came from his pupils, Xenophon and Plato. His work went on to influence generations of scholars, notably Plato, Xenophon, the Stoics, the Cynics, the Sceptics, and Aristotle.

Aristotle was arguably the most famous of Plato's students (384–322 BCE). Aristotle's treatise 'On the Soul' (350 BC) is one of the earliest works to explore differences between animals and humans in a philosophical and scientific form.[3] Aristotle divided souls into three groups: nutritive, sensitive and rational. Nutritive souls are found in all living things and are responsible for the basic functions of nutrition, growth and reproduction. Sensitive souls are found in both animals and humans and are characterised by basic sensations, perception, and movement. Rational souls, however, are only found in humans and relate to deliberate and rational thought and imagination. Aristotle discriminates the senses from imagination, describing sense as a 'faculty' or an 'activity', such as sight and seeing, and that imagination can take place regardless of sense. Humans are distinct from animals in that they possess both practical and speculative thinking, enabling them to reason, deliberate, and plan for the future. In contrast, animals having 'sensitive souls' act by instinct and lack planning and imagination.[4] *Historia Animalium* (the history of animals) is an early attempt by Aristotle at the classification and taxonomy of the animal kingdom, which continues an anthropocentric theme, further outlining man's superiority to animals with gems of wisdom such as 'man being the most erect animal, the only one whose body points toward the universe.' [5]

Historia Animalium further influenced metaphysical and philosophical thinking, inspiring the medieval concept of 'the great chain of being', which illustrates a divinely ordered hierarchical structure of all matter and life. [6] The chain places God consecutively at the peak, followed by angels, humanity, animals, plants, and minerals, an unbroken, finely graduated continuum from the least complex to the *ens per-fectissimum,* the 'highest form of creature'. Indeed, the great chain inspired Carl Linnaeus, the father of modern taxonomy, to produce 'Systema Naturae' in 1735, which introduced binomial naming (two words) into the nomenclature, for example, *Homo Sapiens.* [7] The great chain remained unbroken well into the 18th century, permeating the philosophical, religious and scientific traditions, firmly cementing the divide between homo sapiens and other mammals.

Descartes

Complex machines or 'automata', devoid of a rational soul or consciousness, were how French philosopher, scientist and mathematician René Descartes described animals. Descartes' seminal work *Discourse on the Method*, written in 1637, describes his theories of *mind-body dualism,* where the mind is 'res cogitans' or a non-material thinking substance and the body 'res extensa' is a material extended substance. [8] Descartes used the term 'animal spirits' to explain bodily functions, describing a subtle wind or flame that rises from the heart to the brain, passing through nerves into muscles, which then causes movement. In terms of emotions, these were 'passions of the soul' that differ from other thoughts as being associated perceptions, feelings, or emotions of the soul, which are

13

generated, sustained, and strengthened by some movement of the spirits.[9] With such a rigid, deterministic way of philosophical reasoning of the time, there was little, if any, ethical regard given to animals, as they were considered devoid of a soul and, therefore, incapable of emotions.

Bentham

> *Nature has placed mankind under the governance of two sovereign masters, pain and pleasure. It is for them alone to point out what we ought to do, as well as to determine what we shall do. On the one hand the standard of right and wrong on the other the chain.* [10]

Fast forward 140 years, and English philosopher and the founding father of classical utilitarianism, Jeremy Bentham (1747-1832), laid the groundwork for future animal rights and animal liberation movements. This seems somewhat unusual coming from an individual who once labelled natural human rights as "nonsense on stilts". [11] In Bentham's defence, this was his scathing criticism of the *Declaration of Rights of Man and Citizen,* a mere six weeks after the French Revolution and referred to natural and inalienable rights afforded to all people that exist outside of law, something Bentham deemed dangerous. The above quote, *two sovereign masters, pain and pleasure,* was Bentham's opening statement in the Introduction to the *Principles of Morals and Legislation* (IPML). Bentham's 'maximising utility', or the concept that 'right' actions are contingent on whether they promote happiness or pleasure, was quantified by the 'felicific calculus', whereby the totals of pleasure and pain are weighed against the outcome. Though mainly attributed to human pain and pleasure, Bentham intimated that this should be universally applied to all sentient beings.

> *The question is not, can they reason? Nor can they talk? But can they suffer?*

The above quote is often used by animal activists and ethicists to portray Bentham's stance on animal rights; however, Johannes Kniess of Princeton University argued that the statement was also merely a footnote in the IPML and does not provide a full account of Bentham's thoughts on animal ethics.[12] Kniess explained that although primarily opposed to the mistreatment of animals, Bentham had no problem with them being killed or suffering as long as the act was considered to maximise utility and *felicific calculus.* [12] Although Bentham showed a clear fondness for animals throughout his life, much of his views on animal welfare were based on logically driven philosophy. In Chapter V: *Pleasures and Pains, Their Kinds,* Bentham describes various pleasures and pains of life in regard to wealth, benevolence, memory, imagination and pleasures of the senses. The latter suggests that animals, like humans, are sentient beings. However, unpublished works intended to form part of Bentham's Penal Code suggest that animal cruelty should be punished by law; other writings imply that Bentham had no problem with the killing and eating of animals, with suffering justified in the animal's demise if it served a useful human purpose. [12]

When it came time for his own eventual demise, Benthem left strict instructions for handling his earthly remains, which were carried out to the letter in 1832. Bentham's remains were publicly dissected, then preserved as an 'auto-icon', propped up in his favourite chair, whereby the skeleton was preserved and dressed in his usual attire, stuffed with straw padding [13] Benson's actual head was preserved initially but looked so gruesome that it was decided a wax head would replace it, and the preserved head was placed next to the body in a glass cabinet. To this day, Bentham remains in his auto-icon near the entrance of the University College London, minus his actual head, which was removed after several prank kidnappings by students. Bentham was, however, moved briefly in 2013 to attend a university Council meeting. [14] Rightly or wrongly, Bentham made a significant step forward in understanding animal intelligence and facilitating more humane treatment of animals.

Hume

> And no truth appears to me more evident, than that beasts are endow'd with thought and reason as well as men. The arguments are in this case so obvious, that they never escape the most stupid and ignorant". An Enquiry Concerning Human Understanding, 1748 [15].

David Hume was regarded as one of the most important figures of the Scottish Enlightenment, a prominent philosopher, historian and economist. [16] Hume argued that animals and humans share the same basic "psychological mechanism". Hume proposed that animals possess systems of thought and reasoning similar to those of humans, performing actions directed towards self-preservation and pleasure. Hume also likened instinct in animals to reasoning in humans, one driven by past experiences and observations. "Reason is nothing but a wonderful and unintelligible instinct in our souls, which carries us along a certain train of ideas." [15]

Nietzsche

Observe the herd as it grazes past you: it cannot distinguish yesterday from today, leaps about, eats, sleeps, digests, leaps some more, and carries on like this from morning to night and from day to day, tethered by the short leash of its pleasures and displeasures to the stake of the moment, and thus it is neither melancholy nor bored. The Utility and Liability of History (1874). [17]

Nietzsche went on to describe how animals live "ahistorically," disappearing into the present, unburdened by boredom or melancholy, as they live in the moment. This is an existence that humans envy, one that allows them to escape the weight of the past. In *What Was It Like to Be a Cow?* Erica Fudge describes that, rather than confirming the ahistorical nature of Nietzsche's view on animals, having no concept of past, present, or future, it is possible to view animals as possessing their own culture, history, and traditions, dynamically constructing their own world, much as humans do. [18]

Darwin

By the mid-1800s, the hard-nosed attitudes that animals were soulless creatures devoid of emotion began to soften. The publication of *On the Origin of Species* by Charles Darwin in 1859 marked a significant paradigm shift in understanding the natural world and the theory of evolution. The book well and truly ruffled the feathers of religious loonies, and once the firestorm had finally died down, Darwin published his second masterpiece, *The Descent of Man.* [19] Here, Darwin tackled the thorny issue of evolutionary sexual selection, describing his observations of animal intelligence and the continuity (commonalities) between species rather than a sharp distinction between animals and humans. [20]

Most of the more complex emotions are common to the higher animals and ourselves. Everyone has seen how jealous a dog is of his master's affection, if lavished on any other creature". [20]

Darwin goes on to describe the animals "*manifestly feel emulation*" (emotion). Dogs exhibit fear distinctly from shame and show a sense of humour when playing games such as stick fetching.

A close associate of Darwin, George Romanes wrote extensively on animal behaviour and intelligence, publishing 'Animal Intelligence' in 1882 and 'Mental Evolution in Animals' in 1884. Romanes' introduction to *Animal Intelligence* opens with a statement comparing comparative psychology with comparative anatomy, one examining mental 'structures' and the other bodily structures. [21] Romanes illustrates the difficulties of defining consciousness, explaining that even rudimentary organisms like worms and larvae display levels of perception beyond simple reflexes and further defines reasoning in animals as reliance on cognition rather than automatic reactions. Romanes provides many insightful accounts of the development of reasoning in animals through inherited traits, experience, and reasoning, culminating in his observations of monkeys solving complex problems using tools. *Animal Intelligence* also describes some of the earliest accounts of observational learning in primates, emotions, pro-social behaviour, sympathy, and self-awareness. [22]

Stuffed Pets and Pet Cemeteries

Curiously, Darwin and Romane's efforts to enlighten the great unwashed masses to the intricacies of evolution and animal intelligence helped spark a strange paradoxical movement. From the early 1800s to the beginning of the 20th century, Victorian England saw an explosion of pet ownership, zoological displays and exhibitions, and associated pet paraphernalia, books and newspaper articles. [23] Pet consumerism became big business, with pet connoisseurs purchasing, capturing, trading and breeding all manner of strange and exotic pets, from rats, mice and squirrels to polecats and monkeys. Pet 'bling' was accounted for with elaborate cages for those who could afford them; the plainer the pet, the more elaborate the cage, and the more ornate enclosures transformed into items of ornamental furniture. [23] The Victorian pet craze coincided with a tumultuous era in the empire, marked by social and political upheaval and technological advancements. Pets became symbols of domestication and comfort, deriving pleasure from their company and developing empathy and understanding for another sentient being. [24]

A sad but inevitable part of pet ownership is their eventual and often early demise, which led to two curious practices of the time: taxidermy and pet cemeteries. The prevailing anthropocentrism of the time was giving way to more liberal thoughts on the 'soul', which was no longer considered the exclusive domain of humans but also extended to their beloved pets. It therefore seemed only appropriate that pets should be afforded the same burial rights and customs as their human owners. Pet cemeteries sprang up all over continental Europe, the Americas and Britain; the oldest and one of the largest was the London Pet Cemetery in Hyde Park, established in 1881. Philip Howell describes some of the heartwarming inscriptions on headstones, such as for 'Wee Bobbit', 1901:

> *When our lonely lives are o'er, and our spirits from this earth shall roam, we hope he'll be there waiting, to give us a welcome home".* [25]

The belief that animals, too, might be there to greet us in the afterlife represents a paradigm shift from viewing animals as soulless automatons or objects of utility, as previously described, and a loosening of the church's stranglehold on the sanctity of the human-animal, which was made solely in the image of God.

What better way to remember 'ol Benji' when he finally snuffs it than to have him stuffed, to sit by his master's side by the fireplace, forever ensconced with his loving family? Taxidermy was big business in Victorian England. To provide some context on this strange practice, the death of Prince Albert from typhus in 1861 played a significant role. Queen Victoria's mourning period lasted until her death in 1901; the extravagance of her grief was not lost on the general populace, deeply affecting the mourning practices of the times. [26]In the first year of mourning a close loved one, women were expected to be clad in all-black attire and refuse to leave the house, social outcasts, whereas men, whilst still mourning, were expected to carry on work practices. Death portraits were popular at the time; photos with one's dearly departed, propped up and dressed in their finery, were ways for people to mourn, memorialise, and honour loved ones. It is little wonder that taxidermy began to flourish in this death-obsessed environment.

Strange Arrangements

Three notable taxidermists of the period were Hermann Ploucquet, Charles Waterton and Walter Potter. Potter (1835–1918) maintained a small museum of curiosities that contained whimsical representations of cats, rats, rabbits, birds, and weasels dressed in miniature clothing, all of which were deceased, preserved, and stuffed. [27] These characters are frozen in time, portraying sports, schoolrooms and fairy tale dioramas; his pièce de résistance is the kitten's wedding, which contains around 18 stuffed kittens, all dressed in finery, attending a strange union indeed. Hermann Ploucquet's animal tableaux gained much notoriety after being displayed at the Great Exhibition of 1851. Featuring anthropomorphic figures such as 'Sir Tibert delivering the King's message', a taxidermy cat, bowing reverently to a book-reading fox, a tea party of cats and duelling mice, Ploucquet's works predominantly centred around folk tales and fables. [27]

Charles Waterton (1782-1865) was a naturalist, conservationist and explorer whose unusual take on taxidermy produced some strange chimeras. The 'nondescript' was perhaps his most famous creation, a peculiar, humanoid-like bust fashioned from a howler monkey's skin, with the human-like face likely made from the animal's anus. Waterton took charge of a gorilla's corpse in 1856, preserving the poor animal, adding donkey's ears and calling his creation 'Martin Luther'. [27]

Extraordinary Animals

This new shift from anthropocentrism to anthropomorphism created a strange turn of events, one being the rise of the 'extraordinary animal' phenomenon. The Victorian obsession with pets, death, morbidity and the supernatural cast a strange spell over animals, transforming them from objects of utility, cuisine, or curiosity into creatures of extraordinary abilities. It seems that, finally, the great chain was broken, and now animals were on a continuum with humans, rather than being a level in the chain's hierarchy.

Arguably, the most famous of these 'super' animals was Clever Hans, the counting horse. Wilhelm von Osten, a former German mathematics teacher, taught Hans to do arithmetic, tell the time and date and read, tapping his hoof to indicate an answer. For this, the media went bananas, speculating all manner of contributing factors like telepathy, hypnosis or hidden wires. This was, of course, debunked by Oskar Pfungst, a psychologist who was asked to investigate Hans. When the trainer was not visible to Hans, his counting ability suddenly ceased, and Pfungst deduced that subtle verbal and visual cues alerted Hans when to start and stop counting.[28]

Not to be upstaged, Rolf, the German Airedale Terrier, could apparently spell letters of the alphabet by tapping his paw. Rolf was also a great thinker and amateur mathematician, and spoke several languages. Rolf was so talented that he caught the eye of the Nazis, who were attempting to create a corps of intelligent 'war dogs' that could communicate in human language.[29, 30]

Another clever canine was Don the talking dog, a German setter with a vocabulary of eight words, all in German. Don's notoriety spread from Germany to America, inspiring vaudeville entrepreneur William Hammerstein to sponsor Don's travel to New York, posting a bond, equivalent to over a million US dollars in today's terms, in case Don expired on the journey. Don arrived in 1912 to celebrity fanfare, performing alongside greats such as Harry Houdini and subsequently spending the next two years touring the country. [31] Ironically, it was Pfungst, the psychologist who debunked Hans, who studied Don's behaviour and concluded the dog had no understanding of the words it produced, instead creating the illusion of words in the listener. [32]

Sorting the Animals

Humans have a tendency to seek certainty, clear-cut explanations, and black-and-white terminology. Unfortunately, nature does not kindly abide by those rules, tending to have subtle shades and variations, making it somewhat difficult to nail down particular species and varieties. As mentioned earlier, Aristotle's *Historia Animalium* was probably one of the first attempts at sorting animals into categories, distinguishing creatures by their habitat, reproduction method and simply by lower or higher 'classes'. Carl Linnaeus' *Systema Naturae,* 1735, was the foundational method for modern taxonomy, grouping similar organisms into non-overlapping hierarchies, using binomial naming, genus first, species second. Keeping in mind that this was a hundred years before Darwin's theory of evolution, it was widely accepted that all animals were made by God and named by man. Thus, animal species were seen as static and unchanging.

Animal taxonomy and evolutionary theories also owe much to Jean-Baptiste Lamarck (1744-1829), the French Prussian war hero turned botanist and, later, professor of zoology. Lamarck believed that animals passed on traits acquired in their lifetime to their offspring, a sort of misconceived ultra-rapid evolution. It gets stranger, though; Lamarck believed that two laws influenced this process: the first, use and disuse, and the second, the *inheritance of acquired characteristics*. The first law proposed that organs or structures frequently used would become stronger and more developed; the most infamous example is the giraffe. Lamarck stated the giraffe was originally a much shorter animal that progressively grew taller in its lifetime, reaching up into the trees for tasty leaves (use it or lose it), passing these traits onto offspring and increasing the animal's height over subsequent generations (inheritance of acquired characteristics). These evolutionary processes increased in complexity over generations, influenced by changes in the environment, which in turn led to changes in the organism and its behaviour. Bodily functions were hydraulic in nature, with systems of tubes, pipes, and canals transferring various fluids around the body, enabling 'rapports' between the body and the environment, thus leading to behavioural changes. [33] These concepts sound decidedly kooky today. However, Lamarck's views on evolutionary inheritance laid the groundwork on which theories of organic evolution have been built. Lamarck also contributed substantially to animal taxonomy, separating species previously lumped together, the first to differentiate crustaceans and arachnids from insects and the first to coin the term *biology*. [34]

On Anthropomorphism

Throughout the book, you will encounter the term anthropomorphism, derived from the Greek *anthropos* (human) and *morphe* (form), which refers to the tendency to interpret non-human things by attributing human-like characteristics to them. In the book *Primates and Philosophers: How Morality Evolved,* Frans de Waal describes the struggle between scientific endeavour, such as the cognitive parsimony of behaviourism that favours simple cause-and-effect-like explanations, versus a more liberal view that entertains the thought that animals may indeed possess some human-like traits. De Waal states, *"While it is true that animals are not humans, it is equally true that humans are animals,"*. Since science shifted from a viewpoint of behaviourism to one of complex cognitions in humans, AKA the cognitive revolution, animals became the sole torchbearer of Behaviourism. [35] De Waal explained the misconception that anthropomorphism is a dangerous idea, insofar as it applies only to those who wish to maintain a wall between animals and humans. On the one hand, denying anthropomorphic traits in animals risks throwing the baby out with the bathwater and missing real human-like behaviours and emotions. On the other hand, over-attributing human-like traits skews the reality of what lies behind those behaviours, a delicate balancing act indeed!

The Journey Thus Far

From nutritive, sensitive and rational souls to the great chain of being, animal spirits and passions of the soul, to the two sovereign masters of pain and pleasure and maximising utility, humans have waxed and waned in their views of animals' sentience and intelligence. First, relegating them to mindless automata, then placing them at the pinnacle of collective obsessions, pampering them when alive, interring their bodies in elaborate cemeteries or arranging their small taxidermic corpses in strange anthropomorphic ways. So, it would appear the gap between 'them and us' has sufficiently closed to bring about the next chapter in our long and colourful relationship with animals, the scientific study of intelligence.

The Clever Hominid

Cogito, ergo sum" (I think, therefore I am)

René Descartes *(1596–1650)*

He was so learned that he could name a horse in nine languages, so ignorant that he bought a cow to ride on.

Benjamin Franklin

Intelligence, what is it and where does it come from? Is intelligence equally distributed among humans and individual animal species, and what is normal? Is a goat smarter than a bear, or is a rat cleverer than a parrot? Is a chimpanzee equivalent to a human child in intelligence? These are challenging questions raised by comparative psychology that once again require us to revisit the past to paint a clearer picture of our current understanding.

A Bumpy Skull

Quantifying intelligence in humans, let alone animals, is a science fraught with peril, and its origin story is a fascinating rollercoaster ride of discovery and quackery.

Craniology, or *the science of the head*, was the term coined by Franz Joseph Gall of 18th-century Vienna.[1] Gall partnered with one Johann Christoph Spurzheim on several neuroanatomical experiments, interpreting the outer bumps of the skull to correspond with larger 'muscles' of the 'organ of the mind' and various localised functions. The two eventually parted company, but Spurzheim imagined a potential psychosocial component to the shape of one's noggin and coined the term *phrenology* or science of the mind. He proposed that the lumps and bumps correlated highly with a person's psychological strengths and weaknesses. Spurzheim travelled extensively through Britain and the United States, peddling his pseudo-science quackery; however, by 1832, 11 years after his demise, the concept was unanimously rejected.

George Combe, a young Scottish lawyer, was privy to one of Spurzheim's impromptu brain dissections at a friend's home in Edinburgh and was enamoured with the *faculties of the mind* expounded by Spurzheim's phrenological paradigm. [2] In 1820, Combe and his recently 'converted' physician brother founded the inaugural Phrenological Society. Twelve years later, 29 phrenological societies were scattered throughout Great Britain. Combe went on to publish 'The Constitution of Man' in 1828, which was further published four more times, selling 100,000 copies in the UK and an astonishing 200,000 copies in the US. Combes' appeal lay in the fact that it appealed to the 'great unwashed masses', offering a simplified (pseudo) explanation of the mysteries of the mind. Alas, by the mid-1830s, the phrenology phenomenon had petered out, yet Combe continued to travel and espouse his views, even performing head-bump readings on royal family members.

An adjunct of Gall's craniology experiments was the measurement and documentation of the skull's dimensions. Influenced by Gall and the phrenology movement, physician and naturalist Samuel Morton took a great interest in skulls and their dimensions. [3] In fact, Morton amassed a collection of hundreds of human skulls from around the world via a network of doctors, naturalists and soldiers. This gruesome and eclectic collection included heads from 'idiots', 'lunatics', convicts, prostitutes, pirates and murderers from various poorhouses and hospitals. [4] Morton even enlisted the assistance of the US consul to Cairo to supply him with 100 Egyptian skulls. Morton concluded that different races had distinct

24

cranial capacities relative to intelligence, classifying race in a hierarchy with Caucasians at the top and other races lower on the scale. Despite his penchant for other people's heads, Morton was considered the father of anthropology and a brilliant scientist, arguably also the father of scientific racism.

Another fine example of the influence of phrenology and craniology is Cesare Lombroso, the founder of modern criminal anthropology. Lombroso believed that physical features such as a receding forehead, a large protruding jaw, or facial asymmetry were signs of the *atavistic condition*. [5] Lombroso postulated that atavism indicates criminals are a throwback to a less evolved state of evolution, similar to primitive humans or primates, thus making them vulnerable to criminality. Despite all the monkey business involved in Lombroso's wild speculations, his theories did introduce the idea that biological factors influence criminality.

Measuring Intelligence in Humans

From the bumbling attempts of Gall and the phrenologists measuring skulls with callipers, the journey to establishing a robust way of measuring intelligence is a bumpy road, full of detours and dead ends. Intelligence, particularly IQ, is often referred to as something substantive, like an object. Unfortunately, to this day, no single test or definition of intelligence has been agreed upon, so perhaps the best way to tackle the subject is to examine its genesis. [6]

Beyond the musings of the Greek philosophical schools, Sir Francis Galton was one of the first to have a stab at this elusive subject. *Hereditary Genius,* published in 1869, was Galton's attempt to prove that people differ in their abilities due to inheritance. This was decades before Mendelian genetics was 'rediscovered' and brought to the fore, so Galton's assumption that heredity and not environment were the determinants of intellect was a sound hypothesis for the time. [7] Unfortunately, Galton also bears the unenviable label of being the father of eugenics; his illustrious career ultimately centred on one goal: the improvement of humanity through selective breeding. Strongly influenced by his half-cousin Charles Darwin, Galton was also a keen exponent of measuring everything, and he set the question of intelligence firmly in his sights. Galton's Anthropometric Laboratory in England evaluated thousands of individual cases testing his assumptions, only to have his work ultimately discredited decades later. [8]

IQ

The IQ score or *intelligence quotient* is currently the gold standard of intelligence testing; with many varied flavours of the IQ test, scholars still debate the merits of each flavour. The IQ score had humble beginnings in France at the turn of the century. French law in 1882 decreed that primary education be compulsory for all otherwise healthy children from 6 to 13 years of age. As the numbers swelled in schools, complaints grew louder about the differences in children's abilities and their effect on teaching. A commission was tasked with finding a way to differentiate *normal* children from *abnormal.*

A stoush began between renowned psychiatrist Désiré-Magloire Bourneville, who proposed identifying all children with developmental delays via a physiological assessment and either dispensing them to 'special' classes or institutionalising them in asylums. Physicians of this era typically categorised mentally impaired patients as *idiots* (most impaired) and *imbeciles* (less impaired), and mildly impaired patients were labelled *feeble-minded.* The psychologist Alfred Binet developed a set of assessment guidelines and, together with Théodore Simon, proposed an alternate method of testing children. Using a medical, pedagogical and psychological approach, their methods were finally accepted and passed into law in 1909, and *special* classes were attached to public schools for children with learning disabilities.[9]

Meanwhile, in the US, an influx of immigrants and an almost doubling of school enrolments set about their own homegrown assessment problem. Henry Goddard first introduced Binet's tests in the United States to assist with his research into individuals with developmental disabilities, which later led to an improved version in 1916. [10] Stanford University's Lewis Terman substantially revised the Binet-Simon approach to create the *Stanford-Binet,* which is still in use today, albeit in a refined form. [11] The Stanford-Binet test introduced the term *intelligence quotient* or 'IQ', which is calculated by dividing a child's mental age by their chronological age and multiplying the result by 100. Nowadays, IQ is assessed by a child's test performance compared to the average IQ score of other children their age. [8]

The Army Alpha

As with many scientific and technological discoveries, the military soon took an interest in Terman's and Binet's work. Robert Yerkes, a prominent psychologist, primatologist, and eugenicist, established a committee in 1917, which brought Terman and Goddard

26

on board. [10] The Army alpha and beta were the names given to the psychological testing implemented to screen over a million draftees into the US Army in World War I, primarily to assess potential recruits' intellectual and emotional capacity. Army Alpha was designed for men already proficient in reading and writing and used written instructions and responses. Army beta was aimed at illiterate and semi-literate individuals, utilising simple commands, picture completions and pantomime. [12] The perceived success of these tests and the associated publicity led to an explosion of new intelligence tests, some novel but most based on the army tests, many implemented into schools for assessing student abilities. [8] The results remain a source of contention, with a cohort of scholars contesting the validity and reliability of the results. [12]

Binet believed in a single component of intelligence rather than a combination of 'higher' psychological functions, such as imagination, abstraction, attention and memory. Charles Spearman, however, developed his *two-factor theory* of intelligence, which proposes an overarching factor of general intelligence, or 'G', and specific factors or 'S.' [8] G posits that someone who does well on one type of cognitive task generally does well on others, too. For example, someone with above-average verbal skills is likely to be highly correlated with quantitative and spatial skills.

Gardner's Theory

Howard Gardner took a different approach to intelligence testing; rather than relying on test scores, he drew on studies of child development, gifted individuals, and those with neurological damage. [13] Gardner's theory of multiple intelligences proposes that intelligence is not a single, unified characteristic, such as an IQ score, but rather a distinct type of intelligence that reflects how different people solve problems and process information. Gardner identified nine discrete types of intelligence: linguistic, mathematical, spatial, musical, bodily-kinesthetic, interpersonal, intrapersonal, naturalistic, and existential. [13]

Finally, we arrive at the towering figure of David Wechsler, whose initial work with Spearman and Edward Thorndike led him to develop a theory that encompassed aspects of each of their works and those of other contemporaries. Wechsler's work can be traced back to his assistance, development, and implementation of intelligence testing after WW1, as well as his work in Bellevue Psychiatric Hospital, New York. Wechsler defined intelligence as the overall capacity of an individual to act intentionally, think logically, and handle situations effectively within his environment. [14]

The Wechsler Adult Intelligence Scale (WAIS), the Wechsler Intelligence Scale for Children-V (WISC-V), and the Stanford-Binet are the most widely used measurements of intelligence today. In a nutshell, the WISC-V measures intelligence in children using five indexes: [15]

1. Verbal Comprehension Index: measures verbal concept formation, reasoning, knowledge, word knowledge, abstract reasoning, memory, and verbal expression.

2. Visual-Spatial Index: uses timed block design and visual puzzles to assess nonverbal reasoning, visual intelligence, perception, organisation, simultaneous processing, visual-motor coordination, figure-ground differentiation, spatial reasoning, mental rotation, visual working memory, and analysis of abstract visual stimuli.

3. Fluid Reasoning Index: evaluates pattern recognition, problem-solving, and logical thinking. It includes Matrix Reasoning, Figure Weights, Picture Concepts, and Arithmetic, assessing abstract thinking, visual-spatial, and quantitative reasoning.

4. Working Memory Index: measures ability to hold and manipulate information, with subtests for attention, concentration, memory, mental manipulation, and flexibility.

5. Processing Speed Index: assesses quick, accurate visual information processing via coding, symbol search, and cancellation tasks to test perception, coordination, attention, and decision-making.

This illustrates the difficulties that would arise in applying a human intelligence test to animals, the verbal comprehension test being the most obvious. Nevertheless, scientists have come up with some fascinating and ingenious ways to measure animal intelligence, and the journey to get there has some interesting twists and turns.

Measuring Animal Intelligence

It is a good morning exercise for a research scientist to discard a pet hypothesis every day before breakfast: it keeps him young

Konrad Lorenz, 1903-1989

IF only measuring intelligence in animals was as easy as Spurzheim's phrenology, run the bumps over your pet's skull and mark them out of ten! The previous chapter outlined the difficulties in measuring human intelligence, but imagine the task when your subject cannot speak. Add to the mix our tendency to anthropomorphise animals, especially pets, and our social and cultural ideas about livestock as simply food animals, and the task becomes even more onerous. As described in Chapter One, historical observations of animals often focused on comparisons between animal cognition and human thinking, usually ignoring other external factors that lead to different types of intelligence. Cuttlefish use an amazing array of *chromatophores* or cells that change colour to camouflage themselves or signal their intentions to mates or rivals. Despite being 'simple' sea creatures, bait to some and calamari to others, cuttlefish have shown the ability to delay gratification of a reward for up to 130 seconds, comparable to some higher-order mammals. [1] This demonstrates that even cephalopods, animals usually considered merely as either bait or dinner, show the ability to learn and remember, the central tenets of what we call intelligence.

Aubrey Manning and Marian Stamp Dawkins describe how humans have always pondered on the minds of animals and how or if they 'think'. With rapid advances in science, many researchers are reluctant to broach the subject of animal cognition, preferring to concentrate on behaviour instead. [2] They explain that most serious researchers will have at the back of their minds Morgan's Canon:

In no case may we interpret an action as the outcome of the exercise of a higher faculty, if it can be interpreted as the outcome of the exercise of one which stands lower in the psychological scale. Morgan, 1894.

In other words, sometimes what appears to be reasoning or higher-order thinking might simply be a result of basic reflexes, learning, or conditioning. When asked, are animals as smart as people? renowned animal ethologist, academic and animal whisperer Temple Grandin simply responds that it's a question neither she nor anyone else can yet answer.[3] When tackling issues of animal intelligence versus human intelligence, it pays to pack a 'sceptics toolkit' replete with Morgan's Canon, and a healthy dose of Occam's Razor! Also known as the law of parsimony, Occam's Razor states that sometimes the simplest explanation is the most correct when faced with multiple explanations. For example, when posed with the question "How smart are animals"? It is simply as smart as they need to be! Animals have evolved and adapted to fill environmental niches, with intelligence that allows them to survive and pass on their genes. The Australian koala is not a particularly 'bright' animal, with a small brain for its size and a sleepy demeanour. But the koala is not unintelligent; rather, it is perfectly adapted to the niche diet of toxic, low-nutrient gum leaves.

So, primed with the sceptic's toolkit yet still keeping an open mind, we can now dive in and examine how science has come to measure animal intelligence.

Stone the Crows

One of the earliest recorded observations of animal intelligence involves corvids, dating back to the first century BC. The Greek poet Bianor describes a crow in a graveyard, dropping stones in a funerary urn, giving rise to Aesop's fable of the crow and the pitcher. The fable tells the story of a thirsty crow dropping stones into a pitcher to raise the water level so it can take a sip. [4] Pliny recounts a similar version in the first century; Plutarch describes Libyan crows performing similar feats in the second century AD, and several other permutations of the story arise up until the fourth century AD. At which point does a fable become an ethological observation? Several scientists have attempted to recreate Aesop's scenario, but with mixed results, mainly showing the corvid's ability to learn quickly, as opposed to a level of reasoning and understanding of physics. [4, 5, 6] Therein lies the problem of anecdotal and descriptive observations of animal intelligence versus scientific measuring of intelligence, which did not begin in earnest until around the 19th century.

Drooling Dogs

Not quite a measure of intelligence, but a measure of drool, Pavlov was one of the earliest scientists to study animal behaviour methodically. His famous experiments with a salivating dog laid the groundwork for classical conditioning. Ivan Pavlov (1849-1936) was an eminent Russian physiologist who, midway through his career, found himself studying the human digestive system, often using dogs as his test subjects. Pavlov modified a surgical technique to make a 'miniature stomach' external to the dog to study gastric juices and digestion, dubbed the 'Pavlov pouch.' [7] While studying salivary production, via cannelure placed through an incision in the dog's mouth, Pavlov noticed that once the dog had been fed several times in the laboratory, it would salivate simply when led in. Pavlov labelled this doggy drool phenomenon *psychic secretions*. After noticing unrelated cues that also made the dogs salivate, Pavlov paired a metronome with meat powder, and over time, the dog became conditioned to the sound, or 'higher order conditioning.' [8] Once conditioned, the pooch would respond to the sound stimulus alone, which, contrary to popular belief, was not a bell but a range of different stimulus sounds, ultimately rewarding for Pavlov, who received the Nobel Prize in 1904 for his work. [7]

Clever Cats

Not one to pussyfoot around, Edward Thorndike (1874 -1949) set about measuring learning in cats around the same time Pavlov was conditioning his dogs.[9] Thorndike's junior years at university were spent floating between disciplines, with no particular interest in psychology, until stumbling across the works of William James, who was known as the 'father of modern psychology'. After moving to Harvard, Thorndike juggled English, philosophy and psychology before dropping the former for his PhD candidacy. After some relatively unproductive studies with children, Thorndike suggested he should work with chickens, which was subsequently approved. The birds were kept and experimented on in his lodging room until the landlady's protests could no longer be ignored. [10] Seeing the 'underdog' in Thorndike, William James took a shine to him and allowed Thorndike to 'harbour' his chickens in James's cellar for the remainder of the year. Thorndike muses that he had no particular interest in animal intelligence and completed many investigations to satisfy course requirements. Upon moving to Columbia University in 1899, his two most 'educated' chickens in tow, Thorndike set about studying associative processes in an animal's mind, settling on cats, stating, *"Never will you get a better psychological subject than a hungry cat"*, creating his infamous feline puzzle box. [9] Thorndike fabricated a box with a door that could be opened with a rope or a foot tread; the hungry cat was put into the box, where it essentially freaked out and tried everything in its feline repertoire to escape. Eventually, the hapless tabby accidentally released the door and escaped to freedom and a feed. Placing the cats back in the cage and measuring the time it took to escape, Thorndike recorded the results, plotting the first 'learning curve'.[9] This measure of learning was one of the earliest attempts at measuring animal intelligence, dubbed 'the law of effect', which states that the strength of a behaviour depends on its consequences.

Skinner's Missile

From dogs and cats, we move to pigeons and rats, with psychology's most famous rodent trainer, B.F. Skinner. Born Burrhus Frederic Skinner in 1904 in Susquehanna, Pennsylvania, Skinner is one of the most influential psychologists of the 20th century. Skinner was a prolific writer, publishing 180 articles and 21 books. For a while, he was the hottest item on TV talk shows, and his face was featured on the cover of Time magazine in 1971.[11] An avid inventor, Skinner devised several unusual devices, including the 'aircrib', a large sealed thermostatically controlled box that looks decidedly like a large fish tank, where an infant can enjoy unrestrained movement in an environmentally controlled space; the 'teaching machine' another mechanical box that utilised positive reinforcement to aid student's in their learning and of course his most famous box: the Skinner box.[12] The latter box is a small crate that houses a mouse or rat, with metal bars on the floor and a wall containing a lever that drops a food pellet reward into a magazine when pressed. The metal bars allow an electric shock or 'punishment to be administered to the hapless rodent. The rats first learned to associate the sound of the pellet dropping into the food dispenser; they were rewarded with food each time they pressed a lever. As they continued to press the lever, they learned to associate the lever press with the food reward. The bar was then paired so that the press would dispense the food. Skinner dubbed this 'operant learning' and recorded the rodent's repertoire on a 'cumulative recorder, a graph that measured each level press and the time intervals between.[13] Skinner categorised two operant processes that strengthen behaviour and two that weaken it, leading to the infamous positive and negative reinforcers and punishers. Positive punishment is a well-known phenomenon to many mothers, typically administered with a wooden spoon or a shoe. Spreading out the rewards over different periods led to the 'schedules of reinforcement', further refining the time it took an animal to learn and retain a new behaviour. Skinner also achieved great success with pigeons, training them to discriminate colours and shapes, play ping pong and even guide a missile. Yes, pigeon-guided missiles were nearly a thing in the days before GPS satellite positioning.

Project Pigeon

Skinner's 1960 paper *Pigeons in a Pelican* begins with his own admission, "*This is the history of a crackpot idea, born on the wrong side of the tracks intellectually speaking*", referring to the proposal to use living creatures to guide missiles in the WW2 research program dubbed *Project Pigeon*. [14] Skinner's success in training pigeons led him to believe they could create an effective bio-mechanical interface, observing flocks of birds and the way they synchronised mechanically, which inspired his bird-brained idea.[15] So the capability of a pigeon to steer itself to a target was tested, using a movable hoist; the dashing trainee pilots were secured with a jacket, only their heads able to move and peck at a food dish.[14] The hoist would move in the direction the bird tilted its head; the hoist pushed across the floor toward a bullseye on the wall, which contained a food reward. The pigeons quickly learned to steer the device toward the target successfully, regardless of the starting point or speed. The project was pitched several times to military officials, but eventually lapsed due to a lack of support.

Fortuitously, a young man named Victor walked into the lab in 1942, seeking a psychologist to assist him in his work on steering torpedoes using dogs, which sounds decidedly like a Monty Python skit. Skinner endorsed Viktor's project; however, no one could be convinced that the canine kamikazes were a good idea. One company, General Mills Incorporated, became enamoured with Skinner's 'killer birds' idea and assisted in setting up a bird brain guidance system laboratory in a flour mill in Minneapolis. Problems arose in the pigeons' ability to identify and respond to a distant target, often acting too late. A projection system was used, much like a *camera obscura*, and the pigeon was reinforced (trained) to peck at the projected target. The pigeon pilots became proficient, able to discriminate land and sea targets, ignore clouds and flak, and even hold the 'missile' on target for a street intersection on a map. [14]Further 'serious' testing studied the effects of pressure, vibration, loud noise and special reinforcements, the birds being quite fond of hemp seeds.

The self-guided missile technology of the day was embodied in a bomb called the 'pelican', so called because the guidance system took up so much space there was little room for explosives ('its beak can hold more than its belly can'). The missile was adapted to house the pigeons, with a large lens in the nose of the missile projecting onto a translucent plate in a pressurised chamber that the pigeons could peck at. The pecks sent messages to air valves that steered the missile and required inexpensive and easily sourced materials. Around this time, Skinner's team realised controlling birds was much easier than controlling scientists on committees, so to add another layer of surety, they switched to a multi-bird system, using three pigeons in one missile, the idea being that a missile aimed at a ship might have a consensus of two birds, but one defector. Contingencies of reinforcement would see the other bird punished and quickly drawn into line with his fellow suicide squabs. In December 1943, the Office of Scientific Research and Development visited, accompanied by a demonstration of a three-bird 'bomb' that followed a target around a room. Some inconsistencies were brought up, and the team were given one more chance to correct some perceived problems, working with the MIT tech team who designed the servo motors for the pelican; one MIT member commented on the performance of the bird commenting that they performed better than radar. Alas, a final pitch to a committee of the country's top scientists, despite a glowing performance from the pigeon pilots, was unsuccessful. The Vice-President in Charge of Research at General Mills commented as the project pigeon team left the room, *"Why don't you go out and get drunk!"* [14]

Skinner's deterministic views on behaviourism as the progenitor of almost everything slowly gave way to broader thinking of the (human) mind, culminating with Neisser's book in 1967, 'Cognitive Psychology' and the start of the so-called 'cognitive revolution'. [16] This also had enormous implications for the study of animal intelligence, with more focus on cognition than behaviour.

Harlow's House of Horrors

The final figure whose unabashed contributions to animal cognition, the study of attachment and the inadvertent influence on the establishment of an animal rights movement, is the American psychologist Harry Harlow. Moving beyond Skinner's behaviourism and into the realm of cognition, Harlow demonstrated that monkeys could problem-solve and think abstractly. Working mainly with rhesus macaques, Harlow established a breeding colony of the simians in the 1950s, keeping the offspring in isolated nurseries away from their mothers to reduce the spread of disease. Harlow noticed the monkey behaved strangely, showing thumb-sucking type behaviours, hostility and problems socialising. Hypothesising that macaques need not only sustenance to survive but also maternal bonding and affection led to his infamous wire-frame surrogate experiment. Two 'surrogate' mothers were made from a rolled wire frame with a rudimentary head attached (a box with a couple of dots for eyes), and the other was the same frame, but with a slightly more detailed head, wrapped in soft terry towelling. Alternating both surrogates with a feeding bottle attached to them, the infants overwhelmingly spent more time with the soft towelling surrogate, regardless of where the feeding bottle was placed, a term Harlow coined as 'contact comfort'. [17] The infants even used these robot surrogates as a secure base to explore the world, much like John Bowlby's attachment theory findings in human children.

Despite creating considerable primate mental health issues and winning the prestigious National Medal of Science in 1967, Harlow himself suffered from bouts of major depression. This culminated in his spending time in a Mayo psychiatric clinic in 1968 and receiving several bouts of electroconvulsive therapy. However, the genesis of Harlow's studies into depression began many years earlier with his research into the effects of deprivation in primates. Harlow and his research assistant had been working on ways to speed up despair and depression in monkeys, creating various cages that isolated the simians to induce depression. This took too long, so the monkeys were isolated in an enclosed vertical chamber dubbed 'the pit of despair', a V-shaped, tall chamber made of polished and slippery metal that the poor primate could not climb out of. Along with the pit of despair, the 'tunnel of terror' was also used, in which infant monkeys were scared by toy battery-powered robots and other sinister objects, creating a cohort of chronically and severely depressed monkeys, self-harmers, pacers and chronic masturbators. [18] [19]

Harlow sought to 'reverse' the primates' depressive symptoms, initially experimenting with various early anti-depressive and anti-psychotic medications but with limited success. Harlow drew upon his own experiences at the Mayo Clinic and decided to focus on therapeutic rehabilitation. Harlow joined isolated and depressed monkeys with younger 'therapy monkeys' who were physically and mentally healthy. After a while, the depressed monkeys responded positively, eventually joining in play with their therapist companions. [19] Despite the findings of Harlow's work and the importance of advancing science, the ethical paradox created is rather disturbing. John Gluck describes how Harlow's discoveries on primate cognition and social development show that animals have rich social and emotional lives. Yet, his research seemingly ignored the ethical implications of suffering imposed on the animals. [20] Indeed, Harlow's trusted fellow researcher, Stephen Suomi, waited until Harlow retired from the university in 1970 before tearing out the vertical 'pit of despair' chambers that, in his own words, gave him nightmares. [18]

From those rather depressing accounts of primate studies, I'll move on to how science assesses and measures animal intelligence, focusing mainly on the cognitive abilities of animals rather than on behaviour.

A Theory of Mind

In the field of human cognition, the theory of mind describes the understanding that others may have beliefs, desires, and intentions different from one's own, often used to describe developmental milestones in children. Ironically, the term came from a 1978 study on chimpanzees by comparative psychologists, David Premack and Guy Woodruff. [21] The test subject, Sarah the Chimpanzee, was shown a video of a human actor facing various problems. Sarah was asked to select from a range of photos the one that provided a solution to the actor's problem, to which Sarah consistently and accurately chose the correct answers. The authors assume Sarah assigns states of mind to the video actor that involve positive or negative attitudes.

Five years later, Heinz Wimmer and Josef Permer put Premack and Woodruff's theory to the test with a different kind of species: kids! [22] The researchers posed a series of questions to 36 children aged four to nine about a fictional character named Maxi. Maxi stashes some chocolate in a cupboard (X). In his absence, Maxi's evil mother takes the chocolate and hides it in cupboard Y. The children are then asked where Maxi will look for the pilfered chocolate. Children roughly under four years of age will say cupboard Y, the information the child possesses, unaware that Maxi may also possess his own information. After around four years, most children say Maxi will look for the chocolate in X, a false belief held by Maxi that the chocolate is still there.

Returning once again to chimpanzees, Frans De Waal describes numerous examples of chimpanzee theory of mind. Chimps that observe food stashed somewhere in an enclosure (knowers) often act nonchalantly around others to conceal the location of that food, a form of subterfuge. However, it's not long before the other apes cotton on to the *knower's* caper, closely watching the *knowers* to find the hidden food. [23] Rank order is a big deal in chimp society. When a low-ranking chimp chooses between food that a high-ranking chimp has seen and food that the chimp has not seen, the low-ranking chimp will choose the latter as the safest bet; this behaviour is also observed in macaques. [23] De Waal wrote that he is convinced that apes take each other's perspective; the evolutionary origins lie not in social competition, but in cooperation. This ability centres on emotional bonds common in social mammals, which lead to more complex skills like evaluating others' knowledge and intentions. [24]

Much like the chimp 'knowers' who use tactics to disguise their knowledge of food, ravens are also masters of deception. A 2005 study by Thomas Bugnyar and Bernd Heinrich found that the clever corvids can distinguish between informed and ignorant competitors based on whether those competitors witnessed them caching food. If a raven 'knows' a competitor knows where they stashed their food (witnessed the event), the raven has a higher chance of recovering its food. The pilfering birds also adjust their behaviour, hurrying to steal caches when competing with 'knowing' birds but casually looking for caches when competing against 'unknowing' birds. [25]

Whilst theory of mind is abundantly evident in humans, in the animals it seems confined to higher-order primates, cetaceans and corvids; however, as DeWaal describes, most experiments have only tested the apes' theory of the human mind, whereas it would be more productive to focus on the ape's own theory of the ape mind.[24]

Self-Awareness

The *problem of other minds* is an excellent place to begin with self-awareness. How do we know if other people or animals have minds like our own? This question has haunted philosophers for centuries, but thankfully, with advances in neuroscience, we are a bit closer to an answer; sadly, there is still no consensus.

'Thinking about thinking' is often used to describe metacognition or the process of monitoring one's own thoughts. When you write down a word, second-guess the spelling, and then look it up, that's metacognition in action. Animals demonstrating observable metacognition include apes, monkeys, cetaceans, crows, and, arguably, rats. [26] But how can you test an ape's metacognition or whether a crow is thinking about thinking? Two ways to measure metacognition are perceptual tests, where the animals discriminate between levels of brightness or amounts of dots. The other method is memory tests, where the animal is tested on its ability to remember a series of items. For example, a monkey is shown a bunch of images and will be rewarded if it opts in to take the test and can remember them in the correct order. The monkey is also given the option to opt out and receive a much smaller reward. Opting out reveals a *retrospective mnemonic judgment*, where the monkey accessed its memory and decided it did not have all the information available, thus it's better to opt out. A *prospective mnemonic judgment* occurs when the monkey chooses to take the test and completes it successfully, confident that it has all the necessary information on hand to ace the test and receive the reward. This, in and of itself, does not demonstrate self-awareness but is a pretty darn good indication of self-introspection and metacognition.

Another method to test self-awareness is the mirror test, which comes in three flavours: mirror optics, observations of self-directed behaviour and the mark test. An example of mirror optics is when a monkey has some food obscured by a barrier, but seeing the food reflected in a mirror, it can position its arm to retrieve the food. I recall many times our cattle dog would face a large mirror, barking at my reflection behind him, goading me for a response, apparently aware that the reflection and I were one and the same, turning to look at me to ensure his commands were heard. I can only speculate whether this was the mirror optics or self-awareness. In observations of self-directed behaviour, the animal is simply plonked in front of a mirror, and its behaviour is observed. If it looks intently at itself, examining unseen bits (chimps often examine their butts!), then it's probably self-aware. If the animal screams, barks, or scratches at its reflection, it's perhaps not self-aware. [26] Lastly, the mark test involves placing a mark somewhere on the animal, usually the head and placing the animal in front of a mirror. To rigorously test this, the animal is usually anesthetized before placing the mark and then shown the mirror upon waking. Only chimpanzees, elephants and dolphins have 'passed the test'; however, many other animals show a rudimentary understanding of self and agency. De Waal found that capuchin monkeys were enamoured with their mirror reflection, not treating it in a hostile way as if it were a stranger. Rhesus monkeys, on the other hand, responded to the mark test when a physical sensation was also added. [23]

Problem-Solving

Many species of animals are excellent problem solvers; the most advanced are those who use tools: the great apes, monkeys, corvids and, of course, us. Benjamin Beck first defined tool use in animals as the employment of an external object from the environment to efficiently change the form, position, or condition of another object, organism, or user, where the user must hold or carry the tool and ensure it is correctly oriented. [27]Numerous other species of animals use tools in ambiguous ways, causing ethologists to argue amongst themselves as to what actually constitutes tool use. Here are some excellent examples from Shumaker and colleagues to let you decide: [28]

Throwing Stuff:

California ground squirrels throw rocks and dirt at predators. Elephants throw logs, rocks, dung and novel objects at each other and hapless observers. With surprising accuracy, primates throw pretty much anything, including their faeces, at people, predators and other animals. [28]

Dropping Stuff

There are anecdotal reports of polar bears dropping ice chunks on seals and walruses, and captive bears picking up a beer keg, carrying them up an incline and throwing them. Baboons drop rocks from ledges on people and other animals. Herring gulls drop mussels onto stones to open them. Wild elephants drop logs onto electric fences to disable the fence. Sea otters crack shellfish on rocks balanced on their belly, and Egyptian vultures crack open eggs by dropping stones on them. [28]

Baiting and Enticing

Orangutans that had a taste for coffee would offer up an empty cup or some tasty leaves to get a refill. Primates trade tokens for food or other rewards, even sex! [29] A captive mother wolf, whose pup caught a rat and would not give it up, dug up some meat, enticed the youngster to the far corner of the enclosure, and then stole the rat. Capuchins used food morsels to bait and capture fish in a zoo moat. A captive dolphin used feathers and found objects to attract attention in an underwater viewing area. Bowerbird males decorate their nests with colourful objects to attract a mate. [30] A pet capuchin enticed a young duck with a piece of bread and then killed and ate it. Baboons kidnap other baboons' youngsters and hold them for ransom to solve disputes. [31] Stoffel, the African honey badger, often escaped enclosures by manipulating his environment in incredibly complex ways. When a female companion badger was introduced to Stoffel's enclosure, they used cooperative behaviour to escape. Despite the cage having two latch bolts, one wired in place, Stoffel would climb the gate, open the first, then the second latch, and then hold the gate open so they could escape, a complex behaviour usually only seen in primates. [32]

Hank, a super smart, black-crowned night heron, has a unique bait and entice method. Featured on BBC Super Smart Animals, the heron lives on the grounds of a Hawaiian golf course. [33] Visitors often throw bread to feed the swans in the resort lake, which also entices fish near the shore. Clever Hank places a piece of bread nearby in the water and patiently waits for small fish to surface before pouncing. Seven species of herons are known to bait-fish, out of only twelve known species worldwide.

Reaching Stuff

Spectacled bears used sticks to reach fruit growing outside their enclosure. A female orangutan made a rope from hair plucked from her arms to reach food outside a cage. Sequential tools are used by orangutans, combining different objects to create tools, which they then use to reach another tool to access food. New Caledonian crows use short sticks to retrieve longer sticks to reach food. Elephants often use branches to reach objects, scratch themselves and remove parasites. [28] I recall a school excursion to the Adelaide Zoo, where the class stood admiring George, the majestic male orangutan. Our teacher was also observing George while he ate an ice block, and George motioned to the teacher that he would like it. The iced treat was passed through the bars, and George daintily ate the ice block like a human child would, then gently handed the stick back to the teacher.

Navigating

Edward Tolman noticed something unusual about rats' behaviour in a maze experiment he was conducting in 1948. When a rat learned that turning right in a cross-shaped maze yielded a food reward, you would expect the rat to mistakenly turn right again when starting from a different point. That was not the case; the rodent correctly turned left to get the treat. Tolman surmised that rats develop a 'cognitive map' in their brain of the maze, allowing them to navigate their environment efficiently. [34] In human cognition, these mental maps are referred to as 'schemas' and are utilised in everyday life to navigate the world efficiently. Information about our environment is channelled through the hippocampus and later encoded into various parts of the cortex according to basic geometric representations (spatial schemas) or detailed representations, like the specifics of a street or town (cognitive maps). [35]

Dogs are known to wander great distances and find their way back home; birds successfully migrate halfway around the planet, but Harten and colleagues chose Egyptian fruit bat pups to study navigation and cognitive maps. Several bat pups were tracked via GPS from their first flight outside and then regularly over several months. As the bats gradually expanded their range, they used novel intentional routes as shortcuts between familiar points to find new foraging sites, a key feature of map-based navigation behaviour, indicating that the bats relied on cognitive maps to navigate. [36]

Altruistic Magpies

Australian magpies, known for their pinpoint accuracy in swooping unsuspecting interlopers during nesting season, are also exceptionally intelligent. So much so that a group of magpie research subjects outsmarted their scientific observers, explained Dominique Potvin of the University of the Sunshine Coast. [37] Tracking the movement of birds presents its challenges, as wireless trackers are often too large and bulky for smaller birds. The team developed a tracker that could be attached by a robust harness that released with a magnet. The birds were trained to return to an outdoor feeding station, where the tracker could be wirelessly recharged and data downloaded. Magpies live in highly social groups of up to 12 individuals and often show signs of altruistic-like behaviour, such as helping to raise siblings. Shortly after fitting the final tracker to five of the research subjects, something completely unexpected occurred. The magpies all pecked at their own harnesses, trying to remove them, but then a female magpie, without a harness, was seen actively using her bill and intelligence to remove the harness from a juvenile, which she achieved in around 10 minutes. Other magpies were also observed helping to remove another's tracker, clear signs of cooperative behaviour and a level of problem-solving abilities. Within three days, all the birds had outsmarted the researchers, successfully removing their tracking device harnesses! [38]

Memory

The study of human memory has a long and fascinating history, with some of the earliest attempts at analysing memory performed by German psychologist Hermann Ebbinghaus. In 1885, Ebbinghaus published *Memory*, detailing his theories on how we remember and forget, coining the term *savings curve*. The curve is a measure of how much we initially remember, then over hours and days, that memory (savings) declines in a curve-like manner.

After many theories and much debate, the current consensus divides memory processes into several distinct systems. *Sensory* memory (lasting a fraction of a second), *working* memory (15-30 seconds), *short-term* memory (STM) also lasting 15-30 seconds and storing around 5-9 items, and *long-term memory* (LTM). [39] To complicate things even further, LTM is divided into unconscious or *implicit* memory and conscious or *explicit* memory. *Procedural* memory is a type of unconscious memory for things like learning a skill or riding a bike. Explicit memory is divided into three main categories: episodic memory, which encompasses significant life events; semantic memory, encompassing general knowledge; and autobiographical memory, which combines episodic and semantic components. That is a lot to remember! You have probably forgotten most of it already, unless you went back and reread it, which is called rehearsal and improves memory retention, but that's another whole story. How on Earth do these human cognitive descriptions translate to the animal kingdom? Although notoriously difficult to study, scientists have come up with some ingenious ways to measure the memory abilities of animals, revealing some startling results.

Episodic Memory

'Mental time travel' best describes episodic memory, which involves self-knowing and remembering an event, reliving the details of an event in the past, such as what, where, and *when*. [40] Logic would dictate that animals must have episodic memory; how else would squirrels remember where they stashed their nuts? But how can we measure this in an animal that can't self-report?

Scrub jays were found to remember *what, where*, and *when* of their food caches. The jay's favourite food is waxworms, which decay after a few days and must be retrieved in time accordingly. The clever birds could remember the type of food they stored, the location of the cache, and the amount of time elapsed since they stored it. [41]

In a delayed match-to-sample task, monkeys are shown a sequence of images on a screen, then, after a delay, given a choice of two images to choose from, one seen earlier and one a distractor. The simians were given thousands of trials and not only accurately chose the right images most of the time but also showed primacy and recency effects, much like humans do! [42] Also called the serial position curve, the primacy and recency effect shows we remember things better at the start and end of a list of items but not so well in the middle, where our short-term memory taps out.

Even dogs show evidence of episodic-like memory. A group of canny canines were first trained to imitate a human action, becoming accustomed to expecting that particular action when commanded. The pups were then trained to perform another action, lying down and substituting one expectation for another. The dogs were then asked to switch back to the original imitation behaviour after a one-minute or one-hour interval to test if they remembered the original task that was learned or 'encoded' automatically, without rehearsal, merely by imitating. Many of the dogs indeed repeated the action, indicating that they recalled the action from memory, demonstrating an episodic-like memory. [43]

Animals exhibit examples of behaviour that suggest episodic memory, and their brain structures and functions also show some striking similarities to ours. Rats given a spatial task like a maze have been shown to 'replay' the task in their brain during sleep or rest, using so-called 'place' cells in the hippocampus, which activate in the same order as if they were back navigating a maze. The same neurons 'fire' in the hippocampus of a human when recalling a movie! [42]

The hippocampus, from the Greek 'seahorse', is a brain structure so called because it somewhat resembles a seahorse. It is instrumental in consolidating short-term memories into long-term memories, as well as in spatial memory and emotional memories. A study that tested rats' memory using five different smells in random order, then rewarding them for correctly choosing an odour they sniffed earlier, showed the rats could accurately remember the odour (what) in the correct order (when). When the poor rodents had the hippocampus in their brain lesioned (destroyed), they could remember the smell but not the order, showing the hippocampus is crucial for the memory of 'when', but not 'what'. [44]

Although memory abilities in different animals have evolved to suit diverse environments, social roles, and behavioural functions, there is evidence that animals possess memory capabilities that resemble episodic memory in humans.

Semantic Memory

The other flavour of explicit memory, semantic memory, is difficult to assess, as few goats know the capital of Venezuela and not many pigs know the names of the continents. However, animals are adept at categorising and remembering objects, something akin to human semantic memory. Even the humble pigeon can discriminate between people, furniture, houses, cats, dogs, and even fish![45] Pigeons even learned to appreciate art, discriminating between images of Monet and Picasso paintings. The brainy birds could even generalise paintings as impressionist works like Monet, Cezanne or Renoir or abstract works like Picasso or Georges Braque![46]

Rhesus macaques can accurately categorise fruit as the same or different, for example, apples versus grapes. However, surprisingly, human and monkey faces are categorised as similar. [47] The use of tools in primates and corvids suggests that semantic memory for various objects and their usage must be present. Accounts of chimps collecting and carrying rocks to use later as tools and New Caledonian crows fashioning hooks by bending twigs or grass indicate a semantic memory for that tool and some forward planning, too!

44

Even the humble sheep are experts at discriminating between individual human faces, dogs, and even goats. When isolated and then shown a familiar face of a fellow sheep, their stress levels return to baseline. Even a friendly human face associated with positive interaction is encoded in brain neurons that are usually related to friendly sheep faces! [48]

Our geriatric alpacas, Sundae and Icy Pole, are experts at telling dogs apart, relying primarily on visual cues. One day, Lucy, our border collie, who was well known to the camelids, returned from the vet with a closely shaved 'haircut.' The alpacas went nuts, squeaking wildly until it dawned on them it was the same dog. Seeing the altered shape of the dog violated their previous memory recall of Lucy, leading to activation of their *PANIC* system. Those big alpaca eyes that people find irresistible evolved for a purpose, allowing them to spot a threat from a great distance in the sparsely vegetated high altiplano of South America, giving them ample opportunity to escape potential threats. Despite having cloudy eyes from age and injury, the pair can spot a dog up to a kilometre away, giving off their iconic alarm screech, which sounds like a rubber duck being squeezed, even when the offending dog is in a paddock surrounded by cows and calves.

Long Term Memory

An elephant never forgets is the age-old adage, and with a brain weighing around five kilograms and a lifespan well into the seventies, there's little wonder that is true. Large, long-lived terrestrial mammals are the exception rather than the rule. Daniella Chusyd and colleagues suggest that elephants have evolved mechanisms to combat aging-related diseases, such as cancer and neurodegenerative diseases.[49] A possible clue to longevity and maintaining memory function in elephants is their multiple copies of the tumour suppressor gene, *TP53*, of which humans have one copy and elephants as many as 24. The gene is vital for cells with damaged DNA, causing the cell to temporarily or permanently stop dividing or undergo programmed cell death, thereby assisting in cellular repair, senescence, and tumour growth suppression. Their study of brain tissue from aging elephants also revealed a negligible change in biomarkers for neurodegeneration over time, indicating protective mechanisms that could lead to more effective research and treatment for human age-related neurodegenerative disorders.

Aside from elephants, cows, sheep, pigs and goats all display significant long-term memory capacity. Cows recall the configuration of a test maze up to six weeks later. Sheep can recollect problem-solving tasks for a similar time later, and nanny goats can remember their kids' calls a year after weaning. Pigs raised in 'lean' or 'enriched' environments tested in a maze task performed better after 9 weeks, indicating good long-term memory, although the porkers raised in the enriched environment performed significantly better! [50] [51] [52]

Object Permanence

We take for granted that when an object is in front of us and then covered or obscured, it continues to exist; this is object permanence. Piaget's 1954 groundbreaking studies, many of which are still in use today, found that children from birth to two years old go through six stages of object permanence.[53]

1. No response to an object: self-explanatory!
2. Visually tracking an object: subjects do not actively look for a disappeared object, but do so if it's in the visual field
3. Retrieving partially hidden objects: For example, half an object or a food reward is covered
4. Understanding a single visible displacement: For example, in two cups, A and B, the object is hidden under cup A in front of the animal, and the animal must locate it.
5. Understanding multiple *visible* displacements: For example, the object is hidden under cup A in front of the animal, and it successfully finds it. When the object is placed in cup B, the animal must not make the A not B error, or perseveration error, where it still looks for the item in cup A. This error is seen in children 8-12 months old.
6. Understanding multiple *invisible* displacements: Think of the three cups trick, where the object is placed under one of three cups, the order of the cups is switched around, and the animal must choose the correct one.

Object permanence explains why babies love peekaboo games; one minute, you are there, then magically disappear as they have yet to develop the ability to understand that objects continue to exist, even when you cannot see them. How do animals fare when subjected to object permanence tests? Once again, the star performers are the great apes, parrots, and corvids, all of whom reach stage six.

Another method of measuring animal cognition is the *violation of expectation task*, which is much like it sounds: surprise and shock at an unexpected outcome, or how the hell did that happen? *Object continuity* is much like permanence, where the animal continues to track the movement of an object even when

46

it is out of sight, expecting it to reappear at the tracked location when revealed. For example, if a person picks up a stick and pretends to throw it but hides it behind their back, a dog will look frantically in the direction of the throw; that's object continuity. *Object constancy* is the concept that an item remains the same, even when partly altered or covered. A great example is that dogs recognise us regardless of the clothes we wear, whether we wear a disguise or peek around a corner, only to reveal a face. Object solidity refers to human and non-human animals' abilities to understand that two objects cannot occupy the same space simultaneously. When this is violated by some type of trickery, the animal expresses surprise. [53] Some great examples of these concepts can readily be found in online videos, where monkeys are shown magic tricks and are astonished when the object disappears, or when pet owners hide behind sheets, peek a-boo a few times, then escape unseen and drop the sheet to the poor animal's amazement.

Emotions

Emotions are tough enough to nail down in humans, let alone in animals. Additionally, several theories on the origins of emotions are somewhat at odds with each other. In the field of ethology, or animal behaviour, emotions are believed to be of the 'natural kind', that is, derived biologically from distinct circuits 'hard-wired' in the brain. A giant in this field was Jaak Panksepp, a neuroscientist and psychobiologist who wrote extensively on *affective neuroscience*, the study of neural circuits related to emotion. [54] On the other hand, Lisa Feldman Barrett, Professor of Psychology at Northeastern University, posits that emotions are constructed from basic psychological processes, such as core affect (basic feelings like pleasure or sadness) and conceptual knowledge. Emotions are constructed not in discrete areas or 'circuits' of the subcortical brain, sometimes known as the limbic system, but in diverse regions across the brain. The brain is essentially a prediction machine, running an internal *model* of the world based on past experiences that prepare the body for what may happen next. [55] I highly recommend Barrett's book *How Emotions are Made: The Secret Life of the Brain* if this type of thing interests you. Her well-tested theory challenges many traditional views on emotions in the field of psychology.

To add more complexity to an already confusing subject, Paul Ekman, a renowned psychologist and professor emeritus at the University of California, theorises that some human emotions are universal. Ekman studied multiple cultures throughout the world, from pre-literate cultures of Borneo to subjects in the USA, South America and Japan. Ekman found that certain facial expressions are universal throughout cultures and concluded that there are seven universal facial expressions in humans: anger, contempt, disgust, enjoyment, sadness, fear, and surprise. [56]

However, in the field of animal ethology, most of the studies follow Panksepp's brilliant model, which proposes seven distinct emotional systems in animals and humans:

1. SEEKING: Exploration and goal-directed behaviours that help animals find resources like food, water, warmth, and sex, closely tied to curiosity and motivation.
2. RAGE: Much like anger in humans, RAGE is a reaction to curtailing an animal's freedom of action, leading to aggressive behaviours.
3. FEAR: Survival system that helps animals avoid pain, injury or death, leading to fight, flight or freeze responses to threats.
4. PANIC: Related to social attachment and separation distress, important in the context of social bonding and care between young and their mothers.
5. LUST: Mediates sexual urges and behaviours, with distinct neural circuits for males and females.
6. CARE: Maternal nurturance and caregiving behaviours.
7. PLAY: Rough-and-tumble play and social interactions.

If you come across these terms throughout the book, refer back here for a reminder.
I think it is worth clarifying some of the hormones and brain neurotransmitters associated with these emotions to provide more context for their biological origins. [57]
- Seeking is a positive and rewarding emotion, the urge to explore and is regulated by the dopamine system.
- Rage is a negative emotion and can be triggered artificially by electrically stimulating the hypothalamus.
- Fear is a negative emotion, all about fight, flight or freeze and plays a central role in the amygdala. If this almond-shaped structure in the human brain is stimulated, the person feels fearful; individuals with damage to the amygdala, however, show no fear. Noradrenaline is the key neurotransmitter, along with the hormone cortisol, often called the *stress hormone*.

- Panic is a negative emotion all about separation distress, like when the baby is separated from its mom, with oxytocin being a key hormone.
- Lust, somewhat self-explanatory! It's all about mating; the key hormones are androgens like testosterone.
- Care is a positive emotion, motivating the mom to care for her young, with the oxytocin system being instrumental.
- Play is another positive emotion, rewarding and regulated by the dopamine system.

Measuring Emotions

Discerning emotions in animals is often much more complex than with humans. We have around 20 skeletal facial muscles that display emotional expressions, combined with speech and posture, to convey how we are feeling. We have a fair idea of how dogs and cats feel, able to read their emotional state, having co-existed with them for thousands of years. When a cat or dog growls with its hackles up and ears down, we know it is best avoided. Farm animals are much harder to discern, though. How do you tell if a goat, sheep, cow or pig is happy? *Happy as a pig in mud*, so the saying goes, but how do we know it is happy? Goats do not smile when happy, and sheep do not frown when annoyed, and I'm pretty sure I have never seen a cow show disgust! But perhaps the problem is not a lack of emotion or emotional expression; maybe it is a translational one.

Cécile Arnould and colleagues examined the ability of hens to convey facial expressions and found that chickens express their emotions through facial blushing and feather fluffing. [58] Facial redness, expressed through cheek, earlobe and wattle redness, was associated with situations that were aversive or unpleasant, and feather fluffing was indicative of positive situations and a 'happy' and healthy bird.

Ear movements are considered a facial expression, as many animals with 'mobile' ears use facial muscles to control them. I can gauge the mood of our alpacas by their ear position, having learned the hard way through experience. Walking behind them in their blind spot while eating, combined with flattened ears, is a sure sign you are about to cop a mouthful of foul-smelling alpaca spit. Sometimes I rouse up our big billy goat, and he glances at me sideways with flattened ears, a compelling sign he will rear up and try to butt me. Knowing that is a no-win situation, he often stands up on his hind legs, posturing at me before skulking off and taking it out on some other poor schmuck.

Using animal facial expressions to assess animal welfare is an underutilised tool, according to Kris Descovich and colleagues. [59] They identified many animals' facial expressions in various studies, such as play face, an expression that varies between species but means the same thing: let's play! Bared teeth usually involve a warning; chimpanzees baring their teeth is often mistaken for a smile, but it is a threat grimace. Humans express surprise through an eyebrow raise, as do most primates, but it is also seen in horses and dogs. Dogs at rescue shelters that show high rates of eyebrow raising are rehomed sooner, and eye-widening via the eyelids is an almost universal sign of fear or anxiety. Mice grimace with pain, which led to the creation of the *Mouse Grimace Scale* (I kid, not!). The scale measures aspects such as eyelid, ear, and whisker position, as well as cheek and nose bulges, which can help identify not only the presence of pain but also its intensity.

Other methods are used when it is too difficult to establish an animal's emotional state, such as when the researcher may not understand *chicken-ese* or *goat-lish*. Sound analysis can use animal vocalisations to assess emotional states, and heart rate variability monitors can measure the variability in the time interval between heartbeats, indicating stress. Olfactory and Chemical Sensors can detect chemicals and odours emitted by animals. For example, fearful pigs emit odours that are only detected by other animals. [60] Perhaps our perception that certain animals lack emotions is not that those emotions are absent but simply that we are not speaking the same language.

Conclusions

From pigeon-guided bombs, macaque chambers of horrors, salivating dogs and cats in puzzle boxes, the study of animal intelli-gence has a rich and fascinating history, albeit one tainted with pockets of unspeakable cruelty. Thankfully, we now possess a greater understanding of the intelligence of animals, their rich emotional lives, memory capabilities, self-awareness, and prob-lem-solving abilities. Next, I will delve into how, for better or worse, humans have utilised animals for our benefit

The Utilitarian Animal

Animals are such agreeable friends—they ask no questions, they pass no criticisms. George Eliot: *Scenes of Clerical Life*

The symbiotic relationship between animals and humans is a rich tapestry of predation, cooperation, utilisation, and discovery. Since early hominids evolved in Africa and spread throughout the world, we have eaten animals, worshipped their spirits, clothed ourselves in their hides, made effigies of them, tamed, trained, and selectively bred them, farmed and fished them, and altered their appearance to the point where they barely resemble their wild relatives. Take the humble chicken, for example, derived from the slight and dainty, colourful red junglefowl of Southeast Asia. Modern chickens, with their dizzying array of colours, shapes, and varieties, barely resemble their jungle cousins. Our symbiotic relationship and reverence for animals stretches back millennia and first became apparent when we drew effigies of their likeness on the walls of caves.

Of Gods and Monsters

Adorning the ceilings and walls of the Altamira cave in northern Spain, Neolithic cave paintings reveal clues to this symbiosis we have with animals. Altamira is home to one of the most extensive collections of cave art from the Upper Palaeolithic period, the oldest dating back around 36,000 years. Aside from a few primitive hand stencils and simple shapes, nearly all figures depicted are animals, including horses, deer and Ibex. The steppe bison (*Bison priscus*) is prominently featured throughout Altamira and other European caves, including Chauvet and Lascaux caves in France, where it became extinct around 10,000 years ago. [1] On the far side of the world, a much older cave painting on the Indonesian island of Sulawesi depicts human figures surrounding a pig. It is purported to be the oldest known example of storytelling and representative art in the world, dating back to around 53,000 years. [2] In far northern Australia's Kimberley region, Aboriginal rock art containing naturalistic depictions of kangaroos, echidnas, birds, goannas, fish, possums, and human hand stencils has been radiometrically dated to around 17,000 years ago. [3]

An extensive array of detailed animal motifs adorns the distinctive T-shaped columns of Göbekli Tepe in south-eastern Türkiye. The site features a series of megalithic structures dating back to the Pre-Pottery Neolithic period, between 10,000 and 11,000 years ago, and is one of the oldest known structures of its type. [130] Snakes are the most common carved motif (28%), along with foxes, boars, cranes, aurochs (a large extinct ox), wild sheep and asses, gazelles, lions, and bears. [5] Scientists are uncertain about the exact nature of the pillars and their motifs, whether they served for hunting rituals, rites of passage, or funerary and spiritual practices. However, what is apparent is the importance animals play in early human belief systems.

Ancient Egypt is unsurpassed when it comes to animal gods and deities; its pantheon is replete with some 1500 gods and goddesses. Many of these gods began life as deities manifesting through animals, such as Apis, the bull god, who acted as an intermediary between mankind and the creator god of Memphis. Worship of Apis dates back to the First Dynasty, approximately 5,000 years ago. It was strongly associated with strength and fertility and was used as propaganda during pharaonic rule. Anubis, the canine god of embalming and cemeteries, was represented first as a black, dog-like figure. The black was said to symbolise the discolouration of a corpse during embalming and the resinous coating applied before being wrapped in bandages. Anubis was later anthropomorphised into the human figure with the head of a jackal, one of the most frequently illustrated gods of the Egyptian pantheon. [6]

Herodotus' *The Histories* is considered one of the founding works of historical literature and contains rich and colourful details of his travels through the Nile Valley around 450 BC. Herodotus gave accounts of the lives of everyday Egyptians, including the God-like status afforded to domestic animals. In Book Two, chapter 65, he described, *"Though Egypt has Libya on its borders, it is not a country of many animals. All of them are held sacred; some of these are part of men's households and some not"*. Herodotus described how guardians are appointed to animals via an inheritance system, and townspeople make prayers and offerings to their appointed animal deity, shaving their children's hair and weighing it against a sum of silver, which is then given to the guardian to care for and feed the animal. There were grave consequences for anyone who harmed these sacred animals, stating *"Whoever kills one of these creatures with intention is punished with death; if he kill by mischance he pays whatever penalty the priests appoint."* If a cat died, great pomp and ceremony took place: *"Dwellers in a house where a cat has died a natural death shave their eyebrows."* Of the deceased moggies he wrote *"Dead cats are taken away into sacred buildings, where they are embalmed and buried, in the town of Bubastis."* An account in 59 BC by Diodorus Siculus describes how a man associated with the Roman embassy was put to death for accidentally killing a cat. [7]

A Cat-astrophe

Bubastis was the site of the temple of Bastet, the daughter of the sun god Ra and the goddess of felines. She began life as a ferocious lion figure, later softening and transforming into a female human form with a cat's head. [6] Herodotus provides an account of the wild festivals held in Bubastis, describing the journey to the temple by river, where many people gathered to party, singing, playing flutes, clapping their hands, and using noisy rattles, all indicative of the sacred rattle Bastet is portrayed holding. As they approach towns along the way, they shout and mock townsfolk, dance and stand up and expose themselves! [134] Once they reach the temple, many sacrifices are made, and copious amount of wine are drunk. A thriving trade in sacred moggy 'souvenirs' took place, with many worshippers purchasing a mummified cat for use in ceremonial offerings and possibly to take home. Juliet Clutton-Brock describes the dark side of the sacred cat trade, with thousands of cat mummies created and deposited in temples such as Bubastis. [9] It appears the cats were specially bred, mummified, and sold to the worshippers as ritual offerings. Some of the surviving cat mummies have been X-rayed and found to be less than a year old, usually dying from a broken neck. Skullduggery was also commonplace, with some dodgy embalmers substituting cat bits for other items. One cat mummy was found to contain the skull of a cat, placed on top of pieces of human fibula and tibia bones. [9]

There were so many cat mummies created in Egypt that a cemetery uncovered by local farmers in 1888 at Istabl Antar, 200 miles from Cairo, yielded an incredible 180,000 cat mummies. [10] Researcher Chris Elliot explains how the grave plunder was witnessed by art historian William Martin Conway, who in 1891 described the 'catastrophe' as follows:

> By some chance one day this genius dug a hole, somewhere in the level floor of the desert, and struck—cats! Not one or two here and there, but dozens, hundreds, hundreds of thousands, a layer of them, a stratum thicker than most coal-seams in a series of pits ten to twenty cats deep, mummy squeezed against mummy tight as herrings in a barrel. [11]

Conway described how cat after cat was stripped of its wrappings, the bones piled into yard high heaps and the wrappings sold off by the donkey load for fertiliser. [10] In January 1890, Leventon and Co bought the entire cargo of cats, weighing some 19-20 tons, and shipped them to Liverpool via Alexandria. However, for reasons unbeknownst, the client reneged on the deal, and the cats were sent to auction. A few specimens were sold off as curios, and seven cats were donated to the Liverpool Museum. The fate of the remaining felines was to be sold off for £3 per ton, then ground up for phosphate fertiliser to replenish depleted agricultural soils. [10]

Sugar and Bones

Far from being an isolated incident, in 1882, J.C. McCoan wrote:

> Up to 1872 the shipment of bones had formed a considerable feature of this branch of Egyptian trade, mummy bones contributing nearly as much as those of modern cattle to the yearly total of 10,000 tons sent chiefly to England. [12]

However, prohibitions on tomb raiding soon put a halt to this, and the remaining bones were sent to the sugar refineries of Daïra, happy to take as much as was on offer. [12] The *Daira Saniyya* project was the brainchild of Isma'il Pasha, the Khedive or *ruler* of Egypt and Sudan from 1863 to 1879. The Khedive owned vast land estates, approximately one-fifth of Egypt's agricultural land, where he established massive sugar plantations, including sixteen sugar factories. [13]

On the opposite side of the globe, the French colonial rule of Saint-Domingue came to a crashing halt in 1791-1804, with the Haitian revolution. This ended an exceptionally cruel period of slavery perpetrated by the French and British that saw as many as half of the slaves brought in from Africa die within a year of arriving in Haiti from disease and mistreatment. [14] As Haiti was one of the leading sugar producers of the time, the sugar trade collapsed, leading to a sharp rise in sugar prices. In 1806, Napoleon introduced the *Continental System*, an embargo on all trade from Britain as part of the conflict in the Napoleonic Wars. These further restricted sugar supplies, leading to the rise of the sugar beet trade.

Sugar beets are a nondescript-looking root vegetable in the same family as beetroot. In 1747, the Prussian government funded experiments into sugar alternatives, as sugar cane only grows in warm climates. German chemist Andreas Sigismund Marggraf found that the sugar in beets was the same as that of sugar cane, but the beets were too low in sugar content to be viable. One of his students, Franz Carl Achard, used selective breeding of beets to produce a 'sugar beet', which contained around 5% sugar, making it economically viable. This led to the construction of the first sugar beet factory in 1806 in what is now Poland, and within five years, a further 200 beet refineries had opened across Europe. [15] But what does this have to do with Egypt, mummies, and cats?

The beet sucrose needed to be filtered and refined to transform sugar into the shining white crystals that people desired. Initially, charcoal sufficed; however, a French industrialist discovered that bone char was far superior. Bone char is produced by heating bones in an oxygen-depleted environment, and numerous bone kilns were deployed across the country for this purpose. Also, a valuable by-product of the process is superphosphate, a rich organic fertiliser. The demand for bone char and its dual purpose grew exponentially, which meant that the ubiquitous animal bones littering the countryside were soon snapped up and sold by peasant farmers. [15] Entrepreneurial types, being as they are, soon looked further afield for the dwindling supply of animal bones, which brings us full circle to the cat mummies of Istabl Antar. As the supply of animal bones was depleted, human bones quickly took their place, and restrictions on pilfering the tombs of Egypt forced the bone collectors to look closer to home.

Scottish artist and travel writer Constance Gordon Cumming,

wrote in 1885 of the general disgust at a report that bones from Russian slaughterhouses were mixed with human bones from the battlefields of Crimea, *"all ground up together to enrich British soil!"* [10] Bernard Wilkin, Robin Schäfer & Tony Pollard dug further into this gruesome business and discovered sinister goings-on after the Napoleonic wars ended. [15] They found abundant evidence that the bones of horses and other animals buried on the battlefields were harvested all over Europe. The emergence of the sugar beet industrial complex made bone collecting a highly rewarding business. Between 10,000 and 20,000 men were killed in the Battle of Waterloo in 1815. Despite abundant historical reports of mass graves, the authors describe that archaeologists have yet to find these graves, having excavated just two human skeletons! Through ample evidence, they conclude that the fallen soldiers were dug up by local farmers and sold to the local sugar and animal coal factories. [15] Something to keep in mind when dropping a teaspoon of sugar into your next cup of tea.

The Ritual Animal

Ancient societies revolved around the daily devotion to gods and deities; all manner of day-to-day activities and outcomes revolved around how the gods responded to man's foibles. Failed crops, disease and natural disasters were sure signs that God or the gods were unhappy. What better way to appease, atone, repent or honour the gods than by sacrificing some other poor schmuck? This was commonplace in ancient Meso-America, where human sacrifice and cannibalism were not just commonplace but part of everyday life.

Defining sacrifice is a complicated and messy business, with several theories explaining the underlying motives. In the nineteenth century, Henry Hubert and Marcel Mauss introduced the term 'the sacred and profane', viewing the sacrificial act as having three stages: the consecration of the victim, the killing, and the subsequent offerings to the gods. It also involved three actors: the sacrificer or *sacrifice*, the officiant or *sacrificer* and the priest or individual who performs the ritual. [16] The English terminology of "sacrifice" is derived from the Latin *sacer* (meaning "sacred") and *facere* (meaning "to make"), and is often interpreted as a religious act. Glen Schwartz argues from a more functional perspective that sacrifice is not just a religious ritual but a method of reinforcing social hierarchies, social identity and gender roles, legitimising political power, redistributing resources, and maintaining social order and economic stability. [17]

56

Gabriel Prieto and colleagues' disturbing research describes an archaeological site recently discovered in Peru. The Chimú people lived in the northern coastal regions of Peru from around 900 A.D. until they were conquered by the Inca between 1450 and 1470 A.D. Prieto suggests that sanctioned violence lies at the core of Chimú society as a method of social control. Six sacrificial sites were unearthed in an area on the Huanchaco coast, where hundreds of children, adults and llamas were ritually killed over a period of 500 years. [18] Similarly brutal sacrificial sites have been found over many regions of South and Central America. The Aztecs practised sacrifice as a means of social control and expansion, cutting out the hearts of thousands of (most likely) unwilling participants under the guise of the belief that blood must continuously flow to sustain the Sun god Huitzilopochtli, lest he grow weary and not complete his journey across the sky. [19] The Inca practised capacocha, where outlying communities offered up sacrificial victims, often the children of high-status individuals, which would reinforce social status and good standing with the emperor. They were sent to the capital, Cuzco, and ceremoniously marched up to a mountain to sacred sites or *huacas,* where, unceremoniously, their short lives ended. [19]

The other side of the world saw a sacrifice of biblical proportions almost play out. Genesis Ch. 22 describes how God tests Abraham, instructing him to offer his only son, Isaac, as a burnt offering on Mount Moriah. Before Abraham follows through with this heinous act, an angel appears, instructing him not to harm the boy. Abraham spotted a ram nearby, caught in some thorns, and sacrificed it as a burnt offering in Isaac's place. It is also known as *the Binding of Isaac* in the Hebrew Bible and is celebrated as *Eid al-Adha* in Islam. Abraham's unquestioning obedience to God and God's benevolence are central to this archetypal story, which precipitated a raft of sacrificial burnt animal offerings for many more centuries before Christ of the New Testament atoned for man's sin, putting an end to animal sacrifice in the Christian realm, a much-needed win for the animals! David Janzen outlined the complicated role sacrifice played in biblical stories. He described animal sacrifice as demonstrating obedience to divine command, atonement, purification, and social identity and cohesion that set Israel apart as a society that centres around the temple and its hierarchy. [20] Animal sacrifice was widely practised by the Judaist community; however, the strand of religion dominant at the time held that Jerusalem was the only appropriate place for sacrifices to Yahweh, leading to the centralisation of worship and sacrifice in Jerusalem and the purging of rival cults. This changed with the destruction of the temple around 70 A.D., where hard-line stances to ritual animal sacrifice softened, focusing more on creating and interpreting texts than on stabbing and bleeding animals [21]

The Greco-Roman period was a particularly awful time for animal kind. Both cultures practiced ritualistic animal slaughter, with scholars hotly debating the motives behind the act. In the book *Ancient Victims, Modern Observers*, Fred Naiden disseminates various theories on Greek ritual animal slaughter and illustrates how the term "parasites" was used to describe those who assisted in the ritual, sharing a portion of the meat. Naiden argues that some theories describe Greek rituals as a way of sharing meat with the masses; however, the evidence does not substantiate this. Moreover, the case is that small rituals involving a few animals were carried out, with the potions divided among the parasites, priests, and other rank officials, thereby reinforcing social hierarchies and providing some individuals with honours and rewards. [16] Some notably bloody rituals on the Greek calendar included the annual sacrifice to the goddess Artemis, the goddess of the hunt and wild animals, where 500 goats were slaughtered in remembrance of a military victory at Marathon. The *Panathenaia* was the most important festival celebrated in Athens, lasting around 10 days, during which two major sacrifices were performed. The first group was dedicated to the goddess of health, *Athena Hygieia*, and the meat was offered to the priests, generals, and commanders. The second group consisted of a slaughter of around 100 cattle and numerous sheep at the great altar of Athena. [22]

The Spectacle Animal

The Romans were never ones to shy away from bloodthirsty pursuits, as evident in their expansionist conquests, blood sports, and ritual sacrifices. In the book *Religions of Rome*, the authors give an account of how Roman sacrificial rituals were closely related to the Greek traditions, describing them as follows: The victim (animal) was closely assessed to see if it met the strict criteria of colour, type, age and sex, according to the deity and event. Prayers were offered, and then wine and meal were poured on the head, making the victim 'sacred', which coincided with signs from the god appearing in the animal's entrails. After death, if the entrails were 'acceptable', the animal was cooked and eaten. [23]If the poor animal escaped, it would be considered very inauspicious indeed. The event was said to represent the divide between the gods and men via rules and codes of consumption, the best bits reserved for the gods. But where the Romans surpassed even the most blood-thirsty of cultures was in their entertainment.

The dedication of the Flavian Amphitheatre in 80 A.D. witnessed the brutal deaths of thousands of animals over 100 days. Classical period historian Cassius Dio accounts that battle occurred between four elephants and "*animals both tame and wild were slain to the number of nine thousand.*" Latin poet Martial in *De Spectaculis* described various accounts of a woman fighting a lion, a rhinoceros fighting a bull and a bear, a hunter showing prowess by killing lions, bears and leopards, and an elephant that defeated a bull, then ceremoniously kneeled to Caesar. Emperor Trajan also went all out in a victory celebration in 107 A.D., Dio claiming,

> *And he gave spectacles on one hundred and twenty-three days, in the course of which some eleven thousand animals, both wild and tame, were slain, and ten thousand gladiators fought.* [24]

In the book chapter *Spectacles of Animal Abuse*, Jo-Ann Shelton explains how the Romans viewed civilisation as a rational triumph over nature and its chaos. [25] Animals killing animals was evidence of the rage and violence of a brutal natural world. Exhibiting bouts of humans defeating and killing animals testifies to the superior nature of humans and their constructed environments. Criminals and prisoners of war were also killed as entertainment in the arena (*ad bestias*), retribution for those who chose to 'behave' like animals, contrary to the community and state.

The Romans trafficked in rare and exotic animals for these bloodthirsty *venatio* or hunting events, demonstrating Rome's power and dominion over people in the far reaches of the empire. Big cats were first reportedly used in a venatio in 186 B.C. The Senate later attempted to ban importing African animals to Rome. Still, the public outcry was too loud, and the practice resumed in 169 B.C. with a venatio featuring forty bears, over sixty African animals, and numerous elephants. Another venatio in 100 B.C. featured one hundred lions. Exotic animal importation was so widespread in the Roman Empire that animal populations began to decline throughout the region, making it increasingly difficult to procure animals by the third century. [25] On rare occasions, the animals were the stars of the event, such as the 'camelopard' (giraffe), trained hunting dogs, dancing and dining elephants and, of course, the lions and the Christians. Not all went to plan as revealed in the *Passion of Saints Perpetua and Felicity*, where a graphic account of an *ad bestias* execution of Christians unfolds as follows: In a purpose-built stage, a leopard, wild boar, bear, and a cow were brought in to face their victims. The bear refused to leave its cage, the cow tossed its victims in the air, dazing them, the boar bit its handler, who died several days later and the leopard bit one victim brutally, who eventually passed out! [26]

Sacred Snakes

Harming one particular type of animal in the ancient Huedan kingdom was not a good idea. In the book *Animals and Inequality in the Ancient World*, Neil Norman describes how the Hueda kingdom flourished in the 16th century in what is now Benin, West Africa. Elite Huedans inhabited palace-like complexes, surrounded by artisans and agriculturalists in nearby villages. A vast number of deities (around 140,000) were fundamental to the religious and cultural life of the Hueda. The most important and central to the pantheon was Dangbe. Believed to be a *Python regius* or the African rock python, Dangbe was considered sacred, central to many ceremonies and taboos, and a symbol of the royal family. So important was Dangbe that killing or harming a python was a capital offence, as a group of English traders found out. Not long after landing on the beach, several kilometres south of the town of Savi, the traders were seen to kill a python, the Huedans enacting revenge, killing the whole party and burning their trading lodge. Pigs even bore the brunt of punishment after a European-owned hog killed a python in 1697, the enraged Huedan king issuing a royal decree shortly after that all the pigs in the kingdom were to be killed. The Huedans enacted the decree with fervour, committing rampant *porcicide*. As one European trader discovered, even removing a python from a house was met by threats of violence from an angry mob. Dangbe was the principal *vodun*, or deity, but there were many other hungry vodun to be appeased. Offerings to vodun shrines were interpreted as to 'feast', but the vodun apparently also had an appetite for the latest durable goods. [27]

The spectacular annual parade to the grand temple of Python was an opportunity for the king to showcase his wealth and social status. It was preceded by a parade of musicians, singers, and hundreds of participants carrying an array of silks, food, and European goods. Wealth in the Benin region of the Hueda was measured not in gold or trinkets but in terms of followers with specialised skills and knowledge. Thus, the king's ceremonies often incorporated foreigners, a fanciful display of the king's standing and the kingdom's wealth. The cost of appeasing the vodun, which involved varying degrees of food, drink, trade items, and gift-giving, eventually wore thin as it helped facilitate a shift in social

status. In 1727, soldiers from the neighbouring kingdom of Dahomey marched on the Huedan kingdom, and many Huedans fled in
advance, perhaps due to discontent with the king's shenanigans
and social inequity. Of the magical serpent Dangbe, accounts by
the slave trader William Snelgrave describe the Dahomey invad-
ers finding the pythons in the Huedan houses, holding them up
and saying, " If you are Gods, speak and save yourselves: The poor
snakes, unable to reply, were promptly skinned, cooked and eat-
en. [27]

Animal Currency

*Barter is the natural basis of all dealings between man and
man and the setting up of a common useful article as a medium of exchange-of a currency in the restricted sense of this
discourse-is a natural development.* [28]

This is how Sir Richard Carnac Temple, amateur anthropologist
and Chief Commissioner of the Andaman and Nicobar Islands, described the origins of currency. He explained that real or imagined
articles can be used as substitutes for items in barter, representing
the different values of different articles. For example, X number of
coconuts for one knife or axe, coconuts being the earliest form of
currency in the Nicobar Islands. Temple explained how the Lushai
of North-Eastern India, reckoned the value of goods in buffaloes,
and the Khond peoples of East India valued property in 'lives', such
as those of goats, pigs, chickens and cows. Pigs were the currency
of choice in Tibet, and chooks in the Maldives. Teeth were a popular currency in the South Pacific islands, with sperm whale, por-
poise, and dog teeth found in Fiji, and flying fox teeth and jaws
in Melanesia. Elk's teeth were also used among the Shoshone and
Bannock Indians of Idaho and Montana. [28]

Buffalo Bride Price

Some years ago, I visited one of the megalithic villages of Flores,
also known as Nusa Tenggara, Indonesia, located high in the mountains of central Ngada province. The impressive steep thatched
roofs of the houses, some ten or more metres high, are clustered
around a series of *megaliths* or hewn stone blocks. Despite years
of tourism, modernisation, and the adoption of Catholicism, cus-
tomary practices remain strong in Ngadha culture. The imposing
and sturdy houses endure through time and generations, each clan
owning up to around four or more houses, all given a name and
arranged in a hierarchy. [29] The main clan house or *sa'o*, is the prin-

cipal place of ancestral worship and assembly; the other houses, or *w'oe*, house the rest of the extended family. Marriage is a matrilineal affair, where kinship determines one's social status, often related through the bloodlines of the mother. With such a focus on kin and social structure, understandably, marriage is a complicated business. [30]

Ngadha Bride Price Buffalo Horns, Flores, Indonesia

I noticed many of the houses were adorned with buffalo skulls, some more so than others. Asking a local as to the meaning behind the bovine decorations, they alluded to it being a 'bride price'. Marriage can be an expensive undertaking in Ngadha culture, with the cost measured in terms of horses and buffalo. Archaeologist and historian Tular Sudarmadi describes how the bride price can be a significant expense for the groom, typically in the form of several buffaloes and horses of varying quality, related to the social status of the bride's family. [31] This is a big hit to the groom and his family, but around a third comes back to the groom's *sa'o* in the form of gifts.

Reciprocity is also a prominent feature of bride price in Papua New Guinea (PNG), with pigs often serving as the unit of currency, rather than buffalo. Richard Eves describes how the bride price in the highlands of PNG was originally a reciprocal affair, helping cement bonds between families, generally occurring over a lifetime. The typical bride price before European contact was modest, typically consisting of some cowrie shells, salt, bird-of-paradise feathers, and a single pig. Following European contact, there were greater displays of wealth, with multiple pigs and cash now being part of the exchange. Men now vie to outcompete each other, leaving marriage in the realm of only the wealthiest men. Eves describes how the burden of debt often falls on women, who have to earn money to repay the debt. Men also see the exorbitant price as giving them carte blanche over their spouse, leading to greater amounts of intimate partner violence. [32]

Cattle Without Legs

On the African continent, cattle feature as an important form of currency, wealth and social status. Jean and John Comaroff illustrate the importance of cattle to the Tswana people of Botswana. "*Gods with wet noses*" is how the Tshidi describe cattle, a source of wealth, inheritance, and social status and used extensively in bridewealth transactions. The mining and industrialisation of the late 19th century significantly changed South Africa, and capitalism put a substantial strain on traditional ways of life. Tshidi men were forced to sell cattle to gain cash for goods, and men without cattle were forced into the labour market. Despite these pressures on the Tshidi, many important transactions are still valued in cattle, which the Tshidi call their "Barclays Bank". So enshrined are cattle in the fabric of the culture that 'cattle without legs' is the term they use for cash transactions, a proverbial middle finger to the capitalist system imposed on their culture. [33]

The Wearable Animal

Long before the first synthetic polymer plastics were invented in 1862, animal-derived products were the mainstay of pretty much everything that was not plant or mineral-based. Hair combs were made of horns, elephant ivory for jewellery, billiard balls, sculpture and piano keys. Wearing fur coats and stoles made from minks, foxes, and chinchillas was once fashionable. Briefcases were made from elephant and crocodile hide, and wallets were made from eel skin.

Today, animal skins are still used in clothing, shoes, cars and furniture; their fur to make hats; their innards to make sausage skins and tennis racquet strings; their hooves to make jelly; and their bones to make buttons, fertilisers and collagen-based skincare creams. In fact, the list is somewhat enormous, so I will concentrate on some of the quirkier uses of animals in products.

Top of the list is ambergris, a 'coprolith' (from the Greek meaning *dung stone*) that forms in the guts of sperm whales, usually released after they die and decompose. Some of these dung stones can weigh up to 400kg, but much smaller fragments are sometimes found washed up on beaches. The key component in ambergris is ambrein, which is extremely resistant to microbial or photodegradation, making it highly desirable as a fixative in the perfume industry. For centuries, the royalty of Britain and Europe have perfumed their gloves and pomanders with the unique scent of whale dung stones. [34]

Another unique *eau-de cologne* is castoreum, the dried and macerated contents of beaver anal glands. Castoreum has been used for over 80 years as a food flavour additive, to give a creamy vanilla taste, and as a fixative for soap, crème and perfume, mainly used by men. [35] Another popular anal secretion that is astonishingly valuable is civet musk. Extracted from the perineal glands of the African civet cat, the musky aromas of a cat's anus have been coveted since the time of the ancient Egyptians. Ethiopia is the leading producer of the world's civet musk, exporting around 900 kg annually, valued at approximately USD $450 per kilogram. Despite the value of the musk, the animals are often kept in appalling conditions.[36] Indonesia has its own species of civet cat, which plays a crucial role in producing the world's most expensive coffee. Kopi luwak involves the Asian palm civet, eating coffee berries, partially digesting them and pooping them out. The cat's digestive enzymes alter the coffee's taste; however, I have tasted it myself several times in Indonesia and personally find it rather underwhelming.

Tallow is the rendered fat obtained from animal by-products. Tallow was used as a lubricant, food additive, for frying, soap-making, and candle-making. In 2024, Australia exported over a billion Australian dollars' worth of tallow, making it the world's largest producer of cow fat. The tallow is often used in Australia as an animal feed supplement (yes, cows are fed back to cows), in explosives manufacturing, and in cosmetics, and it is exported to be converted into biofuel. [37]

Fish scales are high in collagen and are used in food additives, wound healing, corneal grafts, sewerage purification, bone grafting, nutraceuticals, and even glitter in cosmetics.[38] To put more yang in your wang, dried seahorses have long been used in traditional Chinese medicine. Purported to treat erectile dysfunction, the fish (yes, a fish, not a crustacean) also exhibits anti-tumour, anti-ageing, and inflammation-suppressing properties. Unfortunately, the poor seahorse is over-exploited, with overfishing dras-tically affecting populations, with 20 million dried seahorses trad-ed globally each year. [39]

The Testable Animal

Lastly, one of the most controversial uses of animals is in testing. Few advancements in science, medicine, and psychology would have been possible without the use of animal testing. There is lit-tle doubt that vivisection causes immense animal suffering, and thankfully, it is on the decline, with many organisations opting for computer modelling and using mouse and insect models over dogs, monkeys, and rabbits. Arguably, one of the most significant uses of animals has been in the development of vaccines.

Smallpox, or the variola virus, has devastated humankind for centuries. Variolation was an early form of inoculation first re-corded in China in the 16th century. In an early medical book from 1695, Zhang Lu described three methods of variolation: placing cloth containing pox pus in a child's nostril, using scabs in the same manner if pus was unavailable, and wearing the clothes of an infected individual. An account in 1713 described blowing pow-dered pox scabs into the nostrils via a tube. [40] By the mid-1800s, the practice was commonplace in China, reducing the spread and severity of smallpox. Thankfully, in 1796, the cow became an in-termediary, and the first smallpox vaccine was created. Edward Jenner had heard tales of milkmaids contracting cowpox and later showing immunity to smallpox. Jenner figured that cowpox pro-tected against smallpox and could be purposefully transmitted as a method of protection. So, he tested his hypothesis on an 8-year-old boy, infecting him with pus from lesions on a milkmaid's hands. After a mild illness, the boy was later infected with smallpox and showed no signs of illness. Thus, the first animal-based vaccine was born. [41]

Cows also assisted humans in the fight against tuberculosis. First described by Robert Koch in 1882 as a *bacillus* or bacteri-um, tuberculosis (TB) was long known to affect cows and humans. However, differences were found between the strains of tubercle bacilli found in cows *(M. Bovis)* and humans *(M. tuberculosis)*. Oddly, though, parallel research between physicians and veteri-narians came up with an ingenious solution that benefited both animals. Initially, the human bacillus was isolated, dried, pow-dered, and treated with phenol and then used to vaccinate cows. Trials showed mixed results but paved the way for the idea of us-ing *M.Bovis* bacteria to treat humans. In 1897, Albert Calmette and

Camille Guérin worked together to attenuate or weaken the bovine bacillus, successfully culturing it through 230 passages over many years. The result was a weakened bacterium that would not cause the disease but would mount an immune response. The vaccine was called 'BCG' or *'vaccin bilié de Calmette et Guérin'* and was trialled in 1921 on a newborn infant. BCG is still used today in the fight against deadly TB. [42]

Quiet and unassuming, few people have heard of John Cade, but his contribution to treating bipolar disorder is immeasurable. Cade was an Australian prisoner of war in the infamous Changi camp from 1942 to 1945, during which time he witnessed many soldiers suffering from both physical and mental illness. Upon his release and return to Australia, Cade weighed only 40kg, but he soon recovered and returned to work at the Bundoora Repatriation Mental Hospital. Here, he set about testing his theory that manic 'insanity' was related to hyper and hypothyroidism, searching for the toxic culprit in urine. Using a battery of guinea pigs (actual guinea pigs), Cade injected the cavies with urine from depressed and bipolar patients. He found that the urine from depressed patients killed the cavies at lower doses than that of a control (normal patient). Cade thought excess urea was the culprit, but this was not the case; uric acid might be. Uric acid is insoluble; to overcome this, he used lithium urate, which, to his surprise, reduced toxicity. Suspecting lithium had protective qualities, he injected the cavies with lithium carbonate, which had no adverse effects other than sedating them. Much of his work was performed from home and at the hospital, his home fridge full of bottles of manic urine and the ward pharmacy housing boxes of guinea pigs lying on their backs contentedly. After taking lithium himself and having no ill effects, he trialled it on 10 patients with mania, six with schizophrenia and two with depression, with the mania patients showing marked improvement. Cade published his results, but it was not until the 1970s that controlled clinical trials took place in Denmark, leading to the widespread use of lithium as a treatment. [43, 44]

In Conclusion

Animals have served us throughout history as food, clothing, companionship and labour. We have immortalised them on cave walls, created gods and idols, worshipped them, honoured them, and embalmed them for all eternity. We have sacrificed animals and organised social hierarchies and structures around their ownership. We have used them as currency, tools of social status, and a cost of marriage. We have made immeasurable goods, clothing, trinkets and tools from their bodies, adorned ourselves with their scent, skinned them, tanned them, ground them into powder to refine sugar, hunted, tortured and extinguished entire species. We have used them for research and testing, and yet, paradoxically, animals have saved millions of human lives. Let's hope the remainder of the Anthropocene sees humans take a more virtuous approach to the lives of animals.

Ploughing a Field the Old Way, the Hi Rise Buildings of Mandalay in the Distance. Myanmar 2022

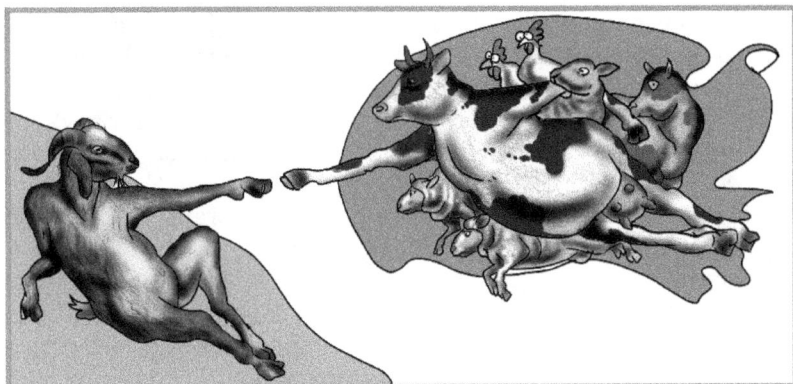

Morality

We are thus impelled to relieve the sufferings of another, in order that our own painful feelings may be at the same time relieved

Charles Darwin

Scratch an altruist and watch a hypocrite bleed

Michael Ghiselin

BAd dog"! You shout. Poor Fido stares glassy-eyed with equal amounts of fear and confusion. Any dog owner will admit, this is a well-worn rebuke, counteracted with "who's a good boy!" Does Fido know he's a bad dog or a good boy? He was happily gnawing on your favourite pair of runners before you rudely interrupted with an angry response. What if Fido ate the neighbour's cat, or worse still, the neighbour? Would that then make Fido a bad dog, or worse, evil?

Marc Bekoff, in his book *The Emotional Lives of Animals*, described animal morality as a social phenomenon emerging from interactions between individual animals, a form of social fabric that binds together social relationships, essentially, to know the difference between right and wrong. [1] Bekoff performed detailed long-term studies of mainly social carnivores, such as wolves, foxes, coyotes and dogs and believes the evidence from these animals supports the claim that animals are moral creatures. Animals display aspects of empathy, fairness and reciprocity, and display certain social standards for behaviour. Play behaviour in animals contains many of these elements; if the rules are broken, play stops. Likewise, if there is no reciprocity (I'll be the aggressor for a while, then we swap) or empathy (I'll stop biting when you yelp), then play is over.

But what is morality? In its simplest form, morality is a concept of right and wrong. From this tree of judgment, sprout many limbs and branches, linking notions of blame, guilt, judgment, punishment, retribution, fairness, and equality. Morality or something that resembles it, appears to emerge in all complex social structures, systems of rules, patterns of thought, and the development of character that benefit cooperation, in both animals and in humans. [2]

Much like our four-legged ancestors, human morality likely evolved from basic aspects of empathy, fairness and reciprocity that benefit reproductive success. Darwin came to the conclusion that moral sense or conscience is the most significant difference between humans and the 'lower animals.' [3] Variously quoting Immanuel Kant, Marcus Aurelius, and others, Darwin stated that firstly, social instincts lead an animal to enjoy the company of their kind, feeling sympathy and helping behaviour for others within the same group and the same species. In other words, *reciprocity* and aspects of *kin selection*. Secondly, as animals and humans developed more sophisticated intelligence, metacognition and rethinking one's actions and motives that were in opposition to social rules and norms, would likely lead to regret and unhappiness, distinct aspects of *fairness*. Thirdly, once humans developed language, people expressed their thoughts, desires and expectations. Shared expectations on group behaviour were then clearly expressed: break the rules at your own peril! However, sympathy forms the "foundation stone" of the social instinct regarding moral behaviour, in essence, *empathy*. [3]

Moral philosopher Richard Joyce supports the view of an innate basis to human morality, explaining the importance of kin selection and the role of maternal bonding in our ancestral past. [4] Joyce describes inhibitions versus prohibitions, where moral judgements rest on the capacity to understand prohibitions; it's wrong to steal or kill, for example. Whereas inhibitions, innate restraints or aversions, don't necessarily rely on moral judgements.

So, where do animals stand amongst all this moral confusion? A chicken can't read Kant; a goat would probably eat the bible, and sheep don't get Socrates! So, are morals innate adaptive behaviours in animals, purely instinctual and automatic? Or are an animal's morals learned behavioural rules, driven by thoughts and social norms, in other words, *top-down* processes?

Frans De Waal argues that morality is an evolved social function that promotes harmonious communities and boundaries on behaviour regardless of age, gender or social status, biased toward one's in-group. [5] He proposed three distinct levels of human morality, with around half sharing parallels with primates. The *First Level* contains the 'building blocks' and includes *empathy, reciprocity, retribution, conflict resolution* and *fairness*. The Second Level concerns the social pressure applied to groups and communities to *cooperate* and play by the rules. The *Third Level* involves judgement, self-reflection and reasoning, well out of the domain of most animals, the careful reflection on what one has done versus what one could or should have done, a distinctly human trait.

With all of the above in mind, we can examine how particular animal behaviours may fit into this complex and highly emotive moral puzzle, starting with how animals cooperate.

Cooperation

Much like humans, animals participate in and benefit from cooperation in different ways. Cooperation can take several forms, such as non-contingent cooperation or *altruism* (I'll help with no expectations), contingent cooperation or *reciprocal altruism* (scratch my back, I'll scratch yours) and cooperation within familial groups or *kin selection*. Whilst cooperation can be seen in hard-nosed deterministic light, such as an evolutionary adaptation to the environment that necessitates reciprocal behaviour, it is also a fundamental aspect of prosocial behaviour. Sharing food, teaching young skills through observational learning, grooming, and cooperative hunting are all prosocial behaviours that help initiate and perpetuate social cohesion in animals. Orcas cooperatively hunt seals by swimming side by side to wash them from ice fragments, wolves hunt cooperatively, as do hyenas, cape-hunting dogs and dolphins.

Humpback whales cooperate in an extraordinarily complex manner, corralling small fish or krill using air bubbles! The whales dive to around 20-40 metres, then swim to the surface in a spiral, continuously expelling air bubbles to create a 'net'. Once corralled, the whales feed on the trapped krill or fish. This has been observed unilaterally and as a cooperative group, with behaviour thought to be reciprocal. Instances of 'freeloaders' have also been observed, cashing in on the haul without blowing bubbles. [6]

Aubrey Manning and Marian Stamp Dawkins give an account of an elephant on a friend's property in South Africa, that had lost about ¾ of her trunk, probably from a hunter's snare. The trunk-less elephant pushed in between her compatriots while they drank at a water trough, and the cow next to her filled her trunk and deposited the water in the trunkless elephant's mouth. The same elephant had also been observed being fed branches by the others. [7]

More complex social systems are usually associated with big brains and greater cognitive ability, but even creatures with small brains cooperate. Birds rally together to chase off marauding reptiles, prairie dogs sound alarm calls to warn others of threats, and meerkat sentinels keep watch for predators. Our chooks will often sound an alarm call if a bird of prey is nearby, sending the rest scattering into hiding under the bushes. Sometimes, this results from an alarm call from an unrelated bird species, like a magpie or crow, which the chooks have learned to associate with danger. They even pick up on alarm calls from alpacas, sending them and the goats into hiding! Is alerting the other chooks and animals entirely altruistic, or is it a way of increasing fitness through survival of the group, or a case of 'I'll help you now, but you better help me later!'

Reciprocity

Robert Trivers first coined the term *reciprocal altruism* to describe the actions of an individual or animal that acts in a way that benefits another individual, with the expectation that the favour will be returned later, which ultimately benefits both individuals' evolutionary fitness. [8] Reciprocal altruism relies on complex cognitive abilities, such as remembering who did what, where and when, as well as the favours received and given, including their intensity or duration, allowing cooperation networks to extend beyond family groups. [9]

The infamous vampire bats of Central and South America show signs of reciprocal altruism in their feeding behaviours, sharing food not only amongst their kin but also between unrelated others. The bats roost in caves and hunt only at night, using sensitive heat receptors to detect other mammals. The bats land nearby and walk up to their victim, biting through the skin and lapping up blood, returning to the roost and regurgitating the blood to feed their young. Bats do not always feed each night, and they will weaken and die if not fed within a few days, so it indirectly benefits the colony to look after one another's kids. Carter and Wilkinson studied vampire bats over several years and found that 64% of sharing episodes were between unrelated bats, supporting a reciprocal altruistic act rather than kin selection. [10] Many primates practice 'allogrooming', where one primate grooms another, with the expectation that the favour will be returned. The bouts of grooming act as a social glue and often last a similar amount of time, further demonstrating reciprocity. [11] Female long-tailed macaques are more likely to help a low-ranking member in a punch-up only if they had been groomed by that member previously. Flycatcher birds are more likely to help their neighbours mob an owl if the neighbours had previously assisted them. [12] Capuchins share food in the wild and captivity, sometimes laying meat down in front of a begging monkey. Frans de Waal describes chimps breaking out into a 'celebration' when novel food arrives, hooting, embracing and kissing each other. Subordinate chimps greet and bow to the alpha male, confirming his status before transitioning to a tolerant and shared feeding session. [9]

Kin Selection

The concept of kin selection is to look after your close relatives, and there is a greater chance of reproductive success for shared genes. William D. Hamilton was the brainchild of kin selection and formulated Hamilton's rule that factors in the benefits and the costs of helping an individual relative to their genetic relationship. Hamilton used the term inclusive fitness, dividing this into *direct fitness* as an individual's own reproductive success and *indirect fitness* as the reproductive success of one's relatives. [11] Fitness refers to one's ability to survive and reproduce, not the ability to run a marathon! Legend has it that British scientist JBS Haldane once announced in a pub, "I would lay down my life for two brothers or eight cousins", a reference to the fact that siblings share 50% of our genes and our cousins 12.5%. [13] Rudimentary evidence of kin selection can be something simple, such as animals sharing food with offspring or siblings and chasing off competitors, increasing the fitness of their kin. Our goats commonly show this behaviour, happy to share food with their kids, but chase away other non-kin goats.

Empathy

Picture a world where no empathy exists; romance novels would disappear, TV shows would all be documentaries, horror movies would not be scary, sympathy and get-well cards would not exist, people would not forgive and forget, and everyone would literally be a psychopath. Ridiculous, yes, society would break down overnight, and we humans would probably go extinct relatively fast. Then why do we find it difficult to believe that animals do not have the capacity for empathy?

Surprisingly, empathy is not a particularly well-defined notion; as Benjamin Cuff and colleagues describe, there are "*as many definitions as there are authors in the field*". [14] Their summation concludes that empathy has both *cognitive* and *emotional* components, with similar emotions present in the target and the observer. Researchers divide empathy into two flavours. Emotional empathy is directly affected by another's emotional state, and cognitive empathy is where the individual imagines how the other feels, even if they are not there. Armed with that knowledge, it's on to animal empathy.

From a brain-based perspective, neuroscientist and psychobiologist Jaak Panksepp focused on emotional empathy and described it as a hierarchy of processes. *Primary* emotional or 'affect' processes are inherent in the (ancient) upper regions of the brainstem with seven basic emotional systems in mammal brains: SEEK/desire; RAGE/anger; FEAR/anxiety; LUST/sex; CARE/nurture; PANIC/grief and PLAY/social engagement. I touched on these definitions in the *Measuring Animal Intelligence* chapter. These primary processes are called '*bottom-up*', and are unregulated subconsciously by the brain. The *secondary processes* involve learning and memory, which help modulate those primal responses, allowing learning, such as fear conditioning and social learning, to occur. Finally, the tertiary processes involve *top-down* (conscious) regulation of these processes, with complex cognitive tasks like taking another's perspective, compassion and sympathy. [15] The tertiary responses are mainly seen in human studies of empathy, as these are often things that can only be described and not measured.

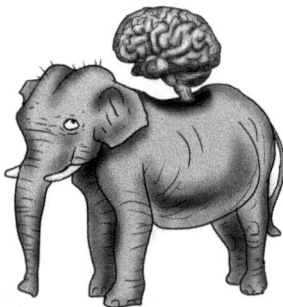

A useful analogy for understanding these processes is the *elephant and the rider* metaphor coined by social psychologist Jonathan Haidt in his book *The Happiness Hypothesis: Finding Modern Truth in Ancient Wisdom*. [16] My take on the metaphor is that the elephant represents the primary process, encompassing unconscious, unregulated bottom-up sensations, while the rider symbolises the conscious, top-down regulator of these sensations and emotions. For example, you are walking in the countryside and see a snake; the immediate emotional response is fear, increased heart rate, narrowing of the field of vision and a surge of adrenaline. The emotion of fear is an automatic, unconscious bottom-up response to a threat (the elephant); however, the rider, the conscious top-down process of the brain, quickly assesses the situation and realises it is a harmless lizard, attempting to steer the elephant back on course, calming it down. However, the elephant is strong and reactive, and it is difficult for the rider to rein in. Meanwhile, your friend, who was walking behind, sees you react and empathetically experiences a fear response (emotional), and later, when you recount the fear felt, they experience cognitive empathy, imagining how you felt.

Can animals experience emotional and cognitive empathy? In a study on empathy and prosocial behaviour in rats, Inbal Ben-Ami Bartal and colleagues explained how rats and mice both display a 'freeze' response (stand very still) when they see another rat/mouse experience distress, an emotional fear contagion. [17] Even hanging out with a ratty friend with a history of fear makes the other rat more prone to fear. Hanging out with a cool and calm rat calms the other rat's fear response levels. Rats have shown helping-like behaviour, intentionally freeing a trapped cage mate, regardless of prior social contact. When a second restrainer containing chocolate was placed next to the restrainer containing the trapped rat, the 'emo' rat freed its cage pal, and they shared the chocolate. These studies demonstrate primal empathy in rodents, but what of more complex forms of empathy?

Frans De Waal describes an extensive range of empathic behaviours in an array of different species and believes that the emotional and cognitive elements of empathy, rather than being disassociated, should be brought together in the study of animal empathy. [18] De Waal describes the importance of using frameworks like the perception-action model (PAM) and mirror neuron theories to assess animal empathic responses. Mirror neurons are brain cells initially found in the brains of macaques and later in humans. These neurons fire both during goal-directed hand movements and when observing similar movements performed by others; monkey see, monkey do!

Mirror neurons give a glimpse into the origins of empathic behaviour, but the PAM model provides a more robust explanation. The PAM posits that as an observer perceives the emotional states of another, the emotional state is automatically 'mapped' onto distributed neural processes, creating a personal representation in the observer of the other's state based on the observer's past experience. This is experience-dependent, so if the observer has no prior experience of that event, empathy may not arise. [18] De Waal goes on to list a wide array of animals that exhibit patterns of behaviour considered to be empathic, including:

- Mirroring or mimicking behaviour: most non-human primates
- Yawn contagion: primates, dogs, birds
- Consoling: primates, birds, dogs, rodents
- Sharing another's emotional state: rodents, chickens
- Learned helping, freeing another or relieving pain: macaques, rats
- Targeted help: capuchins, apes, elephants, dolphins

Of course, this list is by no means exhaustive; as you can imagine, if a rat exhibits consoling behaviour, many other species of rodents and other animals will likely, too.

Evidence that supports the PAM theory is found in neuroimaging studies. Jamil Zaki and colleagues explain the links between empathic and nociceptive pain. [19] They give the example of how hitting your thumb with a hammer is painful! The pain nociceptors in the thumb send messages to the brain that it hurts! Then imagine you see your friend hit their thumb with a hammer; similar brain regions, such as the insula cortex (sensory processing) and even the somatosensory cortex, are activated for both experiences! The somatosensory cortex (sensing) is right next door to the motor cortex (movement) and maps almost directly onto the motor cortex. It is instrumental in sensing pain and sensation and sending signals to motor functions, like quickly yanking your thumb away after being hit by a hammer. This helps explain how, when we see another person hit their thumb, we may instinctively grimace and pull our hand away.

Fairness

Fairness and equity are a big part of an animal's repertoire of behaviours. It is common to see big dogs playing with much smaller dogs, rolling onto their backs and allowing the other to gain the upper hand. They swap roles, being the chaser or the chased, and if it gets too out of hand, a few yelps and growls re-establish equilibrium. When we let one or two goats out into the lush green house paddock, the others look on and bleat with indignation. I used to tease our dog by putting a small dollop of dinner in his bowl. He would look at me in bewilderment, refuse to eat it and protest loudly until an acceptable amount was dished out.

Equity plays a huge role in human society and culture. We constantly evaluate and calculate the worth of our efforts, the cost of investment in people and endeavours, and estimate whether we got a bargain or were ripped off! From gift giving, lending objects and time to friends, relationships and employment, to hobbies and sports, we play by a set of unconscious social rules that guide cooperation. If we receive less than a partner, we get annoyed. Paradoxically, if we get more than a partner, we also act negatively, seeking an impartial 'middle ground'. If we give an expensive gift to a friend and later receive a cheap one, we feel a sense of indignation and inequity. Without even realising it, the rules of cooperation and reciprocity have been breached, placing the benefits of cooperation in doubt. So far, we have seen how animals cooperate to hunt and achieve goals that, as individuals, they could not accomplish. Animals show altruism, reciprocity and kin selection, but what regulates these behaviours and keeps the 'cooperative wheels' turning?

Retribution

Brosnan and de Waal argue that cooperation could not have evolved without systems and frameworks in place. [20] Reciprocal altruism relies on the premise that I'll do you a favour now on the proviso that you return the favour equitably later. This exchange of favours requires checks and balances to compare investment with reward. This is evident in their infamous experiment, *Monkeys Reject Unequal Pay,* conducted in 2003. [21] Two capuchin monkeys were placed side by side in two enclosures and individually offered a token. The token had to be returned to the experimenter within 60 seconds to be exchanged for a food treat. The treat was in a transparent container so both monkeys could see it. Monkey number one exchanges the token and gets a piece of cucumber, happily eating it. The second monkey repeats the procedure but gets a tasty grape instead of a crummy piece of cucumber, monkey number one watching on. Monkey number one is again offered the token, exchanges it, and gets cucumber again. This really pisses him off, and he throws it at the experimenter! So, monkeys exhibit a sense of fairness and respond negatively to inequity, also called inequity aversion. However, inequity aversion seems to only be present in animals with a strong tendency for cooperation, like chimps, bonobos, capuchins, dogs and corvids. Dogs evolved from their cooperative hunting wolf relatives, so equity outcomes are essential when living in a pack. Break the rules, and there will be consequences!

All Work and No Play...

All mammal species, including us, love to play, an integral part of any animal's development. Rough and tumble play is particularly important as it is essential for social bonding, establishing dominance hierarchies, learning boundaries and emotional bonding. [22] One of the best parts of breeding livestock is the joy of watching young animals play. The witching hour, usually late in the day, is when they are at their zaniest best. Goats chase and butt each other and climb and jump on anything that's available, including you! My spouse once taught one of the goat kids to jump off a log into her arms! They tease each other and the adult animals, which the unamused onlookers mostly shrug off. The neighbours' calves chase each other around the paddock playing some sort of bovine tag, often spending the day in 'cow creches'. Our alpaca babies, or cria, were a bit more sanguine but would often take off in a sudden, gangly sprint, running up and down the paddock. One of my favourite memories is sitting on the steps of the Taj Mahal in India, watching as the vast throngs of tourists slowly disappear out the entrance gates. In the middle distance of the Charbagh Garden, there was a lone dog, likely a street mutt that scavenges rubbish to survive. It was having the time of its life, tossing around and retrieving a shoe it had stolen, relishing in the rewarding PLAY brain circuits evolution blessed all mammals with.

After three decades of researching rough and tumble play in young rats, Jaak Panksepp concluded that PLAY urges arise from primary emotional systems deep in the subcortical regions of all mammal brains. [23] Panksepp discovered an unusual phenomenon while rats were playing. They emitted a high-pitched ultrasonic chirp, beyond our range of hearing at around 50kHz. This chirp was a solid indicator that the rat was enjoying social play, to the point that one day, Jaak decided to see if rats emitted the same sound when 'tickled'. Sure enough, rats chirped when tickled, approached the hand that tickled them and came back for more. This behaviour is likely an evolutionary forerunner of laughter, suggesting that if rats 'laugh' when tickled and enjoy bouts of play, it is likely that other mammals do as well.

Gordon Burghardt of the University of Tennessee defines five criteria to identify play: 1. Play is non-functional and does not relate to survival 2. Play is voluntary, spontaneous, deliberate, enjoyable, rewarding, reinforcing, and autotelic or 'just for the hell of it' 3. Play is awkward and goofy, exaggerated and precocious and involves patterns of behaviour that are modified or incomplete. 4. The play pattern is repeatedly performed but not stereotypically. 5. Play generally occurs when an animal is relaxed and free from stress, hunger, or danger. [24]

In a nutshell, play is voluntary, fun, and goofy, but also, like all things in cooperative social groups, it is governed by sets of rules that both parties must abide by. Communication is pivotal in rough and tumble play; for example, Mark Berkoff described how dogs initiate play with the 'play bow', that stereotypical gesture all dogs make, lowering the front of their body and keeping their butt in the air, tail wagging furiously. The play bow can also maintain play or restart play after a play faux pas. [25] Overly aggressive play is a common gaffe that brings a halt to proceedings, the bond of trust momentarily violated until the guilty party 'apologises', play bows once again, and it's off to the races! Role reversal is common in animal play; one party is the aggressor, the other is the defender and vice versa. Self-handicapping allows animals of differing sizes, ages, and strengths to play in an equanimous way, the animal sometimes closing its eyes or lying on its back in a submissive pose. These role reversals and self-handicapping behaviours often follow a set of equitable rules: one animal being the aggressor for a while, the other submissive and then a swap. This is termed the 50:50 rule and is common across the animal kingdom; violate the rule and play grinds to a halt! This differs among species and age groups, with younger, more eager dogs often self-handicapping more to induce play with older dogs. [26]

Conflict Resolution

Another role of play is learning boundaries; just how far can I push you before you snap? Often, when dogs play, things escalate and get more rambunctious until someone bites too hard; a yelp and a snarl indicate, 'Hey, that hurt; do that again, and I won't play anymore.' Peter Smith and Jennifer StGeorge describe how rats deprived of RT play were more likely to turn a playful interaction into something more aggressive, showing a distinct lack of impulse control. [27] In children, RT play between peers and parents has been shown to lessen aggression and externalising behaviours and lead to higher levels of emotional regulation, transferring to other social situations with other children and adults. As with our mammalian cousins, play between children is an enjoyable experience that balances wins and losses, involves self-handicapping and has unwritten social rules. Older children's RT play focuses more on asserting and maintaining dominance, sorting out where they fit in the social hierarchy. The lessons we learn as children in play, sports, and competition generate social skills that tell us just how hard it is to bite before someone else 'yelps.'

But which animals participate more in rough and tumble play, males or females? Males typically invest a lot of energy in intra-sexual competition to win the girls over, but females bear high costs in gestation periods and raising young. One would assume males would participate more in RT play, practice fighting for real combat, form alliances, and sort out who's who in the dominance hierarchy.

Catherine Marley and colleagues found this, with males of various species typically participating more in RT play. Juvenile chimps participated in social play almost twice as much as females, and most primate species had males devote significantly more time to RT play. However, there were also many species where no differences between male and female RT play were observed. These include sheep, cats, wolves, foxes, capybaras and elephants. [28]

Animal play is not all about who dominates whom; it is also adaptive, allowing the animal to develop social bonds, learn social norms, and prepare for unpredictable events. Neuroscientists argue that RT play creates a brain that is more flexible behaviourally, with a greater capacity for learning. [25]Play also helps to strengthen muscles and tendons, develops motor skills and keeps the animal fit and active, as seen in chase play.

A Dish Best Served Cold

Humans are masters of revenge; our history is littered with accounts of creative acts of vengeance and retribution. Books, movies, and TV series are created around the notion of payback, and cultural systems have emerged around honour, blood feuds and retaliation. Do animals also share our lust for a 'dish best served cold?'

Professors Tim Clutton-Brock and Geoff Parker probed the question of revenge in animal societies, or *negative reciprocity,* as it is called in animal ethology. [29] They describe how common this behaviour is, usually in the form of punishing other group members to discourage cheaters and loafers, keep offspring and competitors in line and maintain cooperative behaviour. For example, rhesus monkeys that found tasty food and did not share this information were likely to be punished. Horses given treats in full view of dominant horses were often punished after returning to the group. Relatives are frequently the target of punishment, the guilty party sometimes getting away scot-free, but the relatives bear the brunt of retribution. Baboons form strong friendships and will often attack or threaten other baboons that harass their friend or even attack friends and kin of the perpetrator. Many primates will punish a female who rejects their sexual advances, and dominant males will punish females who flirt with subordinate males! Chimp females have been observed consistently rejecting the advances of low-ranking males whilst the alpha male is around, but once he is locked away for the night, love is suddenly in the air! Often, punishment is meted out toward weaker individuals or redirected to some poor schmuck just minding his own business, often termed displaced aggression.

You have probably seen displaced aggression play out in human interactions: an argument takes place, and some bystander gets an earful, a drunk loses a fight, then goes and beats up the scrawny little guy. Our buck goat often displays displaced aggression. Sometimes he challenges me for authority, one time ending in a wrestling match where I made him submit. Almost immediately afterwards, he goes and takes it out on some other poor schmuck, the hallmarks of displaced aggression!

In the book *Good Natured,* Frans de Waal describes 'quid pro quo' revenge tactics in chimpanzees. [9] Dominant chimps can be formidable adversaries, so acquiring a few fellow rivals to gang up on them makes perfect sense. This can often backfire if the subordinate finds himself alone with the alpha without his backup pals. Shade, a low-ranking captive Japanese macaque, was having a tough time, frequently tormented by a particular male. Eventually, she cracked and faced her aggressor, only to be chased by an angry mob straight into the icy cold moat. After some 20 minutes, she was finally allowed back to shore, where the angry mob bit her repeatedly. Shade was hospitalised but released the next day, limping back to the island colony, straight up to her aggressor and sweet revenge. The brave primate proceeded to beat up the bully for the next 17 minutes, with some of the troop trying to intervene, at which point her two offspring joined the fray.

Conclusions

It would appear that animals display a distinct repertoire of behaviours that keep checks and balances between right and wrong. Reciprocal altruism makes sure you scratch my back if I scratch yours. Cooperation ensures the group survives and thrives; cheaters and social loafers get punished, as do their kin, but you also look after your kin to pass on genes. Play is crucial in learning the rules of the social bargain, and who is at the top or bottom of the social hierarchy, and if you don't play fairly, the game stops. Even rats enjoy play and laugh ultrasonically when tickled. Animals display emotional and cognitive empathy and have a sense of fairness. If you throw a god into this mix, you might even say it looks like a rudimentary religion, but some might say that's barking mad.

CAUCASUS TUR.

Goats

(Capra hircus)

Look for a black goat while it is still daytime

Nigerian proverb

A gentle breeze ruffled his jet-black shock of hair. She inclined her head, and their eyes met, locked in a longing gaze, her long and lustrous eyelashes fluttering with the crescendo of tension building within them both. She shyly turned away, slowly and deliberately directing his attention, leading him to a quiet and intimate place in the shadows. Paolo instinctively knew this was his moment, his desire welling and his heart pounding; it was now or never. He looked behind, gently raising his leg......spraying bountiful amounts of urine over his well-endowed pate, over his rippling body and into his mouth, raising his head in sheer ecstasy and baring his top lip in an orgasmic display of masculinity.

83

Yes, goats can be rather disgusting! At least to us, anyway! Yet the behaviour just described, as disgusting as it sounds (and smells), makes perfect sense biologically to another goat. Goats are prolific breeders, with females coming into oestrus several times a year. Female goat puberty typically starts around 6-8 months, and they often give birth to twins and even triplets. [1] Amongst the dizzying array of stinky odours a billy goat emits, several of these are 'primer pheromones', which act to elicit and even regulate the female goat's ovulation. In fact, just being around ole stinky can bring on oestrus and ovulation in female goats. [2] The other seemingly disgusting act that billy Goats engage in is urophagia: drinking their own pee. Not just a sip but a generous spraying of the head, body, bystanders, the whole shebang. The strange upper lip curl that usually follows this is called the *Flehmen response*. This response is seen in many mammals and is believed to facilitate the transport of scent molecules to the vomeronasal or 'Jacobson's' organ, located at the base of the nasal cavity and near the roof of the mouth. [3] Male goats also do the Flehmen response when sniffing the urine of a female goat, checking to see where she is in the ovulatory cycle. Interestingly, we found that once lover boy was neutered (after siring eight offspring), the behaviour continued when the girls were in oestrus. However, the other males that were neutered before puberty show neither the pee behaviour nor (rarely) the Flehmen response.

Origin Stories

The humble goat, *Capra hircus,* is an Artiodactyl (even-toed) ungulate (hoofed) bovid, a ruminant with four stomachs, two teats, a horizontal pupil, and loads of character. The oldest known common ancestor of the goat is the ancient proto-goat, Capra dalii, whose fossil remains have been found in the Caucasus Mountains and date back around 1.76 million years, sharing similarities with the modern-day Caucasian turs. [4] Goats are one of the earliest domesticated species, with archaeological evidence from the Fertile Crescent of the Near East, or western Iran, dating back 10,000 years, indicating bezoar ibex (Capra aegagrus) were raised and selectively slaughtered by humans. [5] The bezoar is an impressively large and robust wild goat whose habitat extends from the mountains of eastern Türkiye through the Middle East and Central Asia. Although there are no estimates of the number of wild bezoars, an internet search reveals a large number of companies offering hunting safaris for Bezoars, replete with many photos of impressive trophy bucks taken. What is it in the human condition that

drives us to hunt down and take another animal's life, simply because it is rare, endangered, or has impressive horns, antlers, tusks
or teeth? It could well be in years to come; the Bezoar may become
endangered or disappear simply because of its striking, large scim-
itar-shaped horns, which evolved as part of sexual selection and
evolutionary adaptation, attractive to the girls, but unfortunately
also to human trophy hunters.

The Author with a Dodgy Looking Ibex Statue, Kyrgyzstan

March of the Goats

Domesticated goats originated in the Fertile Crescent and spread
through Europe and Greece around 6500 years ago, arriving in the
British Isles around 4000 years ago. They were then traded and
dispersed through the Khyber Pass into India and Asia, and via the
trade routes connecting the Middle East and China. Between the
15th and 18th centuries, goats inadvertently hitched a ride to the
Americas and throughout Oceania, sailors often peppering the islands with goats as a backup food source for later journeys or in
case of shipwreck. [6] Of course, the goats often inadvertently decimated populations of other animals on these islands, upsetting the
ecological equilibrium. Captain James Cook was also complicit in

the goat apocalypse, leaving goats behind in New Zealand and Hawaii, islands that never had populations of mid-sized herbivores before.

One such island recently had its remnant herd of goats declared a heritage breed. Middle Percy Island, a tiny island off the Queensland coast of Australia, was visited in 1874 by Commander Bedwell of the schooner Pearl, who left behind twelve goats for the potential benefit of any unfortunate shipwreck victims. Today, the goats' descendants still thrive on the island, and their population is managed by the island's locals. [7]

Varieties

Goats come in all shapes and varieties, with around 500 different species, from the giant 'Spanish goat' weighing up to 130kg to the tiny Nigerian dwarf goat, popular with children and hobby farmers. Approximately 95% of the world's goat population resides in developing countries, and goats are a vital source of protein. Depressingly, 1.4 million goats and 1.7 million sheep are slaughtered each day around the world. [8] Highly adaptable and able to thrive in most climates on Earth, goats also have the potential to become a pest, as exemplified by the Galapagos Islands' Feral goats. Australia also has its feral goat problem, with the feral goats aptly named *rangeland goats*. The hearty Australian rangeland bears little resemblance to the 19 goats the British colonisers brought over on the first fleet in 1788. [9] Australia now holds the title of the largest exporter of goat meat, 90% of those being rangeland goats, with around 1.63 million head slaughtered in 2011-12, and 24,478 tonnes of goat meat sent abroad. [10]

Domestication, spanning several millennia, means goats have had ample time to evolve and adapt to humans and our behaviours, which may explain how they make eye contact and direct their gaze to a human face. This is common in dogs, as they are acutely attuned to our facial cues, having developed a long symbiotic relationship with humans over the past 20,000 to 40,000 years. However, wolves do not display the same facial scanning characteristics, having diverged from dogs genetically around 11,000 years ago. [11] Domestication has also altered goats' appearance, or their *morphological* traits. These changes include ear and horn shapes, wattles (those dangly things on their necks), long or wavy hair and their diverse range of coat colours. Goats with long curved scimitar horns were selectively bred in ancient Egypt, as were goats with long lop ears. [6]

The Kamori or *Gulabi* goats of Pakistan are a large dairy breed

with an amazing repertoire of colours and some incredibly long ears! The Hejazi of Saudi Arabia is also reported to have ears up to 70 centimetres long and 25 centimetres wide! Some speculate this is an evolutionary adaptation, but it is most likely the result of selective breeding for desired traits.

The Goat Awards

On to the goat world record holders. According to the Guinness World Records, the world's largest recorded goat was a British Saanen that weighed a whopping 181.4 kg! The smallest breed is the dwarf Nigerian, and the most expensive goat was an Angora, which sold for USD 82,600 in New Zealand. The largest litter of goats recorded was seven; a goat with the shortest ears (none actually) is the La Mancha, and the oldest goat was McGinty, who lived for 22 years and 5 months.

Wet Nurse Goats

A social media post grabbed my attention recently that sent me down a series of rabbit holes attempting to find the truth about goat 'wet nurses'. The term "wet nurse" *refers to the practice of feeding a human infant from another human source.* This practice dates back to antiquity and was typically reserved for the nobility and wealthy individuals. The wet nurse, who was also feeding an infant of her own, had to find alternative sources of milk for her child, with cow and goat milk often being the go-to options. The post in question showed a photo of a woman suckling a baby directly from a goat's udder and was originally posted on Reddit in 2022, according to Snopes.com. The story described the photo as "Rural homestead life in 1927", but Snopes traced it back to a photo taken in 1958 on the island of Lanzarote in the Canary Islands, the owner of a cheese shop reporting he had a copy of the photo on his wall for years and knew the boy suckling the goat. There are multiple anecdotal stories across the internet, often citing Pierre Bruzet, the 18th-century French physician, as the source of information on goat wet nurses. However, his translated works barely mention goats. In her 2011 book *Milk: A Local and Global Histo-*

ry, Deborah Valenze explains that past medical authorities agreed that a mother's milk is best for an infant and animal milk from cows and goats has long been a reliable alternative, and essentially what kept the wet nurses alive when their own milk was given to other infants. [12] The prevalence of syphilis in France in the 1500s saw mothers circumvent the wet nurses by employing goats. In the 18th century, abandoned children suspected of having syphilis were put to the udder rather than the breast, for fear of passing on the disease, explained Valenze. French institutions kept goats on their grounds to feed human infants if the need arose. One account from a hospital in Aix described rows of cribs that the goats would eagerly approach, straddling the crib and pushing back the sheets with their horns to suckle the infants. [12] Knowing how rough and boisterous goats are and their propensity to poop anywhere and everywhere, I have some reservations about the last account!

The Judas Goat

A betrayal of almost biblical proportions played out on the Galapagos Islands. Feral pig, goat and donkey populations were scattered throughout the Galapagos, with goats first introduced in the 1800s and eventually released onto 13 islands. The largest island, Isabela, was goat free until the 1970s, when whalers and other mariners released goats on the southern part of the island. Eventually, the goats headed north and crossed a hostile 12-kilometre lava field called the Perry Isthmus, making their way to the southern slopes of the Alcedo Volcano. Here, the goat population exploded, decimating the local ecosystem, a vital habitat and gathering point for giant tortoises in the dry season. This was the catalyst for forming the 1997 'Project Isabela', the brainchild of the Charles Darwin Foundation and the Galapagos National Park Directorate. [13] A highly trained 'hit squad' of park rangers set out to eradicate the goats from Pinta, Santiago and northern Isabela islands, with work beginning on Isabela in 2004. Male goats were selected, sterilised, fitted with a radio collar, and reintroduced to the population. These were the infamous *Judas* goats. The opposite sex did not escape, with select female goats sterilised and placed into long-term oestrus; these were the *Mata Hari* goats who would beguile the males of their herd, ultimately sealing their fate. Following their instinct to rejoin the flock, the Judas goats were tracked, leading the hit squad directly to the herd. The rangers then shot the goats from a helicopter, leaving the Judas goats alive. Over 700 Judas goats were introduced, and over 465 days, 3,439 feral goats were shot whilst associating with their traitorous friends. The last remaining goat was removed from northern Isabela in 2005, and a total of 62,818 goats were killed at a cost of $4.1 million. Although paradoxically, 266 Judas goats were spared and left on southern Isabela Island for monitoring. [14]

The Devil Goat

Goats have featured in religious symbolism throughout history, unwittingly given a bad rap by the notorious image of Baphomet. Most people might recognise Baphomet from the infamous 'the Devil' tarot card, featuring a human-like figure with a goat-like head, wings of a bat, and clawed feet like an eagle, crouched upon a pedestal that male and female human figures are chained to. [15] The iconic 'devil goat' image has been used in popular culture, Hollywood horror films, and in occult practices, most famously by Aleister Crowley. [16] However, the 'devil goat' mystery dates back much further in time, to the 20th dynasty of Egypt, around 1100 BC.

The Ram-God, Banebdjedet, was a deity worshipped in the eastern Nile delta, in the ancient city of Mendes, also known as Djedet and known today as Tell El-Ruba. [17] Banebdjedet is portrayed as a Ram-headed humanoid figure, later exemplified as a four-headed ram-human figure, said to represent the four elements of the cosmos: sun, air, earth, and water. However, a more overt sexual connotation was applied to Banebdjedet, a rather randy ram, described as *"the coupling ram that mounts the beauties"*. [18] Early speculation was that Banebdjedet may have been a goat, but the overwhelming evidence points to the god being Ovid in origin. Sheep were revered in ancient Egypt, with people even refusing to consume the milk. Evidence of such regard for sheep and their ram-headed overlord was the temple of the ram, discovered near Mendes, which contained dozens of unique granite coffins housing the mummified remains of sacred rams. The Greek historian Herodotus (484 – c. 425 BC) gave an account of a visit to Mendes, describing the likeness of Banebdjedet to the god Pan and stating that Mendesians considered all goats to be sacred, especially the male goat, further describing a scene he witnessed, where a goat copulated openly with a woman! [19] It is quite likely that this early account from Herodotus was lost in translation, and the ram-headed god later morphed into a 'goat-headed' god.

Enter the crusades of the Holy Land (1095–1291) and the Knights Templar Inquisition of 1307, and the story becomes intriguing! Founded in Jerusalem in 1120, the Order of the Knights Templar was the Western world's first military order. Comprised solely of men, it had a dual role as soldiers and a religious order, adhering to vows of obedience, poverty and chastity. [20] The order's experience and understanding of the machinations of the holy land, coupled with rumours of a growing political and financial power base within the order, prompted the ironically named 'Philip the Fair', the king of France, to order the arrest of the Templars in France. Charged with heresy, sodomy and 'spitting on the cross', fifty-four Templar Knights were put to the stake after a lengthy series of trials, the order disbanded, and their wealth confiscated. Testimony from the trials was mostly hearsay in nature and purported that all manner of homosexual acts were committed within the order. The Templars vehemently denied this, but strangely, it was admitted under torture. Enter Baphomet, where one of the accusations levelled at the Templars was of idolatry, admonishing an idol named Baphomet, which was vaguely described as a head, a statue or a painting. [21] It appears that the reference to Baphomet originated not from an idol, but from the testimony of two witnesses who described a hieroglyph printed on the head of a statue —a symbol with supposedly 'Gnostic' origins, as published in a 1783 paper by Friedrich Nicolai. [21]

This intrigued Joseph von Hammer-Purgstall, an Austrian scholar of oriental studies, who, during his participation in the British campaign against the French in 1800, made some 'startling' discoveries. Miraculously finding a book on hieroglyphs, translated into Arabic, Hammer-Purgstall postulated that this secret symbol was 'Bahumed' or 'Bahumet', a mysterious incantation invoked by the Templars to address an idolatrous calf statue in secret ceremonies. This gave rise to the idea that the Templars had been indoctrinated by their time in the Orient and had become idolaters and worshipers of Baphomet. [21]French orientalist Antoine Isaac Silvestre de Sacy succinctly pointed out that the ability to read Egyptian hieroglyphic script had been lost long before the Arabs took control of the region. Furthermore, Sacy revealed that *Baffumettus,* quoted in Templar trial records, was most likely a mispronunciation or scribal error of the name Mohammed. Not one to let the truth get in the way of a good story, Hammer-Purgstall went on to publish books and articles on the Templars' idolatry shenanigans, sparking a resurgence of the Templar fable and an almost feverish national obsession with symbolic archaeology. Ignoring the evidence of a simple translational error, he went on to publish a paper titled *The Mystery of Baphomet Revealed*, further connecting the Templars to Gnosticism and esotericism, simultaneously sullying the name of the Freemasons by linking them with the

Templars' idolatrous behaviour. [21] Hammer-Purgstall's 1832 publication contained an illustration of an 'androgynous Baphometic statue' that the Templars supposedly worshipped, introducing the concept of a dualist figure, with male and female sexual organs, incorporating aspects of alchemy, Gnosticism, esotericism, the Kabbalah and ancient Egypt. The illustration went on to inspire generations of pseudo-quacks to shape an archaeological archetype of a goat-headed, androgynous, demon-like God.

Instrumental in fashioning this new devil-goat archetype was Eliphas Lévi, who was born Alphonse-Louis Constant in 1810 in Paris. Constant, the son of a shoemaker and a deeply religious mother, entered a seminary school at 15 but soon discovered his interests lay more in the 'hidden arts'. Constant was beguiled by the principal of the seminary, who was a leading authority on 'animal magnetism', the work of Franz Anton Mesmer. A German physician known for his theory of *animal magnetism*, Mesmer concocted a variety of kooky esoteric ideas, his most enduring creation being the practice of hypnotism, or being *mesmerised*. [22] Mesmer believed magnetism was a universal force, regulating all living beings and that disease was the result of an imbalance of the magnetic fluids of the body. He believed an imbalance in illness could be restored by the penetrating gaze of the therapist, using his animal magnetism, causing the patient to often tremble and faint. [23]

On the cusp of achieving his priestly ambitions, Constant was derailed by a series of life events, spending time teaching, acting with an acting troupe, and as a political dissident, which earned him several stints in prison. Drawn to mysticism from an early age, Constant's stint at the seminary afforded him the opportunity to study Hebrew and dive into the mysteries of the Cabala and Gnosticism. The Cabala, or 'Kabbalah', is an ancient Jewish branch of mysticism that seeks the meaning of life, the universe, and everything. The Gnostics were an early Christian sect that believed salvation comes through knowledge and wisdom, as well as a hidden, esoteric awareness. In 1853, Constant changed his name to Eliphas Lévi, a Hebrew equivalent of his former name, and set upon his infamous journey into the occult. A talented illustrator, Lévi's published work *Dogme et Rituel de la Haute Magie* contained a strange image Lévi drew, a creature with the head and legs of a goat, a male phallus and a woman's breasts. The beast was androgynous, illustrating the balance of masculine and feminine, good and evil, light and dark, with a torch between its horns signifying enlightenment. [22]

But what of the infamous 'the devil' tarot card? This transports us back again to ancient Egypt and the links to the occult symbolism of the tarot. Funnily enough, the tarot has no occult or mystical origins whatsoever, with its roots in a simple card game similar to bridge. The earliest mentions of the tarot come from Florence, Italy, where the tarot sequence or 'Trionfi' first appeared in historical records around 1440. [24] The first accounts of tarot cards becoming fashionable as items of 'cartomancy', or a means to gain insights into the past, present, or future, date back to the late 18th century, when the cards are linked to ancient Egyptian wisdom and divination. [25] Several decades later, Eliphas Lévi's life's work led him to translate the 22 trump cards of the tarot as a series of hieroglyphs that parallel the 22 letters of the Hebrew alphabet, inextricably linking the Jewish Kabbalism, Ancient Egyptian mythology and Western occultism. And so, in 1909, Baphomet, the goat-headed devil, appears as card 15 in the Rider-Waite deck, the gold standard of tarot cards used by spirit botherers, crystal rubbers and mystical morons across the globe. Waite describes Lévi's inspired Baphomet card design as the *"Horned Goat of Mendes,"* replete with bat-like wings, his right hand raised, holding a flaming inverted torch, a pentagram upon his head, and two figures chained to his altar, those of Adam and Eve after the Fall. [15] The Satanic Temple in Salem, Massachusetts, commissioned artist Mark Porter to create an impressive 2.6-metre-tall bronze statue of Baphomet in 2014, based on Eliphas Lévi's earlier-mentioned illustration, of which I'm sure the French occultist would have been impressed by.

Goat Intelligence

And now the circle is complete, with Baphomet, the devil-headed goat, whose sheepish demure began in ancient Egypt, with a saucy Ram-headed God, who was later mistaken for a goat, made a scapegoat for the Templar Knights, adapted by a strange ex-priest who sought the mysteries of the universe, illustrated in an obscure book of high magic, transmogrified to a set of playing cards that morphed into a cartomancers guide to past present and future and finally transfigured into the satanic symbol that Hollywood, popular culture and heavy metal bands have come to love and adore.

Despite the devilish allegations, goats have shared a relationship with humans for thousands of years. We have dispersed goats to all parts of the world, including Antarctica, sometimes with catastrophic results. We have eaten them, milked them, bred them and idolised them, but the question remains: how do they fare in the brain department? Despite having a larger body mass than their wild cousins, domestic goats (Capra *hircus)* have a smaller brain size (0.13 kg) compared to wild goats, Capra aegagrus (0.18 kg). Reduced brain volume is often observed in domesticated animals compared to their wild relatives, likely due to the cognitive demands required to survive in harsh conditions and challenging environments. So, one might expect their pampered domestic goats to be less intelligent than wild goats, but that does not appear to be the case. As with birds and their tiny brains, volume does not always indicate intelligence; therefore, we will examine other ways goats may exhibit intelligence.

Self-Awareness and Theory of Mind

Gordon Gallup devised a test in 1970 to assess animal awareness, known as the mirror self-recognition test, or MSR. [26] Initial research was conducted in chimpanzees, which later expanded to a range of other primates, and then to mammals and cetaceans (whales and dolphins). Initially, chimps, when presented with a mirror, responded as if seeing another animal; however, after a while, they began exhibiting signs of self-recognition. Gallup devised a simple and ingenious test that involved sedating the animal and painting a mark on its face. When the animal wakes up, its response to a mirror is tested. If the animal recognises the mark and tries to remove it (self-directed behaviour), it is classified as self-aware. So, who and what passes this test? So far, the only mammals to successfully pass the MSR are chimpanzees, bonobos, gorillas, orangutans, Asian elephants and dolphins. Birds that passed were Eurasian magpies, other corvids and, amazingly, a fish called the cleaner wrasse! But what about goats? Unfortunately, they fail the MSR, but many scientists believe the MSR is not a true reflection of self-awareness, as many other species demonstrate a 'pseudo awareness, engaged by their reflection, but threatened by a rival's reflection. [27]

Object Permanence

Do goats understand object permanence, the ability to understand objects continue to exist when hidden? Christian Nawroth and colleagues tested this ability in dwarf goats, using the hidden cup method (think the shell game, but with two cups, not three), also known as the A not B task. [28] The task involves hiding a reward in sight of the goat under cup A, with the goat successfully finding it. The reward is then moved to cup B and hidden in full view of the goat. If the animal continues looking for the reward in cup A, it fails the A-B test; most of the miniature goats passed this test.

Next came the old 'bait and switch', where the cups are moved around and crossed over. The goats failed this test when the cups were the same, but several goats passed the test when the cups were different sizes or colours.

Navigating

Goats have excellent spatial abilities, which are part of their evolutionary adaptation to foraging in harsh and diverse environments. Goats are browsers, selectively foraging on trees, leaves, shrubs and grass, unlike sheep, who are grazers. Goats must navigate to foraging areas and remember those routes, with studies showing goats remember navigational routes for many months. Goats' abilities to remember spatial navigational routes and complex topographical details could be explained by an enlarged part of the hippocampus in goats' brains, which is integral to spatial learning. [29]

Goats are also experts in finding and remembering holes in fences, a game our goats often play. They would make excellent Limbo dancers, given the tight spaces they can squeeze under! I've often wondered who leads whom or whether they just browse and move indiscriminately.

Daniel Sankey and Andrew King pondered this problem, measuring the movement of 16 female goats in the Tsaobis Nature Park, Namibia. [30] The goats were fitted with GPS collars that also measured orientation and acceleration; data were collected over a 10-day period. The researchers tested the hypothesis that goats moved by 'voting', that is, making their own assessments and decisions and *voting* by way of their body direction, with the majority *vote* determining which direction they head. This has been observed in African buffalo, where they reach a body-oriented consensus before moving as a herd. The other was via copying, where each individual copies the movement of an adjacent animal, much like a flock of birds. It turns out goats simply respond to their neighbour's cues during collective movement. They noted that goats may also rely on vocalisations or environmental cues when deciding on movement directions.

Problem-Solving

Goats are notoriously adept problem solvers, and as seen in the example of finding and remembering fence holes, they are also expert escape artists, which suggests sophisticated cognitive abilities. Elodie Briefer and colleagues set out to test the cognitive ability of goats via a controlled experiment. [31] Their goaty test cohort of nine subjects performed a two-step task where they first pulled

94

out a lever via a rope using their teeth or lips. Step two involved lifting the lever, which provided a food reward. This procedure was learned in around 12 steps and was remembered by the goats up to 300 days later, with a slight increase in latency (time difference to start). Some goat observers watched on as their goat comrades enacted the experiment, and the researchers tested to see if social or observational learning played a role in response times. However, this did not affect the time required to learn, suggesting that observational learning ability was absent. Overall, the results demonstrated that goats possess excellent spatial abilities and long-term memory, and they learn novel tasks quickly.

Social Learning

On one occasion, I witnessed one of our goats, Frida, learn through observation. Frida was named after the artist Frida Kahlo, as the section of garden hose we taped to her horns to prevent her head from getting stuck in the fencing looked a lot like a monobrow! Frida found it advantageous to plonk herself bodily in the feeding trough so no others could access the food. Being a low-ranking animal in the pecking order, Frida would regularly get beaten up by the other goats. This blocking technique proved quite effective and worked on most occasions. Several weeks later, I witnessed another unrelated animal perform the same behaviour! Occasionally, Frida still pulls this stunt, regardless of the location or the trough shape, showing an ability to generalise that behaviour to other places and contexts.

Not only do goats learn socially from each other, but they are also adept at taking their cues from humans. In an experiment using a simple detour task, where food was placed behind an inward or outward-facing V-shaped hurdle, Christian Nawroth and colleagues found that all the goats navigated the outward hurdle faster than the inward-facing one. [32] However, when a human 'demonstrator' walked the inward hurdle route shortly before the goats performed the same task, their times improved significantly, suggesting social or *observational* learning occurred.

Our goat enclosure has an old security screen door on the front to lock the goats in, which is useful when they are kidding. One day, whilst giving a drench (worming solution) to another goat, Pepe, an almost pathologically curious goat, was mouthing the handle, trying to get in to see what was going on. Was this a completely random action, or a case of covert observational learning? On several occasions, I have seen our billy goat watching intently as I open the gate, observing the latch. It's a big stretch to suggest he is thinking about how the gate latch works, but there seems to be an intense interest in the latch and an association between the latch and the prospect of freedom.

How to Hog the Feed Trough

Memory

Female goats remember their kids' calls long after they've been weaned. Nannies show a strong response to kids around five months old, but also respond to their older kids' calls some 12 months after weaning. [33] Familial bonds are very strong within goat society; our old nanny goat still curls up at night with her large and mature son, Pepe. Although the bond seems weaker with older offspring, the nanny often chases off mature kids so the younger kids can thrive. Millie, one of our middle-aged nannies, still sleeps and grazes with her mature twin kids, but one day I saw her napping with Buck, her much older previous kid.

Dwarf Nigerian goats were the star performers in a study by Susan Meyer and colleagues. Thirteen goats were trained to use a selection of four press buttons in order to receive drinking water. A screen displayed four symbols, category 1: one open-centred ○ (reward) and category 2: the other three symbols all coloured black ● (unrewarded). The goats learned to discriminate between the symbols, even when presented with different sets of shapes that retained the original categories (filled and unfilled). This showed goats can form categories of objects (open-centred but different shapes) based on similarity and are able to generalise this to new shapes and symbols. This was learned over an average of only three training sessions! [34] This suggests that goats can remember visual discrimination tasks, with their performance improving over time, and have the ability to transfer that learning to new and novel shapes, indicating a significant memory capacity. Of course, this makes sense when you need to recall the locations of the best grasses and shrubs.

Recognition

It has been well established in humans that a region of the brain called the fusiform gyrus, or fusiform face area (FFA), is synonymous with facial recognition. This area sits around both sides of the brain, roughly level with and behind the ears. People with damage or abnormalities in the FFA have what's called *prosopagnosia*, or facial blindness. Some well-known people with the condition include actor Brad Pitt, primatologist Jane Goodall and science writer Karl Kruszelnicki. Often, people with prosopagnosia can only identify a person using other cues, such as when they hear their voice.

Laura Cuaya and colleagues at the National Autonomous University of Mexico somehow trained dogs to sit still in an MRI scanner and found brain regions in dogs, similar to the FFA in humans, activated when dogs saw human faces. [35] This was also found to be the case with sheep brains, where populations of cells in similar temporal areas of the sheep's brain encoded for faces and not for other objects! [36] So it would not be a huge stretch of the imagination to suggest that goats also have brain regions that encode and recognise human faces, given their long association with humans.

An important part of recognising faces is combining visual information with other stimuli to determine 'who are you'. Functional MRI imaging has shown that separate brain regions are associated with perceiving faces (FFA) and hearing their voices (temporal gyrus), but when both are combined (multimodal), other brain regions are activated. [37] To investigate whether this cross-modal concept also applies to goats, Benjamin Pitcher and colleagues tested ten goats at the University of Kent in the UK. They found that, indeed, goats do use cross-modal recognition when recognising their friends, with both looking and bleating playing a role in determining 'who are you'. [38] They also found that goats looked longer and more intently when hearing their besties bleat than when hearing less familiar goats. It is also possible that goats may use *inferential reasoning* when trying to work out who is bleating. Psychologist David Premack's work on animal cognition found that animals deal with fragmented information by process of elimination or *infer-*

ence by exclusion, which has mostly been studied and confirmed in chimps, sea lions and dolphins, but as Pitcher et al. imply, perhaps goats too! [39]

Animals in distress or facing insurmountable problems often look to humans for assistance. For example, when playing fetch with your dog, the ball rolls under an inaccessible spot. Often the dog will bark and gesture as if to say, *"Hey, get the ball, dummy, so we can keep playing"*! But do goats also look to humans with an intentional gaze when faced with an insurmountable problem?

Nawroth and colleagues indeed found that goats gaze earlier, longer, and more frequently at a human facing toward them, compared to away, indicating the goat may be thinking something like, 'Hey, human, don't just stand there; some help, please! ' [40] I have witnessed something similar in our goats, often gazing at my face as they try to figure out my intentions, much like a dog watching you for cues to see if you are going for a walk or just staying in. When they are grazing and can't reach a branch with some juicy leaves, the goat will often turn and look you in the eye, intimating you to grab the branch and pull it into reach. Once this happens, it's a free-for-all and the goats all pile on. The biggest goat will often hold the branch down with its body, and the rest of the herd greedily eat up the leaves. Is this cooperative behaviour or reciprocal altruism? Possibly, or maybe just satisfying self-interest, it's hard to tell.

Cooperative Behaviour

As with the gaze experiment above, which looked at goats...looking at us, how about when goats stare at goats? Juliane Kaminski and colleagues at the Max Planck Institute set out to find this with their study of 10 goats in Leipzig, Germany. [41] They mention how primates follow the gaze of other primates and humans to gain information about things such as food locations, but there is little evidence that other species do this. Their trials found that 60% of goats followed the gaze of their conspecifics (goat friends) to look at objects above and behind them. On an object selection task, 23 goats were tested to see if they would follow various cues to alert them to food locations. It turns out that touching and tapping cues yielded two-thirds above chance, a pointing cue about a third above chance, but the gaze-only cue fizzled. Far from a flop, the researchers stated that the results were comparable to those of dolphins and fur seals, which were better than horses but not as strong as dogs' performance.

Emotions

Goats tend to recognise each other through a combination of facial recognition, scent, and social interactions. To test the extent to which they use facial cues, 32 dairy goat volunteers were trained to observe pictures of another goat's face in a positive or negative condition. [42] Bellegarde and colleagues photographed the positive, happy goats while they were being groomed and took negative photos when an ice pack was placed on their udders. The experimenters measured the ear position of the volunteers (forward, neutral or back) as well as the time spent looking at the image on a screen or touching it. Results showed that goats respond differently to images of various emotional states, suggesting they can perceive the emotional valence conveyed in those images. This is quite convincing evidence that goats perceive each other's emotions via facial cues, but what about perceiving human faces?

Twenty willing and tame participants were found at the Buttercups Sanctuary for Goats in the UK, and invited to test whether goats can discriminate against human emotions. [32] Four conditions were arranged via photos of: a happy woman's face on the left and an angry woman's face on the right; a happy man's face on the left and an angry man's face on the right; both conditions were also flipped (left/right). Amazingly, the goats discriminated between happy and sad faces, preferring to approach the happy faces. The goats also spent more time interacting with images on the right. Why the right side? Theories of brain lateralisation (left and right brain hemispheres) suggest that mammals tend to lateralise positive emotions to the left side of the brain, meaning animals will often turn to the left when faced with positive emotions and to the right with aversive stimuli. [43] Whoa, ok, so now goats recognise not only each other's emotions by their facial cues but also human emotions, as well as excellent long-term memory and problem-solving abilities. That sounds suspiciously like a high degree of intelligence.

Personality

Emotions are short-lived expressions of an animal or person's experience; personality is a more enduring trait that determines how, why and when emotions arise. One of the current popular models for personality in humans is the five-factor model, with the acronym 'OCEAN', which includes openness, conscientiousness, extroversion, agreeableness, and neuroticism. Whilst neuroticism fits the profile of several of our goats, can personality traits actually apply to goats?

By testing the social interactions of 30 dairy goats, Miranda-de la Lama and colleagues used a three-factor analysis and divided the goats into avoiders (37%), agonistic (conflict-related 27%) and non-agonistic (28%). They further identified four profiles: *aggressive, affiliative, passive,* and *avoiders.* [44] *Mediators* were the term given to goats that tried to break up fights. Goats that supported each other were called *supporters* and tended to lick, sniff and groom other goats involved in a punch-up. They found that the aggressive goats used (no surprise here) agonistic tactics and had longer feed times than *passives*, which helped resolve conflicts and *support* contenders. The *affiliative* goats showed average dominance and did little in the way of mediating fights, but were highly supportive of contenders. The *passives* were low in dominance, did little in the way of *mediating* or *supporting* conflicts and had the highest resting times but the lowest feeding rates. Lastly, the avoiders were low in dominance, avoided conflict, showed no interest in conflict resolution, and had the lowest resting times and the highest feed times. An explanation for the feed times was probably that they were harassed so much by the others that they had to eat sporadically and had less time to rest. Interestingly, the goats with the longest beards and the biggest bellies were the affiliative goats, and the shortest beards and smallest chests were the avoiders. The sweet spot is the affiliate gals, and the worst place to be is the avoiders at the bottom of the hierarchy!

Robert Sapolsky describes his time spent studying baboons in Africa in *A Primate's Memoir,* where he documented just how miserable it is to be a baboon at the bottom of the social rung. Blood tests from the baboons attest to this, showing massively elevated levels of stress hormones in low-ranking individuals. And if you are low on the ladder and not the direct target of someone else's bad mood, displaced aggression from some other baboon will probably strike! [45]

A similar scenario plays out in our small herd; the big guy at the top gets all the best food and gals, but in rutting season, he loses lots of weight and condition, chasing off all the contenders and worrying constantly about his gals. Life at the bottom of the rung sucks big time, though, constantly being harassed by other high-ranking individuals. The rank order of the hierarchy is easily discerned each morning when they are released from an overnight pen to their grazing paddock, with the same order observed each time. The big guy always goes first (the *aggressive)*, then the second-in-command male, and the middle portion (affiliates, passives) is usually a mishmash, but the tail end is always the same: the *avoider* and her female kid.

Tennessee Fainting Goats

I could not possibly end this chapter without mentioning the famous fainting goats of Tennessee. You may have seen them on social media or YouTube, behaving quite normally until the goat gets a fright, stiffens, all four legs extended, and falls over. It is quite funny to watch, not for the poor old goats, but entertaining, nonetheless. The fainting goat sounds very dramatic, but the real name is myotonia congenita, a hereditary disease that first appeared in goats in central Tennessee in 1880. The culprit lies in a mutation of the ClC-1i chloride channels, which are tiny, microscopic pores in muscle cells that allow chloride ions to flow into the cell after the cells that make up the muscle have contracted. The chloride ions help the muscles relax. So, when the goats get a fright and experience involuntary movement, such as when you jump when startled, the muscles tighten, then freeze up, taking a minute or so to relax again. The goats recover the use of the front of their body first, running away and dragging stiff legs behind them. Oddly, the goats cannot 'faint' again for about twenty to thirty minutes, no matter how scared or excited they are. Despite the goats' comical disabilities, they live a normal lifespan and have no other symptoms apart from their 'faints'. [46] [47]

Conclusions

Goats have coexisted with us for thousands of years, during which time we have spread them throughout the world. Goats have strong social bonds and exhibit and discriminate emotions in each other and humans. They display some human-like personality traits, recognise both goat and human faces, have excellent memory and problem-solving skills and provide us with meat, skins, companionship and milk for infants. What's not to love about goats?

Sheep

(Ovis aries)

Every sheep is slaughtered in the way it lies down

Somali proverb

Sheep and intelligence are not two words that generally share the same sentence, and many puns have been used to insult someone's intelligence or susceptibility to following the crowd. Are sheep truly the dumb animals we have been led to believe, best served up with mint sauce? Read on, and we shall explore the world of ovines.

Origin Stories

Sheep, like goats, are even-toed ungulates, have four-chambered stomachs, chew their cud, live in herds and have slit-shaped pupils for excellent peripheral vision. Sheep, however, are grazers, mostly living off grasses, whereas goats are browsers, preferring shrubs and trees, as well as pot plants, hats, and cardboard. Much like the goat, the origins of domestic sheep can be traced back to the Fertile Crescent, approximately 10,000-12,000 years ago, with a common ancestor of sheep emerging around 2-3 million years ago, roughly the time when sheep and goats diverged from each other. There are eight extant (alive today) species of sheep, differing in things like body size, colouring, horns, and number of chromosomes, including; the European and the Asiatic mouflon from Europe and western Asia, the argali from mountainous areas of Central Asia, the Dall or thin-horn sheep of Western Canada and the USA, the bighorn sheep from the Canadian Rockies to Mexico, the snow sheep of north-eastern Asia and, of course, the domestic sheep.[1] Through genetic testing, Hamid Rezai and colleagues believe sheep originated in Asia and migrated through northeastern Asia across the Bering Strait and into North America, with domestic sheep originating from a common ancestor, *Ovis orientalis*. [1]

Many Flavours

Sheep come in a dizzying array of breeds, shapes and sizes, bred for their wool, milk and meat. The UN Food and Agriculture Organisation lists over 1,690 different breeds of sheep worldwide, from the Afghan Marco Polo Sheep to the Zimbabwean Black-Headed Persian. They vary in size from the tiny 10-20 kg Ouessant sheep of France to the mighty Lincoln, weighing in at 120-160 kg. [2, 3] According to Guinness World Records, the tallest sheep was a Suffolk ram that stood over a metre tall and weighed a whopping 247.2 kg. The most expensive sheep was auctioned in Scotland for £367,500 in 2020. The world's oldest recorded sheep was a crossbred ewe who gave birth to her 40th lamb at the age of 28 and died in 1989 at the ripe old age of 28 years and 51 weeks. In 2012, John Maciver of the Isle of Lewis, Scotland, claimed his sheep *Methuselina* was the oldest living sheep at the time, but that was until *Methuselina* fell off a cliff and died at the age of 26. [4] The heaviest Merino wool sheep recorded was *Chris* the sheep, named after an episode of the comedy series Father Ted. Chris was spotted wandering near the outskirts of Canberra, carrying about 5 years' worth of unshorn wool. Chris was reported to the RSPCA, who arranged for champion Australian shearer Ian Elkins to shear the animal. A whopping

41.1kg fleece was removed and was recorded in the Guinness Book of World Records as the world's 'heaviest sheep fleece'. [5] Chris was adopted and retired to a farm; his fleece is currently on display in the Australian National Museum.

One of the most unusual sheep species I have encountered was in the arid regions of far western China. The city of Kashgar has a history that dates back to the Han dynasty and was once part of the famous Silk Road. The city's bustling livestock market, arguably the world's largest, draws farmers and herdsmen from all around the region. Aside from the cows, yaks, donkeys, horses and goats being traded, the fat-tailed sheep were the star attraction. Packing several kilos of fat on their rumps, it's quite a sight watching them walking in a herd, their fat arses jiggling in unison! The rump fat is highly prized, and street vendors often sell roasted cubes of the glistening fat on shish kebab skewers.

Fat-Tailed Sheep, Kashgar, Xinjiang, China

Polycerates

Sheep have spread globally through wild populations in Europe and Asia, as well as through colonialism in Australia, Asia, the Pacific, and Africa. Most sheep are bred as 'polled' animals, selectively bred to no longer have horns, but there are some extra horny sheep still around today! Polycerate sheep often have four horns, sometimes even up to six! Polyceraty (characterised by more than two horns) is observed in some goat and sheep breeds, including the notable breeds such as the Jacob Sheep, the Sishui Fur Sheep, the Navajo-Churro, and the Icelandic Sheep. Aur'elie Allais-Bonnet and colleagues traced the origins of the multi-horned animals to a gene called HOXD1. This homeobox gene is instrumental in telling what cells to grow where during embryogenesis. They found that ruminants, such as sheep and goats, have the capacity to grow horn buds in specific areas around their heads. A mutation, in this case a deletion, causes the horn buds to split and form multiple horns. [6]

Convicts and Merinos

The rise of the world's largest wool producer began rather inauspiciously in a newly settled penal colony on a largely unexplored continent at the bottom of the world, or 'down under'. Social and political turmoil, along with advances in agriculture and the Industrial Revolution, led to an increase in England's population and crime rate in the late 1700s. The prison system was grossly overcrowded, in part due to the loss of the colonies in America, a common destination for offloading criminals. [7] In 1776, Parliament enacted a law allowing the use of decommissioned warships, known as 'hulks', as floating prisons. Initially, it was only a temporary measure; however, the hulks went on to be used for a further 80 years. To help clear the overcrowded British prison system and overflowing hulks, three separate fleets of prisoner transport and supply ships were arranged to transport convicts to the new colonies in Australia.

The First Fleet of 1787 transported 757 convicts, and the Third Fleet in 1791, over 2000. The Second Fleet of 1789 was infamously named the *Death Fleet*. Michael Flynn's book *The Second Fleet, Britain's Grim Convict Armada*, describes the fateful events leading up to the Second Fleet's departure. [8] The First Fleet had a relatively low prisoner mortality rate of 2.8%. The voyage was overseen by the government and undertaken by a wealthy London merchant, who offered a low tender by subsidising the expenses through a deal to load three of the ships with tea from China, brokered with the East India Company. On the other hand, the second fleet was unscrupulously handled, with a new British home secretary removing the first contractor in favour of a low tender from the former slave traders Camden, Calvert, and King.

Six ships embarked from Portsmouth, England, to Botany Bay in 1789, with only one stop in the Cape of Good Hope. Of those, the *Guardian*, a converted warship, reached Table Bay in Southern Africa and took on supplies of plants, cattle, horses, sheep, chickens, pigs and rabbits. Rounding the cape, they spied an iceberg and thought it a good opportunity to collect some drinking water; however, in the process, the hull was holed, and as the ship began to sink, most of the supplies and the poor animals were turfed overboard. The captain put half of those on board into smaller boats to ensure the ship's survival. Fortunately, the ship survived, but 45 of the 60 souls on the boats did not.

The *Neptune* was the largest of three convict ships, transporting 502 convicts on a journey cursed from the outset. Convicts were shackled at the wrists and ankles, most likely leftover shackles from slave trading. Before even leaving Britain's waters, several convicts had already died and been thrown overboard, along with all the other convicts' possessions and clothes; the bodies were later found floating outside Portsmouth. Neptune's captain was a "*cantankerous sea-dog of the first order*" named Thomas Gilbert, who previously commanded *the Charlotte* on the First Fleet.

Several army officers joined the ship on the voyage: Captain Nicholas Nepean, Lieutenant John Macarthur, and his wife, Elizabeth. Macarthur was a young man with great ambitions and a temper to match, and was soon at odds with Gilbert over his ship's quarters, later leading to a pistol duel in Plymouth on the outward journey. Conditions on board the three convict ships were horrendous, with many suffering from disease and scurvy. Gales and high seas frequently lashed the ships, battering and bruising those on board, the convicts often up to their waists in freezing waters. A virulent fever broke out on board, most likely picked up by Macarthur in Cape Town. A 'black economy' also emerged on the Neptune, involving the crew and soldiers; many of the convicts were extorted with high prices for food and water, which left many on the point of starvation. When the ships finally reached Sydney, of the original 1006 convicts who left England, 267 had died. The Neptune lost 147 men and 11 women, 269 needing hospital treatment on arrival.[8]

Sheep Shifters

But where do sheep fit into this story? Aside from soldiers, convicts and settlers, the First Fleet also arrived in Australia with 29 fat-tailed sheep. The sheep were survivors of the *Guardian*, which was beached at Table Bay, Cape of Good Hope, after the iceberg incident and were put aboard the *Juliana* on the final leg of the voyage to Australia. Unfortunately, the sheep proved unsuitable for harsh Australian conditions, as did sheep later brought in from India. [9] [8] Macarthur had a strong entrepreneurial streak, perhaps driven by his desire to escape the social and financial 'embarrassment' he felt as the son of a simple Plymouth tailor. [8] Soon, sheep would take centre stage in Macarthur's plans to climb the social ladder; however, before sheep, rum was part of Macarthur's playbook.

Not long after he arrived in the New South Wales colony in 1790, Macarthur was soon at odds with the governor, Arthur Phillip. The two had a falling out over a missing cask of spirits, after which time they seldom spoke. Phillip left the colony in 1792 and was replaced by Francis Grose, who became a fellow raconteur with Macarthur in the infamous *rum corps*. In the book *Rum Rebellion*, Herbert Evatt described how the succeeding governors of the colony had to contend with the officers of the corps, who "became an aristocracy" engaged in trade and agriculture, taking control over imports, especially booze. Within 12 months of Governor Philips leaving, rum became the *currency du jour*; even labour costs were paid in rum. [10] Grose allotted his chum Macarthur a prime piece of real estate, 100 acres in fact, which Macarthur named *Elizabeth Farm*, after his wife, and set about building his *ovine* empire. Macarthur purchased a selection of Bengal sheep from India and some Irish ewes, but later found that the Indian sheep only produced coarse hair, and the Irish sheep had low-value wool. Crossing the breeds and the resulting sheep sparked the idea of breeding fine wool in the colonies. [11] Macarthur understood that a small population far from civilisation could only succeed by exporting a raw material, one that was easy to produce, in demand, and capable of covering the costs of a long sea voyage. Wool would fit this bill nicely.

Merino Origins

Merino wool is renowned for the length of its staples (clusters of fibres), fine micron size (fibre diameter), and lanolin oil content. Several theories exist regarding the origins of the Merino sheep, with most pointing to a source in the Iberian region. Elena Ciani and colleagues examined this theory through exhaustive genetic testing of Merino and Merino-derived breeds worldwide. Historical descriptions of fine-wooled sheep from the Apulia region in southern Italy have been recorded during Roman times. Accounts of ewes with fine wool introduced to Spain from Apulia and mated with African coarse-wooled rams were recorded in the first century B.C. Greek authors of the same period also described the distinctive breed. Genome-wide analysis revealed an Iberian origin, admixed with sheep imported from Italy and North Africa, shaping the genetically distinct Merino breed known today. [12]

Spain had a stranglehold over the fine wool industry of the 18th century; the Spanish Merino was banned from export, supposedly upon 'pain of death', with France and England competing enthusiastically for the eight-million-pound annual export of Spanish wool. [13] Around this time, Britain was in the grip of a wool shortage, with a high demand for quality wool, and the English and European fibres were of low quality. This piqued the interest of Royal Society Fellow Joseph Banks, who, between 1788 and 1792, somehow managed to smuggle 73 ewes and 14 rams from Spain to Britain, where eventually they grazed the royal lawns of Kew Gardens and Windsor. In the late 1700s, Spain began to loosen its grip on the Merino monopoly, often using the animals as a means of diplomacy and as gifts to royalty. In 1808, the Spanish Government gifted George III a flock of 2,214 Merinos, several hundred of which were designated as gifts for ministers and nobles. [14]

Another recipient of these woolly gifts was the Dutch prince, William V of Orange, the last *stadtholder* of the Dutch Republic, who was thrust into his princely reign at the tender age of three. William was sent a small flock of Merinos by King Carlos III in 1789, later sending two rams and four ewes to the Cape of Good Hope, South Africa, to be cared for by Robert Jacob Gordon. [9] A remarkable character, Gordon, in the space of twenty years, amassed a wealth of information on the plants, animals and inhabitants of South Africa, all single-handedly. He recorded geological and meteorological information, explored and mapped regions, named the Orange River in honour of William V, and created a vast collection of drawings of local flora and fauna. [15] The Dutch government requested that the Merinos be returned in 1791, but Gordon kept the sheep's progeny. Political turmoil in the Netherlands saw the French seize power in 1795, William fled to Britain, and Gordon, faced with accusations of treason, took his own life. The Merinos, however, survived, and Gordon's wife sold them for four pounds a head.

Macarthur's Dream

Around this same time, Macarthur was formulating his breeding program. Hearing of two war sloops heading to the Cape of Good Hope, he put in an order for any quality wool-bearing sheep at the Cape. The commanders of the sloops were Captain Henry Waterhouse and Lieutenant William, who purchased 26 Merinos from Gordon's widow, selling four ewes and two rams to Macarthur back in Australia. Several years later, Macarthur purchased a further 1200 Merinos of the *Cape common breed* and, in 1801, submitted wool samples to the Committee of Manufacturers, who described the wool as equal to that of any Spanish wool. Colonial Secretary Lord Camden was impressed with Macarthur and his proposed venture. Encouraged by the committee's response, Macarthur sold his coveted position in the army and was granted 10,000 acres on the Nepean River.

Macarthur purchased nine rams and a ewe from the Royal Flock at Kew, where he first met Joseph Banks. Initially, Banks was keen to help Macarthur's Merino breeding endeavours, but relations soured between the two, and Banks later attempted to block Macarthur's efforts. However, Macarthur went on to purchase a ship named the *Argo* and had a figurehead of a golden fleece mounted on the bow. The following day, as the boat was preparing to sail, the London papers reported that it was *"illegal to export sheep from England and that such breach of the law rendered the vessel liable to forfeiture"*. Macarthur promptly called on his mate, Camden, and ran into Banks as he was leaving Camden's office. The matter was settled with a Treasury Warrant and an agreement to split the 10,000 acres into two allotments over an agreed time. By 1803, Macarthur's flock had increased to around 4000 sheep, and the first wool bale was sent to England in 1807. It was not until 1813 that Australia's first commercial shipment of wool landed in England from Elizabeth Farm, marking the beginning of the largest wool-producing nation in the world. [11]

Riding on the Sheep's Back

Since the 1800s and the humble beginnings of the wool industry, Australia is famously said to have *ridden on the sheep's back*, describing the importance of the wool exports that boomed for almost 200 years. More a cycle of boom and bust than a continuous boom, as the Federation drought of 1895-1902 decimated sheep numbers by nearly half, not recovering again until the 1920s. In his book *Breaking the Sheep's Back*, Charles Massey describes riding the sheep's back more as *"Riding off the competitive advantage of 'free' land—courtesy of Aboriginal dispossession"*, a reference to the taking of Aboriginal land by the British colonisers. He writes of the boom in Australian wool production and exports, creating the world's greatest wool e*conomy,* with selective breeding of animals to produce wool suitable for industrial mills, a world first. Massey describes the group of landowners that grew rich and powerful from the wool industry as an Australian *squattocracy* ruling vast estates like English lords, with servants, swanky homes in the city and membership at 'mock-London' clubs. [16]

Indeed, Wool was the backbone of Australia's economy for 120 years, the largest export earner and wealth-builder for the nation. Woolgrowers grew wealthy and were held in high esteem; a ram's head was featured on the shilling coin, and Macarthur was featured on the Australian two-dollar note. Golden Fleece was a ubiquitous petrol station brand that installed its first pump in 1920, featuring a resplendent golden Merino atop. New South Wales even has its own 'Big Merino', a three-storey high concrete and steel sheep on the outskirts of Goulburn.

A perfect storm of events led to the end of the ride on the sheep's back, culminating in the collapse of the wool industry in the 1990s. In 1970, a government-backed Reserve Price Scheme (RPS) was introduced to stabilise fluctuating wool prices, with a floor price set by the Wool Council. Years later, the result was a distorted market, overconfidence, overinvestment in the industry and a massive surplus of wool in the order of millions of bales. Additionally, competition from other fibres, such as synthetics and cotton and global financial pressures resulted in a spectacular collapse in the wool industry, which Massey described as *"the biggest corporate-business disaster in Australian history."* [16]

One-Eyed Sheep and Hedgehogs

Something strange happened in the alpine ranges of southwest and central Idaho in the early 1900s. Ewes grazing in the region occasionally gave birth to lambs with some disturbing deformities. The Basque herders who tended the sheep called these deformities *"chattos"* or *"monkeyface" and were reluctant to disclose the problem,* as they believed it was hereditary. The worst example of lamb *monkeyface* was 'cyclopia', where the poor lambs were born with one large eye in the middle of their head, a shortened muzzle and deformed jaw, a domed head and a nose growing from the forehead! The deformity only seemed to affect ewes grazing above 6000 feet in elevation and later in summer. In 1955, researchers from the USDA tested the sheep for a genetic origin of the deformities, breeding 48 ewes that previously gave birth to gammy lambs with normal healthy rams. None of the lambs born showed abnormalities, so they shifted their attention to the environment. [17] [18] Suspecting a *teratogen* or toxin, likely of plant origin, the researchers set out to identify the culprit plant in the grazing areas. Contemporary studies in rats have identified a toxic plant called the California corn lily, or *Veratrum californicum*, that caused the reabsorption and death of rat foetuses. The plant was also known to cause abnormalities in grazing animals and was endemic to the state of Idaho. Thus, the scientists conducted a series of large-scale grazing and feeding experiments. Forty-eight pregnant sheep were trucked to the Challis National Forest, an area with abundant toxic plant growth and grazed over various periods. Eight ewes gave birth to deformed lambs, and the periods showing grazing of the toxin between 8 and 17 days of gestation caused the abnormalities. The USDA researchers identified three alkaloids responsible: jervine, cycloposine and cyclopamine, the latter of which was named for its cyclops-inducing effects.

Sonic the Hedgehog and Fruit Flies

The humble fruit fly *Drosophila melanogaster* is often used in research due to its fast reproduction rate and the fact that it only has four pairs of chromosomes. In embryology studies, scientists have found that certain proteins affect neighbouring cells and how those cells and structures differentiate as an embryo grows. These proteins are called *hedgehog,* signalling molecules that, in the case of a fruit fly, tell it to form into a leg here or a head there, front from back and top from bottom. Why hedgehog? Because the mutant fly embryos (larvae) that have the hedgehog gene blocked are covered in spikes like a hedgehog! Vertebrates (animals and us!) contain three sets of these genes that signal developmental effects: *sonic hedgehog, Indian hedgehog and desert hedgehog.* [19] *Sonic* (Shh) is named after the video game character and plays a role in the development of the brain, limbs and spinal cord. *Indian hedgehog* plays a role in skeletal development, while the *desert hedgehog* is all about gonads.

What do hedgehogs have to do with Cyclops sheep? Chiang and colleagues studied the Shh gene in mice and found disruptions to the Shh signalling pathway, which created deformed mice with cyclopia (a single eye) and a displaced nose. [20] Suspecting that toxic plant alkaloids like cyclopamine might be involved, Cooper and Beachy found that these teratogens block the Sonic hedgehog pathways, leading to significant deformities. [21] The sheep ate the toxic

V. californicum plant while pregnant; the cyclopamine is mostly contained in the roots and stems that sheep like to eat. Mum ingests the toxin, which travels to the poor lamb as it grows in the womb and knocks out the Sonic hedgehog gene, leading to cells signalling the wrong cells to grow. This results in one eye instead of two, a nose on the forehead, and a brain in one part, not two hemispheres.

Cancer Therapies

With a story that grows even stranger, the discovery of one-eyed lamb mutants and the study of hedgehog genes have led to some promising new anticancer treatments. The hedgehog molecules interact with another protein in the cell, called smoothened (SMO), which initiates a reaction in the cell. This reaction activates target genes within the cell, instructing the cell to divide, differentiate, or form a specific pattern. When this goes haywire, uncontrolled activation of smoothened can cause nasty problems such as basal cell carcinoma. Cyclopamine is a natural SMO inhibitor that has shown promising signs in treating advanced basal cell carcinoma. [17] [19]

The Journey So Far

In conclusion, there are over 400 breeds of sheep, with eight distinct species originating from a common ancestor a few million years ago. Sometimes, sheep are born with two, four or even six horns, depending on their HOX genes, and sheep can live up to 28 years. If the hedgehog genes play up, lambs are sometimes born as a cyclops, but the toxic plants that cause it may offer clues to cancer treatment. The Spanish prized their woolly Merino sheep and tightly held the monopoly until English naturalists smuggled them abroad. Ovine gifts to royalty can end up on the other side of the world, only to be sold and shipped to a penal colony, where entrepreneurial military commanders breed and improve them, then ship them back to old blighty to clothe royalty, the masses and dress the military. The wool can build a nation's wealth and then spectacularly fall from grace. Sheep are certainly more interesting than they would first appear, but are they as stupid as some are led to believe, or do they possess unrecognised intelligence?

Sheep Intelligence

Sensory Abilities

Being a prey animal means you are always potentially someone else's dinner; in order to survive, adaptive fitness evolved some pretty nifty counter-defences in sheep and other small ruminants. The best defence for a prey animal is to spot a predator, preferably from a great distance. Living in a flock or herd means it is essential to know who's who, friend, foe or romantic partner, so it is important to differentiate other animals and remember those guys and gals into the future. Smell or *olfaction* also plays a big role in the sheep's life, whether it's the mating game, working out who's fertile and receptive, detecting a predator, or simply for "hey, you look like my friend, but I'm not sure, I'll just take a sniff".

Eyesight

Sheep have excellent binocular vision, with visual acuity somewhere between that of a monkey and a cat, and can practically see entirely around themselves. Sheep can discriminate between objects and individuals and may even possess colour vision. [22] Sheep can also distinguish between other sheep faces, different breeds, and male and female sheep. They can even differentiate between human and dog faces, as mentioned earlier in the chapter on *goat intelligence*.

Keith Kendrick describes that, like humans and primates, populations of cells in the medial and temporal cortex of sheep brains encode for recognising faces. [23] Not only recognise faces but also recall those faces up to two years later! Kendrick and colleagues trained 20 sheep to recognise 25 pairs of pictures of sheep faces, viewed front on. One sheep face picture of each pair was associated with a food reward, and it took about 30 trials before the sheep were 80% correct. The sheep had no trouble recognising sheep or human faces if they were front-on, but had difficulty if the eyes were obscured or the picture inverted. Apparently, adding horns to the image of a human face made no difference to the activity of the brain cells tested! However, posture and body shape influence the sheep's ability to recognise an individual, so if you ever need to bamboozle a sheep, walk on all fours! But exactly how long can sheep remember their pals, humans and dogs? When the sheep were later retested, performance only began to decline after around 600 days! [22]

Kendrick found that sheep, a highly social animal, had evolved brains that specialised in identifying a small number of categories of individuals from a large group based on emotional salience. This makes sense if you are trying to work out who's who in a giant flock! To test this, the scientists used single-cell electrophysiological recordings, where they inserted tiny electrodes into the sheep's brain to measure the activity of individual neurons (brain cells). They found groups of cells not only code for faces, but also for sheep of the same or different breeds, socially significant animals and even horns and horn size! This is all important stuff if you are a sheep, determining *who is who* in the social hierarchy and the mating game.

Smell

Sheep also use their keen sense of smell not only to alert to danger but to determine who you are and where you rank in the flock. Newborn lambs bond to their mother by smell, and the ewe recognises the odour signature of her lamb's skin and wool within a few hours, rejecting interlopers with a different odour. [22] An old farmer's trick for a ewe whose lamb has died is to skin the dead lamb and place the skin on an orphaned, non-related lamb. After a while, the ewe will associate the smell of the lost lamb with the adoptee and accept it as her own. Rams, not surprisingly, can distinguish ewes in oestrous and, in turn, the smell of a stinky ram can induce oestrus in a female. Not only from the smell of wool, but sheep can also determine other individuals via saliva, poop, glands below the eyes and the interdigital pouch, glands that are between the sheep's toes.

Can You Hear Me?

Sheep have excellent hearing, although not as sensitive as dogs, which can hear much higher frequencies. In fact, sheep's hearing abilities and range are comparable to those of humans, making them great candidates for studying human hearing loss. Po-Yi Lue and colleagues suggest sheep are an excellent model for studying human hearing loss, cochlear implants, and surgical procedures, as sheep have cochlear anatomy and hearing ranges similar to humans. [24] Scott Griffiths and associates suspected hearing loss in infants could occur in the womb, as some previous studies suggested. They used sheep to test the theory and indeed found that some hearing loss occurred in the lambs, as the sound penetrated the uterus and altered the auditory brainstem response. [25] Interestingly, Kendrick found that Dalesbred sheep used auditory cues at a similar level to discriminate between faces, whereas *Clun Forest* sheep could not identify a face with an associated sound. This was likely due to the *Dalesbred* living a more dispersed life on rolling hills, where calling out and listening to who's who is important. The *Clun Forest* sheep are more intensively reared, cheek by jowl, so to speak. [26]

Self-Awareness and Theory of Mind

As in the *Goats* chapter on self-awareness, sheep and goats tend to fail the mirror self-recognition test or MSR. However, this did not stop Sebastian McBride and co from testing the ability of mirrors to assist sheep in navigating. The study tested three breeds of sheep, with around 8-10 animals of each breed. Half the groups were exposed to a mirror, where they generally displayed behaviour as if it were another sheep, with the *Welsh Mountain Sheep* breed spending more time fixated on their image. The sheep were trained to locate a food bucket in a maze; then, a mirror was introduced to aid them in finding it. Neither the mirror-trained nor the mirror-naïve sheep showed any improvement in finding the bucket, although the *Mountain Sheep* had more correct responses overall. [27] This suggests that sheep are incapable of self-recognition through a mirror, unlike other species such as crows, elephants, and pigs, which can use mirrors to locate hidden food. As for the Welsh *Mountain Sheep*, they are either more curious and intelligent due to harsh and challenging living conditions or simply sheep narcissists.

Object Permanence

Goats have been shown to be quite good at object permanence, recognising that something continues to exist even when hidden. To test the abilities of sheep, Megan Quail and Mariecia Fraser tested object permanence and numerical competence in seven animals from each species of goats, alpacas and sheep. [28] Using food hidden under cups and with varying training regimes, they found that all animals passed trial 1, where food was visibly placed under a cup and presented to the animal; the correct response was a tap on the cup with the snout. Experiment two used two cups; the food was hidden under one (A, not B) and tested over training runs. The food is then visibly switched to the other cup; if the animal still selects the original cup, it's an A, not B, error. One sheep passed with flying colours; two sheep, three goats, and an alpaca failed miserably, though! The three-cup A, not B, task saw two sheep pass, but the rest failed. On the transpositional task, where the cups are swapped around, all animals fared poorly, but when the cups were different sizes, one super sheep scored 10 out of 12 times correctly! This was also found by Nawroth in the Goats chapter, where goats fared better when the cups were different colours. [29] In conclusion, the study showed basic object permanence ability in all species, but goats outshone the others. This is likely due to goats being selective browsers and having to remember where the best and most tasty food is located. Nonetheless, sheep have demonstrated a basic ability to recognise that something exists, even if it is hidden.

Navigating

Wild sheep are often migratory in their behaviour, unlike their domestic cousins, who are fenced in and herded around. Moving to new and greener pastures in different locations and altitudes can mean the difference between surviving and thriving or expiring! Wild bighorn sheep inhabit the northwest of America, their numbers decimated by overhunting, domestic sheep disease and habitat destruction. Recent attempts to reintroduce the species have yielded mixed results.

Blake Lowrey of Montana State University and colleagues set out to study the migration patterns of native and restored populations of bighorn sheep. [30] Using helicopter net-gunning and darting, 209 female bighorn sheep covering 18 populations and four states were fitted with GPS tracking collars from 2008 to 2017. They found that all populations migrated to other elevations, but the wild populations showed more variation in their migrations to both elevations and the distances covered. Comparisons of Big Horn sheep reveal that migratory movements are socially and culturally learned and passed on, with relocated or augmented populations covering much less ground than wild populations. Those sheep that maintained a long history in the area had a greater "knowledge" of the region. This knowledge most likely represents an extended evolutionary period in that landscape. The lack of migratory diversity can adversely affect sheep, leading to increased disease risk, lower reproductive success, and reduced resilience. [30] This highlights the effects of climate change and habitat destruction on what remains of wildlife populations, with seemingly innocuous events like migration and navigation having a significant impact on animal populations.

Problem-Solving

I was told a story once by a friend about how they drove past a paddock one day where a sheep stood in the corner where two fences met. It was still there the next day and the day after, until one day, it was dead. I've often thought of that poor sheep. Was it too stupid to turn around, or was it simply sick or injured? Our kid goats would regularly get their head stuck in the fencing wire, their backward-facing horns trapping them, bleating and calling out for help. Once freed, they looked relieved and grateful, but then turned around and did it the next day, the tempting grasses on the other side proving too much.

Which begs the question, can sheep solve problems or inhibit their instinctual drives? Franziska Knolle and colleagues explored this question by testing sheep with a simple, clear plastic cylinder, open at one end and containing a food reward, and measuring the time it took to find the food treat. [31] The sheep were first trained with an opaque cylinder and then tested on a transparent one. If the sheep probed or touched the outside, it was a failure; if they went straight for the opening to find the food, the latency, or time taken, was measured. By approaching the opening and not touching the outside of the clear cylinder where they can see the food, the sheep demonstrate the ability to self-regulate their behaviour and suppress instinctual actions. The test was conducted again seven weeks later to test the sheep's memory. Results showed that younger sheep did slightly better than older sheep, correctly getting the treat 86% of the time.

Maze tests are commonly used to assess the learning, memory and spatial abilities of animals. Caroline Lee and colleagues of the CSIRO Livestock Industries used a maze to test the effects of toxins on Merino sheep. [32] Annual ryegrass toxicity is a terrible and often fatal neurological affliction that affects grazing livestock. The culprit is a bacterium that uses a tiny nematode as a vector, producing corynetoxins on the seedheads of ryegrass. To test the potential effect of these neurotoxins on sheep learning and spatial abilities, 60 Merinos were given a sub-lethal dose of tunicamycin, which acts much like the ryegrass corynetoxins. Also, a group of 30 sheep were administered scopolamine, a compound often used to treat motion sickness, which, at higher doses, affects memory. They found that the toxic tunicamycin (mimics the ryegrass toxin) had no effect on sheep spatial learning or memory. In contrast, the scopolamine sheep had impaired performance, taking longer to navigate the maze. All the control (untreated) animals showed increased speed navigating the maze and fewer errors, which suggests that sheep learn and increase their spatial memory of a maze of relative complexity, with scopolamine adversely affecting learning and memory retention. [32]

Fat-Tailed Sheep, China

Social Learning

As most farmers (self-included) will attest, fencing for livestock can often be challenging. Animals (especially goats) will exploit any weak points in a fence to escape and find greener pastures. Virtual fencing presents a high-tech alternative to traditional fencing, utilising predefined GPS coordinates to define an area and a collar fitted to each animal. If the animal crosses the virtual boundary, an audio cue sounds, prompting it to turn around; if it does not, it receives an electric shock.

Silje Eftang and colleagues from the Norwegian University of Life Sciences tested eight Norwegian White ewes, each with twin lambs, to assess their learning ability in adapting to a virtual fence. [33] Results showed the sheep learned quickly to associate the audio cue with the electric shock and avoid it. When a second virtual boundary was set up at the opposite end of the paddock, the sheep generalised the learning from the first boundary, learning to avoid it in one day. The sheep also demonstrated social learning, as when one sheep's collar sounded the audio cue and turned around, the others responded, sometimes changing direction as a whole group in one movement.

With our own stubborn fence-testing goat herd, we had to acquiesce and stump up for an electric fence. I strung the 'hotwire' slightly above head and horn height, and it was not long before the first goat was zapped. I am not sure how much social learning occurred, but the goats generally required no more than two shocks to avoid the area around the wire, often eyeing it cautiously when approaching the fence for food.

Cooperative Behaviour

Do sheep have besties? Many animals form strong friendships with other animals of the same or different sex, so perhaps sheep do, too. Laura Ozella and colleagues studied 84 Poll Dorset ewes and found sheep do indeed have 'besties', with ewes preferring to associate with the same individuals more often than by chance. We tend to choose friends who share attributes similar to our own, such as age, gender, and common interests, and it appears that sheep also choose similar conspecifics. However, these preferences did change over time, unsurprisingly, as sheep hierarchy can also change over time. One constant, though, was the ewe's preference for sheep of a similar age, which seemed unaffected by size or social status. [34]

Perhaps sheep's most obvious cooperative behaviour is their 'flocking'. Moving as a flock has many advantages, such as protection from predators and the sharing of information, for example, spotting patches of lush grass or warning of danger ahead. Luis Gómez-Nava and colleagues studied the behaviour of sheep. They found that flocking behaviour is a self-organising process, with individuals negotiating and compromising on the travel direction at an average speed until group consensus is reached. They found two distinct behavioural phases, grazing and collective motion phases (CMP). Unlike animal herds that have single dominant leaders, sheep take turns, with each episode of movement being led by a random sheep. The 'temporal' leader moves off, and its motion creates a collective movement, all in a hierarchical line, one following the other. The subsequent CMP might have a different leader and order of followers, but they all follow along....like sheep! [35]

Depressed Sheep

Anxiety and depression are well-studied in humans, with several animal studies showing these maladies affect our animal relatives, too. This would imply that sheep might also experience depression and anxiety, but how would you prove this? Jessica Monk from the

CSIRO and colleagues set out to find the answer, testing 16 Australian Merino ewes. Anxiety manifests in us humans often as an increased fear response to situations, and a hallmark of depression is a reduced interest or pleasure in everyday things. Attentional bias is one way to measure anxiety and depression, particularly in animals, who cannot tell us how they feel! Anxious individuals often pay way more attention to threatening stimuli and shy away from positive stimuli. As predicted, the depressed sheep spent more time looking at a threat than at a positive photo of a sheep friend. Curiously, the anxious sheep went the other way, looking longer at the photo of their friend and paying less attention to the threat. This finding was contrary to their previous results and may be attributed to the reinforcing social aspect of the sheep photo. In case you are wondering how they found depressed and anxious sheep, it was induced by injections of compounds that affect the serotonin system. [36]

Personality

Feeling sheepish, been counting sheep to get to sleep, or do you feel like the black sheep? Do you follow the flock, or are you gentle as a lamb? These common sayings translate to human personality types, transmogrifying across the species boundary. But do sheep actually possess personalities? Studies on animal personality often originate from human personality research, as the definitions of temperament and personality are quite similar across both fields, which often creates confusion.

For example, as mentioned previously, the current gold standard for human personality assessment is the five-factor or *Big Five* model. However, much of the research on animal personality uses a wide range of other, often confusing expressions.

Marie-Antonine Finkemeier and colleagues highlight this confusion and explain that many personality traits in animal species mirror those of the Big Five, such as openness (exploration), consciousness (only found in chimps), extraversion (sociability), agreeableness (aggressiveness), and neuroticism (boldness). [37] Sheep with bold (neurotic) personalities are found to be more reactive to humans and show more explorative behaviour. Animals with bold, aggressive and fearless personalities can be extrapolated to human traits of extraversion. In fact, animal personalities are so apparent that zookeepers reliably rate the personality of animals in their care, which is then implemented into welfare and management practices. Personality traits can also be an effective way of assessing the welfare of farm animals, ensuring efficient production and overall well-being. A unified view on animal personality, like the Big Five, would certainly lessen the confusion when sorting the sheep from the goats!

Temperament

We often describe animals and humans in terms of temperament: an *easy* baby, a *difficult* child, a *slow-to-warm* person. Temperament is another way animal behaviour is assessed, but what exactly is temperament?

Denis Réale and colleagues set out to integrate the concept of animal temperament within ecology and evolution, defining temperament as individual behavioural differences consistent over time and across situations. These are more *innate* characteristics, those present since birth with a strong genetic component. Temperamental traits include behaviours such as novelty avoidance, aggressiveness, risk-taking, exploration, and sociality. [38] Réale explains that temperament variations in individuals appear pervasive across animal species and exert a strong effect on an animal's evolutionary fitness. Temperament can influence ecological processes, including niche expansion, dispersal, and social structure. They provide examples of stickleback fish exhibiting consistent, stable traits of aggressiveness and spiders with varying levels of aggression and anti-predator behaviour, depending on whether they are in food-rich or food-poor environments. Boldness in a bighorn sheep is correlated with reproductive success; the competitive guy with the intimidating horns gets the ladies! Exploration is a trait that a breeder artificially selects for in a sniffer dog; aggressiveness is not a desirable trait, nor is shyness. Boldness is a handy trait for a rooster, affording more access to hens, but if all the roosters have bold/ aggressive traits, it would be a bloodbath!

In their paper, *Social Personality in Sheep*, Genaro Miranda-de la Lama and others set out to identify the existence of sheep personality profiles and how different social strategies can predict differences in abilities, appearance and reproductive success. [39] Using 50 adult ewes, they classify four personality profiles in sheep: *avoider*, *affiliative*, *aggressive*, and *pragmatic*. They also tested cognitive abilities using a simple T-shaped maze and sound cues and found:

•*Aggressive* sheep tend to be bigger, use aggressive tactics to gain dominance, have a higher fertility rate and medium prolificacy (number of offspring) and, as a trade-off, the highest levels of stress, but solved the maze fastest on the second trial (13.6 sec).

•*Pragmatic* animals had the highest prolificacy, all bearing twins, but the lowest fertility, relatively high social rank, and low-stress levels; it took the longest (57.50 sec) to solve the maze.

•The *affiliates* are friendly and cooperative, have moderate stress levels, a moderate social rank and the highest fertility but low prolificacy and moderate cognitive ability with 27.79 seconds to solve the maze.

•The *avoiders* lived up to their name, frequently avoiding other ewes, had the lowest social rank, low-stress levels, a medium fertility rate, in-between prolificacy and solved the maze quickly (18.56 sec).

What to take away from all that information? Low-dominance animals could be displaying a form of social 'survival' learning, by quickly avoiding aggression and confrontation. These sheep are the smallest and scrawniest of the group, which may be advantageous in situations where feed is scarce. The pragmatists employed a combination of aggressive and non-aggressive social interactions, adopting a middle-of-the-road approach to everyday social interactions. The Aggressive girls fared well in most regards but expended a lot of energy on stress; there's a cost to being king on the hill!

The above studies reveal just how evident animal personalities are and how differing terminologies can create confusion in an already confusing and little-studied field. Perhaps a new unified 'Big Five' for our animal cousins is sorely needed!

Conclusions

From their common ancestor *Ovis orientalis,* sheep have diversified and spread throughout the world, migrating on foot and being transported alongside criminals. Sheep were a highly protected commodity of Spanish royalty, smuggled to England to be selectively bred for the finest wool. Their wool clothed and warmed generations of people, dressing soldiers for several world wars, creating an economy that brought prosperity to a former prison colony. Sheep fail the mirror recognition test, but have individual personalities and best friends and can be depressed. Sheep have excellent eyesight, hearing, a strong sense of smell, and a remarkable spatial learning ability. Far from possessing human, primate or corvid intelligence, sheep are perhaps not the 'dumb' animals we make them out to be; rather, they are sentient creatures endowed with all the sensory and cognitive faculties as most mammals. Sheep are highly adapted to, well, being sheep!

Chickens

(Gallus gallus domesticus)

When a chicken is picked up by a hawk, it cries not because anyone can save it but to alert the world of the cause of its demise.

Igbo proverb, Africa

What is not to love about chickens? They are charming little characters; they keep bugs from the garden, turn over the soil, and fertilise the plants. They taste delicious, crumbed and fried, roasted or curried, not to mention a certain colonel made a fortune and built a food empire from them. Chickens are the most numerous domestic animals on earth, with over 26 billion of them as of 2022, inhabiting every continent except Antarctica. The world produces over 123 million tonnes of chicken meat each year and over 93 million tonnes of eggs. [1] In 2024, the average Australian ate more than 50 kilograms of chicken meat, a total of over 8 billion dollars spent on chicken protein, a far cry from the occasional Sunday roast of previous generations. The Australian slang term for a store-bought roasted chicken is a *bachelor's hand-bag*, and Australian supermarket giant Woolworths sold over 20 million such handbags in 2023. Chicken is one of the least expensive meats available in Australia; with the rise of enormous factory farming endeavours reducing production costs, the time to raise a chicken from hatching to slaughter is only four to five weeks. [2] But what of the bird, beyond the plastic-wrapped meat tray or crumbed and fried in a fast-food bucket? We seldom stop to think about the life that an animal may have led. Was it happy, content, distressed, free or confined? Did it suffer or live a relatively normal life? Does it even think or feel, or are chickens just *automata,* as described by Descartes?

Origin Stories

It turns out that chickens are quite the survivors, with their distant relatives being only a handful of birds to survive the asteroid impact in Chicxulub, Mexico, some 66 million years ago. Elizabeth Pennisi explains that many fossils of diverse tree-dwelling birds were found before the impact, but they are absent in sediments laid down after. It appears that five groups of modern birds predate the impact, including species similar to ducks, ostriches and chickens, their surviving ancestors most likely quail-like birds that survived on seeds 'banked' in the soil after the destruction. [3]

There seems little doubt that domestic chickens are descended from the Asian wild red junglefowl and the Indian grey junglefowl, but where and when chickens were first domesticated is hotly debated among scientists. Using DNA analysis, Hai Xiang and others from the University of Beijing found mitochondrial DNA sequences of chicken bones from archaeological digs in Northern China, dating back to around 10,000 years ago. Nanzhuangtou Neolithic site, where the bones were discovered in present-day Hubei province, was much warmer and humid back 10,000 years ago, and it was a habitat suitable for the junglefowl, they explained. [4]

Miao and Peng from Yunnan University, Kunming, China, also conducted extensive DNA analysis of chooks, studying 50 complete genomes from 2000 samples from domestic chooks and red junglefowl from India, China, Myanmar and Laos. They suggest domestication was a more recent event, an independent domestication happening in South Asia and a dispersal of chooks through Austronesia, mainly from Southeast Asia. [5]

Sri Lanka has some spectacular national parks, with an abundance of wildlife. While travelling through several of the parks, I was lucky enough to snap a pic of a wild and elusive junglefowl.

It's fascinating to see how the predecessor of our domestic fowls lived, a much richer life than being confined to a laying cage.

A Colourful Jungle Fowl, Sri Lanka

Record Breakers and Breeds

There are countless chicken breeds, classified by size, shape, plumage, comb, egg colour and so on. The oldest formal classification of chicken breeds is the British Poultry Standard, first published in 1865. The book lists over 60 breeds, giving extensive details on beaks, feet, feathers and combs for those who enjoy the technical aspects of chook taxonomy.

The Guinness World Records lists the oldest recorded chicken as a Red Quill Muffed American Game chicken named Muffy, who lived to the ripe old age of 23! [6] This is in stark contrast to our poor old laying hens, who are lucky to live to three or four; their reproduction system 'falling apart'. The smallest recorded chicken is a bantam breed from Malaysia, called the *Serama*, with birds as small as 15-25cm tall and weighing only 350 grams. The Serama have a distinctive posture, almost like a Queen's guard standing to attention. On the opposite end of the scale, the *White Sully*, a Rhode Island Red hybrid, is the heaviest chook. One White Sully rooster named Weirdo weighed 10kg and was quite cantankerous, killing two cats and injuring a dog that strayed into its territory. Not to be outdone in size, Ricardo "Cano" Tan, Filipino businessman, politician and former president of the Philippine Football Federation, built the world's largest rooster at the family-owned Philippines resort, Negros Occidental. Tan explained that the rooster design was adopted to represent the cock fighting business that saved the region from a downturn in the sugar industry. He claimed the chicken feed business boomed, helping support the local economy and that the rooster was the alarm clock that woke farmers for work and prayers during the Spanish occupation. The rooster-shaped and coloured building stands over 34 metres in height and is a major tourist drawcard for the region. [7]

The Black Chicken

An unusual breed of chicken resides on the Indonesian island of Java; the Ayam Cemani, or literally 'chicken, black down to the bones', is an unusual breed. The highly prized Cemani likely originated from a genetic mutation in a bird, which was then selectively bred from. The Cemani has black feathers, feet, beaks, comb and wattles and even black meat and internal organs, which is the result of fibromatosis, or dermal hyperpigmentation. The key to hyperpigmentation lies in an autosomal dominant trait where only one parent needs the gene to pass on the trait, and the offspring have a 50/50 chance of inheriting it. The gene culprit is called EDN3, a duplication error that causes excessive pigmentation. The Ayam Cemani is not alone in its unusual colouration, with the Silkie and the Kadaknath of India also displaying fibromatosis. The Kadaknath is said to have several health benefits, including treating headaches and asthma, and the meat is thought to have aphrodisiac-like properties. The Kadaknath also displays resistance to several avian diseases, showing robust immune responses, also seen in the Ayam Cemani, which shows high disease resistance to intestinal pathogens and viral infections. [8] Of course, you are wondering what they taste like, apparently like chicken! Though the dark black of the meat no doubt conjures all sorts of thoughts while chewing on the low-fat, gamey bird. However, due to their rarity, slow growth rates, and export restrictions, you probably will not see black chickens turning up on the supermarket shelf anytime soon.

Chicken Ornaments

In case you get your chicken wobbly bits mixed up, the comb is the (often) red fleshy mohawk on the head. The wattles dangle under the chook's beak, and the patch behind the eye, sometimes just a hole, is the ear. But what exactly is the point of the colourful comb and wattles? The comb is essentially an ornament used to indicate health and sexual maturity. Often, when our chooks are unwell, their comb will become pale or dry, indicating underlying health problems. You can also tell a laying hen's maturity by her comb size; they are ready to lay once they reach a certain height/ shape for that breed.

Rose Comb   Pea Comb

The scientific name for chooks is *Gallus domesticus,* where *Gallus* literally means comb, with the wide variety of chook combs originating from two gene variants, the rose comb and the pea comb. [9] The comb plays a role in cooling the chook, as birds lack sweat glands, blood flowing to the comb and wattles acting much like a car radiator. Chickens are sexually dimorphic (the male is larger and appears different), and the rooster often displays an accoutrement of colourful feathers and headgear to attract the girls. In red junglefowl, testosterone has a strong effect on comb size and, importantly, on mating success.

A Not So Well-Endowed Cockerel

Whilst on the subject of mating (go on, admit you wonder how chickens do it!), the rooster has a rather unenviable position in the animal kingdom; it's pecker! Despite its namesake, the feathered pecker does not possess much of a pecker, which intrigued Ana Herera and colleagues at the University of Florida enough to investigate. They describe that in bird evolution, an *intromittent phallus* (capable of insertion during copulation) has been lost in many bird species, with only 3% retaining a peckable pecker. To discover how this came about, they compared chickens (less endowed), waterfowl (well endowed), and an outgroup of emus and alligators. Loss of the sex organ in chooks presents an evolutionary paradox: how on earth does it positively affect reproductive fitness? They suggest several theories, such as sexual selection, where females have more control over paternity, whereby if she does not cooperate, it does not happen, which lays waste to the 'rooster rape' myth. The other is a stabilising effect, if it ain't broke, don't fix it! The third is from pleiotropic effects (one gene affecting several traits), where the pecker reduction could be a secondary effect of developmental changes in other traits, such as limb development. [10]

Just to clarify things here, waterfowl, such as ducks, have rather long and weird corkscrew-shaped penises, part of a duck mating strategy that allows the female (who has a corkscrew-shaped vagina) to separate off unwelcome sperm from ducks who do not measure up. In fact, the world record-holding duck phallus comes from an Argentine lake drake that measured 42.5cm when 'unwound'. [11] Emus and ostriches have a penis that becomes erect, and crocodiles and alligators have a hidden but permanent hard-on. The researchers found a bone growth factor protein called Bmp4, known to cause cell death or 'apoptosis' in some organs, was implicated in the regression of the chicken phallus. When Bmp was inactivated in chicken embryos, they grew a phallus; when it was activated in a duck embryo, it produced cell apoptosis and a chicken-like pecker. They conclude that BMP4 expression, which causes cell death in the genital tubercle and the regression of the penis, likely occurred after chickens diverged from the waterfowl lineage some 90 million years ago. Furthermore, the phallus is one of several parts, including digits and teeth, that undergo partial development in the embryonic stage and then regress. [10] I almost forgot, how do chickens do it? Answer: a cloacal kiss; I'll leave that for you to Google!

Chickenosaurus

The unusual fact that chickens undergo the development of features of their distant ancestors, like teeth, inspired two palaeontologists to embark on an extraordinary project. Back in 2009, Jack Horner and James Gorman set scientific tongues wagging when they published the book *How to Build a Dinosaur: Extinction Doesn't Have to Be Forever*. The book describes Horner's attempts to create a 'chickenosaurus' by essentially reverse engineering a chicken embryo, reawakening dormant genes that once coded for dinosaurian-like traits. [12] A highly accomplished palaeontologist, Horner has struggled with dyslexia, flunking college seven times, reading word by word and having virtually no short-term memory. He describes reading as still presenting considerable challenges. That did not stop Horner from progressing in his career, publishing eight books and over 100 articles, with three dinosaur species named after him. [12]Horner stated on X (formerly Twitter) in 2023 that the "Dinochicken Project has reached a threshold" and that they know how to change teeth, skull shape, alter a wingtip to a hand with three fingers and make a bony tail, the final step needing "an island, with a generous, intrepid donor!" [13]

Several key factors inspired the *chickenosaurus* project, namely the discovery that blocking certain gene expressions in the tail and the beaks of chickens led to dinosaur-like traits. Bhart-Anjan Bhullar and colleagues at Harvard University explain that *Fibroblast Growth Factor 8* (Fgf8) is a crucial gene in the development of facial structures in vertebrates. [14] Birds, including chooks, have distinctive beak structures from fused and elongated premaxillae bones. In humans, our premaxilla is where the four front teeth meet the nose and are fused with the maxilla or facial bones. Archosaurs are the name broadly given to all extinct reptiles and dinosaurs and their still-living relatives, birds and crocodiles. Ancestral archosaurs had shorter snouts and small paired premaxillae, forming the tip of the snout. Using molecules to block and inhibit the *Fibroblast Growth Factor,* the resulting chicken embryos looked much like their ancient cousins, with a short snout and paired maxillae. [14]The birds were never hatched, which is a bit sad, as a *chickenosaur* prototype would have been something to behold.

Matthew Harris and colleagues set out to recreate archosaur-like teeth in chicken embryos. [15] Unlike their ancestors, modern birds have no teeth but may still possess the genetic potential to grow teeth. They used a strain of bird called the *Talpid 2 chicken mutant*, which sounds a bit like something from a horror film. This mutant breed of bird is used in research and does exhibit some pretty awful mutations. They compared the development of teeth in alligators and the mutant chicks, examining the sonic hedgehog (Shh) gene of the two species (remember the hedgehog family from the *Sheep* chapter?). The researchers found the Shh gene expression in the alligator was similar in the mutant chook, with data suggesting the mutant chook can form early tooth structures, similar anatomically to an alligator's first-generation teeth! Interestingly, five of the embryos almost survived to reach the hatching stage.

Further evidence of the chicken's dinosaurian past can be found in the simple chicken drumstick. The chicken leg we so often consume is composed of the thigh, which contains the femur, and the drumstick, which contains the large tibia and the small fibula, that annoying, sharp little bone, dangerous for us and dogs to consume. If you are partial to chewing on chicken feet, which are popular in much of Asia, most of the foot bones (metatarsals) are fused to form the tarsometatarsus bone, leading to the toes. So the long, scaly part of a chicken's foot that is visible when they walk is actually fused toe bones! The human lower leg also consists of a tibia and a smaller fibula, which reaches all the way to the foot; the end of the fibula terminates in the knobby protrusion on the outside of

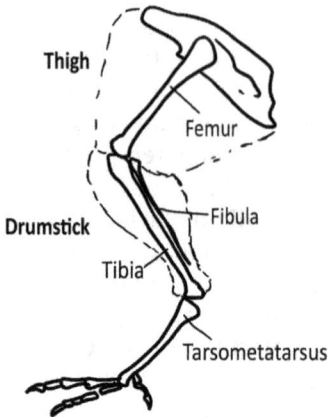

the ankle.

João Francisco Botelho and his team studied the development of the fibula in chicken embryos and found some startling results. [16] Non-avian dinosaurs had equal-length tibia and fibula, but around the Mesozoic period, fossil birds show a fibula almost as long as the tibia, but without the distal epiphysis, the rounded part at the end of the bone that usually forms a joint with the ankle and is important in bone growth and formation. In modern birds, including chickens, the tibia takes all the weight, the fibula is a bit of a remnant, and penguins are the only extant birds to retain a full-length fibula. The authors note that there is no adaptive value in bone shortening; rather, it is a byproduct of other selective pressures that lead to longer tibia growth. At around day five of the chick's development in the egg, the fibula is the same length as the tibia until around day eight, when it significantly shortens and shrinks. To 'reverse engineer' this process, they treated chicken embryos *in ovo* (in the egg) with cyclopamine. Remember cyclopamine from the sheep chapter that caused the Cyclops sheep? Cyclopamine causes downregulation or 'lessens' the gene expression of Indian hedgehog genes (IHH). These genes are responsible for bone growth and differentiation, and the chicks treated with cyclopamine grew a full-length fibula bone, albeit with a shorter and bent tibia. This reveals the dinosaurian evolutionary past of our birds and the humble but tasty chickenosaurus.

Mike the Headless Chicken

From mutant chickenosaurs, black fowls and regressed rooster peckers, to something even more bizarre. In 1945, on a family-owned farm in Fruita, Colorado, Lloyd Olsen and his wife, Clara, were busy preparing chickens to send to market for consumption. Olsen would lop the birds' heads off with an axe, and Clara would clean them; however, after dispatching around 50 of the poor chooks, the couple noticed one rooster was still moving. Not just moving but kicking and running around. They placed the chook in a crate on the porch and left it overnight. In the morning, the rooster was still alive! The struggling farmer took the chickens into town to sell and threw in the hapless and headless rooster, betting with the unbelieving townsfolk that he possessed a headless chicken. Word quickly spread about the miracle bird, and a few weeks later, Hope Wade, a sideshow promoter, saw the money-making potential in the headless fowl and approached the Olsens to exhibit the bird through the sideshow circuit. The first stop was the University of Utah in Salt Lake City, where scientists examined the bird. It turned out the cut removed the chook's head but left enough of the brainstem intact that basic physiological functions remained. The neck was severed in such a way that the jugular vein clotted quickly, preventing the bird from bleeding out. Wade, nicknamed the bird 'Mike' and Life Magazine, ran a story on October 22, 1945, titled *Beheaded Chicken Lives Normally After Freak Decapitation by Axe*. Mike was kept alive by feeding a liquid diet via an eyedropper directly into the bird's oesophagus, and a syringe was used to extract mucus that built up in the stump! One night, whilst travelling through Arizona with Mike, the bird started coughing and spluttering, but the syringe had been left behind, and before another could be found, the chook suffocated. Mike, the Wyandotte rooster, had lived for 18 months without a head.[17, 18]

Mike's spirit lives on today, with Fruita, Colorado, running the *Mike the Headless Chicken Festival* each May since 1999. The festival features a five-kilometre run, live bands, a headless chicken art competition and, oddly, a poultry show.

The Mythological Bird

As chickens have their domestic origins in the Asian continent, it comes as no surprise that ancient folklore is replete with stories of the humble fowl. The egg features heavily in creation myths, such as with the Nakhi of Yunnan and Sichuan, where the story of the human ancestor Chongrenlien tells that the green air of the universe created white light, which turned into sound and then into a god. From this god came an egg, which hatched a white chicken that broke the clouds to reveal the sun, moon and stars. Finally, the chicken spread its feathers on the ground to produce the animals and the grass. The ethnic Miao creation story describes how Pangu was born from an egg, growing only as it could see the wind. Pangu separated the heavens from the earth, but, too tired to live on, fell to earth, where his heart became the sun, his gall the moon and his eyes the stars. [19]

Vietnamese mythology tells the quasi-historical tale *of King An Duong Vuong*, who co-ruled the Au Lac kingdom in the 3rd century BC, which later came to form part of the Vietnamese nation. Au Lac faced threats from a Chinese general named Zhao Tuo, prompting the king to build a fortress to protect his people. But each night, a 1000-year-old chicken that led legions of evil spirits would knock down the walls. The king enlists the help of a magical golden turtle, and together, they defeat the evil chicken. The king builds his fortress, and the turtle gives him one of his toenails to use as a trigger in a magic crossbow, which proves lethal to the king's enemies. General Zhao Tuo sends his son as an emissary to find the secret of this magical crossbow, but the son falls in love with the king's daughter, who gives away the secret of the magical toenail weapon. The general's son swaps out the magic crossbow for a fake and instructs the king's daughter to leave a trail of feathers as she leaves the palace. General Zhao Tuo returns to the kingdom with the mystical weapon, and the king prays to the turtle for assistance. The turtle reveals the daughter's treachery, and the king lops off her head, which the general's son later finds. He is so distraught that he throws himself down a well, and his father goes on to conquer the kingdom. [20]

On the Okinawan islands of Japan, the *kijimuna* are mischievous, elf-like creatures said to be tricksters, often covered in red hair and sometimes possessing gigantic testicles. The kijimuna play tricks on people and can be violent or sometimes benevolent, befriending humans. But in order to break off a friendship with these troublesome tricksters, you must give them something they hate, like an octopus or a chicken. [21]

In ancient China, people often viewed the upset of harmony between humans and heaven as a consequence of changes in their environment, such as fluctuations in celestial bodies, a dog barking or a cock crowing. Restless or distressed dogs or chickens were a bad sign, as the Yilin quote: *"When the cock crows at the wrong time, master will soon have trouble; when the dog barks without ceasing, the traveller should tarry."* [22] Unusual phenomena were often taboo, and the Chinese New Year was particularly auspicious. In the Qin and Han dynasties, around 200 BC, people believed that the nature of the coming year could be divined by events that unfolded at the beginning of the new year, particularly New Year's Day itself. Taboos on killing animals on New Year's Day developed, with one piece of Qin literature stating that wind on the first day of the month is bad for chickens, the second for dogs, the third for pigs and so on. This later led to the concept of a 'chicken day' or a 'human day' and perhaps to the taboo that prevented the killing of chickens or sparrows on New Year's Day.

During the Qing dynasty (1662–1722), it was popular to adorn houses with the *Jin Ji, also known as the "Golden Chicken," or with Jin Ji Zhua, "Golden Chicken's claws,"* which were in fact fossilised dinosaur tracks. Wangzhuang Village, built during the Qing dynasty, is located in northern Shaanxi Province. The original houses were mostly cave dwellings during this period, and people used local sandstone slabs to create doors, fences, house pillars, cistern covers, millstones and even gravestones. Many slabs contained ripples from lakes, mud cracks, fossilised wood and the ubiquitous three-toed golden chicken's footprints. The village still exists today, although in a much more modernised form, and half of the residents who still live in the area report owning fragments of dinosaur tracks. [23]

The Journey So Far

In conclusion, there are around 3.5 chickens for every person on Earth, collectively laying around 1,400 QE2 cruise ships' equivalent weight in eggs. The chicken's distant relatives survived the asteroid extinction event and went on to branch out and populate the world with a diversity of birds, from tiny hummingbirds to giant ostriches. The smallest chickens weigh a few hundred grams, and the largest can weigh up to 10kg, with a diversity of shapes and colours, including some that are completely black, and one that survived without its head for over a year. Chickens can be somewhat reverse-engineered into dinosaurs, whose Mesozoic era tracks adorned Chinese dwellings, where abundant tales and legends were woven around the humble chook. But what of the private lives of chickens? Are they simply bird-brained automatons, a bachelor's handbag, or is there more to this story than meets the eye?

Chicken Intelligence

If you were asked to give an example of a typical bird, how far down the list might the chicken be? With the commodification of chicken, we often associate the word *chicken* with food before even thinking of the animal. A chicken nugget is possibly the first tangible (and edible) example of the bird many children first encounter, taking years before they understand the crumbed tasty snack was once a curious, and highly social, feathered sentient being!

Neuroscientist Lori Marino notes that animals are often categorised by the attributes they possess, which influences how representative they are of a category. When people were asked to rate how typical chickens were as members of the category of birds, most rated them very low, not considering them actual birds. [24]Marino explains how the idea of chicken cognition or 'psychology' is strange to most people; chickens are typically perceived as lacking the characteristics of intelligent animals. Perhaps some of this lies in the 'bird brain' hypothesis, linking cognitive abilities to brain size, which has been thoroughly debunked in the last few decades; research shows avian brains share many of the same functions as mammals, allowing for similar levels of cognition. Before delving into the cognitive ability of chooks, let's first examine their sensory faculties.

Sensory Abilities

Eyesight

Chickens are highly dependent on visual cues and have excellent visual capabilities. Chooks have two distinct visual fields: the monocular lateral field, which detects distant and moving objects like a predatory hawk and the frontal field for resolving static near objects, like a tasty bug. Marian Stamp Dawkins and Alan Woodington explain that hens can even accurately discriminate photographs and choose colours 100% correctly, indicating they have colour vision that shares many similarities with our own. When chooks were shown pictures of another flock mate, they could not recognise it unless they were closer than 30cm, and using the frontal field of vision, often pecking at the comb of the photo as they would a real hen. When viewing the image from a distance using the lateral field, there was no sign of recognition from the bird. [25] When chickens view close objects, around 20-30 cm away, they gaze directly at them front-on but also switch between looking from front to side, swinging their head to get a view from both eyes and their fields of vision. This suggests that chickens, unlike mammals, which fix their gaze upon an object, investigate by moving their heads, perceiving images on different parts of the eye and through different neural pathways. [26] This could also be explained by brain lateralisation, where each hemisphere (half) of the brain performs different functions.

In his book, *The Master and His Emissary,* Iian McGilchrist explains how birds have divided hemispheres much like humans and other mammals. For a bird to discriminate and peck a bug from the dirt, it must narrowly focus attention but, at the same time, keep an eye out for predators, much akin to rubbing your head and patting your belly at the same time. Not just divided attention but also two different types of attention that require a specialised strategy: the right eye (left hemisphere) for finding the tasty bug and the left eye (right hemisphere) for keeping an eye on the sky. Chicks show this behaviour by focusing on local information via the right eye and 'global' information with the left eye. Many birds are better at detecting potential predators with the left eye, so much so that if they spot a threat with the right eye, they will turn their heads to examine it with the left eye. Just a quick biology explainer: in birds and mammals, the eyes are contra-lateralised, meaning the optic nerve passes from the left eye through the optic chiasm to the right hemisphere, where it is processed in the right visual cortex and vice versa. McGilchrist describes detailed discrimination, and topography is associated with the right hemisphere in birds and humans, enabling them to see things in a contextual and holistic manner. At the same time, the left hemisphere sees objects abstracted from their context and broken down into parts. [27] So, left eye on the sky, broad and vigilant and right eye narrow and focused on the tasty bug!

Smell

The idea of a sophisticated sense of smell or *olfaction* in birds was pretty much poo-pooed until around the mid-1960s; in fact, it was once thought chicks lacked any sense of smell or taste. However, an increasing volume of evidence began to surface on the olfactory abilities of birds. Although it is generally believed that birds' sense of smell is less developed than in mammals, studies have found that domestic chooks exhibit greater electrophysiological responses in their olfactory nerves than rats. Familiar smells have been shown to calm fearful chooks, and birds display neophobia (fear of novel things) to smells of unfamiliar food. [28]

It was also assumed that chickens had few, if any, taste buds, which was then revised upward from around only 70 to numbering upwards of 240-360, according to Hong-Xiang Liu and colleagues. [29]In comparison, rats have around 1000 taste buds, and humans have approximately 10,000. Chickens have fewer genes that mediate taste receptors, and it is believed that chooks can only discriminate between salt, sour, bitter and umami. They respond more strongly to bitter tastes, which makes sense from an adaptive fitness perspective, as many poisonous plants are bitter.

We had a nice crop of chillies growing several years back that seemed to disappear over time. It turned out the chooks were the culprits, eating both the leaves and the chillies with no apparent effect! This is because birds lack a receptor called TRPV1, which is activated by capsaicin, giving chillies their burning sensation. If mammals like goats ate the chillies, the seeds would be digested, so the plant's defence is the burning heat, and yes, goats do have the TRPV1 receptors, much the same as us and hate chillies. As birds lack the capsaicin receptors, they can happily eat the chillies and then poop out the seeds, spreading the plant and thereby increasing the chilli plant's reproductive success.

Scientists at the College of Animal Science and Technology in Changsha, China, tested the effect of capsaicin on ducks' egg production. Feeding the test subjects as much of the hot condiment as the ducks desired resulted in an increase in feeding, egg weight, and a moderate increase in egg production compared to the control (non-treatment) ducks. The capsaicin apparently influences follicle growth in the duck ovaries and reduces oxidative stress, though no mention was made of how spicy the duck eggs tasted! [30]

Chicken Speak

Chickens are lively talkers; they love to cackle and make a range of vocalisations whilst going about their business throughout the day. Chooks produce a large repertoire of sounds, around 25 distinct vocalisations that are grouped into eight main types: food calls, single and double clucks, fast clucks, whines, 'gakel' calls, singing, and mixed sounds. [31] Roosters make food calls when finding a tasty treat that could tempt the girls. The tastier and more tempting the treat, the faster he initiates the fast-clucking sound and maintains it. I have observed our hens do this, too; if one gets a treat of some oats and the bird is alone, it lets out a frenzy of fast 'happy' clucks. If a conspecific is nearby, it remains quiet, but not always; perhaps some reciprocal altruism is at play? Fast clucks are like food reward calls, and both seem related to positive emotions, happy clucks, so to speak. Then there are the 'I just laid an egg, everybody' calls, which may be used to maintain social status or could be a tactic to draw potential predators away. The 'gakel' call is usually a 'bloody hell, I'm about to be eaten call'. I vividly remember hearing this call one day, and I raced outside just in time to see a dingo pursuing one of our hens down the hill! The chook escaped and lived to tell the tale, the goats and alpacas on edge after witnessing the event.

In a study to find out how well the average person can interpret 'chicken speak,' Nicky McGrath and colleagues at the University of Queensland surveyed 194 people of various ages. They found that 69% of people could accurately assign chicken calls as rewarded or non-rewarded in context. Previous experience with chickens did not significantly affect the answers, adding weight to the argument that cross-species call recognition may be an intrinsic trait in humans and other creatures. [32]As I wrote the last few paragraphs, I went outside to investigate a cacophony of bird calls coming from a tree near the house. A large goanna was making its way up the trunk, probably searching for eggs, and at least three species of birds were all screeching up a storm! The birds, the lizard and the ape understood what was being said; the lizard gave up and moved on, and the ape returned to his writing.

Can You Hear Me?

Chickens have excellent hearing; they hear me calling *here chook-chook* across the paddock at greater distances than the goats can hear! The sound of our front gate latch often sends the chickens into a frenzy! They often receive food treats near the gate and have learned to associate the sound of the gate latch with the reward. Chickens can even hear infrasound, those low rumbling frequencies below 20 Hz, usually inaudible to humans. Across a range of birds tested, pigeons, guinea fowl, and chickens displayed increased sensitivity to infrasound. Chooks are known to produce low-frequency, closed-mouth vocalisations, which may be beneficial in bird communication. [33] Low-frequency infrasound typically originates from the environment, such as wind, thunder, earthquakes, or meteors. The perception of these sounds could be advantageous to birds, or perhaps this is a collective intergenerational bird trauma related to the Chicxulub meteor impact.

Chicken Cognition

Self-Awareness and Theory of Mind

On reflection, chickens do not appear to pass Gallup's MSR mirror test, treating their likeness as another chook or simply ignoring it. Still, there are some intriguing clues to revealing chicken self-recognition and mirrors. Sonja Hillemacher and Inga Tiemann tested 18 hens to see if they could recognise hidden food rewards via the reflection in a mirror. They note that the MSR mark test, passed mostly by primates and corvids, is the 'top end' of the scale in animal cognition, but other methods can reveal other cognitive abilities. A *mirror-mediated* object discrimination task assesses an animal's ability to associate an object, such as a food reward, with its reflection without requiring an understanding that they are identical. Using this task, the researchers placed the chooks in a box with two food containers, obscured by a covering on the top. A vertical mirror at the back of the box was angled downwards to reveal the hidden food treats in the reflection. The treats were swapped around, and a control group used an opaque background, not a mirror. Eleven out of the eighteen hens successfully solved the task, exploiting the relationship between the real food reward and the reflection in the mirror. [34]

Can chickens anticipate the future? Sounds like a clucky question, but delayed gratification is all about self-control, sacrificing the now for a better payoff in the future. To test this ability in chooks, Siobhan Abeyesinghe and associates tested two groups of hens, one given a two-button task and the other an equivalent task using a spatial maze. The hens chose between a red button (self-control) that gave a 6-second delay with food access for 7 seconds and a green button (impulsivity) with a 2-second delay but only food access for 3 seconds. The birds *fowled* the experiment, being impulsive each time, so the experimenters changed things up, introducing a 'jackpot condition'. Where the birds could hold out for an even greater reward. Birds were given a similar choice as before, but this time, the red key provided a 6-second delay (representing self-control) to obtain a 22-second feed. The hens showed significant self-control in the jackpot condition, with their previous impulsivity attributed to uncertainty associated with the delay. [35] Overvaluing immediate outcomes is probably an adaptive response to a dangerous and uncertain world, akin to 'eat it now while I still can,' and is likely an unconscious action. However, delaying gratification for a bigger payoff requires some cognitive effort and a high degree of awareness, not to mention a basic concept of time differences and quantities. Maybe not so bird-brained after all.

Empathy

Do chickens experience empathy? Do they see one of their friends in distress and also feel distressed, as is often seen in many mammals? Cognitive empathy, or theory of mind, is perspective-taking, walking a mile in another's shoes, whereas emotional empathy is an emotional response to another's emotional experience.

Joanne Edgar and colleagues investigated the emotional empathy in domestic hens. Measuring the physiological response of an observer hen who would watch a conspecific sprayed with a puff of air showed no noticeable differences. When the observers themselves received an air puff, the chooks showed a considerable stress response and heightened alertness. They concluded that there was no evidence of any emotional empathy in chickens in the present context. [36] A couple of caveats here: their previous research, using behavioural and physiological measurements of hens and their chicks, revealed that mother hens exhibited an increase in heart rate, stress-induced hyperthermia, and an increase in vocalisations when their chicks showed distress, indicating the fundamentals of emotional empathy. The researchers also noted that the air puff was a relatively mild stressor, and further study of more stressful situations, and perhaps chooks related to each other, might yield differing results.

So, chickens show emotional reactions to their offspring but not their fowl friends. I am curious to know if the same results would be obtained from testing wild jungle fowl, whose social group structure is very small, compared to broiler chickens, which have been selectively bred to live among thousands of other birds. If the broiler birds showed too much emotional empathy, then factory farms would be full of sick and neurotic chooks, potentially adding Prozac to the antibiotics and anticoccidials they are treated with!

Object Permanence

How do chooks fare in relation to object permanence? For a quick refresher on the stage of object permanence, see Chapter Three. It turns out chickens surprisingly show some aspects of reaching stage four of object permanence, where they recognise that objects are completely hidden. Chicks are often tested by using imprinting, where the first image they see becomes their 'mother'. [24] One famous example of imprinting in birds is Konrad Lorenz's studies using geese, which imprinted him as their mum, following him literally everywhere. In testing baby chickens, chicks are often imprinted to a shape or geometric symbol once hatched, which is then hidden or partially hidden. Stephen Lea et al. found that chicks that were imprinted to recognise a metal rod could still respond to that shape even when it was partially hidden, demonstrating that newly hatched chicks, unlike human newborns, have an immediate response to recognising partly occluded objects. [37]

Justin Wood and colleagues took a more high-tech approach, using a virtual environment to test chicks' object permanence abilities and found some similar, if not startling, results. [38] Newly hatched chicks were placed into a square box with a video screen at each end. In Experiment One, the 'natural world' consisted of a single screen that continuously displayed a shape moving around the screen, which I will call the *Hen* for simplicity. The *Hen* was never hidden and moved if the chick approached it. Soon, the chicks imprinted on this hen shape and followed it around. In the test phase, when the chick tried to move close to the *Hen*, the *Hen* shape would either move 'behind' two square shapes (object move-ment) or the shapes would move to obscure the *Hen* (invisible dis-placement), switching between the two opposing video screens. The chicks demonstrated an understanding of object permanence throughout the entire search period, spending considerably more time near the screen hiding the *Hen* object. The experiment was repeated, but this time, chicks were imprinted and raised in an 'unnatural' world. In this world, when the *Hen* disappeared behind the squares, it was unnaturally teleported to the opposite screen.

Despite the chicks seeing thousands of these 'violations' of object permanence, they remained true believers, exhibiting the same behaviour in both conditions. The researchers concluded that a chick's ability to discern object permanence must devel-op innately whilst in the egg and is unmoved by varying environ-mental conditions. [38] This makes perfect sense if you are a newly hatched chick, keeping close to the mother hen even if she is some-times occluded by objects or learning to chase and catch bugs that run and hide under objects!

Brush Turkeys

Spare a thought for the Australian brush turkey chicks, who, upon hatching from an earthen mound built by the male, burst forth into the world fully formed and with no concept of a father or moth-er. In fact, the turkeys do not imprint like other birds and form no bonds with their parents or siblings. Not a member of the chick-en species, brush turkeys are, however, Galliformes, the order of ground-dwelling birds that includes chooks. Their family name is *Megapodiidae*, basically birds with small heads and big legs that build mound nests.

Matthew Hall and colleagues at the University of Sydney stud-ied the effect urbanisation has had on the turkey population and found some surprising results. [39] The brush turkey typically inhab-its tropical and sub-tropical rainforests; however, with expand-ing urbanisation and habitat loss, the turkeys have slowly moved eastward toward the coast, with populations booming in the cities of Brisbane and Sydney. The birds are often an unwelcome addi-tion to suburban gardeners, as their bizarre nest-building activi-ties generally involve raking all the bark, sticks and leaves within a 10-metre radius into an enormous nest mound. A simple way around this is to spread chicken wire over the garden, which pre-vents the turkey from digging. Despite a healthy population, the birds were pushed to the brink of extinction during the Great De-pression of the 1930s, hunted for their meat and eggs, before the bird became a protected species. Their broad tolerance to disturbance and climatic conditions means the birds are highly adaptable. Enjoying some fish and chips at our favourite place near the foreshore, we were invaded by a bunch of cute baby brush turkeys, probably only a few weeks old. They appear to have taken on seagull-like traits, scavenging chips and crumbs from under the tables. They had some stiff competition, though, from the local ibis, who are often labelled 'bin chooks' for their bin scavenging behaviour, and several water dragons. What was fascinating was how bold the little birds were, showing little fear of people. This is in stark contrast to the occasional 'wild' turkey chick I see on our property, which are extremely shy and flighty. Is the boldness in the urban turkeys a behavioural trait passed on genetically, an example of social learning, or just habituation, I wonder.

Problem-Solving

There is a wealth of information from studies directed at pigeon intelligence and problem-solving (Skinner's pigeon-guided missiles!), but surprisingly little on chicken problem-solving, with most ethologists equating chicken abilities with those of pigeons. However, Martin Schmelz and Tobias Krause investigated cognitive enrichment in laying hens and the potential for improving animal welfare. Fifty feathered test subjects in two groups were given a variety of challenges to access food. First was a simple two-winged door, like in a saloon, that chooks had to push open to access the food, which 80-90% solved. The second, a door hinged at the bottom, held in place by a magnet with a string that chooks needed to pull to open: 100% pass rate. Third was a sliding panel that could be moved left or right: 60-70% success. And lastly, a step panel, where chooks stepped on a long pedal, that opened a hatch to the food: fail! [40] The last test is surprising, given the number of 'treadle' feeders on the market, where chickens stand on a large treadle that opens the food bay door. The study demonstrated that chickens could engage in problem-solving tasks of relative complexity and low-cost devices. A stimulating environment could lead to 'happier' chickens, and as described in the chicken personality section below, happy chickens are healthy chickens, hugely important in the poultry industry.

Social Learning

Chickens are very social animals, able to quickly establish the 'pecking order', who is in charge and who is at the bottom of the rung. Chicken social hierarchies often consist of a dominant rooster, a single dominant hen, and numerous subordinates within the flock. Dominance hierarchies are maintained through posturing and wing flapping, head pecking or rarely all-out chicken combat when the 'feathers' really fly.

Unfortunately, laying hens have relatively short lifespans and need to be replaced from time to time. The first attempt at introducing newcomers into our small flock was rather disastrous, upsetting the chook status quo. The poor new young hens were pecked and harassed for a week or so before the pecking order was re-established and the squabbling settled down. On the advice of a learned chook breeder, we tried a different method. We kept the new chooks hidden from the others until nightfall, then snuck them into the coop, placing them on the perch next to the older birds. Chickens have poor night vision, so they had little idea what was happening. The following morning, the older hens made little fuss over the interlopers, mission accomplished! For the first few days, the new birds huddled in the coop, too scared to leave, but slowly adjusted to their new surroundings. After the third day, they cautiously started to explore, increasing their range over the following days. They quickly adopt the behaviours of the other chooks, learning to come when called for a tasty treat, and when and where to return to roost at night, strong signs of observational and social learning. Aside from simply observing the birds and making assumptions about social learning, how does one actually measure the behaviour in chooks?

In an ingenious experiment using *demonstrator* and *observer* hens, Christine Nicol and Stuart Pope of the University of Bristol, England, tested 36 ISA brown hens for social learning. [41] Demonstrator chooks were trained to receive a food reward by pecking at either of two keys, each with a light above it. If they pecked the correct key four times, a food reward was given. Observer hens were randomly assigned to either observe the experimental group (trained chooks) or the control group (untrained birds or no birds at all). The observers were then placed in an adjacent compartment separated by a clear Perspex divider. The observer chooks who viewed their key pecking friends performed more key pecks than the control group and significantly favoured the key their learned friends had pecked. This suggests that social learning may have played a significant role in the observer hens acquiring the new behaviour.

In a later paper, Nicol explained that observer hens' social learning of pecking responses was greater when they watched dominant demonstrators. Why? Nicol exclaimed that the answer is frustratingly unclear, with possible reasons such as larger size, aggressive behaviour, or simply being the centre of attention, drawing inconclusive results. [42]

What is well established is that birds of prey, like hawks, kites and eagles, are a chicken's worst enemy! When wedge-tailed eagles venture into our valley, frequently soaring hundreds of metres in the air, often barely visible, our chooks always seem to spot them. They will rush for cover under the nearest bushes and shrubs, emitting a low trilling sound whilst huddling together. This contrasts with the 'there's a goanna in our pen' call, which involves running around and cackling at maximum decibels. It is often debated in animal ethology as to who alarm calls benefit: the individual with direct fitness, helping others through reciprocal altruism, or inclusive fitness and kin selection. In giving an alarm call, the caller puts themselves at risk of predation by alerting the predator to their location. Is this altruistic? I'll sacrifice myself for the good of the group! Unlikely, it is more likely kin selection is at play: *'I will risk my life to save the relatives with whom I share my genes'*. [43]

Our chooks respond to each other's alarm calls if a predator is nearby, such as a hawk or an eagle, but they also respond to alarm calls from other birds and even mammals. On many occasions, I have witnessed our chickens scurry off under the bushes when they hear magpies or noisy miner birds sound their alarm calls. I often wondered whether this was a form of social learning or simply habituation of some sort. It turns out Dominique Potvin of the Australian National University and colleagues pondered the same question. [44] The researchers explained that animals often gather valuable information by eavesdropping on other species' alarm calls, so they decided to test whether wild birds also exhibit this behaviour. Using tiny, superb fairy wrens, they tested the birds by playing recorded sounds through speakers. The wrens were trained by hearing a novel sound (a buzz or an unrelated non-threatening bird call) simultaneously with known bird alarm call choruses. After training, the birds learned to associate the novel sound with alarm calls. When the novel sound was played alone, the trained birds responded strongly to it, compared to the control group, despite not having seen a predator or their friends fleeing one. The team concluded that this 'acoustic-acoustic' association process of social learning likely results in an uptake of alarm call recognition in natural bird communities, despite not being able to see the actual predator.

Cooperative Behaviour

Despite being highly social animals, there is a scant amount of literature on cooperation in chooks; however, a rather gruesome example of chicken cooperative behaviour comes to mind. Doves often sneak into our chicken coop to eat the chook feed; sometimes, a few chickens return, and the dove is trapped. The chickens gang up and brutally peck the bird to death within seconds. I've witnessed them beat up brush turkeys several times, often nearly twice their size, combining their efforts to drive off the hapless invader. These are probably examples of territorial behaviour, but they do appear cooperative in nature.

Memory

Whilst working on a piece of machinery one day, a huge grey huntsman spider, about the size of my hand, was dislodged, leaping out onto the garage floor. One of our Australorp chooks was nearby and, quick as a flash, leapt on the poor spider and gobbled it down greedily. Each day for nearly a week, the chook returned to the same spot around the same time and waited patiently for the situation to unfold again, which seems like a possible example of episodic memory in chickens.

As with humans and most other animal species, a stimulating environment is crucial for producing healthy, functioning individuals with properly developed brains. Rafael Freire and Heng-Wei Cheng studied the brains of 16-day-old chicks. They found that birds raised in a stimulating environment with multiple visual barriers had more advanced spatial ability and more and longer dendrites on neurons in the hippocampus. Dendrites are the branch-like connections that bring signals from other neurons into an individual neuron, essentially connecting networks of brain cells together. The hippocampus plays a crucial role in memory and spatial ability, and the right hemisphere showed significantly more hippocampal changes (there is one hippocampi on each side). [45] This is similar to Iain McGilchrist's earlier findings that the right hemisphere in birds and humans is associated with detailed object discrimination and topography. Findings like these in the humble chicken serve as useful models for brain plasticity and development in both animals and humans, highlighting the importance of a stimulating environment, even for chicks.

Personality

The internet is awash with stories of chicken personalities, loving, cheeky, smart, silly, awkward, parochial terms that mostly anthropomorphise chooks in line with our ideals. It may be a long stretch to extrapolate the five-factor personality model to chickens. Most ethologists prefer terms like exploration, boldness/ shyness and aggression.

Anna Favati and colleagues found that personality traits were strong predictors of dominance in roosters. It pays to be the top pecker in the pecking order, with dominant individuals enjoying the spoils of war in the form of access to resources, particularly hens. They found that variations in personality were significant factors in male chooks of similar size, with those obtaining high social status being more likely to be the top chook. Males who showed more exploratory behaviour and remained vigilant longer after a warning call or startle were more likely to achieve high status. More aggressive chooks were more likely to win a duel, but the bolder chooks that explored novel situations and were more vigilant appeared as more salient factors. [46]

Can chickens be happy? Therein lies a can of worms: define happiness! Despite being thoroughly studied and a multitude of books written about the subject, the actual concept of happiness can be somewhat elusive. In antiquity, happiness was at the intersection of luck and the Gods, whereas the Western notion of happiness is something one can pursue and control. [47] To extend that notion to animals has its own set of problems; an animal cannot tell you it is happy, but we can infer that an animal free of stress, healthy biologically and living its 'best life' might be happy. Unhappy animals are usually stressed, and with raised stress levels and elevated cortisol levels come a range of health problems.

Tom Humphrey of the University of Bristol posed the question, *Are happy chickens safer chickens?* [48] Food poisoning from chicken consumption is a global concern, most commonly caused by the bacteria Salmonella and Campylobacter. It was long believed that these bacteria were part of the gut flora of chooks and sometimes contaminated the meat during the slaughter process. Chickens create an antibody response to these pathogens, which would suggest that they are not part of the bird's normal lifecycle. Stress hormones have been shown to alter the immune response and pathogen behaviour, so it's no leap of the imagination to suspect stressed and unhappy chooks are sick chooks. Improving poultry welfare by reducing stressors such as overcrowding, poor diet, and transport stress can enhance chickens' resistance to infections and reduce pathogen shedding, resulting in happier, healthier chickens.

Temperament

As mentioned previously, personality is shaped by genes and environment and can change over the lifespan; however, temperament is innate and remains stable over time. Chooks display personality changes as they mature, but what of the temperament traits that they hatch with? Akira Ishikawa and associates explain that day-old chicks can suffer detrimental and long-lasting behavioural effects when they experience fear and stress during handling. They developed a handling test to assess birds, grouped into three categories: bustle, aggression, and timidity. They tested 96 chicks from seven breeds using 10 behavioural traits, such as vocalisation, biting, escaping and sleeping. These traits were then used to classify the chicks into three categories, from which five distinct temperament groups were identified across the seven breeds. The most aggressive temperament breed, the Oh-Shamo, is a Japanese breed of bird bred for cockfighting, displaying its feisty temperament even in chicks that have just hatched. [49]

Human-imposed selection pressures, through selective breeding, have a huge impact not only on animal phenotypes (appearance) but also on their behaviour. White Leghorn laying hens and their ancestral Red Junglefowl cousins were compared in a study by Karin Schütz and Per Jensen. [50] They found that the laying hens, bred for increased egg production, participated less in energy-demanding behaviours, foraging less and displayed less social behaviour than the junglefowl. The laying chook preferred to freeload on food, eating only where it was freely available, but the jungle chooks were happy scratching and searching for food. This supports the *resource allocation theory,* suggesting that laying hens reallocate energy from demanding behaviours to production traits, such as growth and reproduction. Sadly, those natural traits for 'chicken-ness' are selectively bred out of the birds.

Of the egg-laying breeds in Australia, the ISA brown and Leghorns are the most popular, along with colourful Wyandottes, Plymouth Rocks, Sussex and Australorps. I can attest to the different temperaments of three of these breeds. The ISAs are my favourites: easy-going, neither timid nor aggressive, and easy to train. Australorps are also easy-going but are often timid and tend to get 'clucky' or 'broody' sitting on clusters of eggs all day, fluffing up feathers and growling when attempting to lift them off. This behaviour is a natural part of chicken life; however, the birds also lose condition when clucky, as they eat less and expend a lot of energy warming their body to incubate the eggs. Lastly, my least favourite bird is the Leghorn. Prolific layers, but mad as a cut snake!

Conclusions

From surviving an extinction event to becoming the most numerous animals on earth, chickens have found their way onto every
continent bar Antarctica. They have enriched our lives through
creation stories and fables and provided us with eggs for breakfast
and drumsticks for dinner. Chickens are highly intelligent, curious,
and social, with diverse temperaments and personalities. They can
delay gratification and show the ability to recognise object permanence. Without ruffling too many feathers or counting my chickens before they hatched, this sounds like an intelligent being to
me, not just a walking chicken nugget!

Bovines

(Bos Taurus)

A cow doesn't know the value of its tail.

Hausa proverb, Nigeria, Africa

I Once recall seeing a video on social media of a person lying in a field full of cows; the bovines warily shuffled toward them, and eventually, the cows gathered around the person curiously. It was a warm sunny day, and the neighbour's cows were nearby, quietly grazing yet cautiously keeping an eye on me. I hopped the fence, and the cows scattered, spooked by this strange hairless monkey intruder! I found a clean patch of ground and lay down, and within minutes, I was surrounded by a sea of wet, snorting noses and huge, curious eyes, blinking inquisitively just inches away. There was no fear from them nor me, just curiosity from both parties, albeit one party weighed half a ton and could easily squish me. I slowly stood up, the cows scattered, and we all returned to our business.

Cows, cattle, steers, heifers, bullocks and oxen are all bovine artiodactyl ungulates; that is, they bear weight evenly on two toes, which is essentially a hoof, as do sheep and goats. Cows, as with sheep and goats, are ruminants, named after the largest of four stomach chambers, called the rumen, which is about the volume of a 55-gallon or 200-litre fuel drum! Cows initially stuff grasses into their mouth, passing the roughly chewed mix into the rumen until sufficiently full, then find a place to quietly sit and 'chew the cud' or 'ruminate'. The *reticulum*, a part of the rumen organ, is a muscular pouch lined with a honeycomb pattern that forces the roughly chewed plant material back up the oesophagus, where the cow grinds the vegetation into a finer paste and re-swallows it. The green goop is then passed to the *omasum* pouch, which filters out plant particles from water, keeping them in the rumen. Thousands of diverse species of bacteria allow the cow's rumen to break down the plant material and the tough cellulose to release sugars and nutrients into the gut. From here, the goop passes to the *abomasum*, where acids and enzymes further break down the food before passing it to the small and large intestine, about twenty times the length of the cow, or around 40-60 metres![1, 2]

Cows are the second most abundant domestic livestock on the planet, with chickens being the first, and there are an astounding 1.55 billion cows as of 2022. [3] Brazil topped the cattle population charts with over 234 million bovines, followed by India (193 million) and the United States (92 million). There are over 1600 cattle species, from the Scottish Aberdeen Angus to the Zimbabwean Zwergzebu, with the majority belonging to the species *Bos taurus* or taurine cattle, the others to *Bos indicus*, or zebu cattle. [4]

Some notable record-holding cows are Big Bertha, born on St Patrick's Day in Ireland in 1944 and died in 1993, and holds two Guinness records, one for the oldest cow at 48 years and 9 months, and one for the most productive cow, producing 39 calves over her lifetime. The smallest ever recorded cow was Rani, a Bhutanese cow in Dhaka, Bangladesh, that was a diminutive 50.8 cm (20 in) in height and weighed only 26 kg. Rani was an internet sensation for a while, sadly dying at only two years old. Blossom, from Orangeville, Illinois, holds the record for the tallest cow at a whopping 190 cm from the hoof to the withers. The most expansive width horns were from a Texas Longhorn, measuring a huge 2.84 metres across, and the most expensive cow to date was a purebred Nelore cow, which sold at auction in São Paulo, Brazil, in 2023 for a whopping USD 4.38 million! [5]

A Tail of Two Cows

But what is the deal with all these breeds, and why is categorising them even necessary? As mentioned in the *Us and Them* Chapter, Carl Linnaeus laid the groundwork for the modern taxonomic system in biology, leading to a hierarchical structure of animal classification. Darwin's groundbreaking work on the theories of natural selection and Mendel's discoveries on genetics and inheritance have led to current research that can trace biological lineage back hundreds or even thousands of generations. Classifying animal breeds allows historical reconstruction of that animal's origins. Identifying vulnerable breeds enables the preservation of those lineages, and breeding commercial cattle with other breeds known for their specific traits can result in more robust animals suited to diverse environments.

Cow breeds are surprisingly hard to classify, as written records on cattle before the 18th century simply do not exist. Early classification in the 19th and 20th centuries utilised the Linnaeus style of taxonomy, which relied heavily on differences such as head and horn shape. From 1896 to 1993, coat colour was used to classify cattle. In the 20th century, the focus shifted to the economic factors of cattle breeds, where large swathes of 'economically unviable' breeds were largely ignored. It was not until the 1960s that people began to show interest in local breeds and the conservation of genetically significant animals.

Genetic testing and the fossil record are the only reliable means of tracing ancient bovine ancestry. Evidence of the domestication of cattle dates to around 8300 BC, with taurine cattle predominant in the Fertile Crescent of Western Asia, and the humped zebu becoming ubiquitous throughout the Indus Valley around 1500 years later. As mentioned in the previous chapters, the Fertile Crescent was the heartland for the domestication of sheep and goats during the same period. [6] Both the taurine and zebu cattle descend from a common ancestor, the *auroch* or wild ox, *Bos primigenius*, which diverged from yaks and bison around 1.65 million years ago. [7]

The auroch was one of the last surviving remnants of the European megafauna, which included spectacular animals such as giant cave bears, dire wolves, woolly mammoths, and giant one-horned rhinoceroses, which went extinct in the late Pleistocene, around 50,000 years ago. The auroch was a formidable beast, standing around 1.8 metres at the shoulder, with horns over a metre wide and a striking dark-coloured coat with a white stripe down its back.

Julius Caesar gave a somewhat exaggerated eyewitness account of the auroch in 51 BCE, stating: [8]

A little below the elephant in size, their strength and speed are extraordinary; they spare neither man nor wild beast which they have espied.

In the Lascaux cave, France, the *Great Hall of the Bulls* contains paintings of wild aurochs, estimated to be around 17 - 22,000 years old. Since their gradual domestication some 10,000 years ago, the Auroch was on a slow path to extinction, being selectively bred over generations into the more diminutive and docile cattle breeds of today. The last surviving animals were kept on game reserves for royalty to hunt, the only remaining beast taking its last breath on one such reserve in Poland in 1627.

Nazi Bovines

In the early 1920s, brothers Lutz and Heinz Heck hatched an ingenious plan inspired by the work of zoologist Feliks Paweł Jarocki; the duo planned to resurrect the extinct auroch. In the book *Hitler's Geographies: The Spatialities of the Third Reich,* Clemens Driessen and Jamie Lorimer tell how the brothers grew up surrounded by animals on the grounds of the Berlin Zoo, where their father was the director. [9] Lutz studied the natural sciences at the University of Berlin and was keenly interested in German colonial exploration and the African continent, travelling to Ethiopia to collect specimens for the Berlin Zoo. The brothers began researching the auroch, studying cave paintings, artworks and fossil auroch skulls to determine the physiological properties of the animal. Using the notion of *back-breeding*, the brothers sought to 'breed backwards' to eliminate the phenotypic traits created through domestication. The violent character of French and Spanish fighting cattle was of particular interest to Lutz, and he travelled throughout Spain and France in the 1920s to garner specimens, eventually cobbling together a collection of breeds to create their 'Franken-auroch'. [9]

This all sounds somewhat altruistic in nature, but more sinister motives were behind the resurrection and rewilding of aurochs. Lutz Heck was also an avid hunter and fascinated by Germanic mythology, finding a kindred spirit and ally in Hermann Göring, Hitler's second-in-command. Lutz and Göring would often go on hunts dressed in traditional garb, carrying spears, attempting to relive some strange fable of the noble aristocratic hunter. Göring introduced the *Nature Protection Law* of 1935 to protect property rights and create vast nature reserves, undoubtedly for his own pleasure and prestige. This was also part of Germanic Lebensraum, or living space, tied to Nazi ideology and expansionist plans, which involved rewilding animals for hunting, restoring natural landscapes, and safeguarding agricultural and industrial self-sufficiency. Göring's first encounter with an auroch bull led him to revel in the beast's violent nature, describing it as *Sinnbild der Urkraft, or a* symbol of the primal force. [9]

During the invasion of Poland, Heck travelled to the Warsaw Zoo to oversee the transfer of all the 'valuable' animals to other zoos in Germany; the remaining ones were shot. Diane Ackerman's novel *The Zookeeper's Wife* is based on the unpublished diary of Antonina Zabinska, wife of Warsaw Zoo director Jan Zabinska, who assisted hundreds of Jews to escape Poland via the abandoned zoo. Ackerman gives a damning account of Heck, illustrating how a private hunting party was organised by Heck and his SS mates, who, full of booze-fuelled bravado, shot the penned animals for entertainment and sport. [10] Heck would later return to Berlin in 1932 to assume his father's role as director of the Berlin Zoological Garden. As the Red Army rolled into a defeated Berlin in 1945, Heck turned tail and fled the zoo that had been a part of his family for over 50 years, although not before transferring 600,000 Reichsmarks of the zoo's funds into a Swiss bank account. [10]

Though to be fair, the Heck brothers did contribute to the rewilding of the auroch (also called Heck cattle) and bringing the wisent, or European bison, back from the brink of extinction, albeit to populate Göring's Nazi-hunting estates. The brothers also attempted to revive the extinct tarpan, a Eurasian wild horse, by creating the Heck horse, which bore a vague resemblance to its extinct relative.

Mighty Milkers

I have fond memories from my childhood, waking up early to be the first to retrieve the milk delivered to the front door, and claiming the thick wad of cream that sits at the top of the bottle when it's opened. When you stop and consider the current dizzying array of milk varieties on offer, full cream, no cream, A2, lactose-free, organic Argentinian beaver's milk, it is difficult to believe that only a few decades back, a 'milkman' delivered bottled milk (one variety only) to your door each morning, retrieving the glass bottles to be later refilled.

Worldwide, cows produced 930 million tonnes of milk in 2022, equivalent to around 360,000 Olympic-sized swimming pools full. The thirstiest consumers were Europeans, at 200kg per person per year, followed by Americans (181kg), then Australians (147kg). [3] American dairy cows yield the most milk, averaging around 10,000 kg a year, an increase of 223% from what they produced in 1961! Surprisingly, this was more than double the output of New Zealand cows, which made around 4,400 kg per cow. Whoa! That is a huge difference; what could be driving the output of these American mega-milkers?

Heather White and colleagues examined the genetic differences between New Zealand (NZ) and North American (NA) dairy cows and how they affect milk production. [11] They describe that NA cows have been selectively bred to produce more milk, but NZ cows produce milk with a higher fat and protein content, as well as a longer lifespan. This was due to NZ cows showing higher levels of liver enzymes that burn energy differently than the NA cows, leading to higher lipogenesis (fat creation).

In the book *Are We Pushing Animals to Their Biological Limits?*, Temple Grandin expounds on the dangers of over-selecting for specific traits, such as milk production. [12] Dairy cows have been bred to become 'super-producers', with milk yields per cow more than doubling in just 40 years; many cows produce over 20,000 kg of milk between calving and 'drying off'. Grandin describes scientists' concern over animals bred for high productivity, stating that they may display more metabolic, physical, and psychological problems. Large increases in milk production are found to reduce fertility in cows, increase lameness and have problems maintaining body weight, all likely a result of over-selecting for a particular trait, a practice highly detrimental to the animal. According to reports, approximately a quarter of all milking cows are lame, have less fat cushioning in their feet, poor body condition, and low-fat reserves. Grandin suggests that rather than breeding large, high-producing animals with short lifespans and only two milking years, smaller cows with lower milk production will yield 3 to 4 years of milk, as demonstrated by the New Zealand cows. [12]

Another factor contributing to the difference in milk production may be *bovine somatotropin* (bST). First discovered in the 1920s when bovine pituitary tissue was found to stimulate growth in rats, Dale Bauman of Cornell University explains that not only did it promote growth, but also lactation in rabbits and goats. The protein responsible was later isolated and identified as a peptide hormone called somatotropin. [13] Early Russian experiments on cows proved highly effective, and scientists in the UK investigated the ability of bST to alleviate wartime food shortages. However, the tiny amounts of bST that could be retrieved from cow brains were insufficient to affect milk shortages. Rapid advances in DNA technology in the 1980s led to the creation of a synthetic form of bST, using recombinant technology, inserting cloned bovine genes into E—coli bacteria, which produces large amounts of the bST hormone, creating rbST. [14] The synthesised rbST varies slightly from natural cow bST in their amino acid sequences but produces essentially the same effect. The US Food and Drug Administration (FDA) first approved the use of rbST in 1993, stating it is safe for human consumption, but it does have some adverse effects on cows. [15]A 2013 WHO report stated that the risk of cancer from rbST-treated milk was negligible, as they are not bioactive or absorbed in the human gut. However, cows given rbST to increase milk production tend to suffer from more (25%) udder infections, often treated with antibiotics. The WHO committee suggested no evidence of an increase in non-compliant drug residues in milk samples from the USA. [16] Despite the evidence, many countries, including Canada, the EU, Japan, Australia, and New Zealand, have banned bovine growth hormones from increasing milk yields. This is one possible explanation for the difference between the American mega milkers' milk output and the NZ cows, but that is up for debate.

Bio-impacting Bovines

What is not in dispute is the effect of large-scale bovine farming on the environment. *Livestock's Long Shadow* was the title of a 2006 report by the Food and Agriculture Organisation of the United Nations, or FAO, that assessed the impact of livestock on the environment. [17] The report highlights the importance of the livestock sector, which accounts for 40% of global agricultural GDP, employs 1.3 billion people, and creates livelihoods for over a billion of the world's poorest individuals. The trade-off is in the projected doubling of meat consumption from 229 million tonnes in 1999/01 to 465 million tonnes in 2050, with milk predicted to grow from 580 to 1,043 million tonnes. They note that the livestock sector is changing, trending towards more regionalised and peri-urban areas, with a rise in intensive, industrialised farming that focuses on efficiency at the expense of marginalising small landholders and pastoralists, and increasing waste and pollution. On land degradation, the report describes that the livestock sector is the largest land user, occupying 26% of the ice-free terrestrial surface with grazing and 33% of arable land for feed crops. Overall, livestock accounts for 70% of agricultural land and 30% of global land.

The expansion of livestock production significantly contributes to deforestation, particularly in Latin America, which experiences the highest rates. Around 70% of former Amazon forest land is now used for pastures, with feed crops dominating much of the rest. [17] Furthermore, the livestock sector accounts for eight per cent of the world's water usage, primarily for irrigating feed crops, with significant pollution from animal waste, antibiotics, hormones, fertilisers, pesticides, and chemical residues from tanneries. The scale of leather production worldwide is jaw-dropping! The International Council of Tanners, the self-described global organisation for the leather-producing industry, lists the top producers of bovine hides as Argentina (11.5 million) and Australia (8.8 million). The largest leather producer is China, with a whopping 5.9 billion square feet produced in 2015, equivalent to approximately 135,000 acres or 102,000 football fields. [18] Regarding biodiversity, the FAO report states:

Livestock now account for about 20 per cent of the total terrestrial animal biomass, and the 30 per cent of the earth's land surface that they now pre-empt was once habitat for wildlife. Indeed, the livestock sector may well be the leading player in the reduction of biodiversity, since it is the major driver of deforestation, as well as one of the leading drivers of land degradation, pollution, climate change, overfishing, sedimentation of coastal areas and facilitation of invasions by alien species. [17]

Sobering facts to consider: the price we are now paying for our love affair with bovines, their milk and their flesh. This love affair is also leading to a greater biomass in people in the form of obesity. The report describes how past hunter-gatherer societies consumed more meat than developed countries do now. However, developed countries now have a more varied and balanced diet. Still, developing countries are now playing 'catch-up', a term named the 'nutrition transition', a shift from being undernourished to overnourished. The shift to a Western diet of pre-processed food containing high sugar and fat levels, combined with a sedentary lifestyle, has led to developing waistlines in developing countries. Interestingly, the report states that:

Worldwide, the number of overweight people (about 1 billion) has now surpassed the number of malnourished people (about 800 million). [17]

That report was in 2006; however, since then, things have

somewhat changed. The WHO now states that *"Worldwide adult obesity has more than doubled since 1990, and adolescent obesity has quadrupled"*. [19] They list that in 2022, 43% of adults 18 years and over were overweight, and 16% suffered from obesity.

Along with the burgeoning waistlines also come burgeoning health problems, with a rise in developing countries of all the diseases that plague affluent Westerners. South Africa is not immune to the obesity epidemic; Steffen Otterbach and colleagues describe the country as experiencing an unprecedented rise in obesity, where 68% of women and 31% of men are overweight or obese. [20] Data suggests that eating a healthy diet costs 69% more than an 'average' diet, with healthier food options more expensive in lower-income regions. According to their 2017 study, nearly all of South Africa's fast-food offerings were meat-based! Using a combination of household surveys and Google geospatial information, they found that for each kilometre closer to a supermarket or fast-food restaurant an individual lives, their BMI increases.

Cultural factors also play a significant role in meat consumption rates. Brazil and Thailand have similar per capita income and urbanisation rates, but the consumption of animal products in Brazil is roughly twice that of Thailand. [17] Unsurprisingly, Brazil, home to the Amazon rainforest, is the world's largest beef producer; consequently, local consumption is also high. Deforestation of the Amazon, partly due to increased grazing land, is undoubtedly a slow-motion train wreck. According to a 2020 study, that year saw the most significant rate of deforestation in a decade in the Brazilian Amazon, with 11,088 square kilometres of forest clearcut. [21] This was 182% higher than the target set by Brazil's National Policy on Climate Change, yet still an improvement on the historic peak of clearing in 2004, when over 27,000 km2 of forests were clear-cut. Much of the illegal deforestation occurs to produce farmland, with significant amounts devoted to browsing bovines, which in turn produce, you guessed it! Hamburger patties.

Bovines between buns

The fast-food industry is one of the biggest consumers of beef worldwide, and the growth of the industry shows little sign of slowing down. McDonald's is one of the world's largest fast-food chains and a major buyer of beef. Their UK website states: *"McDonald's has around 34,000 restaurants in 118 countries and territories across the world, serving more than 69 million people every day worldwide.* [22] Exactly how much beef McDonald's uses for its hamburger patties is a little tricky to nail down. However, to offer some clues, in 2022, Meat & Livestock Australia reported:

"In its 2021 Annual Shopping List, released last November, McDonald's reported it purchased more than 30 million kilograms of Australian beef for use in 970 stores across the country. On the global stage, Australia is also crucial to the supply of beef to around 39,000 restaurants in 109 nations." [23]

McDonald's purportedly passed the 300 billion burger mark in 2013, but as Nancy Folbre of the University of Massachusetts explained, only *ballpark estimates* can be made, as McDonald's stopped releasing details of cumulative burger sales in 1994, when they reached 99 billion. [24] Folbre described McDonald's as almost a "culinary country of its own" with revenues that exceed the GDP of Ecuador, a testament to Ray Kroc's description of the company he built as his own *"personal monument to capitalism."* [24] Although it appears that chicken consumption by McDonald's patrons may be catching up to that of the iconic beef burgers, Hannah Ziegler of The Washington Post reported in 2024 that McDonald's serves around 300 million pounds, or 136,000 kg, of chicken each year, with sales split equally between bird and bovine. [25]

Of course, McDonald's is only one of several global fast-food franchises that supply our seemingly insatiable appetite for beef burgers. According to industry data, as of 2024, there are over 84,000 burger restaurants in the US alone, that is an awful lot of beef! [26]

But where on earth is all that beef supplied from? A little-known fact about hamburger meat is that the 'mighty milkers' described previously often end up between two bread buns. Marcy Lowe and Gary Gereffi from the *Centre on Globalization, Governance & Competitiveness* at Duke University explain that one in four dairy cows are removed from dairy farms each year, four out of five of these are 'cull cows' removed because of lower milk yields or the end of their productive lives of four to six years, despite the fact many cows live to 20 years. [27, 28] Proceeds from the cow cull amount to around 5-15% of dairy income, the meat is mostly ground up into hamburger mince for the fast food industry, with historical data revealing fast food restaurants used 60% dairy cull cow meat and 40% fed-beef trimmings. Ligia Moreira and colleagues of The Department of Animal and Dairy Sciences, Wisconsin, explain that in the U.S., around 3 million dairy cows were slaughtered in 2019 to supply the food industry with various cuts and ground beef. [29] The researchers expressed surprise at the lack of research into dairy cows and the food system, with concerns over cow welfare and economic losses related to lameness and poor body condition scores, stating, "Cow *welfare should be an emphasis for all cow handling from the farm to the harvest event*". [29] Would you like a milkshake with your burger?

Besides dairy cows, what exactly is in some of the *five billion* hamburgers that Americans consume each year? Brigid Prayson and colleagues tested eight undisclosed fast-food burger brands, which yielded disturbing results. [30] Using histological methods, they found that water content averaged 49%, meat content ranged from 2.1% to 14.8%, and a variety of anatomical bovine bits and pieces were found. These included connective tissue, nerves, blood vessels, adipose (fat), bone, plant material and cartilage. Unexpectedly, they also found parasites in two of the burger brands, *Sarcocystis*, an intracellular parasite that often affects various animals, including cows and sometimes humans. The parasite forms cysts in the muscles of the infected cows, which are passed on through faeces or by eating raw meat. They also conducted protein staining to test for brain tissue, due to concerns about bovine spongiform encephalopathy, also known as mad cow disease; however, none were found.

Bovine Bacteria and Palaeolithic Poop

It is hard to fathom that fast food might impact a microscopic bacterium that was passed from cows to humans over millennia. This is precisely what Sarah Moraïs and colleagues of Ben-Gurion University of the Negev found in a study on a new species of bacterium they discovered. [31] Cellulose, the complex carbohydrate found in plant cell walls, is particularly difficult to break down and digest in the gut. Cows have diverse colonies of ruminococcal bacteria in their gut and rumen that allow them to break down the tough plant cellulose. The researchers identified a specific gene (cttA) that encodes proteins that bind the bacterium to cellulose cells, allowing bovines to break down cellulose. They then scanned thousands of human gut DNA samples for the same cttA gene, eventually narrowing down three samples that closely resembled the cow gut bacteria. The team suggests that these were passed initially to humans from cows, most likely when they were first domesticated some 10,000 years ago. To assess the prevalence of the bacteria, they tested reconstructed samples of DNA from paleo-poop around 1-2000 years old and found a 43% prevalence of the bacteria; samples from modern-day hunter-gatherers showed a 21% occurrence, present-day rural societies showed 20% and modern industrialised populations, a meagre 4.5% of people harboured the bacteria. The key factor here is fibre; hunter-gatherers consume the most plant fibre, and the industrialised fast-food nations consume the least amount of food fibre, leaving no need or place for the beneficial bovine bacterium.

Plant-based Cows

"It's time to address the cow in the room", stated Melita Jazbec and the team from *The Institute for Sustainable Futures*, UTS, Sydney. They explain that food production is responsible for more than a third of human-made greenhouse gas emissions (GHG), with Australia having the highest GHG emissions per capita from food among the other G20 countries. [31] A huge 60 per cent of those emissions come from the production of meat and dairy. The team's report, *Shifting the Menu*, suggests that replacing meat products in fast food will have a beneficial effect on the environment and greenhouse gas emissions. They claim that simply replacing 25% of the beef used in fast food with plant-based alternatives would cut CO2 emissions by 150,000 metric tons, equivalent to removing 150,000 cars from the road. Australia is often called the driest continent in the world, and water is an extremely valuable resource. From 1981 to 2010, water availability for cattle consumption dropped by a third due to competition from other agricultural endeavours. Their analysis revealed that replacing beef burgers with plant-based alternatives would result in a 94% reduction in water and land use. Replacing the mozzarella cheese used on a 12-inch pizza with plant-based cheese would result in a 47% reduction in water usage and a 77% reduction in land use. A meat patty accounts for 6.4m² of land use and 126 litres of water, whereas a plant-based patty uses just 0.4m² and 7 litres of water. [31]

Some of the fast-food giants have tested the market with beef-free, plant-based alternatives, finding mixed results, with many eventually withdrawing the bovine-free products from sale. Burger King, however, seems to have bucked the trend with its 'Impossible Whopper', replacing the traditional beef patty with a plant-based alternative. [33,34] Clearly, the public still has an ongoing love affair with meat burgers, which begs the question: how much, if any, information about eating less unsustainable beef and meat is filtering through to the media and influencing the collective masses? Rimante Ronto and colleagues at Macquarie and Curtin Universities pondered the same question.[35] They looked at how sustainable plant-based diets in Australia were portrayed in the news media between 2018 and 2020 to assess their impact on perception and dietary behaviours. The study revealed that over half of the articles encouraged increasing plant-based food intake and reducing animal-derived food intake; however, challenges persist in public perceptions of plant-based food. Those centred around the high sodium content of many plant-based alternatives, with one study finding that plant-based mince contained six times more sodium than meat mince! Issues around nutrient content were also a concern, with some products providing fewer nutrients than meat but greater amounts of fibre and beneficial fats.

There seems to be a lot of talk about switching away from meat, but very little sign of it happening. For a while, my spouse and I tried to go plant-based, buying the veggie-based make-believe burgers and schnitzels, but that novelty wore thin after a while. I have also noticed the supermarket giants' offerings of plant-based food alternatives have dwindled. On one visit to a Woolworths store, I counted out roughly 40 metres of fridges containing meat, and one fridge one metre long containing plant-based alternatives! Maybe our innate primal instinct to hunt, kill and eat animals eventually wins out in the mental battleground of attempting to do 'the right thing.' Or perhaps there are other factors at play, which will be revealed in chapter eleven.

Lab-Grown Cows

One possible solution to animal ethics concerns, such as methane gas pollution from cow farts and burgeoning grazing land usage, sounds like the content of a science fiction novel. Cultivated meat, also known as lab-grown, cell-based, and slaughter-free meat, is slowly gaining traction as technology advances. Way back in 1894, a French chemist first speculated that by the year 2000, milk, meat and eggs could be factory-synthesised, explained Marline Kirsch and colleagues of *Cultimate Foods*, Germany.[36] Even in 1930, the British Secretary for India, Frederick Smith, envisioned a time when juicy self-replicating steaks might become popular.

According to Neil Stephens of Brunel University London, the origins of cultivated meat have indeed been inspired by science fiction, with initial work starting in the 2000s, including one enterprise funded by NASA. The goal at the time was to develop a muscle-based protein system suitable for feeding astronauts on long-term space travel. Another contemporary development was an artistic project conducted by bio-artists Oron Catts and Ionat Zurr, who initially used cells from sheep and later from frogs. The pair grew frog muscles on biopolymer scaffolds, which were exhibited right next to the healthy living frog donors. The muscles were later prepared into tiny frog steaks and then served at the French cuisine exhibition in 2003, L'art Biotech, Le Lieu Unique. The live frogs were later released into a pond. [37] The first fully formed, in-vitro (outside of the body) produced burger was cooked and served in a globally broadcast event in 2013 by Professor Mark Post of Maastricht University. The burger took two years to produce and cost 300,000 euros, bankrolled by a sizeable financial donation from Google co-founder Sergey Brin. [36] In 2003, PETA (People for the Ethical Treatment of Animals) offered one million dollars to the first group to create and sell an in-vitro chicken that tasted like real chicken. More of a publicity stunt than actual reality, the money was later channelled into grants to fund lab-grown meat projects. Stephens suggests that there are two distinct waves in the cultivated meat movement: the first, funded by universities and academically based, and the second, via startups with Silicon Valley backing and slick promotions that claim cell-based meat will change the world. [37] Stephens postulates that the third wave may consist of the big multinational meat companies themselves, seeking to vertically integrate the lab-grown meat industry or smaller companies licensing the technology. Watch this space; who knows where lab-grown meat may lead! I wonder whether lab-grown chickens would come in a chicken-shaped form or just a blob, the concept of an animal almost wholly erased from the equation.

The Journey Thus Far

From Nazi henchmen who tried to resurrect a giant extinct beast to then kill them for sport to thousands of diverse breeds that cover the planet, munching their way through the Amazon rainforest, cows are an undeniable success story. There are over one and a half billion of them on the planet, and they supply us with leather for our clothes and furniture, and burgers for our fast-food restaurants. They shared an important cellulose-busting bacterium with us and helped to create the most obese population the world has known. We have modified their morphology and their psychology and created mega milkers through selective breeding and hormone injections. Knowing that, ultimately, this is environmentally unsustainable, we have attempted to duplicate their meat through plants and cell biology so far with limited success. These are the extrinsic cow factors; let's now examine the intrinsic ones.

A Cow Taxi! Myanmar

Cow Intelligence

Playing the Zither to a Cow

Gongming Yi was an infamous and skilled player of the stringed zither or guqin, who enchanted crowds wherever he played his melodious tunes. One day, whilst walking in the countryside, he spotted a grazing cow and decided to sit near the browsing bovine and play his guqin. No matter how beautifully he played, the cow gave no response. Frustrated, he got up to leave and inadvertently plucked a string that sounded something like a calf calling, to which the cow responded briefly before going back to grazing. It dawned on Gongming Yi that humans appreciated human music and that cows only responded to sounds their own kind made. [38]

This *mooving* Chinese fable from the Warring States period illustrates that sometimes our anthropocentric views of intelligence often clash with actual animal intelligence. Our beliefs skew our perceptions of an animal's behaviour as unintelligent, whereas perhaps it was simply lost in translation; all that was needed was the right 'note'. Unfortunately, much of the scientific literature on cows is focused on an applied setting, such as training cows to access chutes and automatic feeding stations, in order to make a more manageable and profitable food commodity, with scant mention of the comparative psychology of cows. However, there is a wealth of information from one of the leaders in animal behaviour,

165

Temple Grandin, whom I have already quoted numerous times and whose fascinating story deserves to be told.

Temple Grandin

Born in 1947 in Boston, Massachusetts, Mary Temple Grandin also shared her first name with an employee, so Temple became her preferred name.[39] At the age of two, doctors advised Grandin's mother that Temple would likely need to be institutionalised due to her autism, a diagnosis her mother refused to give in to, enrolling Grandin in intensive speech therapy classes that later proved successful. Grandin had a special connection with animals from an early age, though she struggled to understand why a small dog is not a cat, categorisation being a problem many autistic children struggle with. Teased incessantly throughout her school years, Grandin would often lash out and was eventually expelled for fighting. Temple's mother eventually enrolled her in a special boarding school for gifted children with emotional problems. The school had a stable and a selection of behaviourally troubled horses, with whom Temple spent a great deal of time. Despite the joy the horses brought her, school life was hard and the 'tidal wave' of anxiety she experienced as an adolescent never ceased. One summer, Grandin was visiting an aunt in Arizona and saw cattle being herded into a squeeze chute, a V-shaped contraption hinged at the bottom, that the cattle walk into the V, which closes securely, holding the animal in place. Temple saw that instead of being frightened by the device squeezing the cows, they calmed down, allowing the ranchers to treat or vaccinate the cows. Returning to school, she enlisted the help of a teacher to build Grandin her own 'squeeze box', which worked a treat, making her feel calmer. The box is still in use today, according to Grandin, who states, *"Animals saved me"*. Temple went on to finish college, earning a PhD and eventually a faculty position at Colorado State University, designing innovative systems for livestock handling in the meat industry and becoming a leading spokesperson on autism. [40]

Step into your squeeze chute, and we'll explore the machinations behind those big eyes and endearing eyelashes and attempt to discover what goes on in a bovine brain.

Sensory Abilities

Eyesight

Cows, being prey animals, have eyes positioned on the sides of their heads and have evolved to scan their environment for threats. In their book *Cow Talk*, John Moran and Rebecca Doyle explain that cattle, much like sheep and goats, have a 330° field of vision, with a limited area of binocular vision directly in front of them.[41] This area of vision is where cows see most clearly and have good depth perception, which is why cows will often lower their head to face an object of curiosity or threat. A cow's remaining visual field is monocular, great for detecting predators, but poor for judging distances, the authors describe. This is why it's best to approach a cow from the side rather than from the front, albeit slowly so as not to spook the animal. Cows are less perceptive of red colours than we are, which tends to increase colour contrast, making shadows and bright areas appear more extreme. To a cow, a solid shadow may look like a hole in the ground, which explains why they often baulk at shadows, lowering and raising their head, attempting to determine if it's safe to proceed. [42] This makes evolutionary sense; falling into a hole and breaking a leg is essentially a death sentence for wild cattle. People suffering from Alzheimer's dementia also have problems differentiating shadows from holes, likely a result of degradation in visual-spatial processing in the brain.

Cows have oval-shaped pupils, as opposed to the horizontal slit-like pupils of goats and sheep, and once again, they are adapted to scan the horizontal horizon. This is evident in the visual streak seen in ungulates, such as cows, sheep, and goats, an area of higher density of photoreceptor cells in the retina that allows for greater visual perception in a horizontal plane. Humans have the highest density of receptor cells in the fovea, mostly cones, which enables us to read and view objects directly in front of us with high acuity. Studies have shown that cows see the world dichromatically, in just two colours, as they have only two types of colour cone receptors, as opposed to our three, which enable colour vision. Interestingly, the way to assess stress or fearfulness in a cow is by the amount of eye white visible! Cows, like most mammals and even birds (see the chapter on chickens), exhibit brain lateralisation, with the left eye associated with the right hemisphere of the brain and novel or threatening stimuli, and the right eye connected with familiar and safe objects. Cows will purposefully pass an unfamiliar object with their left side, but the eye preference switches once that object is familiar. [43]

It is hard to imagine what experiencing the world would be like as a cow, but a researcher in Germany has made a step toward this by inventing an ingenious way to see the world through cow goggles. Benito Weise created a virtual reality (VR) headset that allows people to see the world from a cow's perspective. Used in agricultural training and education, the device will enable users to better understand cow behaviour through their perception of the world. The prize-winning inventor hopes that the cow glasses will enable people to better understand the lives of bovines, thereby increasing animal welfare, and plans to incorporate cow acoustic perception into the VR experience. [44]

Smell & Taste

Writing this brings a vivid memory of a wet market somewhere in Central Asia, where I photographed a row of buffalo noses, minus their owners. I often wondered what the recipe would call for buffalo noses. Soup, stew, or hot pot? The mind boggles! It also reminds me of the joke about the fellow who owned a dog with no nose; his friend inquired, *"How does it smell?"* Awful, he replied.

As one might expect from a prey animal, cows have a keen sense of smell and can detect odours many kilometres away. They are sensitive to the smell of urine from other stressed cows, and much like goats, males (bulls) display the Flehmen response, lifting the head and curling the upper lip. Cows can perceive four primary tastes, sweet, salty, bitter, and acidic, and have two to three times the number of human taste buds. [41]

Ever woken up with a stray tuft of hair at odds with the rest of your coiffure? Often called a 'cow lick', the term was first used by a physician in 1598, according to the Oxford English Dictionary; clearly, not a modern problem! If an actual cow has ever licked you, it's a mooving experience, and feels like being caressed by a large eel covered in sandpaper. When cows eat, they wrap their long, leathery tongue around a clump of grass and bite off the clump with the lower incisors, grinding the tough grasses with the molars at the back of the jaw. Bovine tongues are nearly a foot long, so unsurprisingly, cows can also lick their own nostrils! Cows do not have upper front incisors, but rather a leathery pad, much like sheep and goats, and their upper lip is relatively immobile, whereas sheep and goats have very dextrous upper lips. The rough, sandpapery feel comes from the large filiform papillae on the tongue's surface, which vary in shape and size according to their function.

The rough sandpapery filiform papillae are a mechanical form useful for grasping and manipulating, whereas other varieties of papillae are gustatory, containing taste cells. [42] Something to ponder if you are fond of ox tongue soup!

Hearing

Cows have excellent hearing and can interpret a range of sounds that fall outside the range of our hearing abilities. Humans typically hear in a range from 20 Hz to 20,000 Hz (20 kHz), whereas cows have a hearing range from 23 Hz to 35 kHz, hearing that is more acute than that of horses. Hertz is the unit that measures the vibration of a sound per second. Low rumbling noises typically range around 20 Hz, while birds chirping typically fall within the range of 2-20 kHz. [45] Many milking sheds are noisy environments, with noise levels often up around 96.10 dB at 500 Hz. A chainsaw is typically around the 100 dB mark, and considering that dairy cattle find noises above 70 dB stressful, it must surely affect the cows.

Daniel Mota-Rojas and colleagues explain that loud noise, particularly high-frequency sounds, can have a negative impact on the quality and quantity of milk yields. [46]Music has been shown to positively affect many animals, and studies on cows have found that music reduces stress levels, irregular behaviours like tongue rolling and mooing, and increases social interactions. Holstein cows that listened to classical music had reduced levels of stress hormones and significant increases in milk yield. Holstein, Friesian, Jersey, and Ayrshire cows exposed to over 50 different rock, blues and jazz pieces showed an interesting variety of reactions. Enriched cows, those that listened to music as opposed to their control group, which did not, showed higher milking frequency and higher levels of serotonin, the mood-regulating feel-good neurotransmitter. Some cows showed no difference in milk production to certain sounds or music, yet crossbred cows listening to classical music with a slow to moderate tempo of 75–107 bpm showed a 50–65% increase in daily milk production! [46] It just goes to show that a little Mozart in the milk or Brahms in the butter goes a long way.

Calling

It is well-established in folklore that cows...moo. But is a moo just a moo, or do the bovines really have something to say? How the heck would you even test such a thing? By living with a herd of 18 Holstein-Friesian heifers over the course of five months and recording their moos, which is what PhD student Alexandra Green from The University of Sydney did! [47] Analysing 333 cow vocalisations, two distinct types of call were identified: low-frequency nasalised moos for low distress at close range and high-frequency calls when aroused or calling over long distances. Cows have individually distinct vocalisations, much as humans do, due to the size and shape of their laryngeal tract and physiological changes impacting the movement of their vocal folds. Cow calling is beneficial for calves to identify their moms and for cows to alert their conspecifics (friends) and inform them of their emotional state. Mooing is also useful for calling for social support from other herd members. Green found that cows maintained their individual 'voice' over both positive and negative valence (pleasantness or unpleasantness). This stable trait is beneficial for other herd members to identify them, but also presents opportunities for farmers to identify individual cows to further improve farming practices.

Temperament

Imagine if you could simply appraise the appearance of an animal before witnessing any of its behavioural patterns and work out what sort of temperament it has. Oddly enough, the hair whorl is a hidden clue to not only animal temperament but also our own! The patterning of scalp hair in humans occurs around 10-16 weeks in the foetus, secondary to the shape and formation of tissues under the skin, particularly the brain, explained Temple Grandin and Mark Deesing in their book *Genetics and the Behaviour of Domestic Animals.* [48] Irregular scalp patterns can be an indicator of brain abnormalities in human foetuses before 16 weeks. They can also indicate handedness in adults, as well as hemispheric language dominance, sexual preferences and some mental illnesses. Yousefi-Nooraie and Mortaz-Hedjri examined differences between subjects with schizophrenia and bipolar disorder. They found a high correlation between the location of the hair whorl and asymmetry in skin ridge patterns (fingerprints) on the hands, indicating a higher incidence of brain lateralisation problems in people with the disorder. [49]

An awful, debilitating disorder with an equally debilitating social stigma that affects 1-2 per cent of the population, schizophrenia was first described in 1893 by Emil Kraepelin. *Dementia praecox,* or 'senility of the young', was the term Kraepelin gave to the progressive neurodegenerative disease, which leads to an early onset of loss of cognitive functions. In 1908, Eugen Bleuler renamed the disorder schizophrenia from the Latin *split mind*, describing the fragmented nature of the mental processes of those with the disorder. Patients with schizophrenia commonly show enlarged ventricles, fluid-filled spaces in the brain, and a difference in the size of the hippocampus. The seahorse-shaped structure strongly associated with memory and hippocampus sizes in schizophrenia patients differed not only in volume but also in symmetry. [50]

Animals are used to model schizophrenia-like symptoms to better understand the disorder and find new treatments. Some commonly used animal models use amphetamines (a stimulant), ketamine, a horse tranquiliser and well-known illegal party drug, and MK-801, an NMDA receptor antagonist much like ketamine, to induce psychosis-like effects and cognitive symptoms in animals like rodents and zebrafish! Why would someone stone zebrafish with potent party drugs? The answer is relatively simple: they breed prolifically in a lab environment and share a significant part of their genome with us! Scientists also use genetic models in animals, deleting or duplicating certain genes, and neurodevelopmental models, like damaging the brain of the developing rodent foetus, to induce schizophrenic-like symptoms. [51] Incredibly, it was commonly believed, right up until the 1960s, that schizophrenia was the result of bad mothering or the *schizophrenogenic mother,* before genetic testing and brain imaging blew that theory out of the water.

I am not suggesting that cows suffer from schizophrenia, as evidence so far shows it is only a human affliction. Instead, it is the biological association between hair and skin patterns and brain development, such as the hair whorls described, that transcends species. These patterns and their relationship to temperament in horses were observed hundreds of years ago in Arabia, with contemporary observations showing horses with a whorl high on the forehead or two whorls were highly reactive. It turns out that horses and cattle have similar whorl patterns on their heads, and indeed, studies of cattle show that a whorl located above the eyes is associated with a more vigilant and highly reactive temperament. [48] A 2007 study compared the hair whorl position (high, middle and low) of 58 Holstein heifers and found that cows with a high hair whorl gained weight significantly faster than the other cows. [52]

Skittish Animals

Highly reactive animals are often fine-boned, like antelopes, whippet dogs or Arabian horses, whereas strong, big-boned animals, like draught horses, often exhibit less reactive temperaments. The trade-off is that those big, strong animals, though less reactive, tend to be dangerous if you piss them off! Temple Grandin explains that large and heavily boned animals within a species usually originate from colder northern climates and are better adapted for energy conservation. Their cousins from the warmer south tend to be slightly built and more reactive, an evolutionary effect known as *Bergmann's rule*. [48]

A fine example of how humans exert evolutionary selection pressures on animals comes from the story of Beefmaster cattle. Grandin describes how, in the early 1930s, Tom Lasater created the Beefmaster breed by crossing half Brahman, a quarter Hereford, and a quarter Shorthorn. [48]. The resulting cattle were left to fend for themselves; cows unable to birth independently or chase off coyotes did not survive. The cattle were then selected based on temperament, and newly weaned calves were assessed by observing them in their pens. If the calves would approach and eat from a person's hand, they were kept; the others, as many as 25%, were culled. The resulting generations of cows were very docile and approachable yet staunchly defensive of their calves. Selecting for traits like low *fear*, high maternal care, and high *panic*, or separation distress, created an easy-handling cow with a temperament favourable to us humans, who were also good moms to their calves.

Self-Awareness and Theory of Mind

Does a cow mental time travel? thinking beyond the present and into the future. This is a difficult question to answer and even more difficult to prove, but Gary Comstock of North Carolina State University gave it a solid go. Comstock explains that thinking about the future involves prospection, directing attention to things that are yet to come, suggesting that rather than asking if this prospection in cows is conscious, one should ask if it is similar to ours. [53] In a striking video, a line of Holstein cows is locked in place at a feeding trough, each via a stanchion, a metal frame that loosely holds the cow's neck while they are milked. The cow in question (Betsy, for want of a better name) observes an attendant throwing a bucket full of grain in front of Betsy's neighbours. Unable to reach the grain, Betsy unlocks the metal stanchion via a clasp at the top, using her horn, then backs out and proceeds to unlock the neighbour's stanchion using her tongue. The neighbour backs out, and she repeats the unlocking sequence on the second neighbour's stall. The second neighbour also backs out, giving Betsy access to the second neighbour's stall. The clever bovine then reaches out, grabs the bucket and pulls it towards herself and the tasty grain reward.

But is this a result of deliberate cow planning, unconscious prospection or intuitive prospection? The cow is unable to tell us much, but the comparative brain structures of a bovine may hold some clues. Anatomically, cows have a mesolimbic dopamine pathway (MDP) that shares many similarities with the human brain. The MDP is a collection of circuits involved in motivation, reward and reinforcement. These circuits are either automatic, like seeking water when thirsty, or mediated by conscious thought, as in imagining or desiring. Comstock reasons that if these pathways are similar in humans and cows, in conjunction with past evidence for bovine intelligence and problem-solving abilities, then *"the weight of evidence lies on the side of the assumption that cows seek, anticipate, and look forward"*. [53] The author concludes that the bovine mind most likely employs intuitive prospection, utilising past experiences to achieve goals without consciously deliberating the steps. This contrasts with humans and apes, which possess autobiographical prospection, with a narrative of self, beliefs that other people have beliefs and a theory of mind. This ultimately raises a whole raft of ethical and moral questions about the treatment of cows, given the evidence that they can likely look forward to the future.

Empathy

As Alexandra Green's study showed, cow calls contain information about the sender and their emotional state, so it is fair to assume that cows discern emotions in their bovine friends. Does discerning those emotions then affect the receiver, that is, do they experience empathy? Frans De Waal illustrates how Empathy is often confused due to two contrasting views: biologists focus on what behaviour is good for, and psychologists concentrate on what gives rise to behaviour. [54] Casting aside motivational factors, as in psychology, emotional contagion is the *lowest common denominator* of the empathic process; one individual is affected by another's emotional state. This phenomenon is observed in most mammals and humans: dogs nervously shadowing their anxious owners, cattle stampeding in fear, people sharing emotive content on social media, or newborn babies in a nursery all spontaneously crying after one baby starts crying.

Alain Boissy and colleagues found that cows fed alongside a conspecific that had been previously subjected to an electric shock themselves showed increased levels of cortisol, took longer to start eating and fed more slowly. [55] Cows exposed to urine from a stressed animal also showed a similar physiological reaction, which is pretty good evidence of emotional contagion. The flip side of showing empathic-like behaviour to stressed bovine friends is social buffering, where cows surrounded by happy, unstressed conspecifics exhibit much less intense responses to negative stressors. [56] Stressed cows are also known to seek out non-stressed bovines, calves actively seek out other young calves and weaner calves licked more by other cows thrive better than other 'unlicked' calves.

Of course, this is not indicative of cognitive empathy, sympathy, or 'walking a mile in another's shoes', but it does demonstrate the rudimentary hallmarks of empathy in cows.

Object Permanence

There is a wealth of studies with sheep and goats in relation to object permanence, but sadly, none that I could find on cows, so for the moment, this one is up for conjecture!

Personality

Lowlands & Highlands

Assessing the personality of a slow and lumbering beast like a cow is no easy feat! As mentioned in previous chapters, emotions are short-lived expressions. However, personality is a more enduring trait that determines how, why and when emotions arise. Maggie Creamer and Kristina Horback of the University of California, Davis, studied cow grazing patterns and found some interesting results. [57] Cows display 'grazing personalities', enduring patterns of behaviour much akin to a personality trait. Cows could be grouped into hill climbers or bottom dwellers, the latter being suited to more open rangeland pastures, with those traits stable and independent of environmental changes. Hill-climbing cows were more flexible in their grazing patterns and showed more variability in their behaviour compared to their lowland friends, personality traits that aid in their adaptive fitness.

In humans, people who like to travel and explore tend to be high in openness (open to novel experiences) and low in neuroticism (low in anxiety and fear), personality traits the travel industry values, but also adaptive strategies important when we once lived in tribes. Just enough adventurous explorers and new hunting grounds can be discovered; too many risk-takers and the cumulative toll of misadventures might wipe out the tribe. It is to a group's advantage or *adaptive fitness* to have a bunch of different personalities, with stable individuals left to tend the flock, introverts to grind the flour, neurotics to keep watch for danger and extroverts to hunt and kill a small deer and return to tell stories of how big it was. All under the seductive power and influence of the tribe's shaman, the fellow with schizophrenia!

Pessimistic Dairy Calves

Rats have been shown to exhibit pessimistic personality traits, which makes them more prone to anhedonia (the inability to feel pleasure) when under stress. Does this also translate to other species, such as cows? Benjamin Lecorps and colleagues at the University of British Columbia also pondered that and tested a cohort of 24 dairy calves to see if personality traits affected judgment bias. [58] When faced with ambiguous situations, personality traits such as optimism or pessimism influence the choices we make, and it turns out that cows also exhibit this behaviour. Using a spatial learning task, the calves learned to associate one side of a pen with a milk bottle reward and the other side with an empty bottle and an air puff to the face. Bottles were placed in ambiguous locations around the pen, and the animals were tested multiple times over a four-week period. Two personality groups were established in the calves: pessimistic and social. The social group showed no differences in outcome. The pessimistic calves, however, showed more reluctance to novel objects and unfamiliar humans, used avoidance behaviours and showed less exploration. These results remained consistent throughout the testing period, indicating that they are stable and enduring traits, with implications for animal welfare. Specifically, pessimistic cows respond less well to enrichment and, like humans, struggle when faced with challenging emotional situations.

Problem-Solving

There is a distinct paucity of studies on bovine problem-solving, no doubt partly due to the logistics of building a maze large enough and studying the large ungulates. As mentioned earlier, there is a wealth of information on the farming practices of cattle, but realistically, the cognitive ability the meat industry might be most interested in is how well cows navigate the chute to the captive bolt gun.

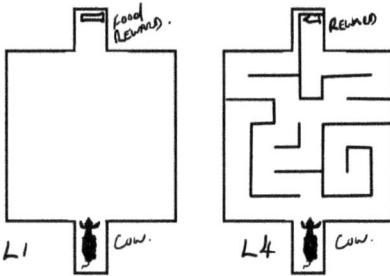

Nonetheless, Masahiko Hirata and colleagues at the University of Miyazaki, Japan, tested a bunch of Japanese Black cows and found the cows could navigate quite complex mazes and remember the maze configuration for up to 6 weeks. [59] The initial level one maze (L1) was a simple 14-metre square arena with an entry point at one end and a food reward at the other. The following levels increased in complexity, culminating in the 'L4' maze, which featured many twists, turns, and dead ends. Not all cows could navigate the L4 maze, with only 20 per cent completing the task, and all cows needed to complete it step by step. The bovines could not complete the L4 maze if they jumped straight from the L1 maze, indicating that gradual learning is needed to master complex tasks. One fascinating finding was that personality significantly affected who passed the maze test. Cows with bold risk-taking personalities were more exploratory and less affected by social isolation, quickly finding the food reward in the simple maze L1. Sounds suspiciously like the example of humans living in tribes in the previous section, with bold personalities akin to extraversion and exploratory behaviour, such as openness in the five-factor OCEAN model in humans.

Not quite a maze, but cows sure are clever at finding ways through fences. It seems to be a never-ending game of cat and mouse with our neighbour's dairy cows; find a hole, bust through, patch up the hole, rinse and repeat. The calves are particularly cheeky, seeking novelty and breaking through in small groups to go and explore.

Temple Grandin tells a wonderful story of an infamous bull in the Arizona high country that was an expert fence buster. [39] The bull could knock down the fences faster than the forestry service could build them. The bull once walked through four separate five-strand barbed wire fences completely unscathed, possibly by knocking the posts down with his head, an example of cognition rather than accidental learning. Holstein cows are extremely curious beasts, testing any and all novel items with their long tongues. Often, this exploratory behaviour results in a gate latch opening, a 'happy accident' that results in learning. Grandin explains that cows and horses, despite watching a gate opened countless times, will not try to test the latch. But if the animal accidentally unlatches a gate, it will learn and cannot be trained out of that behaviour. What's worse is that other animals witness this and learn the bad habit, an example of observational learning. Cows and other large animals can also work out that busting through an electric fence hurts for a few seconds, but has a huge reward in the gained freedom. This is shown in pigs, who will squeal before they hit the fence, indicating they know they will be shocked but make a conscious decision anyway.

Enormous Pets

Author, journalist and photographer Jon Katz tells the heartwarming story of Elvis, the 800 kg bull that Katz inadvertently acquired from Peter, his farmer neighbour. [60] Peter was rather impassive about livestock, milking and sending them to the slaughterhouse for many years. However, this cow grabbed Peter's attention, following him around like a dog and cleverly working out how to avoid the slaughter truck. After some haggling over price, Katz purchased the monstrous pet-to-be and named him Elvis. The giant bovine was curious about the world around him and accepting of his adopted family's affection, but seemed anxious about being alone. The bull soon found companions in the other reluctant farm animals, who were decidedly taken aback by the large and playful bovine. Katz laments how *"cows have never been allowed to be smart"*, lacking the stimulation other pets receive, mostly regarded as milk factories or *walking steaks*. Becoming rather boisterous, Elvis's love of apples could be a means to train the belligerent bovine, Katz realised. Soon, the lumbering Elvis was trained to come when called, stop and stay when asked. Elvis also trained Katz to bring him an apple each morning by repeatedly mooing until his demands were met. Elvis coexisted happily with all the other animals and whoever visited the farm, enthusiastically giving them a bovine tongue bath.

Social Learning

Lick-a Lot

Cows are highly sociable animals, and being an accepted member of the herd means your allogrooming skills better be top-notch! Allogrooming, or social grooming (think monkeys grooming each other), is a way to cement social bonds, establish and maintain social hierarchies and also pleasure!
Inès de Freslon and colleagues at the Austral University of Chile studied cow grooming and social structure. They observed 38 dairy cows over 30 days to examine how their social structure, popularity and individual attributes change over time. [61] They found reciprocity in cows, with cows more likely to lick and groom cows who had previously done the same. Older cows licked more often than younger cows, possibly indicating that grooming is related to seniority, and cows generally licked others of a similar age. The group size was gradually increased over time, and the new cows on the block tended to lick a lot, possibly to facilitate their acceptance into the herd. Despite adding new cows to the group, the social dynamics stayed stable over time.

Cow Cuddling

Animal-assisted therapy (AAT) is currently all the rage, as you may have noticed when boarding a flight with a fellow passenger and their emotional support otter. The physiological and emotional effects of AAT using domestic animals like cats or dogs have been well established, but do farm animals have a similar effect? Katherine Compitus and Sonya Bierbower studied the effect on eleven human participants in their interactions with two Holstein rescue steers, one and a half years old Magnus and one-year-old Callum. [62] The human participants reported overwhelmingly positive experiences, petting, watching and talking to the animals. Individuals reported comments like *"There is something about cows that is so therapeutic"* and *"It is so amazing to be near an animal that is so big and yet so gentle"*.[62] The surprising result came from the steers, showing a strong preference for interacting with women rather than men! The females also reported strong attachment-like behaviours to the steers, though what is behind those results is unclear. Overall, the cow-cuddling experiment showed that bovine-assisted therapy may be an effective treatment for both humans and their bovine assistants.

Herd Instinct

A wonderful lecture by Robert Sapolsky on *behavioural Evolution* in 2010 described a scenario often seen in wildlife documentaries where a herd of wildebeest gather nervously on the edge of the river, infested with crocodiles. [63] From behind, pushing his way through the throng, comes a noble beast, who, sacrificing himself for the greater good of the species, leaps into the river to the delight of the waiting crocodiles. This is completely fictitious, according to Sapolsky; the sacrificial beast was some poor old schmuck, who didn't force his way through; he was being pushed in by the others, 'let's get this old guy in the river so we can get across'! Sacrifice for the species is a myth; animals behave in a way that maximises their chance of passing down their genes to future generations, not for the good of the group.

It is dangerous being the leader of a herd, according to Temple Grandin, and high social rank holds many privileges, with animals high in the pecking order seldom at the front of a herd. [48] So higher-ranking cows let the lower-ranking suckers take that position, hiding out in the comparative safety of the middle herd.

Learn with the Herd

Grandin described that most people who handle and raise horses and cattle are familiar with social learning, social fear and social recognition of those animals. Calm-trained horses are used to ease fear in young and inexperienced horses, and tame 'coacher' cattle are used in Australia when mustering wild feral cattle. The coacher cattle, often up to 100 animals, are conditioned to be calm and moved slowly, usually by stockmen on horseback. The rest of the feral cattle mob is driven to the *coachers* by helicopter or vehicles. The 'Old West' style cattle drives preserved herd leaders with a calm temperament but culled off any excitable ones, reducing the possibility of a stampede. Cows learn from each other (social learning) in things as diverse as observing how their friends are handled and treated, to detecting fear or pain in other cows. Cattle that are trained to do tasks learn much quicker with an 'educated' conspecific, as seen with goats and sheep. [48] Cows that are treated well and conditioned to human interaction are easy to handle, much easier to lead an 800kg cow into a chute than to attempt to wrestle it in!

Memory

In the maze test previously mentioned under Problem Solving, Masahiko Hirata and colleagues discovered that cows were able to remember the various maze configurations for up to six weeks. A 2002 study took a slightly different approach, asking the question of how well cattle remember food locations over time. [64] In an open pasture setting, an 8-row by 8-column grid was constructed with a container in each grid, 5 metres apart. Four of the 64 containers were randomly 'loaded' with feed. Six steers were trained to find the food within the containers and then tested 5, 10, 20 and 48 days later. The steers all showed excellent spatial memory recall, remembering the location of the feed containers with little difference between five days and 48 days later.

From an evolutionary perspective, it makes perfect sense to have good memory capabilities if you are a grazing animal. Ungulates like sheep, goats, and cows often suffer high levels of parasitism, particularly intestinal worms. We have firsthand knowledge of these nasty little beasties, fighting a never-ending battle with blood sucking worm infections in our goats, losing two young kids to the parasitic helminths. Mostly, this is down to grazing practices, where the animals re-infest themselves with the worm eggs on infected pastures; the eggs lay dormant in the faecal matter, and the hatched worm larvae climb the grass stalks, waiting to be eaten to repeat the cycle.

Animals, understandably, try to avoid being eaten and have evolved a range of defences to achieve this, as have plants. Defences such as spines, thorns, and chemical toxins prevent or deter grazers, such as cows, from eating them. Some of these toxins, called secondary metabolites, also provide protection from parasites and anti-bacterial properties. [65] Cattle learn to selectively browse on these beneficial plants to reduce parasitic load. They also prefer sparse patches of vegetation where the chances of picking up ticks are much lower. So, what do all these parasites have to do with memory? Cows must remember a large repertoire of plants, their appearance, taste, texture and catalogue that away. Along with the type of plants, they may need to recall where they found those plants, and which plants counteract the toxic effects of other beneficial plants. This is hard to achieve without possessing good short-term, long-term, and spatial memory capabilities, as demonstrated in the maze experiments. Memory also plays a crucial role in remembering who is who in the herd!

Recognition

Animals clearly recognise each other; otherwise, social and dominance hierarchies would not exist. Animals also recognise other species; without such cognitions, predators could not discern each other from prey. Cows are essentially prey animals, but also inquisitive creatures. Several times, I have seen our alpacas covertly observing the cows next door. They sidle up to the fence, pretending not to look at the large and peculiar bovine standing a few feet away, nibbling indiscriminately at some leaf or twig, their subterfuge embarrassingly apparent. Our goats sometimes do the same; why? I can only guess they see another non-threatening being and just want a closer look, something novel, something to break the monotony of chewing grass; who knows?

So, how well can cows discriminate between their cow friends, other cow breeds and other species? Marjorie Coulon and colleagues tested 10 Prim' Holstein heifers to assess how well they could tell printed pictures of cows from other cows and different species. [66] When given a food reward for correctly choosing a bovine face over that of a sheep's face, the heifers were surprisingly accurate, with only one out of ten cows failing to meet the criteria of 80% correct responses.

Do cows have similar abilities in detecting human faces? Eight Holstein cows were trained and assessed by Pierre Rybarczyk and colleagues at the *Dairy and Swine Research and Development Centre,* Canada. [67] Two people, one a *rewarder*, the other a *non-rewarder*, were dressed in identical overalls and stood in front of a lever. The cows that pressed the lever in front of the rewarder received a food treat, and nothing if pressing the *non-rewarder* lever. All cows passed the test when only the *rewarder* was present, and five of seven passed when both the rewarder and non-rewarder were present, standing upright and fully visible. However, all cows failed when only the people's faces were visible. When both people were fully visible and wore identical masks, all cows passed the test once again. Bizarrely, when both people were *identical in height* and had their faces visible, the cows passed with flying colours, but when they covered their faces, all the cows failed! Rybarczyk concludes that cows can discriminate between two people using multiple cues like body height and faces, but have difficulty when using faces alone.

This is much like the findings in sheep and goats, where the animals use multiple cues to discern faces in humans and their pals. However, there is little to no research available that focuses on brain regions associated with facial recognition in cows.

Conclusions

Cows have excellent hearing, long sandpapery tongues that can lick their own nostrils and 330-degree eyesight, with a blind spot that is best avoided. They have distinct 'voices' and can recognise each other's calls and whether the caller is stressed. Cows show empathy to stressed cows, elevating their own stress levels and seeking calming friends to feel better. Best to check the whorl on a cow's head before approaching it, which, unlike the out-of-place 'cow licked' tuft on a human head, was formed in vivo and is related to calmness, skittishness and schizophrenia, albeit in a roundabout way. Cows show distinct personalities and, in all likelihood, can 'mental time travel', using forward thinking to solve complex tasks to get to food. Cows have good long-term memory, make great, if not enormous, pets or therapy animals, can be trained and can recognise their cow friends and humans, though not if they are the same height and their faces are covered!

Pigs

(Sus scrofa)

Dogs look up to you, cats look down on you. Give me a pig! He looks you in the eye and treats you as an equal.

Winston Churchill

A LL ANIMALS ARE EQUAL, BUT SOME ANIMALS ARE MORE EQUAL THAN OTHERS: the words famously scrawled on the barn wall of Jones' farm, replacing the seven commandments of animalism, concocted by *Snowball, Napoleon* and *Squealer*. The role of the pigs in the rebellion that led to the renaming of the property to Animal Farm and their subsequent oppression of the other animals alludes to the cunning and intelligence that Orwell, and in fact many of us, attribute to pigs.[1]

Indeed, popular culture is awash with an array of intelligent and fantastical pigs, *Babe*, the sheep-herding pig, *Kermit's* Muppet love interest *Miss Piggy*, the famous singing warthog of *The Lion King*, Charlotte the spider's friend *Wilbur*, the pig with a speech impediment from *Looney Tunes*, and *the Simpsons'* unforgettable *Spider Pig*. Pigs are interwoven into fairy tales and folk stories, such as the *Three Little Pigs* and their questionable building standards, the *Little Piggies that went to Market*, and the twelfth animal of the Chinese zodiac. The fecundity of sows with their large litter sizes and ample mammary glands, gave rise to porcine symbols of

183

fertility in the ancient world, explains David Fontana in *The Secret Language of Symbols*. [2] Greek legends described Zeus being suckled by a sow, and sacrifices to Ceres and Demeter, the fertility goddess, often involved pigs. Christians linked pigs to the seven deadly sins, with porkers exemplifying gluttony. Jesus healed the hermit living amongst the tombs by casting his tormenting demons into a herd of swine, who promptly jumped into the sea and drowned. Jewish traditions see pigs as unclean animals that must not be consumed, as does Islam, which states that consumption of pork is *haram*, or forbidden.

As for the rest of the world, it seems our predilection for bacon is insatiable, with around 964 million live domestic pigs on the planet at any given time in 2023. [3] China is the world's largest producer of pork, breeding an estimated 434 million pigs annually and producing around 58 million tonnes of pig meat. Collectively, the world produced around 124 million tonnes of pig meat in 2023 from approximately 1.5 billion pigs. Pigs, however, are more than the sum of just their bacon! Reducing an animal to the raw data values of protein in tonnes, describing them as merely pork or bacon, deindividuates that animal, obscuring the fact that they are intelligent and highly social creatures often kept in cruel and appalling conditions.

The social structure of domestic pigs is similar to that of their wild predecessors, living in hierarchical matrilineal groups consisting of around two to four related sows and their juvenile offspring from previous litters.[4] Males typically split off from the herd at around 7-8 months of age, forming 'bachelor' groups of two or three individuals during the non-breeding season. Mature boars, however, are solitary critters and during mating season, form a breeding group with sows, becoming 'boss hog' for a short time, the younger pigs staying on the periphery of the group. Despite the assumption that pigs are dirty, they maintain a 'dunging' area around 5-15m away from where they sleep, unlike goats and sheep, who poop wherever and whenever! Of course, if they are penned up or in sow stalls, this is not possible, and this is probably where the negative trope originates.

In commercial production, piglets are often weaned suddenly from their moms around 3-5 weeks of age, in stark contrast to natural weaning that occurs around 4 months. Failure to form a secure attachment bond with an animal's mom can cause all manner of problems in all mammals, including us! British psychologist John Bowlby famously described the importance of infant attachment bonds back in the 1960s, expanded on by Mary Ainsworth in the 'strange situation' experiment with babies. Four attachment styles were proposed, which are still accepted today: *secure, insecure-avoidant, insecure-anxious,* and *disorganised* attachments. Anything other than a secure attachment style can lead to behavioural and psychological problems throughout the lifespan, so it's reasonable to assume this also might apply to piglets. Joy Campbell and colleagues tested weaned pigs at various ages of separation, ranging from 15 to 32 days.[5] They described weaning as the most stressful event a pig endures (bar being made into bacon) and found startling differences in the biological processes of the piglets. Animals weaned early experience intestinal mucosal barrier problems and inflammation, as well as high levels of stress hormones, which affect feed intake and growth rates, and can persist into later life. Piglets weaned later also experienced a stress response but recovered more quickly and tended to thrive compared to their counterparts.

Piglets that were weaned at two weeks and at four weeks were compared in a study by Daniel Weary and colleagues, who found that piglets weaned at just 2 weeks vocalised more and performed more belly nosing behaviours than their older counterparts.[6] Belly nosing can be a real problem, a sign of suckling-seeking behaviour and a sure sign of activation of the PANIC basic emotion, producing a range of stress-induced hormones that help the pig to reunite with its mother. This in turn leads to SEEKING, the piglet trying to find its lost mom, which, if successful, leads to a whole swathe of feel-good molecules such as oxytocin, vasopressin, dopamine and endogenous opioids.[7] This natural adaptive behaviour to keep mom close during crucial developmental stages has evolved to increase the probability of young animals (and humans) surviving to reproductive age. Young pigs grouped together after weaning with unfamiliar pigs, likely experiencing PANIC and SEEKING emotions, are notoriously aggressive to each other, with tail and ear biting and belly-nosing commonplace. The other piglets don't appreciate being belly nosed and often fight back, explained Temple Grandin.[8] Commercial pig growers often group weaned pigs into nursery *10–25 kg*, grower *25–60 kg*, and finisher *60–120 kg* phases of production, often housing the pigs separately. Some growers may lump some or all the pigs together to reduce costs and improve efficiency. All pigs fight when first grouped together, according to Grandin, the sows just as much as the boars. Often, the pigs are covered in superficial lacerations, but after around four days, things have settled down.[8]

Industrial Pigs

Production value and investor return are top and centre for large-scale producers of pork, and as mentioned earlier, China is the world's biggest producer of pigs and their meat. In 1961, China had around 82 million live hogs compared to 434 million in 2023. That is a massive leap forward, not surprising given China's successful Great Financial Leap Forward, which lifted millions out of poverty and into the middle class. As with most people who gain greater financial freedom, there also comes the desire to eat better food and the Chinese love their pork! Pig domestication in China can be traced back approximately 8000 years, during which changes in pig morphology, particularly in tooth shape and size, indicate human management. Brian Lander of Brown University and colleagues describe how pigs likely shared a commensal pathway to domestication with dogs, both animals scavenging rubbish and excrement on the verges of settlements, with increasing contact leading to eventual domestication.[9] Studies of stable isotopes contained in pig bones from Neolithic sites confirm that pigs ate loads of human rubbish and waste, with the by-product of the pig also becoming a valuable commodity. As farming increased and the amount of arable land per family decreased due to growing population densities, pig manure became an important fertiliser, with most farmers raising pigs for this purpose rather than for consumption. In fact, most households rarely ate pork, raising only a few pigs per year, slaughtered only for important celebrations and festivals.[9] At the end of the Cultural Revolution, Deng Xiaoping set about developing a set of cultural and economic reforms that would eventually lead to China's 'economic miracle', opening up trade with the West, and eventually creating the world's largest economy by GDP. Agribusiness received vast amounts of investment in the late 1980s, with a focus on scaling up production for urban populations. [9] Rural farmers gave up pig farming and other small-scale ventures and headed to the cities in droves to join mass labour markets, often in low-skilled, poorly paid jobs. By 2015, the pig industry consisted primarily of medium-scale household farms of up to 500 pigs per year, to mega operations, producing more than 10,000 pigs per year. This can be seen on data plots that show an exponential rise in pig slaughter rates from 1980 (198 million) to 2023 (726 million pigs). [10] Paradoxically, the mass movement from rural areas to China's megacities has resulted in people's only interactions with farm animals being when they eat them, with meat consumption around three times higher compared with people in rural areas.

The scaling up of agricultural production in China is unprecedented, with mega production facilities becoming the norm rather than the exception. The early days of China's reforms favoured so-called 'Dragonhead Enterprises' to lead agricultural development and grow markets. [9] These government-supported enterprises were 'vertically integrated', controlling supply chains, production and product distribution, leading to some of the largest pork producers in the world. High-rise hog hotels have been popping up all over China, culminating in the granddaddy of all hog hotels in Ezhou, Hubei province. Yating Yang of the South China Morning Post described how social media labels the new vertical farming projects as 'Bajie Buildings', a reference to the pigs as "the second elder brother living in a high-rise", a play on words from the character *Zhu Bajie,* otherwise known as Pigsy, from the classic novel Journey to the West. [11] The two 26-storey skyscrapers employ an army of 800 workers and have an area of 390 square metres per floor, the facility producing around 1.2 million pigs per year. The pigs are transported to their appropriate floor via elevator according to their age, beginning in the gestation area, to the farrowing, then the nursery, and finally the raising area, where they spend 6-8 months before being shipped off to their forever home... pork sausages. Cleanliness and hygiene are paramount to reduce the risk of disease, and food is transported to the roof before being distributed automatically throughout the building. No doubt, a mountain of pig waste would be produced, which is also processed on-site.

Despite the fastidious quarantine measures these vertical

farms implement, the risk of disease is a very real threat. Lander and colleagues described how the rise of Confined Animal Feeding Operations (CAFOs) has led to some of the most conducive places on earth for the transfer of pathogens, such as influenza and other viruses, between pigs and people. [9] The breeding of commercial hogs has also drastically reduced genetic diversity, compromising the pig's ability to resist disease and leading to the overuse of antibiotics. This, in turn, has led to an increase in antibiotic-resistant, disease-causing organisms in the soil and waterways surrounding large-scale pig farms. Several large-scale disease outbreaks have led to the mass culling of pigs, with one such incident making international news in 2013.

"There are more pigs than fish in Jiapingtang river", joked a 48-year-old fisherwoman from the sleepy country village of Xinfeng, reported Nicola Davidson of The Guardian. [12] The long-time resident recounts how, in her youth, she played in the pristine waters of the river, which is now inky black and smells of a sewer. Bobbing along the surface nearby, float the bodies of several pigs and piglets, only several of an estimated 16,000 dead pigs that were discovered floating in tributaries of the Huangpu River in Zhejiang province, around 60 miles from Shanghai. The Huangpu is a major source of drinking water for Shanghai, a city of around 24 million people. Mystery surrounded the origin of the pigs, one likely culprit being the rise of mega pig farming. With mortality rates of around 2-4%, pig farms must dispose of dead pigs, which necessitates the construction of dead pig processing plants that struggle to keep up with demand. Some unscrupulous farmers simply throw the pigs in the river, reported one local official. Another explanation could be the crackdown on black market hogs, where rogue operators butchered diseased animals for human consumption rather than disposing of them. A Government crackdown on the practice most likely led to additional dumping of pigs. Not only do the dead pigs end up in the river, but also their manure.

An Ocean of Poop

The massive explosion in pig numbers has predictably also led to an explosion in poop, creating a mountain of waste in the Chinese countryside. Some of the approximately 7 billion tons of swine shit also end up in rivers and waterways, causing toxic algal blooms and rendering drinking water unsafe. [9]

One creative solution to this problem is to turn crap into cash! In a joint project between the People's Republic of China and the Asian Development Bank, 118 farms were assisted to convert their pig waste into biogas and organic fertiliser. The biogas, in turn, produced electricity that was sold back into the grid, and the organic fertiliser helped both small and large farms produce better yields and reduce reliance on chemical fertilisers. [13]

The US is not immune to the vagaries of mass hog production and the resulting byproducts. Chloe Sorvino, in her 2022 book *Hidden Corruption, Corporate Greed, and the Fight for the Future of Meat*, describes how you smell a hog plant, long before it comes into view. [14] Enormous hog processing plants, hundreds of thousands of square feet in size, pack thousands of breeding sows into small metal cages, so tight that the pigs must lie on their sides, with rapid reproduction being the main aim. Slatted floors allow the urine and faeces to fall through, to be washed into enormous waste lagoons, often the size of several football fields. Sorvino describes how an Illinois plant owned by the world's largest beef and chicken producer and second-largest pork producer was ranked the country's worst water polluter in a 2018 study. These industrial-scale hog processing plants and their colossal poop lagoons not only smell bad, but the gases that escape contain large amounts of hydrogen sulphide, ammonia, methane and carbon dioxide; significant greenhouse gases. [14]

In 1995, an eight-acre pond containing 25 million gallons of liquid pig poop burst its containment wall and spilled into the New River, North Carolina, according to David Robinson Simon in his 2013 book *Meatonomics*. [15] The pond, which was 12 feet deep and contained the liquid poop from 10 thousand pigs, washed into fields and nearby tributaries, creating the worst hazardous spill in the state's history. Toxic nitrogen and phosphorus levels caused mass algal blooms and regions devoid of oxygen that killed around 10 million fish and closed hundreds of square kilometres of wetlands. This is hardly surprising, given the 10 billion land animals that create one trillion pounds of excrement each year in the US, the manure forming vast ponds and lagoons around the country. The animal waste can eventually find its way into groundwater supplies, with the 2024 *EPA National Water Quality Inventory: Report to Congress* revealing that across the country, 24% of lakes were in poor condition and almost half contained poor levels of nitrogen and phosphorus, often byproducts of farm runoff, fertilisers, and human and animal waste. [16]

Beyond the stench and the pollutants, there are also significant ethical and moral questions regarding the mass production of pigs in this manner. The unfortunate porkers never see daylight or experience an enriching environment, such as rooting around in a mud wallow, but rather spend their entire lives in an industrial high-rise hotel from hell, or an enormous factory plant surrounded by lakes of their own poop. These are highly modified domestic breeds that have been artificially selected to quickly grow either lean hogs, in the case of the US, or fat hogs in Asia. But this is not the typical phenotype of a pig, as a diverse array of wild pigs of all shapes, sizes, colours, and warts inhabit our world, with a fascinating and unexpected origin story.

Origin Stories

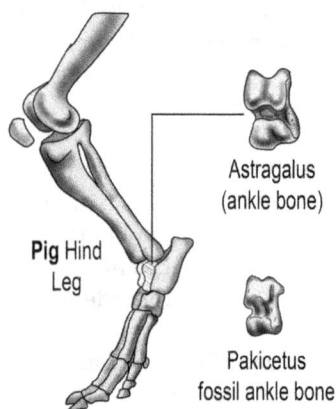

Astragalus (ankle bone)

Pig Hind Leg

Pakicetus fossil ankle bone

Fig 1

All modern pigs are of the genus *Sus*, the family of *Suidae* and of the order *Cetartiodactyla*. Wait, what in the heck is a Cetartiodactyla? Pigs, like sheep, goats and cows, are artiodactyls or even-toed ungulates (mammals with hooves) as mentioned in the previous chapters. The first part of Cetartiodactyla originates from Cetacea, which includes whales and dolphins (Cetaceans), but how in the world are pigs and whales connected?

Molecular data (genetic studies) suggests that artiodactyls and cetaceans are closely related, much to the ire of some scientists, who argue it's overly confusing; however, a landmark fossil find in 1977 inextricably linked the two. [17] Philip Gingerich described his chance discovery in Pakistan of one of the earliest known fossil whales, the land-dwelling, semi-aquatic *Pakicetus*, a small wolf-sized, dog-like creature that bears scant resemblance to Flipper! [18] Examining the skull of this strange 50-million-year-old fossil, Gingerich noticed structures of the middle ear bones bore striking similarities to modern-day cetaceans. The *tympanic bulla*, a hollow, bowl-shaped bony structure, protects the inner ear in mammals. It has a thickened portion called the *involucrum* in whales and dolphins, which assists in amplifying and detecting sounds underwater. [19] Gingerich and his team noticed this ancient land mammal fossil also had a thickened involucrum and bore teeth that both resembled other ancient proto-whales and land mammals. Another intriguing feature is the animal's ankle bones, which bear a shape and features synonymous with those of artiodactyls. The ankle bone or *astragalus* showed the familiar *'double pulley'* shape (Figure 1), which allows the animal to walk on its toes with efficient flexion and extension, whilst keeping the joint stable.

You may have heard of the game 'knuckles' or jumping jacks, which was traditionally played with, yep, the ankle bones of artiodactyls, usually sheep. Other intermediate fossils, like Basilosaurus, reveal the evolutionary path from Pakicetus to modern whales and dolphins. The fully aquatic 30-40 million-year-old 'king lizard' possessed vestigial feet and astragalus ankle bones, distant echoes of its artiodactyl relatives. [18] One last wrinkle to iron out, pigs are not 'more' related to whales than are other ruminants like deer or goats, or camels, as was once believed; rather, the hippopotamus holds that distinction. [17]

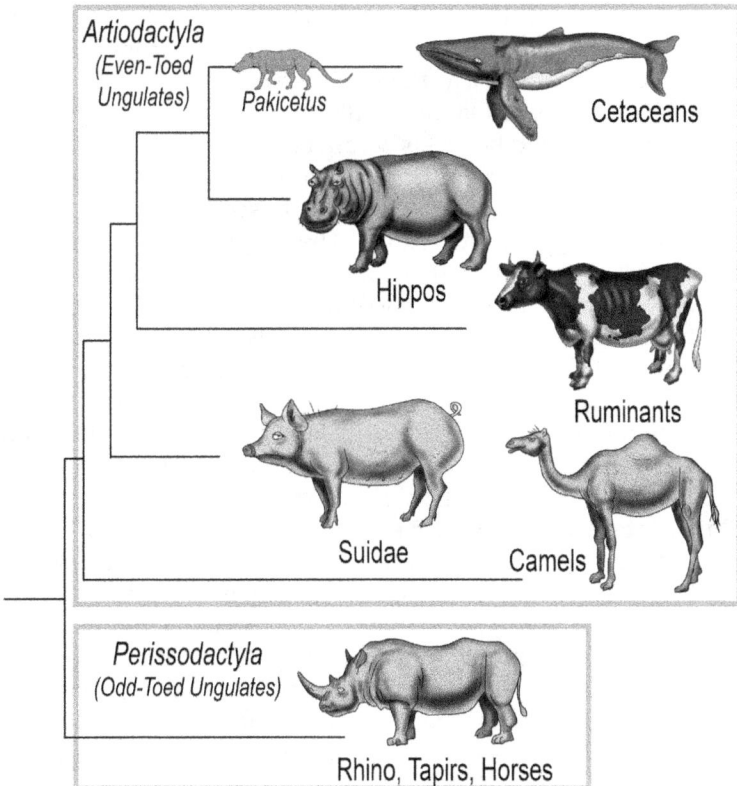

Fig 2 Ungulates Family Tree

Here a Pig, There a Pig

Pigs inhabit all continents of the globe, except Antarctica, and come in all shapes and sizes, due to the selection pressures of their environment and domestication. Laurent Frantz and colleagues of the University of Oxford explain that Suidae (all pigs, hogs, or 'suids') were once believed to be closely related to hippos; however, recent genetic analysis shows hippos are more closely related to whales, and they all fall under the label of Artiodactyla. From a common ancestor, the New World pigs of the Americas, the *Tayassuidae* or *Peccaries,* diverged from the New World pigs of Eurasia around 34-39 million years ago. By around 20 million years ago, suids had radiated throughout Africa, Europe, and Asia. By the end of the Pliocene and the start of the Pleistocene, only the subfamily called Suinae, survived and diversified into: warthogs, bush pigs, and forest hogs in Africa; the babirusa or 'deer pigs' of Sulawesi; warty pigs, and bearded pigs in SE Asia, and the origins of the domestic pig, the wild boar Sus scrofa of Eurasia.[20]

Max Price and Hitomi Hongo estimated that there are around 200-300 pig breeds worldwide and described several potential pathways to pig domestication. [21] They explain that clear evidence shows that independent domestication of pigs occurred in northern Mesopotamia around 8700–7000 BC and in China by around 6600–5000 BC, the porkers in the Near East changing slowly over thousands of years, due to weak selection pressures. They suggest that a *commensal pathway* where pigs were attracted to human settlements, combined with a prey pathway, where hunter-gatherer societies practised both hunting and managing herds, was likely behind the slow evolution of hog change. On the other hand, in China, intensive farming, feeding and penning of animals led to much faster morphological changes in pig shapes and size.

A significant factor in the change of pigs and other mammals is called *domestication syndrome,* where heritable physical and behavioural traits begin to appear in animals that have been domesticated. For example, animal faces become shorter, ears become floppier, teeth become smaller, coat colours become more diverse, with spots, stripes, and patches, and importantly, brains become smaller. Why? Well, living in large social groups in challenging environments where you are often someone else's potential dinner requires extra cognitive abilities. As environmental stressors decrease and behaviour changes to a 'tamer' animal with reduced fearfulness, brains tend to shrink, of course, not in a lifetime, but over many generations. [21]

Ten thousand years of hunting, selective breeding and domestication have led to a diverse range of pig varieties, and some of the more unusual varieties include: The curly-haired *Mangalica,* which somewhat resembles a pig crossed with a sheep and sports a variety of coiffures, including a 'blonde' variation. The *red wattle hog,* whose distinctive red hair is overshadowed by a giant pair of wattles that hang from its neck like a pair of testicles (would they be called necksticles?). The incredibly fertile *Meishan* pig of Southern China, with its enormous floppy ears, low-hanging belly and Shar-pei dog-like wrinkles. The *Meishan* can produce large litters of 15-16 piglets and were imported into the USA to be studied at research facilities in Nebraska, Illinois and Iowa. [22] Researchers initially believed that the sows would have higher levels of follicle-stimulating hormone (FSH), but they found that the levels were similar to those of other pigs. However, the males had 5-7 times more circulating FSH and smaller testes than most hogs. They found that the sows reached puberty much earlier than most pigs, ovulated more eggs per cycle, and had a greater uterine capacity than other pigs, which might explain the large litter sizes. Beyond the man-made selection pressures that produced an array of interesting porkers, Mother Nature has moulded a far more interesting and diverse assortment of fantastical porcine, and I'll start with the smallest.

Tiny Porcula

The pygmy hog (*Porcula salvania*) is the smallest and rarest wild Suidae, weighing around 8 kilograms and standing a mere 20-25 centimetres tall, hoof to shoulder. The mini porkers are only found in the subtropical grasslands of an isolated area of Manas National Park in the Indian state of Assam. [23] Genetic analysis of pygmy hogs reveals that populations of around 500 individuals have persisted for tens of thousands of years, resulting in low genetic diversity and the accumulation of harmful mutations in the petite porcine. The pygmy hog is critically endangered, with fewer than 250 individuals remaining in the wild. [24]

The Pig-Deer

The babirusa, which means 'pig-deer' in Bahasa, is one strange porker. A medium-sized, mostly hairless pig with slender deer-like legs, the babirusa is best known for its impressive facial adornments. The male grows an elongated pair of canine teeth in the upper mandible that extend vertically, piercing through the skin and curving backwards towards the skull; a lower pair of canines grow upward and outward from the jaw. There is little known about the evolutionary history of the babirusa, as there are no known extant (alive) or extinct relatives and only pockets of the rare porker are scattered throughout Sulawesi, Buru and the Togean Islands of Indonesia. Cave paintings discovered in Sulawesi, dating back approximately 35,000 years, depict a babirusa alongside an older human hand stencil. Balinese masks featuring demonic faces are said to be inspired by the babirusa's tusks. [20]

The Bearded Pig

Sus Barbatus or the Bornean bearded pig, is a distinguished-looking pig sporting an impressive beard of coarse hair that grows the length of its head, along the cheeks and lower jaw. Various subspecies are scattered throughout the Malay Peninsula, Borneo and Sumatra, and other smaller islands. Sea level fluctuations that have occurred since the Pliocene (approximately 5.2 million years ago) likely led to the formation of temporary land bridges between islands, resulting in the highest diversity of pig species in the world. Unfortunately, vast amounts of habitat loss due to logging and palm oil plantations have placed pressure on bearded pig populations, with Kerinci Seblat National Park in Sumatra holding the largest remaining population of these unique Suids. [25] [26]

Warty Swine

194

The Javan warty pig *Sus verrucosus (meaning many warts) is an endangered porker* endemic to the Indonesian island of Java. Once feared extinct, it faces pressures from uncontrolled hunting and habitat loss. Often, the pigs are poisoned, explained Raleigh Blouch, with an account from 1981 describing how a group of men allegedly poisoned and sold 160 wild pigs for meat, with most buyers of wild pig stating they would not buy poisoned meat. However, the poachers often stab the carcasses with spears to disguise the toxic porkers as hunted and not poisoned. [27]

Hakuna Matata

Perhaps the most famous warthog in popular culture is Pumbaa, who, together with his meerkat sidekick Timon, provided comic relief to the animated Disney series *The Lion King*. The warthog is endemic to Africa, with two recognised species: the desert warthog *Phacochoerus aethiopicus*, which is localised to the Horn of Africa, and the common warthog *Phacochoerus africanus*. Renowned for their striking good looks, the warthog is so named for the large warty protuberances on the male's head. They are not actually warts, but *callosities*, three pairs of thickened skin pads, that help protect the males' eyes and muzzle during fights, where they "tusk wrestle" and thump each other's skulls, often resulting in fractures or even death. Despite their relatively long lifespan of up to 18 years, only around one out of four males survives to reproductive age. Warthogs, unlike domestic pigs, lack insulating surface fat and often hide out in aardvark holes to escape the searing African heat. Both sows and boars will often back into these burrows, the sow placing piglets in first, then backing in to face any potential threats. [28]

Despite their fearsome appearance, warthogs are surprisingly cooperative animals, with sows displaying many altruistic-like behaviours. Angela White and Elissa Cameron studied 32 breeding groups of warthogs in the Hluhluwe–iMfolozi National Park in KwaZulu-Natal, South Africa and found some surprising reproductive strategies by the clever Cetartiodactyla. [29] Sows in communal groups would often 'babysit' piglets of other conspecifics in their absence, likely as an adaptive benefit to reduce predation of piglets at their most vulnerable time. But not only babysit, if mom ended up as someone else's bacon burger, the babysitting sows would often adopt the orphaned piglets. There was also a degree of reciprocity in the babysitting arrangements, where *alloparenting* (care of non-biological offspring) increased the overall fitness of the group. Even though we have a distinct fondness for pigs, their perceived intelligence, zany antics and representation in folk tales and children's stories, there is a brooding dark side of the pork that we often choose not to think about or discuss, which is precisely why I will.

Pigs to Market, Cambodian Style

The Dark Side of the Hog

The tranquillity of Laon, a picturesque farming community in Aisne, northern France, was abruptly shattered one quiet morning with a crime that would shock the tight-knit community. [30] A young child was brutally strangled and mutilated in his crib whilst his father, Jehan Lenfant, was away tending the livestock and his mother, Gillon, was away running errands. Witnesses Jehan Benjamin and Jehan Daudancourt testified under oath that the child was left in the care of his nine-year-old sister, who was distracted and left to play, leaving the infant unattended. This was when the heinous attack took place, the child dying from his injuries shortly after. The perpetrator was hunted down and detained in the Saint-Martin church abbey, where he was subsequently tried and sentenced to be hanged.

A similar travesty of justice played out in the town of Savigny in Burgundy, where a five-year-old child named Jehan Martin was murdered. The perpetrator was caught in the act, captured, detained, and presented to the court; her six children were charged as accessories. The honourable and wise Master Benoît Milot d'Ostun, a licensed lawyer, bachelor of canon law, and counsellor to the Duke of Burgundy, decreed that for the 'murder and homicide' committed against the child, the offender is to be executed by being hanged by the hind legs from a thorn tree. The question of the involvement of the six children was postponed for a later hearing. Shortly thereafter, Master Étienne Poinceau was appointed the official executioner, and the sentence was carried out within the jurisdiction of Lady Savigny's estate. Twenty-four days later, the six offspring were brought before the judge of Savigny, Nicolas Quarroillon, squire, and on behalf of the noble lady Katherine de Barnault, lady of Savigny. They were found not guilty and discharged into the care of the Lady of Savigny. The year was 1457, and the two cases, though not unusual for the time, were in and of themselves very unusual.

The perpetrators in both cases were, you guessed it, pigs. These cases and more were faithfully researched and recorded by Jacques Berriat-Saint-Prix (1783–1852), a French legal scholar, historian, and magistrate. Berriat-Saint-Prix is best known for his research into the animal trials of medieval Europe, which saw the trials and summary execution of a range of animals, including:

In 1403, a pig was executed for devouring a child; the expenses for the execution included imprisonment, transportation, rope, and gloves for the executioner.

In 1499, another pig was sentenced to be hanged for killing a child; the pig was formally notified of the sentence before execution.

In 1386, the judge of Falaise, Normandy, condemned a sow to have her leg and head mutilated and then hanged, for having killed a child. The sow was dressed as a man and executed in the town square.

The bailiwick of the abbey of Beaupré, Cistercian order, near Beauvais in 1499, ordered the execution of a bull, sent to the gallows for having, "in fury", killed a young boy.

But it gets even stranger. Take, for example, the case of the blister beetles, small insects that release a nasty, poisonous chemical called Cantharidin, which causes blistering of the skin, hence their namesake. Apart from the noxious chemical, the beetles also devastate crops, which transpired in Mainz's Electorate in the 15th century. Frustrated farmers summoned the insects before the local judge, appointing a spokesperson for the tiny defendants, considering their diminutive size and lack of legal maturity. The curator performed a successful defence, and the tiny perpetrators were excommunicated, expelled from the land, but to a designated area to which they could retreat. A similar fate befell a cohort of caterpillars, who in 1585 were brought to trial in the Diocese of Valence. The vicar general summoned the caterpillars and appointed them a defence lawyer, who argued vehemently for their case, with a lenient sentence subsequently handed down, ordering the larcenous larvae to leave the diocese.

But what in the heck is going on here? Surely, even back in medieval Europe, people would have had a basic understanding that animals cannot be *Criminis reatus*, or culpable of human-like crimes? Sven Gins of the University of Groningen, the Netherlands, studied the case of the sow and her piglets and concluded that a multiplicity of motivations were behind the trial and other similar trials in the medieval period. [31] The trials were a way to restore order to the community after a traumatic event, through public rituals that also serve as a stark reminder not to leave children unattended, particularly around pigs. The trials were also a response to an increasingly centralised legal system, demonstrating that the country folk can still successfully pursue and enact justice. There were also the religious aspects of violations of human sanctity, and the horror around the idea of eating an animal that had consumed a child and the moral conviction that all creatures have their assigned 'place', the pig overstepping that boundary when we become the bacon! [31] The theatrics of the trials and the rituals of prosecution and punishment, perhaps, violate the myth we create around our perceived superiority above animals and the myths we create of our illusory control over our world. Nothing breaks that illusion of control better than seeing a loved one eaten by, well, our lunch!

Edward Payson Evans tackled the thorny issue of animal trials from several angles: that animals were moral agents, therefore capable of committing crimes, contemporary religious beliefs and superstitions and the desire to project control onto animals via legal and ethical structures. [32] Evans argued that as Christianity supplanted paganism, animals that were once revered were transformed into agents of Satan or incarnations of devils. *"Chief of the stenchy beasts is the pig"*, a source of adoration of the pagans, which early Christians viewed simply as devil worship, explained Evans. In a fable reminiscent of the times, *"the farrow of the sow is supposed to number seven shotes, corresponding to the seven deadly sins"*, shotes being the piglets, corresponding to the seven deadly sins of the bible, transforming the symbolic creature of pagan culture into a moral allegory of sin. In fact, any animal that displayed 'irrational' behaviour was back then considered as an agent of the devil, *"who makes use of irrational creatures to our detriment"*. [32]

Pigs, most notably wild boars, were once important symbols of fertility and identity in Anglo-Saxon Pagan culture, according to Aleks Pluskowski of the University of Reading. [33] In the book Signals *of Belief in Early England: Anglo-Saxon Paganism Revisited,* he explains that boar symbols not only adorned the helmets of 7th-century warriors from England and Scandinavia, but boars were represented on men's and women's jewellery, buckles, clasps and swords, and commonly incorporated into funerary practices. The symbolism likely centred around concepts of aggression, protection, self-identity and fertility. As paganism gradually gave way to Christianity, lingering on in regions of Scandinavia up to the 13th century, views on the power and nobility of the porcine diminished, reduced to being seen as an unclean animal, most likely from the influence of early Jewish settlements and their strict adherence to biblical dietary beliefs. [34]

Dale Spencer and Amy Fitzgerald of the University of Manitoba and the University of Windsor, Ontario, approached the issue from a criminologist's viewpoint. [35] They describe the punishment of animals by proxy as symbolic acts to maintain and create social order and to punish the animals' owners. If the animal is deemed a problem (for example, murderous pigs), breaching the "culture/nature divide", then it was tried and punished publicly, that is, humanised. The message being sent is that humans must control their animal property, and if the 'stupid' animals commit a crime, their 'stupid' owner should be held liable. The researchers claim this created a bridge to later 'animalise' humans within the field of criminology, labelling them as inferior or stupid and leading to the eugenics movement and the pathologisation of certain groups.

There are certainly contemporary examples of animal behaviour being held accountable by owners who are ultimately liable for their actions. Think of the multitude of dog attacks that occur, or people keeping unsuitable pets that eventually cause all manner of problems. One extraordinary example that comes to mind is the Colombian cocaine hippos. Drug cartel leader Pablo Escobar thought African hippos would make a fine addition to his small private zoo; however, after his death in 1993, the hippos escaped into the nearby Magdalena River. Luke Taylor in *Nature* described how, without natural predators, hippos have proliferated, causing untold harm to the environment and posing a risk to human life. [36] Accounts of serious attacks on humans and a vehicle crash that left a hippo dead on a highway prompted the government to take action. Darting the hippos with contraceptives was one strategy that was ultimately slow and costly. With a 2022 census count of 181-215 of the three-ton beasts, the largest population outside Africa, culling may become the country's only option.

Attack Pigs

Occasionally, fatal animal attacks make the evening news, such as shark attacks, which, despite popular beliefs, occur far less often than people might believe. According to the Taronga Conservation Society Australian Shark Incident Database (yes, it's a real thing!), There were an average of 20 shark incidents per year over the last decade. [37] Of these incidents, most were attacks with injuries; however, seven were uninjured, and on average, 2.8 were fatalities. Comparing those figures to the roughly 600 million people that visit the Australian coast each year, the odds of becoming a 2.8 are pretty slim compared to the 125 coastal drownings and the 1,266 road fatalities that occurred in 2023. But let not the facts stand in the way of retribution! Often the alleged perpetrator, frequently a great white shark, is hunted down, killed and hung up proudly for the evening news. No trial, despite the overwhelming evidence, no stupid owner bearing responsibility for an animal's wayward behaviour, just a violation of our perceived illusory control over the world, a shattering of our beliefs of superiority and an overarching desire for retribution.

But hold the bacon! There is another fearsome predator that takes more lives each year than sharks! John Mayer of the Savannah River National Laboratory, James Garabedian, and John Kilgo of the USDA, Forest Service, researched wild pig attacks on humans worldwide between 2000 and 2019 and found some astonishing results. [38] Over the two decades, they found 163 separate reports of fatal wild pig attacks, 172 of which resulted in human deaths. That's an average of 8.6 human deaths annually compared to 2.8 deaths from shark attacks in Australia and 5.4 deaths by shark attacks worldwide in the same time period. In fact, wild pig attacks trumped that of brown bears (6.3); however, the Indian Tiger wore the biggest grin, snacking on 34 poor souls in the same period. Most of the porcine assaults were from incidents where the pig was threatened, provoked, chased or wounded (36%), while many of the non-hunting incidents were from wounded animals or sudden unprovoked attacks. Despite the apparent murderous nature of *Sus scrofa*, of the thousands of reported wild pig attacks each year, very few resulted in fatalities. In most cases, the pig was merely reacting to a perceived threat.

Temple Grandin described how pigs can be extremely vicious, especially mother pigs protecting their piglets. [39] Grandin believes pigs do not possess a bite inhibition, being chewers more than biters, often chewing on her boots with increasing intensity, ignoring her attempts to stop them. Juvenile pigs often fight violently, and as Grandin explained, simply spraying the scent of a dominant male pig amongst the unruly teenagers would often calm things down. This was tested by introducing a mature male boar into the herd, and sure enough, the unruly delinquents settled down. When a couple of pigs started fighting, merely the presence of the boar walking toward them made them stop; the juvenile delinquents even looked around to see if the male boar was in view before picking a fight. Temple described this behaviour as "the Boar Police"!

When We Become the Bacon

An uncomfortable thought that raises its ugly head is that perhaps we may be as tasty to pigs as bacon and pork are to us. Movies in popular culture depict the bad guys feeding victims to the swine, but how much of that is based on fiction versus reality?

One of Canada's worst serial killers, Robert Pickton, brought female victims to his pig farm over several years, once bragging to a prosecution witness about strangling his victims and feeding their remains to his pigs. An intensive search of the farm revealed the DNA of 33 women, with Pickton caught boasting that he had killed 49 women to an undercover police officer. At one stage of the investigation, health officials issued a warning to the community that some of the pork purchased from Pickton's farm may be tainted with human remains, ground up and mixed with pork mince. In 2007, Pickton was charged with the murders of 26 women and ultimately convicted of six counts of second-degree murder and sentenced to life in prison. Pickton died in 2024 as a result of injuries sustained from a fellow inmate. [40]

An Oregon pig farmer and Vietnam War veteran who suffered from post-traumatic stress disorder, found solace in farming, his brother describing the hog farming practice as a lifesaving. Unfortunately, when well-liked veteran went missing, all that was found were his dentures and pieces of his body; investigators postulated that the hogs may have knocked over the farmer before devouring him. [41]

Pigs are omnivores and usually graze on grasses or dig for roots and tubers, but will happily eat meat when it's available. On several occasions, I have encountered mobs of wild pigs in outback Australia, feeding on kangaroo carcasses along the roadside. The kangaroos come to the roadside in lean times, to eat the green grass on the verges at night and are often hit by trucks. On inspection, the pigs had chewed through the leg bones of the kangaroo, probably the same thickness as a human arm bone or *humerus*. That's some bit force!

When Pets Turn Bad

There is little doubt that pigs make wonderful pets, intelligent, affectionate and curious. However, many people have been misled by the unscrupulous claims of some breeders, who spread their misleading terms such as 'micro pigs', 'mini pigs', or 'Teacup pigs'. The fact of the matter is that all pigs are born small, weighing around one kilogram, little bundles of cuteness and joy, all those neotenous features we love, short snout, large head and large eyes! This is short-lived, though, as James Paras of ABC explained, with Teacup pigs often promoted as the perfect pet for children in suburban homes. [42] The perfect pet, often, turns into a 200-300 kg monster. Kathie Anderson, founder of *The Contented Pig Inn,* has around 120 pigs on her NSW property and often takes in surrendered pigs from dismayed owners who mistakenly believed their tiny piglets would remain mini but later transmogrified into 300kg hogs. Exotic pig breeds, such as the Vietnamese pot-bellied pig and the miniature Juliana or spotted pig, have also become increasingly popular as pets, although if well fed, they too can also turn into 100kg+ monsters.

Exotic pets, unusual, desirable, and often highly profitable, can often become problematic, as Shannon Tompkins of the *Houston Chronicle* goes on to explain. [43] The Texas Parks and Wildlife Department (TPWD) regulates native wildlife but has no authority over exotic species, which has allowed landholders to import exotic animals such as oryx, sambar deer, antelope, and African warthogs, resulting in the development of self-sustaining populations. Warthogs, being highly intelligent and tenacious creatures, eventually escaped their enclosures, with the first escapees spotted around 2014. The fugitives, despite the best efforts of the TPWD and hunters, have increased their population size and become a localised pest. The warty porcine competes with the native collared peccary, causing damage to fences, crops, and degrading local habitats. [44] [43]

Many years back, whilst travelling through Africa, I came across a tame pet warthog at a campsite in Zimbabwe. I was surprised at how docile and affectionate the animal was, although not entirely pleasant to pet, as its hair and skin are incredibly coarse. Numerous videos on social media show people who have adopted warthogs as pets, showcasing how readily they adapt to life in a suburban household, often cohabiting with dogs and other pets, and in one video, wreaking havoc on the furniture. However, when pets turn bad, it can often be with catastrophic consequences, as was the case with an animal-loving boy and his adopted orphaned warthog from an exotic Texas animal ranch.

Peter Holley of the *Texas Monthly* recounted the story of an unbreakable bond that formed between Austin and his pet warthog, Waylon. [45] The warthog was raised as a bottle-fed orphaned piglet, but Waylon quickly grew into a rambunctious 250-pound pet with sharpened tusks up to seven inches long. Waylon happily followed his owner around the farm until one fateful day, the warthog was startled and violently attacked Austin, inflicting serious damage that required multiple surgeries and a lengthy rehabilitation. [45]

Why does an animal turn so violently on a person to whom it has formed such a strong bond? We have co-evolved with dogs for around 10,000 years, yet every so often, they turn on us. Only several generations removed from a wild creature, all it took was an unknown environmental trigger to likely activate the *RAGE* circuits in Waylon's brain, turning him from a trusted companion to a 250-pound killing machine.

As humans, we have evolved the theory of mind to 'best guess' what others are thinking. What is that person's intention? Are they friend or foe? Are they part of my social group or a potential threat? As mentioned in previous chapters, many animals do not exhibit a similar theory of mind to humans but rather send and receive social and intentional cues in different ways. As we often anthropomorphise animals, it is easy to fall into the trap of believing that we know an animal's thoughts, motivations, and intentions. My wife's four-year-old niece visited recently and was intent on making friends with our alpacas. The two geriatric camelids still barely trust us, but a mini human was a bit too much. Despite her best efforts to feed the wary animals some pellets, it all ended in tears. As humans do not fully develop a theory of mind until around 5 years old, young Ellie likely believed the alpaca had the same thoughts and desires that she did, 'I want to be friends and feed and pet you'. When the alpacas ignored the request and stood aloof, Ellie probably assumed they did not like her. Of course, who knows what the alpaca was thinking? Most of its behaviour is likely driven by fear of a novel mini-human. But even as adults, we often fall into the trap of believing that we know an animal's thoughts and intentions, projecting our human theory of mind onto another, completely different species. Looking at the sad dog with widened glassy eyes and backward-facing ears, we believe the dog is thinking "I'm sad, I need a pat", whereas the dog is really signalling "I don't know you, back off bucko!"

Kinky Hogs

But enough of dwelling on the 'dark side' of the hog, it's time to switch to some more positive attributes of pigs, starting with their kinky side. In a long list of appallingly bad dad jokes lodged somewhere in my long-term memory, there is the one about the pig farmer who lost his favourite boar. The farmer lamented to his neighbour that his prize boar had died and commented on how good his neighbour's pigs looked. The neighbour explained he serviced them himself. With his mouth agape, the farmer asked how on earth he achieved this. "I just holler to them, they jump in the truck, and I take the sows up the top paddock". Reluctantly, the farmer decided to try this and loaded the sows into his pickup and drove them up to the top paddock. On returning home, he asked his wife, "Let me know if the hogs start acting weird." Several months passed with the farmer patiently applying his technique, but to no avail. One morning, his wife announced, "You know how you asked me to let you know if the pigs are acting funny?" Yes, said the farmer with mounting enthusiasm. "Well, they're all out front in the back of your pickup truck, and one is sitting in the driver's seat, honking the horn."

Never short of an amusing animal story, Temple Grandin describes the gentle art of artificial pig insemination, which is usually applied to pigs. [39] Brahman cattle are relatively straightforward, she explained, the girls are easy, just insert a catheter into the uterus and inject the semen. Brahman cattle are very affectionate and love a good scratch, but when it comes to collecting semen from them, a lot of foreplay is involved! Some brahman will delay giving semen for around 20 minutes until they have successfully had their throat and butt scratched. Pigs, however, can be harder work and have their subtle nuances that can sometimes border on perversion. One highly successful breeder recounted to Grandin that each boar had its own little perversions. Some liked their flaky dandruff-coated backs scratched vigorously, while others had more intimate needs, like having their penis held or stroked exactly the right way before they deliver the goods. But one particular boar would not give up the goods until the breeder played with the boar's butt. *"I have to stick my finger in his butt, he really loves that"!* Exclaimed the breeder, shortly thereafter turning red in the face. [39,] Female pigs also had their peculiarities. Unlike the brahman, the pigs needed to be 'turned on' before the semen could be drawn up into the uterus; less arousal equals smaller litters with fewer eggs fertilised. Arousal is made apparent when the sow 'pops', that is, her ears suddenly pop straight up. Sows also require pressure on their backs to simulate when the boar mounts them, often performed by the breeder sitting on the sow's back while artificially inseminating them. The image of the hogs in the truck, honking the horn, suddenly comes to mind again....

But enough of the porcine porn, and onto the subject of

Pig Intelligence

For an animal that humans have devoted vast amounts of time hunting, domesticating, and selectively breeding over the last 10,000 years, there is surprisingly little research done into their cognitive abilities and emotional lives. Mountains of research have been done on producing tastier pork faster and more efficiently, but sadly, research into the animal itself, its inner world of 'what it is like to be a pig' is rather paltry. However, a few dedicated researchers into the porcine inner world have created some wonderful glimmers of insight into the mind of a pig.

Oh, the Smell!

No doubt, the sensory ability most people would associate with a pig is its sense of smell. Not the foul odour that emanates from their sty, but the pig's amazing olfactory capabilities. And along with their incredible sense of smell, unsurprisingly comes a dizzying array of odours emitted from no less than nine different glands on a pig, including: Digital glands in the feet, vulvar, preputial (penis) and anal glands, mental glands near the chin, salivary and buccal glands in the mouth, and pre-orbital and harderian glands near the eyes. [46] Peter Brunjes and colleagues of the University of Virginia studied the olfactory components of pig brains, noting that the olfactory bulb accounts for around 7% of a pig's brain, compared with only around 0.01% in a human brain. Whilst similar in structure and organisation to a rat olfactory bulb, the pig has 1,113 functional olfactory receptor genes, which is much larger than most mammal species, including dogs, giving pigs an exceptional sense of smell. Interestingly, around 3% of human genes are dedicated to smell, but strangely, only 390 olfaction genes are active; the other 465 are *pseudogenes*, rendered inactive due to mutations. [47] Some scientists figure this is due to the evolution of our reliance on colour vision, but the jury is still out on this one.

One use of the exceptionally sensitive snout of *Sus scrofa* is in truffle detection, but there is a peculiar link between truffles and boar's balls! Kirsten Allen and Joan Bennett of The State University of New Jersey explain that truffles are the underground reproductive structures of a large range of fungus species of the class Ascomycetes. [48] Known for their pungent flavour and aroma, truffles can command exorbitant prices. Depending on the species, truffles can fetch prices up to US$3000 a kilogram for white truffles and slightly less for black truffles. In 2014, Australian truffle producer Ted Smith struck underground gold when he unearthed a whopping 1.172 kg French black Perigord truffle on his farm, according to ABC News. [49] Apart from their super olfaction capabilities, why are pigs so efficient at finding the rare fungi, even when it is buried up to a metre underground? The answer is *5a-androst-16-en-3a-ol,* which is a steroid pheromone in the androstanol family that produces a distinct musk-like odour. Where is it produced? In the testes of boars, of course, where it is transferred to the salivary glands and secreted in mating behaviour, a key factor in prompting the sow into the 'standing position' or lordosis, ready for action!... is that the truck horn honking? [50] This would explain why female pigs have traditionally been used to seek out truffles and why truffles have long been considered a human aphrodisiac. [48] Discriminating between whether the pigs are drawn to the musky scent of boars' balls or the prospect of a tasty snack is yet to be established. An interesting side note is that the androstanol is also produced in human male testes and is found in saliva, as well as secreted through sweat glands.

Eyesight

Although pigs primarily rely on their keen sense of smell, touch, and hearing, they also have excellent vision. Johan Zonderland and colleagues tested the visual acuity of pigs, and explained that despite sharing similar size, shape and anatomy with a human eye, pigs have far fewer cone cells than humans and have difficulty discriminating shapes smaller than 20mm even at close range. [51] Pigs' eyesight is suited to both diurnal and nocturnal life, which requires a combination of both rods (black and white and low light detection) and cones (colour and fine object discrimination), explained Jay Neitz and Gerald Jacobs of the University of California. [52] Studying pig vision, the researchers found that pigs possess two types of cone classes, with maximum light wavelength values of around 439 nanometres (nm) and 556nm. What that means is that pigs see the world through two colour ranges (dichromatic), where 439nm is the short wavelength blue-violet spectrum and 556nm is the medium wavelength of yellow/ green. Humans have trichromatic vision, with short, medium and long-wave cones able to discriminate colours from around 420 nm to 560 nm. Okay, while you are feeling all superior to pigs and other ungulates with your superior colour vision, just keep in mind that we have three types of photoreceptors, but the tiny mantis shrimp has up to 16 and can see not only a similar colour spectrum, but also ultraviolet light. If their eyestalks are somehow damaged, they also possess a third eye, consisting of photoreceptor cells that detect both dark and light, enabling them to escape prey even if blinded. [53]

Sooie Pig!

Pigs can hear a broad range of frequencies, from low 42Hz sounds up to 40.5 kHz (40,500 Hz), which is in the ultrasonic range. To put that in perspective, we hear sounds that range from 20Hz to 20kHz. Rickye and Henry Heffner of the University of Toledo, Ohio, tested hearing in pigs and goats and found that pigs can hear both the lower and higher ranges of frequencies than goats.[54] They postulate that ungulates like pigs evolved high-frequency hearing as a means to localise sound position and direction. Sometimes sound direction can be ambiguous; this is when the animal may experience *front-back locus reversals*, where it cannot tell if the sound is in front or behind. Binaural cues (from both ears) provide clues about the side and distance from which the sound is emanating, but not about its direction in front or back. This is where monaural (one ear) cues come in handy to reduce reversal errors. The fleshy part of the pig's ear, the pinnae, is highly mobile and alters the incoming sound waves as it moves, localising the sound source. High-frequency hearing works best in this system, a handy adaptation when many other animals are after your bacon!

Self-Awareness and Theory of Mind

Theory of mind, discussed in previous chapters, involves the ability to imagine others have differing thoughts and beliefs from ours, notoriously hard to establish in animals. Visuospatial perspective-taking, or imagining how a scene looks from another's perspective, shares many overlapping features with the theory of mind and although similarly different...is a good place to start.

To test the perspective-taking abilities of pigs, Suzanne Held and colleagues used 18 juvenile pigs in a controlled experiment. [55] Companion pigs were trained to enter one of four chutes consistently. Then, the two companion pigs were held in a pen, while a trainer walked over with a bucket and pretended to bait one of the chutes with food. Only one companion, the 'seeing' pig, could see the baiting; the other pig was hidden from observing this. The whole time, the test pig was watching on and was released shortly after the companion pigs. If it followed the *seeing* pig into the chute, it would indicate perspective-taking. Unfortunately, only one pig out of ten consistently followed the *seeing* pig; the others followed their companions less than would be expected by chance. This pig was either exceptionally good at perspective-taking, or some prior learning may have influenced its behaviour.

Michael Mendl of the University of Bristol suggests that our understanding of pig cognition is still in its infancy, with the sophisticated learning abilities of pigs, capacity for episodic-like memory and possible theory of mind, only beginning to come to light. [56] In a 2009 foraging experiment conducted by Mendl and Christine Nicol, pigs were tested daily in a specially constructed foraging area, where Pig 1 scouts around and finds the food stashed randomly that day. Later, Pig 1 (informed) is reintroduced to the area with a bigger and burlier naïve friend (Pig 2). As this trial is repeated over time, both pigs' behaviour begins to change, with the naïve pig learning to follow the informed pig, something resembling a theory of mind, "hey, this guy has useful information I don't". The informed porker is none too happy with this and adapts its behaviours to bamboozle its freeloading friend. The informed pig will often only go to the baited site (food) when naïve Pig 2 is a distance away, facing away from them or out of sight behind a barrier. When a non-exploitative friend is introduced, the deceptive behaviour stops, and when two known food sources are present, one bigger and tastier, the clever porkers suppress their desire to visit the large stash if an exploiter is present. This deceptive behaviour is typically only seen in primates and ravens, perhaps lending weight to Orwell's depictions of the devious, porcine characters that ruled *Animal Farm*.

Object Permanence

As mentioned in previous chapters, a variety of animals, such as primates and corvids, have passed the object permanence task, identifying that an object continues to exist even when hidden or displaced. Christian Nawroth, Mirjam Ebersbach and Eberhard von Borell tested a cohort of young porkers to establish if pigs showed signs of object permanence. Pigs were shown three cups with a rewarded object hidden under the cups (like the old shell game). When the object was visibly placed under the same cup in front of the pig, called a *fixed single visible displacement*, three out of four pigs chose correctly more often than chance, with one pig correctly choosing the baited cup in three trials. When they upped the ante to an A-not-B error trial, where the bait is visibly switched from the original cup to a new cup, the pigs failed to choose the correct cup, returning to the original cup, indicating they have difficulty following the movements of hidden objects.

In stark contrast, Alina Schaffer and colleagues tested five different species —goats, llamas, guanacos, zebras, and rhinos — and found that all the animals showed basic object permanence abilities, recalling the location of a baited cup up to 60 seconds after. [57] However, only two cups were used in this trial, and the A-not-B error was not covered. Megan Quail and Mariecia Fraser tested a cohort of sheep, goats, and alpacas and found that goats demonstrated a superior capacity for object permanence compared to their woolly counterparts. [58] In fact, the goats often passed the A not B error task, and one goat chose the correct cup 10 out of 12 times in the three-cup transposition task (moving the cups around randomly, like in the shell game).

This raises some interesting questions as to why the pigs performed so poorly in object permanence compared to other ungulates. This could be the result of different foraging behaviours in pigs, being omnivores as opposed to herbivores. Until further research is conducted, the jury is still out on this one.

Navigating

Can pigs use cues reflected in a mirror to help find hidden objects? In 2009, Donald Broom and colleagues of the University of Cambridge set out to answer this question. [59] Their porky test subjects were 4-8 week-old pigs, seven of whom were placed in a pen with a mirror for 24 hours, while 11 pigs were mirror naïve, meaning they had not been initially exposed to the mirror. The researchers noted that no mirror self-recognition tests have been performed on pigs in the past, and their test subjects showed some interesting inquisitive behaviour. At first, the young pigs reacted to their reflection as if it were another pig, but they would often stop and stand still, intently watching in a way that suggests they were monitoring and comparing their movements with their reflection. The test subjects were placed in a holding pen where they could see a food bowl reflected in a mirror, which was in fact obscured behind a partition. When released, seven of the eight pigs found the food bowl by using cues reflected in the mirror within an average of 23 seconds. The mirror naïve pigs, however, looked behind the mirror for the bowl, believing the reflection represented the food reward. However, within around five hours, the naïve pigs learned to locate the bowl by way of its reflection.

In an experiment aimed at replicating the above study, Elise Gieling and colleagues obtained differing results. Using similar-aged pigs and a setup that corresponded to the prior study, only 3 out of 22 pigs successfully used the mirror to locate the hidden food bowl. [60] The researchers concluded that not all pigs of certain breeds or ages may share the ability to use a mirror effectively to find hidden objects, and the experiment likely tested the upper limits of the pigs' cognitive capacity. Of course, this is the foundation of the scientific process as proposed by philosopher Karl Popper, that a theory or hypothesis should be falsifiable, that is, it can be contradicted or disproven by empirical testing. Like the findings of Broom et al, they also noted that the pigs learned that their perceptions of the mirror reflections differed from their surroundings after around 5 hours. Additionally, older pigs may have passed more developmental milestones, much like children, which could yield different results worth testing in the future.

Perhaps visual cues are not the whole picture here, as most animals use a combination of sight, sound and smell to navigate their worlds. Candace Croney and colleagues from Oregon State University tested the use of olfactory and spatial cues in pig navigation behaviour. [61] They hypothesised that pigs that learned to associate a reward with spatial, visual and olfactory cues could also independently rely on visual or olfactory cues alone, disregarding the spatial cues stored in memory. Using a cohort of older porkers, the pigs were given a search trial task to find a pot of a certain colour amongst an assortment of pots, rewarded when it knocked over the correct pot, increasing in complexity from 2 up to 10 choices. For the olfactory test, plastic bottles were placed on the same-coloured pots, one containing a coconut or almond scent, and a similar regimen to the sight test was played out. Results showed that the pigs progressively learned to discriminate between the correct objects, both by sight and by smell, independent of spatial cues. This is important in the handling and transport of pigs, as negative visual and olfactory events would likely negatively affect the pigs and their behaviour. Temple Grandin explained that the person involved in breeding and artificial insemination cannot be the same fellow who does 'nasty' stuff like vaccinations and vet visits, testament to the visual and olfactory cues pigs take on board.[39] I'm that bad guy with our animals, the one who gives the injections and foul-tasting worming drench, so our alpacas are acutely wary of me. It's much easier for my wife to catch them rather than for me to chase them around the paddock!

Problem-Solving

Piglets appear to be attracted to human voices, spending more time gazing toward human voices than artificial noise, according to Sandy Bensoussan and colleagues. [62] The porkers also seemed attracted to higher-pitched slow voices and voices with a rapid rhythm. They showed no difference in behaviour with angry or commanding voices, likely due to limited human interaction. Why does this matter? With the rise of pigs as pets and companions, in part due to the miniature pig swindle, it raises the question of whether pigs respond to human cues in the same way as dogs.

A novel study by Pérez Fraga and his team aimed to answer the question of whether companion pigs look to their human hosts in the same way as dogs when faced with an unsolvable task. [63] If you have owned a dog or cat before, you may be familiar with the look the animal gives you when the task is impossible, like the ball under the lounge or the food in the unopened tin. Cats probably won't look to their owner, trying to solve the task on their own, as do wolves. On several occasions, our goats will stare intently at me if I'm close to a tree with tasty leaves. They will even follow me, predicting that I will pull down a branch for them, eventually giving up when that does not eventuate. As dogs and pigs have taken different paths to domestication, one as a companion, the other as bacon, it came as no surprise that the researchers found that pigs rarely look to humans for help, while dogs spend way more time alternating their gaze between the unsolvable test device and their host.

Cooperative Behaviour

An exceptional example of problem-solving ability and cooperative behaviour was shown by wild boars in the Voděradské Bučiny
National Nature Reserve, the Czech Republic, in 2020. Captured
for the first time in a series of over 90 photos, Michaela Masilkova and colleagues described how two juvenile boars were trapped
in a box cage with two drop-down doors, which, when triggered,
were held in place by large wooden logs. [64] After several hours, an
adult sow and around seven other pigs arrived, the sow showing
clear signs of distress with distinct piloerection (her hair standing
on end). The sow and the other boars showed immediate interest
in the logs securing the door, examining it and touching the log
with their snouts. The sow charged at the front log, partially dis-
lodging it, then attacked the rear log, also displacing it, until, eventually, after 29 minutes, the log was completely removed, and the
prisoners made their escape. Some fascinating things are going on
here. Let's break that down. Back in 2010, Nowbahari and Hollis
created a set of four criteria to define rescue behaviour, which was
clearly met in the case of the trapped wild boar. Firstly, the victims
were in distress: the two trapped boars charging against the walls
and their mane hair standing erect, a sign of acute arousal. The
sow was also clearly emotionally aroused, indicating an empathic
state, and keeping close to the trapped boars also suggests awareness and concern. Secondly, the rescuer put herself at considerable
risk to save the boars. Thirdly, the sow's actions were adequate to
rescue the other hogs; her actions were precisely directed at removing the logs. Lastly, the rescue was of no immediate benefit
to the sow. So here in a bunch of wild boars, certain behaviours
appear to show aspects of empathy, perspective-taking, theory of
mind, advanced cognitive abilities in problem-solving and altruistic-like tendencies. The trapped juveniles may well have been her
offspring, which would also imply aspects of kin selection. The
other boars also showed intense interest in her behaviour, possible
signs of cooperation and social facilitation.

In a controlled experiment to assess helping behaviour in pigs,
Liza Moscovice and colleagues tested 75 porkers to see if they
would help a fellow boar escape from a confined room. [65] The other pigs could see their friend through a small window, and there
was a handle on the door that the pigs could manipulate. A 'control' room was provided that was empty. Results showed pigs were
more inclined to help their trapped hog friends than to enter the
empty room, and pigs that paid more social attention to their im-
prisoned pals were more likely to free them. Squeals and escape

attempts from their confined conspecifics also increase the speed and likelihood of rescue, and there was no preference shown for kin over strangers. They concluded that their results show partial support for targeted helping, but other selfish motivations could also be a factor.

Social Learning

Pigs form strong, long-lasting social bonds, but how much of their rich social lives is derived from observing their porcine friends? It has been established that animals that observe their conspecifics receiving positive human interaction, such as being stroked and spoken to gently, have reduced stress levels. Daniela Luna and colleagues tested 75 young pigs, separating them into a control group, a dominant or high-ranking animal demonstrator group and a subordinate, low-ranking demonstrator group. [66] The test subjects observed their dominant or subordinate porcine friends being treated kindly, stroked, spoken to and fed by a human. Findings revealed that observer pigs had lower levels of stress during aversive events and developed positive perceptions of their human hosts, indicating a level of social learning. The results were the same for observers of both high- and low-ranking animal pampering, whereas the no-treatment or 'control group' exhibited higher amounts of restlessness, vocalising, and biting behaviour around their human hosts. Interestingly, pigs discriminated between a familiar human who pampered their friend and an unfamiliar human; the calming effect was only observed when the pig recognised the one treating their friend well. No doubt, the opposite would also apply to animals observing their friends being treated cruelly, punishment often translating into learning and behaviour faster and more strongly than rewards. I'm pretty sure that one would not pass an ethics committee, though.

A funny example of social learning in pigs is the use of electronically controlled feeding stations. Pigs often get into nasty fights over food, explained Temple Grandin, so producers like to use automated isolating stalls to feed the pigs individually.[39] Nowadays, these systems rely on small RFID ear tags; however, several years ago, the pigs had to wear bulky radio collars. Pigs would approach the stall door, the collar triggering the door to open. The hog then walks in, and the gate shuts. The pigs move their head near the feeding station, which dispenses a measured amount of food for that individual pig. Sometimes the collars would fall off, and the other pigs learned to pick up the collar and wave it to get access to someone else's dinner. Some pigs exhibited very odd behaviour, walking into the enclosure and approaching the feeding trough, then performing unusual movements or foot stomping before the collar eventually triggered the food release. This is termed *superstitious behaviour,* coined by BF Skinner when he was training pigeons. Skinner noticed that when birds were placed on a fixed schedule of reinforcement, where they were given food every 15 seconds regardless of their behaviour, they started doing odd things such as turning in circles, bobbing their heads, and other unusual actions. The pigs likely lifted their leg in a certain way when the collar triggered the food reward, and if it happened a second time by chance, that behaviour was reinforced. Of course, human animals also make this error; perhaps the worst perpetrators are sportspeople who attribute some behaviour, trinket or piece of jewellery to a winning match or goal score, religiously repeating the ritual each game.

Memory

We often put our memory to the test. Children play hide and seek games, using short-term or working memory to remember 'who hid where' and not to look in the same place twice. Card games like *concentration* or 'pairs' test short-term and long-term memory to match the hidden cards. But what is the best way to test memory in pigs? Spatial hole board tests were initially used in measuring rodents' behaviour and cognition, consisting of a small square arena, with a floor containing equally spaced holes in which food or bait is placed. For example, the board has 9 holes, and 3 have bait. In a short-term or working memory trial, the bait position is changed with each trial. A rat enters the arena and searches for the food, eating the baits as it goes. If the rat returns to the same hole where it previously ate a bait, it has committed a short-term memory error. In the reference memory trial, something akin to long-term memory, the bait is placed in the same spot each time, and the rat should theoretically get better at finding the food as it commits the spot to long-term memory. Pigs require a much bigger arena, 8 x 8 metres and buckets containing the food bait are screwed to the floor rather than using holes. Johanna Arts and colleagues tested working and reference memory in 20 pigs across a series of different trials. [67] In all the tasks, 4 of the 16 buckets were baited with chocolate raisins in a manner that pigs cannot find the tasty treats using their keen sense of smell. In Task A (reference memory), pigs had to find the raisins hidden in the same spot in each of the 25 trials, performance measured as the percentage of all visits to the baited set of holes. Task B was the same except that the bait locations were changed on each of the 13 trials (working memory). The porker's performance increased dramatically over the course of the trials, task A going from around 300 seconds to around 50 and with similar results for task B, the experimenters concluded the pigs "learned to learn".

Several years later, Elizabeth Bolhuis and her team replicated the above study and found very similar results, but with an interesting twist. [68] Half of the 32 piglets were raised and weaned in an enriched environment containing wood shavings, peat, straw, and three branches, while the other half were raised in a barren pen. The piglets from the enriched environment showed better working memory, solving the tasks faster and making fewer errors than their barren-raised pals. Reference memory was, however, unaffected. This suggests that a stimulating environment improves the cognitive abilities of pigs, something which has been demonstrated in many other animal species, including humans.

Personality

So how does one work out the personality of a porker? How do you discern an extraverted pig from an introvert, or a happy-go-lucky hog from a melancholy hog? According to Charlotte Goursot and team from the Leibniz Institute for Farm Animal Biology, from the curl of their tail! [69] Well, there is more to it than that, but basically, the direction of a pig's tail and the preference for using one side of their snouts are what's called motor biases, key indicators of brain lateralisation. There is some evidence that left hemisphere dominance (right tail and snout) is associated with approach behaviours and positive emotions, whereas right hemisphere dominance (left tail and snout) is linked to withdrawal behaviours and negative emotions. Eighty piglets were assessed to determine their personality types, measuring: Boldness, Exploration, Activity and Sociability. *Boldness* was the time it took pigs to approach an unfamiliar person in the pen (sounds much like Ainsworth's Strange Situation test for children!) *Exploration* included assessing, exploring, and touching novel objects and the Activity measured duration and frequency of movement. Sociability was measured by the number of oinks and the levels of testosterone and cortisol in saliva; the latter has been previously linked to human sociability. The other method was back-testing, where the pigs were placed on their backs and held down to determine how much and how long they struggled, thereby distinguishing between active and passive coping styles. These are behavioural strategies that animals use to respond to stress or challenges. It turns out that piglets with both a right-sided tail and snout motor bias oinked more in an open-field test, calling for their friends, indicating high sociability, showed bolder approach behaviours, and struggled longer on their backs, suggesting an active coping style. On the other hand, piglets that showed left biases were less bold, showed less exploration, more akin to withdrawal behaviours.

Strangely enough, the teat rank order might also be related to pig personality. Piglets who suckle on the sow's teats closest to her front scored much higher levels of active traits (approach behaviours) compared to siblings who suckle in the middle or at the rear, explained Kristina Horback and Thomas Parsons. [70] Sows secrete more nutrient and antibody-rich colostrum at the front teats, and the piglets form a rank teat order early on in life. The front suckling piglets are bigger and tend to be more aggressive and dominant than piglets that suckle from the last row of teats, which are typically smaller and more submissive. More of a chicken-and-egg problem, the dominant piglets were probably predisposed to their behaviour by their genes, giving them an advantage to grab the best spot to suckle. The researchers tested 36 sows from birth through to their second parity (litter of piglets) and found that personality characteristics at birth significantly predicted their adult personality style. This sounds an awful lot like human personality traits, which are also relatively stable and fixed over time. Ultimately, pigs, like humans and other mammals, have both a genetic and an environmental component in the development of their personality, although it's often difficult to differentiate between the two.

Temple Grandin described an incident that highlights the influence of genes on personality and temperament. [8] Some breeds of fast-growing lean hogs, which are preferred in the US, can be particularly vicious and mean-nasty fighters, explained Grandin. Recounting how one producer had to completely change his hogs' genetic lines to calmer, more robust sows after tearing out his sow stalls and letting the pigs intermingle. Sow stalls are a particularly cruel way of keeping breeding sows, which is being phased out in the industry, albeit slowly. Grandin lamented that many of the aggressive sows need to be culled to make way for calmer pigs that can mix in large pens.

Conclusions

Pigs are much-loved, intelligent animals, both for their antics and their tasty bacon. Fables, fairy tales and movies are awash with porcine characters that exemplify the cleverness and cunning of hogs. We have coexisted with pigs for 10,000 years; they were once believed to be close relatives of whales, and their incredible sense of smell helps us find rare and expensive fungi. Pigs also have a dark side and can be incredibly violent to each other and sometimes to us, to the extent that they were once put on trial and publicly executed. Cooperative problem-solving behaviour, social learning, and strong cognitive and memory abilities put pigs somewhere in the realm of canine intelligence. Yet despite all this knowledge, we still confine them to life imprisonment in factory farms, some of them up to 26 stories high, and kill and process sows after 3-4 years, separate their piglets after three weeks and slaughter those after 7 months. So many pigs are farmed that they produce billions of tons of excrement, some of which is cleverly turned into biofuel and fertiliser, while much ends up in the environment. Our obsession with pork and the scaling of production to industrial levels leaves so many questions unanswered as to the long-term viability of mega-scale pig farming and the ethical treatment of intelligent, sentient animals. Perhaps it's we who have ultimately made pigs of ourselves, in our gluttonous quest for the perfect bacon burger.

What Does it all Mean?

The real problem of humanity is the following: we have Palaeolithic emotions, medieval institutions, and God-like technology.

Edward O. Wilson

Whilst a rock-solid definitive answer to *just how intelligent are the animals we eat?* is somewhat nuanced, I hope this book has provided some insight into what intelligence is, how it's measured and how the different animals that we often call food measure up. Science is still playing catch-up with animal intelligence and cognition, particularly in the realm of livestock animals, with most research directed at how quickly they grow and how nutritious they are, not necessarily how they think.

Throughout the book, I have highlighted what science currently knows and how we may have arrived at our beliefs and worldviews regarding animals. The research and experiments I have covered are by no means exhaustive, but I chose the more interesting and relevant pieces of investigation and, in some cases, the only ones. In this chapter, I will examine why, biologically speaking, we eat animals, and what psychological, social and cultural factors motivate this behaviour. I will highlight why it is having disastrous consequences for the planet, and what, if anything, we can do about it. Before doing so, here is a brief synopsis of the journey so far, along with a slight detour back several million years.

How Did We Get Here?

Since we diverged from the chimpanzee lineage around 5 to 10 million years ago, humans have co-evolved alongside a huge diversity of animals; some species still exist, many are long extinct. Some of the oldest known *hominins*, that is, bipedal primates which include humans, were called *Australopithecines*, who walked the forests and savannahs of Africa around four million years ago. Studying the fossil teeth of these ancient humans, primatologist John Fleagle explained that the robust jaw, large molars and premolars with thick enamel layers suggest the ancient hominids dined on hard foods such as nuts, seeds, grains and other plant material. [1] Ancient humans were often themselves dined upon by other animals, as bite marks in several hominin fossils have revealed. One such discovery was in the famous *Taung child*, a fossil skull of an *Australopithecus* juvenile, found in a Quarry in Taung, South Africa. Lee Berger described that holes in the eye orbits of the skull indicate the child was likely taken by a large bird of prey like an eagle, after comparing similar wounds in monkeys, a morbid sign that we were once part of other animals' diets. [2]

Global climate change around 2.8 million years ago led to a dramatic shift in East Africa, from closed-canopy wetlands to drier, open grass savannahs, explained Neil Mann of the University of Melbourne. [3] Digestible plants were much more difficult to find in the dry grasslands; however, animals were abundant. Australopithecines likely scavenged on animals' carcasses, gradually shifting to hunting practices over several million years. We know this from samples of stable isotopes taken from fossil bones and teeth, such as carbon isotopes C13 and C12, and the strontium-to-calcium ratios (Sr/Ca). Carnivores have the lowest ratio of Sr/Ca, and studies have shown that early hominins were around midway, a sure sign they ate a considerable amount of meat. Further evidence is found in cut marks and evidence of butchery in animal fossils dating back 1.5 million years, pointing to our hominin ancestors moving from energy-poor, highly fibrous food to energy-rich animal food, resulting in our movement to the peak of top-level carnivores. [3]

In the book *Catching Fire: How Cooking Made Us Human*, primatologist Richard Wrangham argues that cooking was behind our great leap forward in brain size. [4] Cooking food raises the energetic quality of food, reduces the amount of chewing needed and requires less digestion time, allowing for more energy to be directed to expensive organs like the brain. Wrangham suggests *Homo Habilis*, a transitional species between the Australopithecines and Homo Erectus, most likely cooked food, evident by the small reduction in the tooth sizes in habilines, which became much more pronounced in Homo erectus. Brain size also increased significantly in Homo erectus, 42% larger than that of habilis.

Biological anthropologist and evolutionary psychologist Robin Dunbar offers an alternative hypothesis. Dunbar believes complex social interactions are behind the rise in our expanded craniums and proposed the *Social Brain Hypothesis* to explain large brain sizes in humans and primates. [5] In primates, there is a distinct relationship between brain cortex volume and social group size, likely due to the complexities in social and mating systems. Lifelong pair-bonding in species of birds and other mammals also appears to lead to larger brains in those animals compared with their more promiscuous counterparts.

Evidence suggests that a rise in toolmaking and more sophisticated hunting practices saw early humans venturing further afield in search of both vegetable foods and game. Cooking and fire management elevated the consumption of animal and vegetable matter to new culinary levels, killing off harmful pathogens, and making food easier to chew, more nutritious and tastier too. As Wrangham suggests, less mastication of tough meat and plants led to a gradual reduction in our jaw and teeth sizes. Is cooking of food or an increase in social interactions the cause of our capacious craniums? Or is it perhaps a combination of both? The jury is still out on a definitive answer, but either way, some precipitous event in our ancient past led to a distinct increase in our brain size and power. [3][4]

Of course, this did not happen overnight, but over the passage of around 3 million years. In this time, our neocortex, the wrinkly, folded part of the brain that sits atop more ancient structures, grew way out of proportion to the rest of the brain, tripling in size over that period. [6] Containing around 86 billion neurons, our cortex neuron count is arguably the highest in the animal kingdom. Before you let those facts go to your head, the human brain is essentially a linearly scaled-up primate brain in terms of cells, according to Suzana Herculano-Houzel of the Federal University of Rio de Janeiro. [7] That is to say, if you took a tiny marmoset brain, weighing just 8 grams, and scaled it up to the size of a human brain, the number of neurons would be similar. And in the case of brains, oddly, size does not matter; it's all about the neurons! A capybara, a large member of the rodent family, has a brain that weighs 76g and contains around 1600 neurons. Compared to a capuchin monkey, which has a brain of only 52g but around 3690 neurons. Humans tick both boxes, in terms of brain size and density of neurons, with the highest Encephalization Quotient (EQ) or expected brain size compared to mass, of any animal, at around seven, compared to chimps at two to three and dogs at around one. This means our scaled-up, densely packed primate brain is the largest in the known world compared to body size, from which we derive our scaled-up cognitive abilities. Despite our highly evolved noggin, our primary motor, sensory and emotional circuits are not that dissimilar to those of many mammals. Where we differ is in our cognitive abilities, theory of mind, ability to imitate and social cognition. [7]

Big brains are also metabolically expensive to run, a bit like a thirsty V8 motor using more fuel than a small four-cylinder car, burning up around 20% of the body's total energy requirements at rest. To what degree cooking or social group size influenced brain size increases in humans is still up for debate, but the evidence strongly points to the change to a more meat-intensive diet in our evolutionary history. Animal protein and, particularly the long-chain fatty acids found in meat, fish and eggs feed our metabolically expensive noggins, likely leading to or enlarged craniums. [3]

However, something odd occurred in the last 50,000 years of our evolutionary history: our brains stopped increasing in size and began to shrink! Compared to fossils of our ancestors, both our bodies and our brains have decreased in size, the latter by around 5.4%. [8] On the other hand, paradoxically, our IQ has increased! Jeff Stibel of the Natural History Museum in Los Angeles explained that, despite these changes, IQ rates have risen steadily over the last century, increasing by approximately 0.4 points per year between 1935 and 2006. Called *the Flynn effect*, named after New Zealand intelligence researcher James R. Flynn, the phenomenon can be explained by short-term environmental factors that offset long-term genetic trends. Access to education and increased years of attainment, a reduction in disease and pathogens and importantly, improved nutrition are all factors that likely led to increases in our general intelligence, despite our shrinking grey matter. [8]

Pass it On

It seems highly likely that meat eating, cooking of food and larger social groups all contributed to our growing brains, enhanced cognitive abilities and greater intelligence. What also propelled humans to stratospheric heights in intelligence was the development of culture and language. In his book *The Gap, What Separates Us from Other Animals*, Thomas Suddendorf explained that language, particularly by way of cultural transmission, allowed the passing of skills and knowledge onto future generations, no longer having to 'reinvent the wheel'. [9] Along with the transmission of knowledge came networks of cooperation that, despite all odds, overcame obstacles, allowing us to expand our sphere of knowledge and build communities, towns, and cities, and develop trade and commerce. As humans expanded out into the world, carrying with us artifacts of cultural knowledge, we also brought with us the animals we called companions, workers and food. We created religions and gods, assigning mystical powers to animals, and decorated caves with their images. We created artwork and jewellery in their forms, and legends emerged around their fertility and prowess.

As we discovered in Chapter One, the Greek philosophers created some of the earliest recorded musings on what distinguishes humans from animals. Monotheistic religions placed God squarely at the centre of the universe, and man, made in his image, took centre stage, the animals created merely to be used and dominated. Polytheistic religions viewed animals as proxies for divine entities and sources of entertainment, whereas the Dark and Middle Ages regarded animals as beasts of burden, automata, and entities devoid of a rational soul. Not devoid enough to be put on trial for their perceived crimes, though appropriately represented by somewhat biased legal entities. The Victorian era saw the importance of pets rise in popular culture, although domestic farm animals continued to be treated in cruel and repressive ways. Stuffed animals and pet cemeteries became all the rage in old blighty, but it was not until Darwin's *The Descent of Man* that humans really began to examine our relationship to other animals.

Around the same period, the new science of psychology began to flourish as humans began to explore what lies behind our thoughts, motivations and behaviours. The early studies of classical conditioning, using various animals such as dogs, cats, rats and primates, soon led to the startling realisation that we are not all that dissimilar. In later studies termed 'behaviourism', B.F. Skinner found that reward and punishment shape and modify an animal's behaviour, much in the same fashion as humans. The cognitive revolution of the 1960s saw a greater focus on memory and cognition, with experiments adding further weight to the similarities we share with animals. Even the field of emotions could not be partitioned entirely from the domain of humans, as animal ethologists such as Niko Tinbergen, Frans de Waal and neurobiologist Jaak Panksepp made abundantly clear.

Despite our large brains, many subcortical structures (those areas below the wrinkled cortex) share ancient evolutionary pathways with animals. Panksepp described wonderfully how basic emotional systems in brains, serve an adaptive function, which emerged as mammals evolved, allowing us to change physiological and behavioural mechanisms in response to survival problems. [10] Indeed, we share many similarities in our emotional systems with our fellow mammals. Panksepp's SEEKING, FEAR, RAGE, PANIC, PLAY AND LUST systems overlap and share many parallels with the Big Five personality trait model of openness, extroversion, neuroticism, conscientiousness and agreeableness.

PLAY is a big deal, and all mammals love to play. It's an integral part of growing up, learning social rules and boundaries, developing coordination and generally having fun. Children love rough and tumble play as much as a puppy, a goat, a kitten or a piglet. Other components of animal intelligence also show parallels in our repertoire of abilities. As mentioned, scrub jays, primates, dogs and rodents have shown episodic-like memories for what, where and when, a form of mental time travel. Sheep and goats can discriminate between human faces and their friends' faces, and macaques can sort fruit into categories, demonstrating semantic-like memory. Cows can remember the location of feed containers for nearly two months, and goats can learn tasks for food rewards that are retained for up to 300 days, providing strong evidence of long-term memory. Sheep, goats, chickens, and pigs all exhibit basic levels of object permanence, typically up to level 4, similar to what is observed in human infants up to 12 months of age. Some animals demonstrate levels of self-awareness through the mirror self-recognition test, primarily primates, corvids, and cetaceans; however, most ungulates fail this test. Sheep, goats, pigs, and cows exhibit levels of cooperative behaviour and display empathy for their conspecifics, behaviours that we might, at some level, call moral.

No Denying We Are Different

There is, however, no denying the unique abilities of the human mind. Our powerful cognitive abilities, large capacity for memory, and mastery of language afford us distinct advantages over our mammalian cousins. Through *episodic memory*, we can 'mental time travel', recalling what, where, and when in vivid detail. We develop the ability to discern object permanence from an early age and develop the *theory of mind* through 'mind-reading' capabilities, to best guess what the other person is thinking. We exhibit altruistic behaviours and often look after our most vulnerable members of society, despite them not being kin. We share complex language abilities and can exchange ideas across time and distance, via culture and the written word. We cooperate at high levels to imagine, build, invent and produce music and art; behaviours and abilities our primate relatives never achieved. Suddendorf proposed that the uniqueness of the human mind rests on 'two legs': Our expansive capacity to construct layered mental scenarios, and our fundamental urge to connect with other scenario-building minds. [9] Beyond the incredible capacity of our 'scaled-up' primate brain and our advances in language and culture, there also remain within us stark reminders of our evolutionary biological heritage.

But are we that Different?

Beyond the similarities we share with non-human animals insofar as brain functions, emotions and behaviours, there are also some strange and somewhat disturbing similarities in our anatomies. In 2004, Edward Daeschler, Neil Shubin, and Farish Jenkins made a groundbreaking discovery on Ellesmere Island, in the far north of Canada. [11] The late Devonian era rocks (385–359 million years ago) contained an unusual fish fossil, which, when painstakingly cleaned back at the lab, revealed a transitional species of fish, one that also showed features of a land animal, later named *Tiktaalik*. Why is this relevant? The fossil revealed frontal fins capable of supporting the fish's body weight, but importantly, it is one of the earliest known animals to have the bones of our upper arm, forearm, wrist and palm, but also had scales and webbing. [12] In his fascinating book, Your Inner Fish, Neil Shubin described this as the *one bone, two bones, lotsa blobs* phenomenon, referring to the same limb pattern in many ancient and all present-day animals. The *one bone* is the humerus or upper arm bone, and the femur, the long leg bone. The *two bones* are the radius and ulna of the arm and the tibia and fibula of the leg. The *lotsa blobs* are the small bones of the wrists and ankles.

Not only are bones similar, so too are organs! The 'gold standard' in heart valve replacements in humans is using bioprosthetic leaflets, which are typically made from animal tissues. For example, bovine pericardium (the fluid-filled sack that surrounds the heart) and pig aortic valve tissue. These are genetically modified to knock out the GGTA-1 gene, thereby avoiding rejection by our bodies, and are then sewn onto synthetic fabric or stents. Hundreds of thousands of pig heart valve replacements are performed successfully each year, saving many people's bacon! The pig's heart is a similar size and shape to a human heart, but we also share some other strange similarities with fish!

Shubin describes the early discovery of embryo formation by Karl Ernst von Baer and Christian Pander in the 19th century. [12] Von Baer deduced that all the organs in a developing chicken embryo can be traced to either one of three layers, later called the *germ* layers. This intrigued Von Baer who set about examining all manner of different embryos and concluded that all animal embryos; fish, reptiles, birds and mammals, all develop in the same way: the outer layer the *ectoderm* (skin, brain, eyes, teeth), the *mesoderm* (muscles, bones, organs) and the *endoderm* (lungs, liver, glands). Interestingly, we all started life as a bunch of dividing cells that first form a ball, then a frisbee-shaped two-layer disk that folds in on itself, forming a tube within a tube, one end the head, the other the anus. Here's the kicker: we are all *deuterostomes*; that is, our anus forms before our mouth does! Another strange remnant of our ancestral past is the four branchial arches or *gill arches* of the head region that all developing embryos share, from humans through to sharks. Each of the arches differentiates into diverse organs. In sharks, these transform into organs and nerves, eventually developing into gill slits. In humans, into cartilage and nerves, bones of the ear, muscles of the face and neck and the cranial nerves. Sometimes in humans, the gill arch fails to close over, resulting in a branchial cyst —a fluid-filled, bulging pouch in the neck. [12]

We are all animals evolved from a primitive ancestor, lucky enough to have somehow survived, evolved, developed a big brain, and formed cohesive cooperative societies that pass on rich information and knowledge through language and culture. As the sociobiologist Edward O Wilson so succinctly put it:

"We have Palaeolithic emotions, medieval institutions, and God-like technology."

The Palaeolithic emotions we have covered make sense in terms of evolution and biology. The medieval institutions, so far as animals are concerned, could be construed as the industrial-scale farming, growing and slaughtering facilities we have built using our giant brains, which we combined with God-like technology to streamline the production of animal-based food. The resulting proteins and fats go back into fuelling our demanding, energy-hungry

226

big brains and ever-expanding waistlines. A fascinating thought experiment is once AI reaches human-like self-awareness, posing the question: *is it the right thing to do to breed, kill and eat all these animals?* Most likely, the answer would be the number 42!

Our Carnivorous Addiction

Despite our big brains with Palaeolithic emotions and our medieval institutions and mountains of technology, humans have still failed to address the vast amount of meat we consume. If you have ever visited an all-you-can-eat buffet, you may have noticed that people generally help themselves to the meat and seafood, piling their plates high like there is no tomorrow! The Aussie barbecue is a quintessential Australian institution, where two things are set in stone: alcohol and loads of charred meat. Most often, a variety of salads are laid out to make us feel better about the half a cow we just ate, but more often than not, the meat is all eaten, and the salads are taken home again!

There seems to be little financial incentive not to eat meat. You may have noticed that takeaway, fast food or restaurant prices of meals containing meat are usually the same or similar price to the vegetarian or vegan alternative. Difficult for our energy-craving Neolithic brains to take that option when the animal protein version is so cheap and tempting!

So, why do we 'hog' the meat? After all, we have evolved to not only eat meat, but also a vast range of other plant and fungi-based foods. Why do we choose the beef burger over the salad bowl? Why is the first bite of food on our dinner plate usually the meat, and the best bits we save for last? The short answer is it's rewarding.

Our big complex brains are wired on primitive reward systems evolved over millions of years to favour high-energy, protein-rich food. Those reward systems drive behaviours beneficial to our survival and reproductive fitness, that is, to pass on our genes. These mechanisms have also evolved to detect the nutrient content of food, as Amber Kelly and colleagues explain. [13] Nutrient information is rapidly communicated to the brain, and in particular, to the hypothalamus, which regulates hunger and satiety among other things. Fats and sugars use distinct pathways to the hypothalamus, and the nutrient content affects learning pathways via the dopamine reward system. A case in point, rats were fed either raw or cooked sweet potatoes and ate similar amounts of both. Once the brain's learning and reward systems kicked in, they preferred the higher-nutrient cooked potatoes. Our brains also learn by flavour and nutrient combinations; the brain senses both the nutrient content and the taste, with winning combinations driving learning, motivation, and changes in behaviour.

This is how fast-food companies hijack your reward system. Take a nutrient-rich material (fat), combine it with minced animal protein, flavour enhancers, sodium and sugar, place it between two high-calorie buns, throw in a bit of lettuce to fool you into believing it's healthy and voila! One addictive, dopamine-inducing burger! Ashley Gearhardt and Erica Schulte describe how not only fats and sugars are highly addictive, but also *ultra-processed* fats and sugars. [14] The combination of the fats and sugars creates a *supra-additive* response in the brain, greater than either single ingredient. Ultra-processed food nutrients are also absorbed quickly, due to the removal of fibre, water and protein, replaced with texturisers. This adds to the addictive nature of these foods, almost like a cocaine burger! In contrast, slow-release whole foods do not stimulate our reward system as dramatically, think chewing on a raw carrot versus biting into a tasty steak! Gluten-containing high-energy foods like bread produce opioid peptides called *gluteomorphins* when digested, which can cross the intestinal barrier and enter the bloodstream, possibly explaining why eating delicious cakes and bread feels so satisfying.

These food-brain reward systems served us well in our hunter-gatherer past. In periods of feast and famine, it made sense to stuff yourself with as much tasty animal meat and fat as possible; it might be weeks before it happens again, and raw yams might be the only alternative. The Khoisan, also known as the 'Bushmen,' of the Kalahari Desert are an interesting example of adapting to feast or famine. The San are known for their 'steatopygia' or ability to store larger than average amounts of fat on their butts, handy when your next meal might be a while off. It makes sense when you are a child or teenager to binge on high-protein, high-energy foods, as growing bodies and brains require energy. Not as important as you grow older, as evidenced by the way people have less desire to eat sugars and fats as they age.

How We Rationalise Eating Animals

So far in the human journey, we have seen that we evolved big brains and increased cognition facilitated by hunting and eating meat. High-energy foods such as meat and fats are both nourishing and rewarding, humanity clearly benefiting from consuming animals. Now that we no longer live on the savannah, the freezing steppes of Central Asia, or the jungles of Asia, and live a more sedentary lifestyle, we no longer require the high-protein, high-fat diet of our Palaeolithic cousins. So why do we continue to eat so much meat? The answer is a multifaceted one at best. On the one hand, our genetically determined nutritional needs, desires, and reward systems have evolved over millennia and will persist well into the future. Alternately, we have the influence of culture and tradition, but most pernicious is the powerful effect of corporate greed and big business, which I will discuss later.

Our large craniums, however, are also blessed with substantial top-down abilities, that is, the capacity to reason, make decisions and suppress our wants and desires. And yet, still, we collectively stuff our mouths with a combined 350 million tons of animal meat per year as of 2023. [15] So why in the heck, despite our increasing IQ, powerful reasoning abilities and abundance of education, do we still eat way too much meat? There is a myriad of possible psychological culprits that explain our carnivorous cravings, the first I will start with is culture.

Culture

As described in the previous chapters, we have a strange capacity to categorise and compartmentalise animals as food or non-food. Dogs and cats are a category of pet, as are colourful birds, hamsters, and guinea pigs. Yet in some parts of Asia, dogs and cats were, and to some degree, still are a category of food. In many developing parts of the world, any bird is potentially food, and in South America, guinea pigs or cavies run around under the house, not as pets, but dinner that requires no refrigeration. Yet in Western culture, colourful birds are only pets, but chickens, and to a lesser degree pigeons, ducks, and turkeys, are categories of food.

This implies a significant cultural effect on how we categorise animals. In outback Australia, dogs are indispensable workmates. In Vietnam, eating dogs has long been popular in the north of the country. Nir Avieli of Ben Gurion University explained that eating dog meat, or *Thit Cho*, is often an expression of class distinction and modernisation, tinged with political idealism. [16] But overarchingly, eating of *Thit Cho* is linked to masculinity, social dominance and sexual potency. Sadly, I admit to having once attended a Thit Cho restaurant in Hanoi many years ago. After the meal, which was possibly the worst thing I have ever eaten, my masculinity was down in the gutter along with my self-esteem and libido!

India is a vast continent with a population of over 1.4 billion people, more than 17% of the world's population. Yet around four in ten Indian adults describe themselves as vegetarian, according to Travis Mitchell of the Pew Research Centre. [17] One of the driving factors is religious beliefs, with Jains almost universally abstaining from meat eating, 83% of Hindus are vegetarian or restrict meat intake, whereas around 50% of Christians and Muslims abstain from certain meats. The term *Holy Cow* certainly holds currency in India; the photo I took in Rajasthan is typical of the bovines that wander the crowded streets of towns and cities, unhindered and unharassed by humans. Surveys found that most Hindu's believe you cannot identify as Hindu if you eat beef, and likewise, a Muslim cannot be Muslim if they consume pork. Unfortunately, chickens lucked out on the sacred status; the consumption of chicken meat has increased a whopping 1,700% in India since 1980!

Australia has long had a culture of meat-eating, the famous institution of the Aussie meat pie, a shining example of our love affair with meat. Residents of Adelaide even marched in force to complain about a lack of beef! Dubbed the *Beef Riot*, in 1931, over 1000 unemployed men took to the streets to protest the replacement of beef with mutton (sheep) on their ration tickets. [18] This was, of course, during the Great Depression, and the public was incensed that good beef was replaced with inferior mutton, thought to be full of bone and gristle. As the protestors approached the city with a view to confronting the Premier, the police set upon them, some mounted on horseback, some on motorcycles. A wild brawl erupted that lasted some 20 minutes before the mob was dispersed. Never get between an Aussie and his meat pie! The Aussie meat culture appears to have mellowed in recent years, with research by Roy Morgan showing that in 2019, 12.1% of the population had a diet entirely or mostly made up of plant-based food. [19]

Utility

Often, when faced with uncertainty, we make decisions based on a mental economic calculation to find the best option, a concept economists refer to as expected utility theory. [20] What is this animal's utility, and does it have a benefit monetarily, aesthetically, or emotionally? Can it be eaten? If yes, it is relegated to the industrial food complex and priced according to supply and demand. Is it intrinsically rewarding, entertaining, and rare, like a macaw? Then, it's priced based on its novelty and scarcity. One person may view a rat as nothing more than a filthy pest to be poisoned or trapped, whereas a herpetologist may see the utility in a rat as food for their reptile. In contrast, a child might see a rat as a highly intelligent and clean rodent that makes a wonderful pet and companion.

Chickens have great utility in producing eggs and meat, but chickens can also become much-loved pets. Some chook owners will pay hundreds of dollars to treat and save their feathered friend, our local vet relaying one such story. The utility of that animal then is valued emotionally, on its worth as a companion and fellow sentient being, not merely a chicken dinner. Fortunately for our goat with the broken leg in the *Introduction* section, Rosie, our emotional valuation of a goat's life exceeded the market value of a goat (about $100), seeing more utility in saving her life and reducing suffering than saving money. We use similar cost-benefit analyses when deciding to purchase a pet. How much will this dog cost? How much will the food and vet bills be? Would it be more cost-effective to buy a guinea pig? Although often blatantly clear economic decisions are ridden over roughshod by emotional decisions, where we may choose entirely the wrong pet! Do we make similar cost-benefit analyses of animals based on their intelligence or appearance? More than likely so. The *Halo effect* is a cognitive bias exhibited in humans, where we tend to judge attractive people more favourably. Perhaps this also carries over to attractive or *neotenous* featured animals.

Speciesism

Introduced by Richard Ryder in the 1970s and popularised by animal rights activist Peter Singer, *speciesism* is a term loosely used to explain the assumption that humans are inherently more worthy of consideration than other species, that is, animals. Lucius Caviola and colleagues of the University of Oxford demonstrated that this assumption, essentially a form of prejudice, is also a psychological construct, comparable to sexism and racism and sharing ideological roots. As a construct, it can therefore be measured, which is what the researchers did, creating a *Speciesism Scale.* [21] Sampling a variety of people to assess links between speciesism and other constructs such as racism, sexism, homophobia and right-wing authoritarianism, the scale is described as able to pinpoint differences in speciesist attitudes. The researchers noted that they did not explicitly explore how these prejudices occur, stating the possibility that categorisation of animals such as food or pets could play a role.

If indeed the speciesism prejudice is a real and present pernicious effect throughout human society, what would an anti-speciesist world look like, where equal moral and ethical rights were afforded to all sentient beings?

Australian biologist Allen Greer argues that speciesism itself is a form of unjustifiable discrimination, and the arguments put forth by the animal liberation movement are untenable. [22] The anti-speciesists argue that all sentient beings, that is, humans and animals, share interests, most importantly, the avoidance of suffering. Humans also share a moral obligation to give equal consideration to animals and humans. However, this goes against the basic tenets of human social cohesion, kin selection, empathy and the social contract "do unto others". Greer explains that we inherited the rudiments of empathy from our primate cousins, yet that empathy is very much contained within the species, not to individuals of another species. This makes perfect sense as an adaptation to facilitate intra-species cooperation and cohesion.

On the surface, the speciesism argument seems attractive, but from a biological perspective, it runs contrary to evolutionary theory. But as Greer points out, extending our concern for another species also deepens concern for our own, which suspiciously sounds like an adaptive function. Unfortunately, speciesism has arguably shown little if any effect in swaying the people's opinions on animal suffering. No doubt it has equally had little impact on curbing our insatiable appetite for animal meat.

An Ugly Animal

Would you rather eat an ugly cow or a cute poodle? Does the thought of a chimpanzee burger or a gorilla steak horrify you? There is a good reason for reactions to these questions, as Aurélien Miralles and colleagues explained. [23] The researchers surveyed 3500 people to garner their empathic perceptions or their compassionate reactions to a set of 52 photographs of animals, plants and fungi. They found that phylogenetically, the further away from us a species is, the less empathy and compassion we ascribe to that animal. In other words, the more an animal resembles us, the more empathic and compassionate we are to that creature. Called the *anthropomorphic stimuli hypothesis*, this concept is explained by evolutionary forces that shape our perceptions, leading us to believe that species resembling us likely share similar traits. Think about that for a moment! It is easy to attribute human-like traits to a monkey, but challenging to do the same with a sheep, or even worse, a tortoise, regardless of what we know of their intelligence. Taking culture, religion and morality out of the equation, the *anthropomorphic stimuli hypothesis* certainly helps explain why we have no problem eating meat from animals that in no way resemble us.

Neoteny

From ugly animals to adorable baby ones, *neoteny* is a significant factor in our animal preferences. Features such as big eyes spaced far apart, small and blunt noses, and large, rounded heads are all neotenous characteristics that humans are predisposed to respond to in a caring and nurturing manner. [24] Perhaps these evolved responses that encourage nurturing and discourage harming our offspring are carried over to other species. There are very few baby animals we eat, partly because of a lack of sufficient meat and partly because of the disgust factor. Although suckling pig and the Philippine tradition of *balut*, a boiled, partly developed duck embryo, are exceptions that come to mind.

Neoteny also plays a significant role in our mental classification of an animal's importance. Is a cute, furry koala more important or worthy of saving than an ugly naked mole rat? A panda is likely less intelligent than a warthog. Yet, we take delight in warthogs being eaten by lions on nature documentaries, but shudder at the thought of a panda being harmed. Perhaps this is the *Halo effect* in action! From childhood, we are taught the objective value of animals with neotenous features through picture books, stuffed toys, video games and cartoons. Classic books like *The Wind in the Willows* and *Beatrix Potter's tales* have enthralled children for generations with their anthropomorphised, neotenous characters that get into all sorts of human-like mischief. Still, strangely, they never end up on a plate. When we wrestle with the reality that many of those fabled animal characters do indeed end up on a dinner plate, *cognitive dissonance* can strike.

Cognitive Dissonance

Have you ever experienced the discomfort of holding a particular belief, yet acting or portraying yourself in a different light? According to Leon Festinger's 1957 theory, *cognitive dissonance* is the psychological discomfort we feel when we hold contradictory thoughts compared to our actions. [25] There are several methods humans employ to reduce cognitive dissonance, removing or reducing that belief, adding a new consonant belief in line with our values, or increasing the importance of that belief.

People the world over consume meat, often experiencing some psychological discomfort in the process, chewing over the fact that the meat on their plate was once alive, eating and breathing, and presumably enjoying its life. Steve Loughnan and Brock Bastian summed it up nicely with the *meat paradox*: People enjoy eating meat but feel conflicted about harming animals. Their study revealed that meat consumption tends to lead to a withdrawal of moral concern for animals and a reduction in the perception that meat animals can suffer. This helps resolve the cognitive dissonance between enjoying one's steak dinner and caring about animals. [26] [27] They further describe that as humans, we employ a multitude of tactics to reduce dissonance when faced with the moral conflicts that interrupt our self-serving behaviours. For example, people may experience dissonance when faced with the realisation that their actions have caused harm to another individual or animal. Adjusting one's view of that animal as 'dumb' or lacking a soul helps minimise that psychological discomfort, allowing one to carry on as usual.

Many people morally care about and express concern for animals, yet ironically, they also eat them, as described by Hank Roth-gerber and Daniel Rosenfeld. [28] Research has shown that most Americans believe animals deserve protection from exploitation and harm, and a third believe animals have the same rights as people in this regard. Most people surveyed were concerned about animal treatment and the cruel modern production systems, with many supporting bans on factory farming. However, their behaviour tells a different story, with as few as 5% of Americans identifying as vegetarians! Although most people said they disapprove of slaughter methods, 41% indicated they would still eat meat from these methods. This disconnect between our beliefs and our behaviours is at the heart of *cognitive dissonance* theory. Rothgerber and Rosenfeld also describe mechanisms we use to avoid dissonance regarding eating animals, including *Avoidance:* actively avoiding information that reveals animal welfare, or locating farms and slaughter facilities away from urban centres. *Wilful Ignorance:* making it easier to buy and eat meat without knowing the source. *Dissociation:* such as the clean, bloodless packaging of meat and the disconnecting of names like hogget or bacon. They also identify a host of indirect strategies, such as moral outrage, blaming third parties like the government, denigrating vegans and vegetarians, or simply convincing themselves they consume less meat than they actually do.

Other Mental Gymnastics

Another theory that may explain why we so easily absolve ourselves of our carnivorous predilections is the *Self-Perception Theory,* coined by Daryl Bem in 1967. [29] Bem suggested that people form their own attitudes and beliefs simply by observing their own behaviour, much like the tail wagging the dog! For example:

> *I enjoy fried chicken, my friends and family enjoy fried chicken, and it tastes good, so it can't be cruel and must be ok to eat!*

Forming attitudes by observing our own behaviour or external cues, such as watching friends and family members, leads to normalising those finger-licking good behaviours. This can also lead to moral disengagement, rationalising our beliefs that 'animals are stupid' or 'they do not suffer much', or 'what difference will one more chicken make?'

Diffusion of responsibility, rationalisation and reframing are also methods we employ to reduce our psychological discomfort. We are 'meant to eat meat', 'everyone does it', and it is 'necessary for survival' or 'oh well it was going to die anyway' are some of the stories we tell ourselves. Paleo, carnivore and keto diets, mass advertising, and ubiquitous and plentiful stock of meat in supermarkets normalise the behaviour of meat eating, making it not only socially acceptable but also expected. Of course, the meat and livestock industries have a vested interest in high meat consumption, the bottom line being much dependent on our waistlines!

Deindividuation is a common way to strip an individual of their unique attributes and qualities. Think prison uniforms and numbers, not names, and identical uniforms in the military. Deindividuation can help us reduce the dissonance between that cute pig we just watched on TikTok and the crispy bacon we had for breakfast. Stripping away the characteristics that make that animal an individual entity with intelligence, behaviours and emotions, and relabelling it simply as a commodity. Renaming animals as beef, yearlings, mutton, veal, broilers and spatchcocks, and animal parts as topside, rump, sirloin, and shanks helps to disconnect us from the mental image of that animal and its demise for our dinner.

Wrapping it all up, the eating of other animals likely drove the evolution of our big brains, leading to cooking, toolmaking, language, culture, animal husbandry practices and the evolution of the industrial farming complex. We utilised science to study animals and selectively breed them for our plates and profit reports in corporate boardrooms. All the while, a combination of mental gymnastics, clever corporate marketing, ultra processing and government policy has convinced us we have to eat meat, not just a small quantity, but vast mountains of animals, which, in the next chapter, I will explain, comes at a price.

The True Cost of Meat

In 2022, on average, 10 cows, 47 pigs, and 2,400 chickens were slaughtered for meat every second. [1]

Read those figures again and let that marinate for a while. In the time it took you to read that sentence, 12,000 chickens were likely placed live upside down hanging from a moving conveyer belt, stunned in electrified water, run through a throat slashing machine to exsanguinate them, dipped into boiling water to remove the feathers, eviscerated by a suction machine and packaged up to be distributed around the country. [2]

Those sobering figures highlight the rather obese elephant in the room. It is not only the meat we consume, or why we consume it, nor the questionable treatment of the animals we raise, but the sheer volume of meat we consume that is disturbing. Over the last 60 years, worldwide per capita meat consumption has doubled from around 20 kg per person to over 40 kg per year. The figures are somewhat distorted by the increased production and consumption in China, which went from below 10 kg in the 1960s to over 60 kg in 2022. However, many countries have remained static or increased only marginally, with Australia maintaining totals of around 100kg of meat per year, and the USA increasing its waistlines from around 90kg to 120kg per year. Interestingly, most European countries appear to have peaked in meat consumption in the 1990s and 2000s and are now trending downward. Despite being the cradle of mankind, Africa has one of the lowest per capita meat consumption rates, at around 17kg per year. However, the safest place to be an animal appears to be India, where consumption has been around 4kg per person for decades. [3]

We currently live in a world of over 8.2 billion, energy-hungry brains, vying for calorific intake in a changing climate and a planet that is replete with domestic animals, mostly ungulates, that are essentially our food. Our giant cave-man brains, hardwired to seek high-energy, high-fat foods, have been hijacked by mega-industrialised, processed, and fast-food companies. The industrial complex has taken over the production of most foods in the developed world, including the raising and slaughtering of animals. Our hardwired, feast-or-famine instincts subconsciously direct our behaviours toward seeking and obtaining these highly rewarding, high-fat, energy- and protein-rich foods, which lead to a multitude of health problems.

Clearly, our big brains give us an advantage over many other mammals, enabling us to think, reason, and plan for the future. We can use our cognitive abilities to modulate desires and delay gratification; otherwise, when shopping, we might arrive at the checkout with a trolley full of chocolate bars. Decades of campaigns promoting healthier eating have pummelled into us the notion that eating a balanced diet is essential to maintain health. There are also a myriad of other mitigating factors that affect diet choices, such as socioeconomic status and access to healthy food. In the current economic climate, fresh fruit and vegetables are often more expensive than processed food or even meat.

With our array of cognitive abilities, we are, to some extent, in full control of the thirsty V8 motor in our head, able to decide what, when and how much we eat. Hunger is driven by hormones like ghrelin, produced in the stomach, which signal the brain to increase food intake. [4] Glucose-sensing cells of the pancreas, liver and gut alert us to falling blood sugar levels, tempting us to reach for the chocolate bar, but our cognitive abilities allow us to make decisions based on learned experiences. A recent health campaign might still be fresh in your mind, reminding you that bananas can deliver a quick energy boost without the excess sugar and weight gain. We gather information on what to put in our mouths from a vast array of sources, including education, culture, the media, and social media influencers. However, one pernicious entity is an expert at bypassing our evolved decision-making mechanisms: big business.

The Meat Machine

On the surface, one might assume that our Palaeolithic emotions and appetites, along with our predilection for animal meat, are solely driven by our own desires and instincts, as well as changes in lifestyle factors, that is, demand-driven.

David Simon, author of *Meatonomics*, argues that this is not the case; rather, demand is heavily influenced by falling prices, government policy, and meat producers. [5] Research has shown that a shift from traditional farming methods in the US to industrial low-cost factory farming has resulted in declining meat prices, a significant factor in consumer behaviour. So-called 'check off' programs, government-authorised initiatives, collect funds (less than one per cent) from producers to fund research and marketing programs. Simon explained that these programs are extremely effective at making people buy more meat than they might normally. Clever marketing campaigns with catchy slogans, such as "Beef." *It's What's for Dinner: Milk. It Does a Body Good: Pork. The Other White Meat* helps convince people it's in their interest to get *some Pork on your Fork*! The last slogan was a successful Australian marketing catchphrase from the Australian Pork organisation. A highly successful Australian marketing campaign in the 1990s was a series of TV adverts for lamb. In the most well-known ad, over the phone, actress Naomi Watts wins a date with Tom Cruise only to decline so she can stay home with her mum for a lamb roast dinner.

It is little wonder that US marketing campaigns are so effective at convincing people to buy and eat more meat, with checkoff programs providing annual budgets of over $ 500 million. The 2023 US milk industry dairy checkoff financial report shows Marketing Plan Program Revenues totalling $262 million, with 46.8% spent on 'Reputation', which it describes as including 'marketing and communications, Fuel Up to Play 60, youth wellness programs and scientific affairs and outreach.' [6] The *Fuel Up* is a youth and school program, focused on "improving the school milk experience and expanding access to school meals".

The U.S. Department of Agriculture (USDA) states on its webpage, "Industry Insight: Checkoff Programs Empower Business," that checkoff programs provide strength in numbers, allowing individual farmers and businesses to increase revenue, market share, and raise awareness. The page describes the checkoff programs as solely funded and operated by industry stakeholders, allowing groups to pool resources for advertising, research, product development and education. *"For every $1 spent in a research and promotion program, the return on investment can range as high as $18."* [7]

Australia has its own pseudo-checkoff program under the guise of Commonwealth-funded transaction levies. Meat and Livestock Australia (MLA) states that they are funded via transaction levies collected by the Australian Government upon the sale per head of sheep, cattle, and goats. The levies go toward supporting marketing, research and development activities, with the Government matching dollar for dollar any money that MLA spends on research and development (R&D). Confusingly, a lot of that levy allocation is spent on marketing, with the $5 levy per head of grassfed cattle divided between $3.66 for marketing and 92 cents for R&D. The marketing allocation for lambs is around 60% and grain-fed cattle around 61%; however, goats are only around 27% of marketing. [8]

A media release in February 2025 exemplifies Australia's commitment to its burgeoning beef industry with a joint statement affirming the Labor Government will invest $12 million in Beef Australia, an event held in Queensland each three years to showcase all aspects of the beef industry. The release further states: *"The investment underscores the Albanese Labor Government's iron clad commitment to Australia's almost $16 billion beef industry, which is our most valuable agricultural export."* [9] [10]

Arguably, farmers, particularly individual and small-scale farmers in Australia and the US, are doing it tough and need all the assistance they can get. It is questionable, though, how much government support should be given to large multinational, multi-billion-dollar companies that dominate the market, flooding the world with more cheap meat that exceeds human nutritional needs. This push by governments to support and fund increasing amounts of meat production also runs counter to the medical community's advice on reducing meat consumption.

Figures from the Meat Institute's 20th annual Power of Meat report indicate that in 2024, meat sales in the US reached a record high of $104.6 billion. [11] According to the report, nearly 98% of American households purchase meat, with consumers buying it more than once a week on average. Additionally, 73% of consumers view meat as a healthy choice overall.

Australians are not far behind in the meat consumption race, eating 2.3% more meat and poultry in 2023-24 compared with the previous financial year, according to the Australian Bureau of Statistics. [12] Australians are eating 13% more chicken than they did six years ago, accounting for 44% of total meat consumption, with less of a rise in beef, lamb and pork consumption at 1.8%. In fact, worldwide, chicken meat production and consumption have surpassed all other animal meat products. Figures from *Our World in Data* show that in 1961 Australians consumed just 4.80 kg of chook per person per year, rising to a staggering 49 kg per year in 2022, a 922 per cent increase! [13] A similar story played out in most regions of the world, with the US consuming 213% more chicken meat, increasing from 16.96 kg to 53.03 kg between 1961 and 2022. Most people born before World War II will recall that chicken was once a luxury, something eaten on special occasions, unlike the plethora of cheap chicken meat we now have on offer.

Global demand for meat seems unrelenting, with production over the last 50 years more than tripling, to an astounding 350 million tonnes per year, according to Hannah Ritchie and colleagues at Our World in Data. Asia currently holds the title of the world's largest producer of animal meat, overtaking Europe and America, with poultry production increasing exponentially from 9 million tonnes in 1961 to a feather-ruffling 144 million tonnes in 2023.

There is a hidden cost to all this excess, one that is shouldered by the public, claims David Robinson Simon, with *meatonomics* shifting the costs of production onto taxpayers and consumers. [5] According to Simon, meat products may be cheap at the cash register, but downstream, the toll exacted on health systems, home devaluations caused by proximity to factory farms, and environmental effects impose externalised costs of around $414 billion on the US economy in 2012.

The Health Costs

There are, however, some distinct benefits to eating meat, which is an important source of protein, iron, B vitamins, zinc, retinol, and selenium, as explained by Alison McAfee and colleagues. [14] Meat also contains beneficial Long-Chain Omega-3 Polyunsaturated Fatty Acids such as: *eicosapentaenoic acid* (EPA) and *docosahexaenoic acid* (DHA), found in meat and particularly oily fish and known for its beneficial effects in heart, brain and eye health: *docosapentaenoic acid* (DPA) found in red meat, and is suggested to have beneficial effects on heart health: and *conjugated linoleic acid* or

CLA, primarily found in ruminants, has shown potential in reducing cancer risk in animal studies, with some evidence it also positively influences immune function in humans.

The flip side of course, is that in 2015, the International Agency for Research on Cancer announced that after reviewing the scientific literature using a group of 22 experts from 10 countries, red meat consumption was *"probably carcinogenic to humans"* (Group 2A), based on limited evidence, but *"strong mechanistic evidence supporting a carcinogenic effect."* [15] Processed meat received a much worse rap, being *"classified as carcinogenic to humans (Group 1), based on sufficient evidence in humans that the consumption of processed meat causes colorectal cancer."* According to the experts, for each 50 grams of meat consumed each day, the risk of colorectal cancer increases by 18%. The report states that red meat has nutritional value; however, it recommends limiting meat intake.

This is in stark contrast to how Western governments seem to operate, funding and assisting livestock growers, factory farms and abattoir operators to expand production and increase supply into a society already bursting at the seams with meat and dairy products.

Meat and dairy products are becoming increasingly cheaper, driven in part by government subsidies and partly by more efficient factory farms, which externalise the costs to others. [5] Significant increases in meat consumption in the US over the last century have also been accompanied by a substantial rise in obesity, with per capita meat consumption increasing from 91kg per person per year in 1961 to 121kg in 2022 and poultry consumption more than tripling. [3]

Although meat consumption is not a single contributing factor to obesity, indeed *ketogenic diets* that consume mostly protein and low carbs can induce rapid weight loss, it is the combination of ultra-processed meat and dairy products, combined with high carbohydrate ingredients, that has contributed significantly to worldwide obesity. Adult obesity rates in the US have more than doubled from 18.6% in 1990 to 42% in 2022, with Australia not far behind at 32%, Argentina at 35.4% and, surprisingly, Egypt at 44.3% as of 2022. [16] In fact, obesity rates worldwide have more than doubled since 1990 and quadrupled in adolescents, according to the World Health Organization. Unbelievably, undernutrition and obesity are found to co-exist within the same country, even the same households! Low- and middle-income countries are most susceptible to inadequate diets, with low-cost, energy-dense foods high in sugar and fat, along with decreased levels of physical activity, being the main culprits. The double whammy that accompanies this double shit sandwich is, of course, the associated rise in non-communicable diseases such as cardiovascular disease and type 2 diabetes.

The Environmental Cost

The impact on the environment that comes from feeding 8 billion humans is truly staggering. Whilst livestock farming contributes 30% of dietary protein and 18% of calories, it takes up 75% of agricultural land, emits 14-17% of human-induced GHG emissions, utilises more antibiotics than does human medicine and uses 70% of the world's freshwater, accounting for 78% of freshwater pollution. [17] [18] No doubt, different farming methods would account for varying amounts of water usage and GHG emissions, but results from studies reveal some surprising and conflicting findings.

Organic meat is often more expensive, priced at a premium compared to non-organic meat, due to its higher production costs and limited demand. Organic, grass-fed beef is said to taste better, and undoubtedly, pasture-raised cows have a better life than their corralled feedlot cousins. But one of the hidden trade-offs comes in cow farts! David Robinson Simon explained that grazing cows rely much more on intestinal bacteria to break down and digest grass, making them much more flatulent than grain-fed cows. [5] This results in organic cattle emitting four times the amount of methane, a potent GHG, than do grain-fed cows. Grass-fed cows also require a larger amount of land, leading to a greater 'hoofprint.' [19]

Grazed and Confused? Was a creatively titled report released by the Food Climate Research Network (FCRN) of Oxford University in 2017. [20] The authors aim to provide clarity on the often extremely polarised debate between the doomsayers, who believe ruminants to be the cause of all our environmental woes, and the idealists, who argue that grass-fed cattle are the solution. There are no apparent, clear-cut solutions. Ruminants such as cows require more land per unit of edible food output than pigs, but pigs consume large amounts of grain and soy, which also require arable land to grow. Grazing on pastures also depletes nitrogen, necessitating the addition of chemical fertilisers or nitrogen-fixing legumes, both of which create their own sets of problems. The authors state that the current and future challenges are to "figure out the environmentally 'least bad' way of using land and other resources to nourish ourselves and meet our other developmental goals." Current livestock systems create enormous environmental damage, release vast amounts of GHG, and have literally transformed the face of this earth." The report concludes that grazing livestock has a limited role in a sustainable food system. Regardless of perspective, any growth in the industry becomes harder by the day to tackle environmental and climate challenges.

Challenges to sustainable meat production are by no means limited to bovines. In the Chapter on pigs, I mentioned the trend to vertical farms in China, which minimise land use and maximise production, but is this truly the answer? Harriet Bartlett of the University of Cambridge and colleagues studied a sample of 44 UK and 20 Brazilian pig growers, classifying them as either none, Red Tractor (a quality assurance scheme), RSPCA, Free Range, Woodland and Organic. [17] Examining four critical external factors, they found that the land use cost, which is the total area of land required over 1 year to produce 1 kg of pork, was almost five times higher for organic pigs than for RSPCA-certified pigs and more than double that of free-range pigs, with a similar finding for GHG emissions. Pigs in free-range, Woodland Organic environments had the best quality of life and lower use of antibiotics, whereas pigs in Brazil had lower overall welfare levels. There is no silver bullet or magic solution; reducing land and GHG emissions leads to a decline in pig welfare, and vice versa. One can only imagine the welfare of a pig born into a 26-story high-rise hog farm in Ezhou, China, as described in the Pigs chapter, spending its entire life confined indoors in a multi-storey building.

The Eat Less Meat Paradox

It would seem logical that the simplest solution to the growing waistlines of populations and the environmental effects of factory farming would simply be to eat less meat! Or so I thought; it turns out to be much more complicated and nuanced.

There is a growing movement toward 'flexitarianism' or the semi-vegetarian diet (SVD), a primarily vegetarian diet that also sometimes includes meat and fish. This is likely a more socially acceptable term, as vegans often cop a lot of flak. Just for example: *Why did the vegan cross the road? To tell you they are vegan,* and: *Why did the vegan become a cyclist? Because he wasn't hated enough already.* As flexitarianism is a relatively new phenomenon, there are few studies on the effects of an SVD diet. Emma Derbyshire of Nutritional Insight Ltd found evidence that SVD diets are associated with lower bodyweight, reduced blood pressure, lower rates of cancer and less diabetes risk. [21] The literature review of 25 studies shows some promising results, but future randomised controlled trials are needed to give a more accurate view of the effects of flexitarianism.

One thing we do currently know about flexitarianism is roughly how many people are adopting that behaviour. Edouard Mathieu and Hannah Ritchie explain that there is a growing interest in the ethical, environmental and health implications of our diets. [22] A 2025 UK poll asked six questions about dietary preferences: meat-eater, flexitarian, pescetarian, vegetarian, vegan, or none of these. 72% identified as meat eaters, 13% as flexitarians, 6% as vegetarians and only 3% as vegans. The results were similar to a 2018 US poll, which revealed that only 5% of Americans identified as vegetarian and 2% as vegan. Comparable results were found across 28 countries, with India being the exception, where one in five people is vegetarian.

Common sense would dictate that adopting a more flexitarian diet would at least decrease the number of animals being farmed and killed for meat, thereby improving animal welfare, the environment, and reducing greenhouse gas emissions (GHG). To produce one tonne of beef, 499 tonnes of GHG emissions are produced, compared to only 57 tonnes of GHG to produce a tonne of chicken meat. Easy solution: order a chicken burger rather than a beef burger, right? Yes, but there is a massive trade-off, as Hannah Ritchie explained. What might be good for the planet often conflicts with what's good for the animal. An average chicken yields around 1.7kg of meat, whereas a cow produces around 360kg of meat. To obtain the same amount of meat, you would need to kill around 200 chickens. Most cows are raised in either feedlots, pasture-fed, or in outback Australia, free-ranging, whereas chickens have a rather shit life. Most chickens around the world are factory farmed, packed in small cages or spaces to minimise energy expenditure and maximise growth. Chickens have been selectively bred to grow super-fast; in the 1950s, they reached around 900 grams in 56 days, compared to now reaching 4200 grams at the same time.

Single-trait breeding focuses on improving a particular trait, for instance, increasing the size of breast meat on a hen. The flip side of this is a loss of genetic diversity and unintended deletions of certain traits. In her book *Animals in Translation*, Temple Grandin explained that in the early days of selectively breeding bigger chooks, an unintended consequence was a high incidence of *flip-over disease,* so-called because the poor chooks tended to have weaker legs and hearts, flipping over when they dropped dead from cardiac failure! [23] Single-trait breeding for larger breasts on the chooks also led to a different type of flip-over. The resulting birds were so top-heavy that their legs could barely support them, and the chickens often became lame. They were also likely in pain, with studies showing the birds preferred food laced with painkillers! Not wanting lame, in pain and deformed chooks with gammy drumsticks, breeders concentrated on breeding chooks with good strength and 'liveability'.

During the 1990s, some strange effects of trait breeding began to emerge. Increasing numbers of broiler breeding males were being reported as being overly aggressive to hens. [24] Dubbed 'rooster rapists' by some, the behaviour was highly unusual, as male chooks of most species, including aggressive fighting strains, almost never show aggression to hens. The females were being harassed, injured and even killed by the roosters, which began in one breeding strain but soon spread to others. All other things considered, researchers concluded that trait selection for breast size or fertility likely led to a genetic defect affecting rooster courtship behaviour! Deficiencies in the rooster courtship dance meant the hens were confused and tried to avoid the rooster's romantic advances, often hiding in nest boxes or sheltering on perches. The jilted roosters often took out their sexual frustrations on the poor hens, pecking and slashing them with their claws. [24] [25]

Examples like this highlight the fact that increases in production and efficiency often come at the expense of animal welfare and suffering. Behind the huge increases in meat production lies a global system of 'industrialised' factory farming, driven by big business and supported, in part, by government funding. Advertising budgets that rival those of Hollywood movies create adverts and catchy slogans to encourage us to eat ever-increasing amounts of meat. Vegans on average represent only around 3% of the global population, and vegetarians around 5%, varying across countries, and perhaps have the least impact on the environment compared with meat eaters. Evidence shows meat production is inextricably linked to environmental degradation, habitat and species losses, genetic modification of animals beyond anything they once resembled and welfare issues that defy comprehension. Swapping from beef to chicken saves one beast and reduces environmental impact, but 200 chickens, living in horrid conditions, must die to take their place. Logic would dictate that there remains only one answer: eat less meat!

Just Eat Less Meat!

It sounds easy: just eat less meat! But this can be problematic if you enjoy meat and live in a society bursting at the seams with cheap meat products. Slick marketing tactics, funded by eyewatering budgets and government funding, encourage greater meat production and disincentivise consumers from reducing their meat consumption. Consumer behaviour change in this current climate would likely face significant resistance from meat producers and their government lobbyists.

But would eating less meat truly have any impact, or have we passed the point of no return? Bruce Kidd and colleagues of the University of Auckland used modelling to determine the costs and benefits of a vegan, vegetarian, healthy and current diet on GHG emissions. [26] Comparing average GHG emissions, measured as kg/ CO_2 over an estimated 20-year period, the 'current' diet, that is, what people were eating in Aotearoa, NZ at the time, indicated the worst emissions (597), due to a high consumption of meat and processed foods. Whereas flexitarian (263) and vegan diets (203) were associated with the lowest emissions. The flip side is that the vegan diet was the most expensive of the diets, costing around NZD\$789 per fortnight, compared to NZD\$584 for the current diet, although much of that cost was associated with the expense of dairy alternatives.

A large study by Peter Scarborough of the University of Oxford and colleagues examined data from 55,504 fish and meat-eaters, vegans, and vegetarians, covering more than 38,000 farms in 119 countries. [18] Standardising the number of calories to a similar level (2,000 kcal), they found strong relationships between environmental impacts, GHG emissions, water and land use, nutrient spillover into waterways, and biodiversity, as well as the consumption of meat. Vegans, vegetarians, and low-meat eaters all showed significantly lower levels of all the above measures. For example, comparing GWP20 CO_2e, which is basically the *Global Warming Potential over 20 years* expressed in terms of carbon dioxide equivalents (CO_2e); vegans averaged 441% less GHG compared with high meat eaters. Land use for high meat eaters was 283% greater than a vegan diet, water use was 117% less, nutrient pollution was 281% less, and biodiversity impact was 229% less for a vegan diet. These are significant differences comparing vegan and high meat-eating, surely even a reduction in each of us eating meat will lead to a positive benefit to the land, the environment and the animals.

Inevitably, there have been strong pushbacks from livestock industries and some sections of the scientific community against the notion of reducing meat production or its environmental effects. TABLE, a collaborative organisation of partner universities that includes The University of Oxford, The Swedish University of Agricultural Sciences (SLU), and Wageningen University & Research, describes itself as working with *"food system stakeholders to explore the future of food."* Irina Herzon describes the fallout from a published article titled "The Dublin Declaration of Scientists on the Societal Role of Livestock," which was the product of an International Summit on the Societal Role of Meat in Dublin, Ireland, in 2022, hosted by the Irish state agency for agriculture. [27] The declaration underscores the vital role of livestock in health, nutrition, sustainability, and socio-economic development and advocates for scientific evidence-based solutions to global challenges, while promoting sustainable livestock systems. [28] Herzon is highly critical of the report, stating that of the 36 co-authors, virtually all are experts in meat sciences and similar disciplines, with experts in other fields, such as biology or environmental sciences, decidedly absent. [27] Most of the authors and half of the 1,223 signatories come from countries with large livestock industries and high meat consumption, stacking the deck much in favour of the meat industry. TABLE goes on to list the multitude of claims that are misleading or inaccurate, making for some interesting reading, too much to mention here; I will leave that up to you.

It has been quite a challenge to find information in this space that is not unduly influenced by the meat industry. Many of the journal articles I have encountered are either directly or indirectly supported by funding bodies from the meat industry. In fact, a good proportion of the research on animal cognition and behaviour is also sponsored by food industry bodies, a bias that cannot be ignored.

Whilst writing this last chapter, an article dropped on ABC News by reporter Gareth Hutchens. Former Australian Treasury Secretary Ken Henry blasted the media, arguing that it must hold Australia's political system to account for failing to ensure a better future for younger Australians. [29] Henry highlights issues such as environmental degradation, biodiversity loss, and industries contributing to the destruction of the natural world, adding, *"I am angry at our failures. But we should all be angry at our collective failure to design economic structures, including environmental regulations, that underpin confidence in a better future for our children and grandchildren"* Henry refers to the important role played by the 'Fourth Estate', a colloquial name for the news media, the first three estates being the parliament, the government, and the courts. The fourth estate should monitor the other three to ensure accountability. However, with trust in mainstream media at an all-time low, people are increasingly turning to the Fifth Estate. The Fifth Estate, of course, is the internet, the blogosphere, influencers, podcasters, and literally anyone online who has an opinion.

Although Ken Henry did not mention animals, meat, or farming, he did succinctly describe our failures to address environmental degradation, climate change, and the legacy that will be left for future generations, all notions tied to livestock practices, the meat industry, and our carnivorous addictions, that fill our bellies at the cost of animal welfare.

Be Kind

At the start of writing this book, I made a conscious decision not to go down the road of animal ethics, as that is outside my field of psychology and would probably constitute a whole other book! However, in light of what I have learned researching journal articles and books, I believe that ethics and animal welfare are such an important part of the animals we consider food, that it warrants attention.

Throughout the book, I have highlighted published studies that repeatedly show that sheep, goats, chickens, cows and pigs all display sentience, emotions, social cognition, bonding, empathy, play, cooperation, and problem-solving abilities. Yet despite the evidence, these animals are still often simply categorised as *meat* and dismembered, cleaned, packaged in plastic film, made into sausages, hamburgers, hot dogs and pies, pizzas and tacos. We are shielded from the live product, sequestered away on large factory farms, intensive piggeries, high-rise hog mansions and poultry grow-out houses. Trucked to abattoirs often hundreds of miles from cities, animals are killed, broken down, packaged and distributed around the country. The clean, hermetically sealed packages on the supermarket shelf offer little indication of the horrors that animals likely endured.

Sure, the eventual destination for most livestock is the dinner plate; however, my argument is that the sheer amount of animals bred for that fate, their negative impact on the environment, and the treatment of those animals, along with their subjective experience, are all significant concerns. As Peter Singer describes it, "lives well lived."

When Singer first published *Animal Liberation Now* in 1975, animal rights movements did not exist, and welfare concerns mainly were centred around cruelty to dogs and cats. [2] As the book gained popularity, animal activists started leaving copies behind after rescuing animals from labs or filming cruel animal practices and releasing the videos. This influenced the growth of the animal movement, applying pressure to factory farming practices and experimental studies to help reduce animal suffering. In the Introduction of Singer's book, Yuval Noah Harari sums things up beautifully, stating that needs shaped by evolutionary selection pressures countless generations ago are still felt subjectively by animals, despite no longer being necessary for an animal's survival or reproductive fitness. [2] In other words, even though pigs no longer resemble their wild boar relatives and live in artificial man-made structures, their evolved instincts, desires, motivations and reward systems are still the same, stymied, stifled and unfulfilled. When animals cannot carry out normal patterns of instinctual behaviour, it adversely affects those animals, leading to an array of physiological and psychological problems.

I spoke with Rimini Quinn, a Queensland-based animal behaviour veterinarian, who described how many animals develop stress responses to not only aversive stimuli, such as crowded poultry farms or packed pig breeding facilities, but also to a lack of stimuli, such as barren captive environments. [30] When an animal's natural repertoire of behaviours cannot be carried out to completion, the animal can become chronically distressed. Most animal behaviours, and indeed also our own, are highly evolved mechanisms that increase evolutionary fitness. For example, a pig's searching and rooting behaviour using its snout to dig and explore, or a chicken's scratching and pecking behaviour. When these instinctual patterns cannot be performed, animals often develop strange or destructive behaviours to fill the void and reduce psychological stress.

Slatted flooring in piggeries that allows urine and faeces to fall through deprives pigs of rooting and nest-building behaviours. Overcrowded poultry broiler farms are often stocked with 25 chickens per square metre, resulting in toxic levels of ammonia buildup and dropping laden floor litter, which offers no room or incentive for scratching and pecking behaviour. [2] Piglets attempting to suckle from each other, fighting behaviour, tail biting, pecking in chickens, and increased aggression are all tell-tale signs that those animals are stressed and deprived of natural stimuli.

Stereotypic behaviour can also be a sign of poor animal welfare. Repetitive and unvarying, functionless behaviours like head shaking or feather pecking in chickens, pacing, sham-chewing or bar-biting in pigs, tail chasing in dogs, and windsucking on stable edges or poles by horses are examples. These behaviours are not always reliable indicators of poor welfare, explained Mason and Latham of Oxford University. [31] Some animals in stressful environments may not show low or no stereotypies but still suffer poorly in terms of welfare. Some animals use stereotypies as self-soothing behaviours, falling into the *won't stop* category, whereas others fall into the *can't stop* category, performing these functions unconsciously due to suboptimal environmental conditions. In either case, they estimate 68% of environments that cause stereotypical animal behaviour also likely contribute to poor animal welfare.

Animal welfare concerns came to the fore in the 1960s, in reaction to the UK Government's Brambell Report into animal welfare under intensive livestock husbandry systems. [32] In response, the Farm Animal Welfare Committee proposed the 1979 *Five Freedoms model*:
1. Freedom from thirst, hunger, and malnutrition.
2. Freedom from discomfort.
3. Freedom from pain, injury, and disease.
4. Freedom to express normal behaviour.
5. Freedom from fear and distress.

Early versions of the model specifically focused on assessing and grading the impacts of research, teaching and testing (RTT) on animals. Later revisions were renamed the *Five Domains model* and saw the inclusion of affective states (emotions), the importance of pleasurable experiences for animals, and the embodiment of the concept of "a life worth living." The latest (2020) update of the Five Domains is simplified to nutrition, environment, health, behaviour and mental domains. The model also includes positive and negative effects of human interactions and methods to grade those interactions. For example, scenarios of human-animal interactions that cause positive or negative emotions, physical environmental conditions, nutritional and health conditions and behavioural interactions and their associated effects on animals. Also added is the aspect of 'agency', conscious behavioural choices made by those creatures. [33]

The use of the model has also spread to other domains, including Australia, New Zealand, and Europe, where it is used to assess a variety of livestock, companion, wildlife, and research animals. However, it is far from a one-size-fits-all approach, with little uptake in the Americas, Asia, and Africa. The Cambridge opinion paper *Rethinking the utility of the Five Domains model* describes the strengths and weaknesses of the Five Domains, concluding that it sees great value in the model "as a way of thinking about animal welfare." However, the authors contend that as an assessment tool, it is not fit-for-purpose, lacking repeatability, transparency, and the possibility of being open to misuse. [32]

Nonetheless, there is evidence that after years of advocacy and animal rights campaigns, the tide has begun to turn. Around the time of writing this chapter, Swedish animal welfare group Project 1882 announced that Sweden has gone completely caged egg-free. [34] What sets this apart from other countries is that this was achieved without a legal ban. Through dialogue with businesses, political advocacy, public education campaigns, and international efforts, the group convinced egg producers, policymakers, and the public that caged hens are a bad idea. Although this did not happen overnight, the process of explaining this began around 50 years ago.

A Cagey Practice

The *Open Wing Alliance*, a self-described global coalition of organisations working to end factory farmed animal abuse, claim that cage-free is becoming the global norm. [35] According to their 2024 Fulfilment Report, "as of April 2023, an overwhelming 89% of cage-free egg commitments with deadlines of 2022 or earlier were fulfilled." Despite this progress, they state that four billion chickens are still confined to laying cages, affecting hens' physical and mental health. The report lists some of the major companies that fulfilled their commitments in 2023, including Hershey (Global), Woolworths (South Africa), McDonald's (US), TGI Fridays (US), and The Cheesecake Factory (US). [35]

Moving at its usual glacial speed, the Australian Government has committed to phasing out caged egg farming practices by 2036, according to ABC News. [36] Thankfully, the supermarket giants, Coles, Woolworths and Aldi are more committed, stating they will phase out caged eggs later in 2025. Not everyone shares this positive sentiment, with the Victorian Farmers Federation (VFF) highlighting that egg shortages are an ongoing concern with consumers, due to bird flu outbreaks the previous year. The federation's president explained eggs are an inexpensive, high-value protein way to feed a family, and "People buy eggs because of those reasons, "not always for animal welfare reasons." [36] A third-generation poultry auctioneer expressed concern that free-range farms will lead to greater incidences of bird flu, stating that chickens were "designed" to be caged. Thankfully, not everyone shares these sentiments, as evidenced by the shift in public opinion from a preference for cheap caged eggs to slightly more expensive free-range varieties.

The egg industry in the US appears to be moving forward at a faster rate than its Australian counterparts, with animal rights group The Humane League reporting in July 2025 that 45.7% of all egg-laying hens in the US are now cage-free. [37] The number of caged chooks had dropped to 154.9 million, the lowest on record. The argument that disease rates are higher for free-range birds was also debunked, with figures revealing both caged and free-range chooks were equally affected by avian flu.

Frankenchickens

So named because of the grossly distorted anatomy of broiler hens, Frankenchickens have been selectively bred to grow to reach slaughter size in the shortest time possible, reaching 2.2kg in around 35 days. The RSPCA report *Eat.Sit.Suffer.Repeat,* explains that just three broiler breeding companies dominate the global supply of broiler or *meat* chickens. [38] The birds are genetically selected based on traits with the highest economic value, such as growth rates, breast meat size, and feed conversion rates, which essentially measure how efficiently the chicken converts food into meat. The trade-off is that compared with slower-growing breeds, the modified chooks have a much higher mortality rate, much poorer health, poor leg, hock, and plumage health, and spend much less time, basically being a chicken. Hence the title, many of the birds are incapable of walking and moving around, much less scratching or dustbathing. They basically eat, sit, suffer, rinse and repeat, hardly a life worth living.

In 2024, the culmination of a David versus Goliath battle that spanned four years saw the UK Court of Appeals deliver potentially radical changes to animal welfare laws. According to The Humane League, a global nonprofit animal welfare organisation, *"the impact of this judgment on chickens could be seismic."* [39] The Humane League UK originally challenged the government over the extensive use of the genetically modified fast-growing chooks in the UK, which the court ultimately dismissed. The win they claim came in the form of the clarification of a key piece of regulatory legislation, explaining that farm animals that are purposefully bred to suffer are likely already unlawful under the act. The group claim the ruling potentially opens the door to criminal prosecutions directed toward farmers who grow the genetically modified fast-growing chooks.

It remains to be seen if this has an impact downstream, but it caught the ire of one UK politician. Green MP Adrian Ramsay raised the treatment of the *Frankenchicken* broiler hens in the UK parliament in June 2025 in a debate on animal welfare. Ramsay described how the government should set procurement targets to cut meat from industrial systems, promote plant-rich diets, and reward farmers working with nature. In his opening statements, Ramsay says of the treatment of animals and recent undercover footage revealing mistreatment:

> *However, we must be clear: these are sadly not isolated incidents, but a symptom of policy and enforcement failings in our food and farming systems. The way we treat farmed animals is not only the biggest animal protection issue we face here in the UK, but deeply entwined with the climate crisis, nature loss and the viability of our food systems. It speaks to a moral failing, a disconnection from the suffering hidden behind supermarket shelves. Ultimately, we need a food system that recognises the need to reduce demand, raise legal baselines and support better farming systems.* [40]

A Shameful Export

Back in Australia, fortunately, public opinion has also shifted on the heinous practice of live sheep exports. The country I call home has the unenviable reputation as the world's largest exporter of livestock. We export around 900,000 cattle and 1.8 million sheep to nearly 20 countries around the world, on enormous, crowded, repurposed export ships. Kuwait and Qatar are our largest markets for sheep, driven by demand for fresh meat, high processing costs in Australia, and religious and cultural reasons. [41] Once the animals land, they are no longer subject to Australian animal welfare laws, often with disturbing results.

In 2011, ABC Australia TV show Four Corners aired 'A Bloody Business'. An industry and government report published in January of that year painted a rosy picture of livestock slaughter conditions in Indonesia. At the time, Australia sent around half a million cattle each year to Indonesia, a trade valued at more than $300 million, with six million cattle sent in the last two decades. Unconvinced, activists infiltrated the abattoirs and filmed slaughter practices so appalling that they led to the Australian Government suspending live exports to Indonesia. [42] The footage revealed horrifying slaughter practices and inadequate training, animals repeatedly smashing their heads against the concrete floor, their throats slashed clumsily, taking many minutes to die whilst tied in place by ropes. The workers also kicked, hit, gouged the eyes of the cows and broke their tails. All of this in spite of industry and Australian Government involvement and supposed training of the workers.

The record on animal welfare for live sheep exports is also embarrassingly poor. According to the RSPCA, over the last forty years, there have been a string of major disasters around exporting animals, many involving Saudi Arabia. [43] In 1983, a ventilation breakdown onboard the *Mukairish Althaleth* caused the death of 70 sheep each day. Approximately 30,000 sheep died from heat stroke and dehydration after arriving in war-torn Kuwait, likely due to poor infrastructure and feedlot inadequacies. Boasting of its abilities to provide high standards of animal welfare, the *MV Becrux,* on its maiden voyage in 2002, lost 1,400 sheep and 880 cattle to heat stress after the vessel encountered high temperatures and humidity in the Arabian Gulf. However, the icing on the cake was the cruise from hell of the *MV Cormo Express,* which in 2003 was turned away by Saudi Arabia, allegedly on the grounds of disease fears. No other country would take the stricken ship and its alleged cursed cargo. It was eight weeks before Eritrea agreed to take the sheep, after which time, 6000 of them had died. At that point, Australia suspended all live exports to the Saudis until 2005. The exports and the animal attrition continued unabated until finally, in July 2024, Australia's Senate passed the *Export Control Amendment Bill 2024* into legislation, putting a well-deserved end to the live sheep exports by sea in 2028. [43]

There is a wealth of easily accessible evidence online that leaves no doubt about the cruelty of animal factory farming. However, there is also growing evidence that the tide is turning on the antiquated view that animals are mere soulless non-feeling objects or just meat. The early work of the animal rights movements of the 60s and 70s is now paying dividends, with more young people joining those movements to champion the cause of animal welfare. Pushbacks from government-assisted mega meat corporations have been fierce. Still, public opinion and the consumer's wallet ultimately can sway these monolithic institutions to change their methods, or they themselves go extinct.

You might have noticed I have failed to mention cruelty in animal testing, but that heinous subject would consume another whole chapter. According to Peter Singer, big advances in regulating the use of animals for science and the cosmetic industry have taken place, beginning in the 1980s and gathering pace in the 1990s. [2] These wins were achieved through large institutions like the OECD and the US Environmental Protection Agency (EPA). In 2013, the European Union announced a blanket ban on the sale of animal-tested cosmetics, regardless of which country they were tested in. In 2019, the EPA announced that it would reduce and then cease all testing involving mammals by 2035. These wins are often punctuated with other losses, but the tide has most definitely turned against the cruel practices involved in animal testing.

I will conclude with the sage-like words of Charles Darwin from *The Descent of Man* (1871), where he succinctly describes the last stage of moral evolution, sympathy for non-human animals.

This virtue, one of the noblest with which man is endowed, seems to arise incidentally from our sympathies becoming more tender and more widely diffused, until they are extended to all sentient beings. As soon as this virtue is honoured and practised by some few men, it spreads through instruction and example to the young and eventually becomes incorporated in public opinion. [44]

Animals are wonderful. Stop, look, notice, and observe. When you take time and really observe an animal, think back to the previous chapters describing their rich emotional lives, human-like cognitive abilities and amazing sensory capabilities. Imagine yourself as that animal. What would make you happy? As a chook, contentment may lie in busily scratching through the soil looking for bugs. A goat might find happiness lying in the warm sunshine, chewing its cud. A cow's sense of satisfaction and pleasure might simply be in the company of its besties, happily grooming each other with a leathery tongue. The lives of animals we call food do not need to be miserable and bleak, and our plates do not always need to be filled with their flesh; the planet, though blessed with their presence, would fare much better with less livestock.

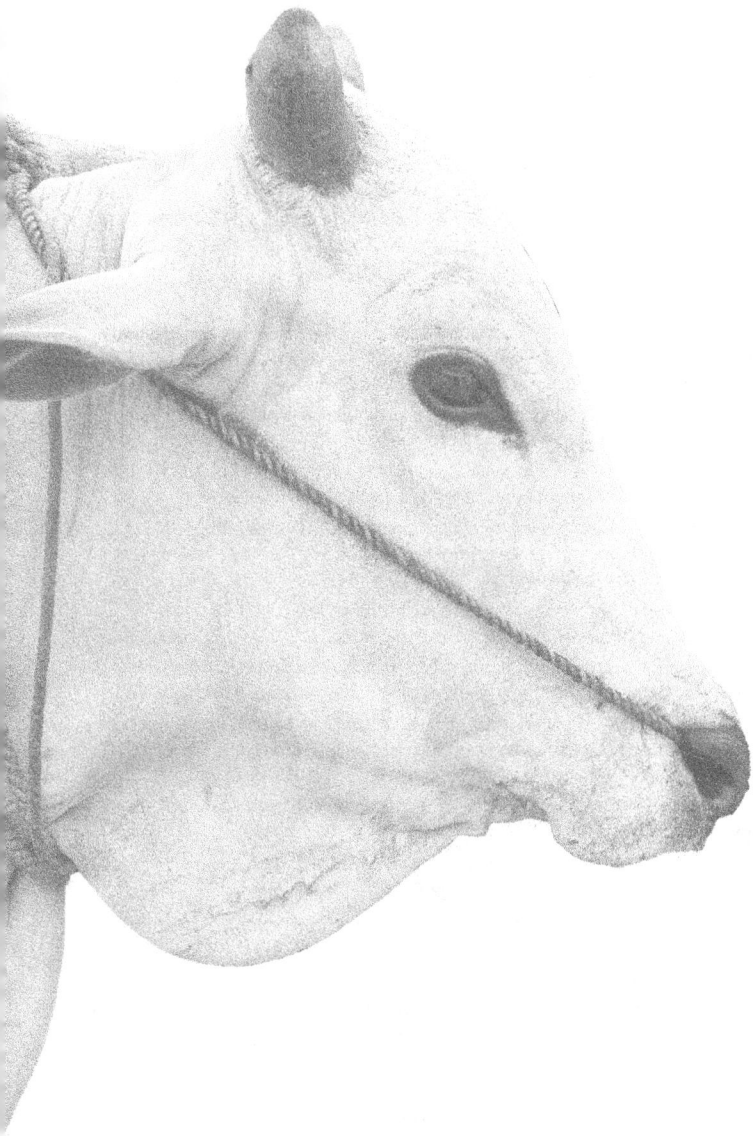

References

Introduction

1. Our World in Data. Meat Consumption. [Internet]. 2024. Available from: ourworldindata.org/grapher/daily-meat-consumption-per-person

2. ABC. Emu farming is making a comeback amid renewed interest in health properties of their oil. [Internet]. 2018 [cited 2025 February 5]. Available from: www.abc.net.au/news/2018-03-24/emu-farming-takes-off-in-australia/9564246

3. Animals Australia. Understanding the issues: kangaroo shooting. [Internet]. 2024. Available from: animalsaustralia.org/our-work/shooting-and-hunting/kangaroo-shooting/

4. Victorian Government. Department of Jobs, Skills, Industry and Regions. [Internet]. 2024. Available from: djsir.vic.gov.au/game-hunting/kangaroo-harvesting

5. Albizuri S, Nadal J, Martín P, Gibaja JF, Cólliga AM, Esteve X, et al. Dogs in funerary contexts during the Middle Neolithic in the northeastern Iberian Peninsula (5th–early 4th millennium BCE). Journal of Archaeological Science: Reports. 2019; 24: p. 198–207.

6. Te Velde H. A Few Remarks Upon the Religious Significance of Animals in Ancient Egypt. Numen. 1980; 27(1): p. 76–82.

7. Francis Crick Memorial Conference. Francis Crick Memorial Conference. [Internet]. ND. Available from: https://fcmconference.org/img/CambridgeDeclarationOnConsciousness.pdf

8. Career Harvest. New figures reveal Aussies' shocking disconnect with life's essentials – NFF. [Internet]. 2017. Available from: https://www.careerharvest.com.au/new-figures-reveal-aussies-shocking-disconnect-with-lifes-essent

9. Smeds P, Jeronen E, Kurppa S. Farm education and the effect of a farm visit on children's conception of agriculture. European Journal of Educational Research. 2015; 4(1): p. 1-13.

10. Simon DR. Meatonomics: how the rigged economics of meat and dairy make you consume too much-and how to eat better, live longer, and spend smarter San Francisco: Conari Press; 2013.

11. Lawton A, & Morrison N. The loss of peri-urban agricultural land and the state-local tensions in managing its demise: The case of Greater Western Sydney, Australia. Land Use Policy. 2022; 120: p. Article 106265.

12. Compitus K, Bierbower SM. Cow cuddling: Cognitive considerations in bovine-assisted therapy. Human-Animal Interactions. 2024.

13. Davies J. The Birth of the Anthropocene: University of California Press; 2016.

14. Harari YN. Homo Deus: Penguin Random House, UK; 2015.

15. Ritchie H, Roser M. Our World in Data. [Internet]. 2024. Available from: https://ourworldindata.org/wild-mammals-birds-biomass

16. Why isn't the world covered in poop? - Eleanor Slade and Paul Manning. [Internet]. [cited 2024 December 26]. Available from: https://ed.ted.com/lessons/why-isn-t-the-world-covered-in-poop-eleanor-slade-and-paul-manning

17. Alexander P, Brown C, Arneth A, Finnigan J, Rounsevell MDA. Human appropriation of land for food: The role of diet. Global Environmental Change. 2016; 4: p. 88–98.

18. Sutton P, Walshe K. Farmers or hunter-gatherers? the dark emu debate: Melbourne University Publishing; 2021.

19. Thompson BA. Concern for Animals among Hunter-Gatherers. Cross-Cultural Research. 2024.

20. Meat Institute. Industry at a Glance. [Internet]. [cited 2024 November 30]. Available from: meatinstitute.org/Industry_at_a_Glance

Us and Them

1. KJV. GC1. kingjamesbibleonline. [Internet]. 2024. Available from: www.kingjamesbibleonline.org/Genesis-Chapter-1/

2. Ahbel-Rappe S. Socrates: a guide for the perplexed (1st ed.): Continuum; 2009.

3. Smith JA, Barnes. On the Soul. In Aristotle. Complete Works of Aristotle, Volume 1.: Princeton University Press.; 2019. p. 641–692.

4. Sorabji R. Soul and self in ancient philosophy. In From Soul to Self.: Routledge; 2012. p. 8-32.

5. Pellegrin P, Preus A. Animals in the World : Five Essays on Aristotle's Biology. (1st ed.): State University of New York Press; 2023.

6. Lovejoy AO. The great chain of being : a study of the history of an idea : the William James lectures delivered at Harvard University, 1933 : Harvard University Press; 1964.

7. Callahan D. Systema Naturae (10th edition). In Linnaeus C. A History of Birdwatching in 100 Objects.: Bloomsbury Publishing; 2014.

8. Descartes R, Maclean I. A discourse on the method of correctly conducting one's reason and seeking truth in the sciences: Oxford University Press.; 2006.

9. Descartes R. The philosophical works of Descartes (Vol. 1, E. S., Trans.). In Haldane ES, Ross GRT..: London: Cambridge University Press.; 1975. p. 16.

10. Bentham J. An Introduction to the principles of morals and legislation.: Batoche Books; 2000.

11. Bedau HA. Anarchical Fallacies: Bentham's Attack on Human Rights. Human Rights Quarterly. 2000; 22(1): p. 261–279.

12. Kniess J. Bentham on animal welfare. British Journal for the History of Philosophy. 2019; 27(3): p. 556–572.

13. Marmoy CFA. The 'auto-icon' of Jeremy Bentham at university college, London. Medical History. 1958; 2(2): p. 77–86.

14. UCL News. [Internet]. 2024. Available from: ucl.ac.uk/news/2013/jul/jeremy-bentham-makes-surprise-visit-ucl-council

15. Hume d. Of the reason of animals. In Hume d. A Treatise of Human Nature.; 1739. p. section 16.

16. Morris WE, Brown CR, Hume D,. Zalta EN,. Nodelman U. The Stanford Encyclopedia of Philosophy (Winter 2023). Metaphysics Research Lab, Stanford University. [Internet]. 2024. Available from: https://plato.stanford.edu/archives/win2023/entries/hume/

17. Nietzsche F. The Utility and Liability of History, in Unfashionable Observations. In The Comnplete Works of Friedrich Nietzsche, vol. 2 , ed. Richard T. Gray. Palo Alto, CA: Stanford University Press; 1874//1995. p. 87.

18. Fudge E. What is it like to be a cow? In The Oxford Handbook of Animal Studies.: Oxford University Press, Incorporated.; 2017. p. 258-267.

19. Darwin C. The descent of man [2nd ed.]: Prometheus Books; 1997.

20. Spencer J. Love and Hatred are Common to the Whole Sensitive Creation. In Richardson RA, Martineau RB, Amigoni D. After Darwin : animals, emotions, and the mind (1st ed.).: Brill; 2013.

21. Romanes GJ, Darwin C. Mental evolution in animals with a posthumous essay on instinct: D. Appleton and Company; 1884.

22. Romanes GJ. Animal intelligence : the International Scientific Series, Vol. XLIV. D: Appleton and Co; 1912.

23. Amato S. Beastly possessions : animals in Victorian consumer culture: University of Toronto Press; 2015.

24. Roussillon-Constanty L, Thornton S. Comforting Creatures: Changing Visions of Animal Otherness in the Victorian Period. Cahiers Victoriens & Édouardiens. 2018; 88: p. 1–11.

25. Howell P. A Place for the Animal Dead: Pets, Pet Cemeteries and Animal Ethics in Late Victorian Britain. Ethics, Place and Environment. 2002; 5(1): p. 5–22.

26. Tucker HF, Boxall R. Passing On: Death. In Gerhard J, Tucker HF. A new companion to Victorian literature and culture (1st ed.).: Wiley-Blackwell.; 2014.

27. Henning M. Anthropomorphic taxidermy and the death of nature: the curious art of Hermann Ploucque. t, Walter Potter, and Charles Waterton.Victorian Literature and Culture. 2007; 35(2): p. 663–678.

28. Lachapelle S, Healey J. On Hans, Zou and the others: wonder animals and the question of animal intelligence in early twentieth-century France. Studies in History and Philosophy of Science. Part C, Studies in History and Philosophy of Biological and Biomedical Sciences. 2010; 41(1): p. 12–20.

29. Coren S. Psychology Today Australia. [Internet]. 2024. Available from: psychologytoday.com/au/blog/canine-corner/201105/the-school-teach-nazi-war-dogs-speak

30. Włodarczyk J, Harrison J, Kruszona-Barełkowska SL, Wynne CDL. Talking Dogs: The Paradoxes Inherent in the Cultural Phenomenon of Soundboard Use by Dogs. Animals 2024. 2024; 14: p. 3272.

31. Daugherty G. Smithsonian Magazine. [Internet]. 2024. Available from: smithsonianmag.com/history/when-don-talking-dog-took-nation-storm-180968867/

32. Johnson HM. The Talking Dog. Science. 1912; 35(906): p. 749–751.

33. Gissis S, Jablonka E, Zeligowski A. Transformations of Lamarckism: from subtle fluids to molecular biology (1st ed.): MIT Press; 2011.

34. Damkaer DM. The Copepodologist's Cabinet A Biographical and Bibliographical History: American Philosophical Society; 2002.

35. De Waal FD, Macedo S, Ober J,.. Primates and Philosophers: How Morality Evolved (Princeton Science Library): Princeton University Press. Kindle Edition.

The Clever Hominid

1. Greenblatt SH. Phrenology in the science and culture of the 19th century. Neurosurgery. 1995; 37(4): p. 790–80.

2. Wright P. George Combe – Phrenologist, Philosopher, Psychologist (1788-1858). Cortex. 2005; 41(4): p. 447–451.

3. Michael JS. An "American Humboldt"?: Memorializing Philadelphia physician and race supremacist Samuel George Morton. Pennsylvania History. 2020; 87(2): p. 279–312.

4. Sommer M. A diagrammatics of race: Samuel George Morton's 'American Golgotha' and the contest for the definition of the young field of anthropology. History of the Human Sciences. 2024; 37(3–4): p. 34–63.

5. Ferracuti S. Cesare Lombroso (1835-1907). The Journal of Forensic Psychiatry. 1996; 7(1): p. 130–149.

6. O. Willis J, Dumont R, Kaufman AS. Factor-analytic models of intelligence. In J. R, Kaufman SB. The Cambridge handbook of intelligence (1st ed.).: Cambridge University Press.; 2011. p. 39-57.

7. Gillham NW. Cousins: Charles Darwin, Sir Francis Galton and the birth of eugenics. Significance. 2009; 6(3): p. 132–135.

8. Mackintosh NJ. Tests of intelligence. In Robert J, Kaufman SB. The Cambridge handbook of intelligence (1st ed.).: Cambridge University Press.; 2011. p. 3-19.

9. Nicolas S, Andrieu B, Croizet JC, Sanitioso RB, Burman JT. Sick? or slow? On the origins of intelligence as a psychological object. Intelligence (Norwood). 2013; 41(5): p. 699–711.

10. Urbina S. Tests of intelligence. In Robert J, Kaufman SB. The Cambridge handbook of intelligence (1st ed.).: Cambridge University Press.; 2011. p. 20-38.

11. Sternberg RJ, Pickren WE. Intelligence. In Sternberg RJ. The Cambridge handbook of the intellectual history of psychology.: Cambridge University Press; 2019. p. 267–286.

12. Warne RT, Burton JZ, Gibbons A, Melendez DA. Stephen Jay Gould's analysis of the army beta test in the mismeasure of man: Distortions and misconceptions regarding a pioneering mental test. Journal of Intelligence. 2019; 7(1): p. 6.

13. Gardner H. Frames of mind: The theory of multiple intelligences: Basic Books; 2011.

14. Wechsler D. The Measurement and Appraisal of Adult Intelligence (Fourth edition.): Williams & Wilkins Co.; 1958.

15. Weiss LG, Saklofske DH, Holdnack JA, Prifitera A. Chapter 1 - WISC-V: Advances in the Assessment of Intelligence. In WISC-V Assessment and Interpretation.: Elsevier Inc. https://doi.org/10.1016/B978-0-12-404697-9.00001-7; 2016. p. 3–23.

Measuring Animal Intelligence

1. Schnell AK, Boeckle M, Rivera M, Clayton NS, Hanlon RT. Cuttlefish exert self-control in a delay of gratification task. Proceedings of the Royal Society. B, Biological Sciences. 2021; 288(1946): p. 20203161–20203161.

2. Manning A, Stamp Dawkins M. Introduction to Animal Behaviour: Cambridge University Press; 2012.

3. Grandin T, and Johnson C. How animals think. In Grandin T, and Johnson C. Animals in Translation: Using the Mysteries of Autism to Decode Animal Behaviour.: Harcourt; 2006. p. 248-249.

4. Hansen W, Barker B., Povinelli DJ. The early tradition of the crow and the pitcher. In The Aesop's Fable Paradigm (pp. 23-).: Indiana University Press; 2024.

5. Bird CD, Emery NJ. Rooks Use Stones to Raise the Water Level to Reach a Floating Worm. Current Biology. 2009; 19(16): p. 1410–1414.

6. Jelbert SA, Taylor AH'CLG, Clayton NS, Gray RD, Addessi E. Using the aesop's fable paradigm to investigate causal understanding of water displacement by new caledonian crows. PloS One. 2014; 9(3): p. e92895–e92895.

7. Smith GP. Pavlov and integrative physiology. American Journal of Physiology. Regulatory, Integrative and Comparative Physiology. 2000; 279(3): p. 743-R755.

8. Pavlov IP, Dennis W. Scientific study of the so-called psychical processes in the higher animals, 1906. In Readings in the history of psychology.: Appleton-Century-Crofts; 1948. p. 425–438.

9. Thorndike EL. Animal intelligence: The Macmillan Company; 1898.

10. Thorndike EL. Edward Lee Thorndike. In Murchison C. A history of psychology in autobiography volume III.: Clark University Press; 1936. p. 263–270.

11. Foundation BFS. Full Bibliography. [Internet]. 2024. Available from: bfskinner.org/publications/full-bibliography

12. Bjork DW. B.F. Skinner: a life: BasicBooks; 1993.

13. Skinner BF. The behavior of organisms: An experimental analysis New York: Appleton-Century-Crofts; 1938.

14. Skinner BF. Pigeons in a pelican. The American Psychologist. 1960; 15(1): p. 28–37.

15. Włodarczyk J. Beyond Bizarre: Nature, Culture and the Spectacular Failure of B.F. Skinner's Pigeon-Guided Missiles 1. Polish Journal for American Studies: Yearbook of the Polish Association for American Studies. 2020; 14: p. 7–140.

16. Neisser U. Cognitive psychology: Appleton-Century-Crofts; 1967.

17. Harlow HF, Zimmermann RR. Affectional responses in the infant monkey. Science. 1959; 130: p. 421–432.

18. Blum D. The monkey wars NEW YORK, NY (USA): OXFORD UNIVERSITY PRESS; 1995.

19. Rosmalen L, Luijk MPCM, Horst FCP. Harry Harlow's pit of despair: Depression in monkeys and men. Journal of the History of the Behavioral Sciences. 2022; 58(2): p. 204–222.

20. Gluck JP. Harry F. Harlow and animal research: reflection on the ethical paradox. Ethics & Behavior. 1997; 7(2): p. 149–16.

21. Premack D, Woodruff G. Does the chimpanzee have a theory of mind? Behavioral and Brain Sciences. 1978; 1(4): p. 515–526.

22. Wimmer H, Perner J. Beliefs about beliefs: Representation and constraining function of wrong beliefs in young children's understanding of deception. Cognition. 1983; 13(1): p. 103–128.

23. de Waal F. Are We Smart Enough to Know How Smart Animals Are? London: Granta; 2016.

24. De Waal F, Macedo S, Ober J. Primates and Philosophers: How Morality Evolved (Princeton Science Library): Princeton University Press. Kindle Edition.; 2006.

25. Bugnyar T, Heinrich B. Ravens, Corvus corax, differentiate between knowledgeable and ignorant competitors. Proceedings - Royal Society. Biological Sciences/Proceedings - Royal Society. Biological Sciences. 2005; 272(1573): p. 1641–1646.

26. Vonk J, Shackelford TK. Self-Recognition. In Encyclopedia of Animal Cognition and Behavioor.: Springer International Publishing; 2022. p. 6320–6320.

27. Beck BB. Animal tool behavior New York: Garland Press; 1980.

28. Shumaker RW, Burghardt GM, Beck BB, Walkup KR. Animal tool behavior : the use and manufacture of tools by animals (Revised and updated edition.): Johns Hopkins University Press; 2011.

29. Chen MK, Lakshminarayanan V, Santos LR. How Basic Are Behavioral Biases? Evidence from Capuchin Monkey Trading Behavior. The Journal of Political Economy. 2006; 114(3): p. 517–537.

30. Cortés Zulueta C, Weber K, Velasco J. Bowerbirds and Their Bowers: Bird Art before Bio Art. In Bio-Art.; 2024. p. 101–130.

31. Sapolsky RM. A Primate's Memoir: Scribner; 2002.

32. BBC. Stoffel, the honey badger that can escape from anywhere! [Video]. [Internet]. 2014. Available from: youtube.com/watch?v=c36UNSoJenI

33. BBC Earth. Super Smart Animals. [Internet]. ND [cited 2025 August 3]. Available from: https://www.bbc.co.uk/programmes/profiles/2RBBmQ1crzp2ZZdjsjrHTj9/hank

34. Tolman EC. Cognitive maps in rats and men. Psychology Review. 1948; 55: p. 189–208.

35. Farzanfar D, Spiers HJ, Moscovitch M, Rosenbaum RS. From cognitive maps to spatial schemas. Nature Reviews. Neuroscience. 2023; 24(2) (10.1038/s41583-022-00655-9): p. 63–79.

36. Harten L, Katz A, Goldshtein A, Handel M, YY. The ontogeny of a mammalian cognitive map in the real world. Science (American Association for the Advancement of Science). 2020; 369(6500): p. 194–197.

37. Potvin D. Altruism in birds? Magpies have outwitted scientists by helping each other remove tracking devices. The Conversation. 2022; 22.

38. Crampton J, Frere CH, Potvin DA. Australian Magpies "Gymnorhina tibicen" cooperate to remove tracking devices. Australian Field Ornithology. 2022; 39: p. 7–11.

39. Goldstein EB. Cognitive Psychology: Connecting Mind, Research, and Everyday Experience. (Fifth edition): Cengage; 2018.

40. TULVING E, Annis HM. MEMORY AND CONSCIOUSNESS. Canadian Psychology = Psychologie Canadienne. 1985; 26(1): p. 1–12.

41. Clayton NS, Dickinson A. Scrub jays (Aphelocoma coerulescens) remember the relative time of caching as well as the location and content of their caches. Journal of Comparative Psychology. 1999; 113: p. 403–416.

42. Templer VL, Hampton RR. Episodic memory in nonhuman animals. CB/Current Biology. 2013; 23(17): p. R801–R806.

43. Fugazza C, Pogány Á, Miklósi Á. Do as I ... Did! Long-term memory of imitative actions in dogs (Canis familiaris). Animal Cognition. 2016; 19(2): p. 263–269.

44. Eichenbaum HB, Fortin NJ, Agster KL. Critical role of the hippocampus in memory for sequences of events. Nature Neuroscience. 2002; 5(5): p. 458–462.

45. Aust U, Call J, Snowdon CT, Pepperberg IM, Zentall T, Burghardt GM. Perceptual and functional categorization in animals. In APA handbook of comparative psychology.: American Psychological Association; 2017. p. 89–116.

46. Watanabe S, Sakamoto J, Wakita M. Pigeons' discrimination of paintings by Monet and Picasso. Journal of the Experimental Analysis of Behavior. 1995; 63(2): p. 165–174.

47. Sands SF, LCE, Wright AA. Pictorial similarity judgments and the organization of visual memory in the rhesus monkey. Journal of Experimental Psychology. 1982; 111(4): p. 369–389.

48. da Costa AP, Leigh AE, Man MS, Kendrick KM. Face pictures reduce behavioural, autonomic, endocrine and neural indices of stress and fear in sheep. Proceedings - Royal Society. Biological Sciences. 2004; 271(1552): p. 2077–2084.

49. Chusyd DE, Ackermans NL, Austad SN, Hof PR, Mielke MM, Sherwood CC, et al. Aging: What we can learn from elephants. Frontiers in Aging. 2021; 2: p. 726714–726714.

50. Knolle F, Goncalves RP, Davies EL, Duff AR, Morton JA. Response-inhibition during problem solving in sheep (Ovis aries). International Journal of Comparative Psychology. 2019; 32: p. 1–14.

51. Briefer EF, Padilla de la Torre M, McElligott AG. Mother goats do not forget their kids' calls. Proceedings of the Royal Society. B, Biological Sciences. 2012; 279(1743): p. 3749–3755.

52. de Jong IC, Prelle IT, van de Burgwal JA, Lambooij E, Korte SM, Blokhuis HJ, et al. Effects of environmental enrichment on behavioral responses to novelty, learning, and memory, and the circadian rhythm in cortisol in growing pigs. Physiology & Behavior. 2000; 68(4): p. 571–578.

53. Zewald J, Jacobs I. Object Permanence. In Vonk J, Shackelford TK. Encyclopedia of Animal Cognition and Behavior.: Springer International Publishing; 2022. p. 4711–4727.

54. Panksepp J. Affective neuroscience: the foundations of human and animal emotions (1st ed.).: Oxford University Press; 1998.

55. Barrett LF, Lindquist KA, Bliss-Moreau E, Duncan S, Gendron M, Mize J, et al. Of Mice and Men: Natural Kinds of Emotions in the Mammalian Brain? A Response to Panksepp and Izard. Perspectives on Psychological Science. 2007; 2(3): p. 297–312.

56. Ekman P, Friesen WV. Constants across cultures in the face and emotion. Journal of Personality and Social Psychology. 1971; 17(2): p. 124–129.

57. Grandin T. My reflections on understanding animal emotions for improving the life of animals in zoos. Journal of Applied Animal Welfare Science. 2018; 21(1): p. 12–22.

58. Arnould C, Love SA, Piégu B, Lefort G, Blache MC, Parias C, et al. Facial blushing and feather fluffing are indicators of emotions in domestic fowl (Gallus gallus domesticus). PloS One. 2024; 19(7): p. e0306601.

59. Descovich KA, Wathan J, Leach MC, Buchanan-Smith HM, Flecknell P, Farningham D, et al. Facial expression: An under-utilized tool for the assessment of welfare in mammals. ALTEX, Alternatives to Animal Experimentation. 2017; 34(3): p. 409–429.

60. Neethirajan S, Reimert I, Kemp B. Measuring farm animal emotions—sensor-based approaches. Sensors (Basel, Switzerland). 2021; 21(2): p. 1–23.

The Utilitarian Animal

1. Massilani D, Guimaraes S, Brugal JP, Bennett EA, Tokarska M, Arbogast RM, et al. Past climate changes, population dynamics and the origin of Bison in Europe. BMC Biology. 2016; 14(1): p. 93–93.

2. Oktaviana, A. A, Joannes-Boyau, R., Hakim, B., et al. Narrative cave art in Indonesia by 51,200 years ago. Nature (London). 2024; 631(8022): p. 814–818.

3. Finch D, Gleadow A, Hergt J, Heaney P, Green H, Myers C, et al. Ages for Australia's oldest rock paintings. Nature Human Behaviour. 2021; 5(3): p. 310–318.

4. Centre UWH(d). Gobekli Tepe. [Online]. [cited 2024 November 20. Available from: whc.unesco.org/en/list/1572/.

5. Peters J, Schmidt K. Animals in the symbolic world of Pre-Pottery Neolithic Göbekli Tepe, south-eastern Turkey: a preliminary assessment. Anthropozoologica. 2004; 39(1): p. 179–218.

6. Hart G. The Routledge dictionary of Egyptian gods and goddesses: Taylor & Francis Group; 2005.

7. Clutton-Brock J. Animals as Domesticates: A World View Through History (1st ed.): Michigan State University Press.; 2012.

8. Rawlinson G. LacusCurtius • Herodotus—Book II: Chapters 1 98. In History of Herodotus. London: John Murray; 1880. p. 104.

9. Clutton-Brock J. The British Museum Book of Cats Ancient and Modern: British Museum Press; 1995.

10. Elliott C. Cats, Commerce, and Cemeteries: The Mummified Felines of Beni Hasan. Journal of Egyptian Archaeology. 2023; 109(1–2): p. 147–158.

11. Conway WM. Dawn of Art in the Ancient World: An Archaeological Sketch London: Percival; 1891.

12. McCoan. JC. Egypt as it is. In Egypt. New York: Peter Fenelen Collier; 1882.

13. Bodenstein R. Sugar and Iron: Khedive Ismail's sugar factories in Egypt and the role of French engineering companies (1867-1875). ABE Journal, 5. 2014.

14. Dubois L. Avengers of the New World: the story of the Haitian Revolution: Belknap Press of Harvard University Press; 2004.

15. Wilkin B, Schafer R, Pollard T. The real fate of the waterloo fallen. Revue Belge d'histoire Contemporaine. Belgisch Tijdschrift Voor Nieuwste Geschiedenis. 2023; 53(4): p. 8–29.

16. Faraone CA. Greek and Roman animal sacrifice: ancient victims, modern observers: Cambridge University Press; 2012.

17. Schwartz GM, SK, Brenneis D. The Archaeological Study of Sacrifice. Annual Review of Anthropology. 2017; 46(1): p. 223–240.

18. Prieto G, Verano J, Rowe AP, Castillo F, Flores L, Asencio J, et al. Pampa La Cruz: a New Mass Sacrificial Burial Ground during the Chimú Occupation in Huanchaco, North Coast of Peru. Ñawpa Pacha, ahead-of-print(ahead-of-print). 2024; p. 1–86.

19. Ceruti MC, Nerlich AG. Frozen Mummies from Andean Mountaintop Shrines: Bioarchaeology and Ethnohistory of Inca Human Sacrifice. BioMed Research International. 2015; 2015(2015): p. 1–12.

20. Janzen D. (2004). The social meanings of sacrifice in the Hebrew Bible: a study of four writings: W. de Gruyter; 2004.

21. Ullucci D. Sacrifice in the Ancient Mediterranean: Recent and Current Research. Currents in Biblical Research. 2015; 13(3): p. 388–439.

22. MIKALSON J. Erechtheus and the Panathenaia. American Journal of Philology. 1976; 97(2): p. 141–153.

23. Beard M, North J, Price S. Religions of Rome: Volume 1, A History: Cambridge University Press; 1998.

24. Cassius D. Roman History, Volume I: Books 1-11. Translated by Earnest Cary, Herbert B. Foster: Loeb Classical Library 32. Cambridge, MA: Harvard University Press, 1914.

25. Shelton JA. Spectacles of animal abuse. In The Oxford handbook of animals in classical thought and life.: Oxford University Press; 2014. p. 461-477.

26. Rossiter J. In ampitζatru Carthaginis: The Carthage amphitheatre and its uses. Journal of Roman Archaeology. 2016; 29: p. 239–258.

27. Norman NL, Arbuckle BS, McCarty SA. Pythons, Pigs, and Political Process in the Hueda Kingdom, Benin, West Africa AD 1650–1727. In Animals and Inequality in the Ancient World.: University Press of Colorado; 2015. p. 295.

28. Temple RC. Beginnings of Currency. The Journal of the Anthropological Institute of Great Britain and Ireland. 1899; 29(1/2): p. 99–122.

29. Cole S. Appropriated meanings: Megaliths and tourism in Eastern Indonesia. Indonesia and the Malay World. 2003; 31(89): p. 140–150.

30. Smedal O. Ngadha relationship terms in context: description, analysis, and implications. Asian Journal of Social Science. 2002; 30(3): p. 493–524.

31. Sudarmadi T. Between colonial legacies and grassroots movements: exploring cultural heritage practice in the Ngadha and Manggarai Region of Flores. [PhD-Thesis –. Research external, graduation internal, Vrije Universiteit Amsterdam]. Eigen Beheer. 2014.

32. Eves R. "Full price, full body": norms, brideprice and intimate partner violence in highlands Papua New Guinea. Culture, Health & Sexuality. 2019; 21(12): p. 1367–1380.

33. Comaroff JL. Goodly beasts, beastly goods: cattle and commodities in a South African context. American Ethnologist. 1990; 17(2): p. 195–216.

34. Rowland SJ, Sutton PA, Knowles TDJ. The age of ambergris. Natural Product Research. 2019; 33(21): p. 3134–3142.

35. Burdock GA. Safety Assessment of Castoreum Extract as a Food Ingredient. International Journal of Toxicology. ; 26(1): p. 51–55.

36. Desta TT. Enhanced enrichment is inevitable to carry on the legacy of African civet (Civettictis civetta) captive farming. Biodiversitas (Surakarta). 2019; 20(6): p. 1575–1579.

37. ABC. From dripping on bread to biofuels and skincare, demand for tallow is surging. [Online].; 2024 [cited 2025 January 1. Available from: abc.net.au/news/rural/2024-02-04/tallow-exports-have-exceeded-one-billion-dollars/103408312.

38. Salindeho N, Mokolensang JF, Manu L, Taslim NA, Nurkolis F, Gunawan WB, et al. Fish scale rich in functional compounds and peptides: A potential nutraceutical to overcome undernutrition. Frontiers in Nutrition (Lausanne). 2022; 9: p. 1072370–1072370.

39. Chang CH, Jang-Liaw NH, Lin YS, Fang YC, Shao KT. (2013). Authenticating the use of dried seahorses in the traditional Chinese medicine market in Taiwan using molecular forensics. Yàowu Shìpin Fenxi. 2013; 21(3): p. 310–316.

40. Plotkin SA. Variolation" and Vaccination in Late Imperial China, Ca 1570–1911. In History of Vaccine Development.: Springer; 2011. p. 5-8.

41. Riedel S. Edward Jenner and the History of Smallpox and Vaccination. Proceeding Baylor University. Medical Center. 2005; 18(1): p. 21–25.

42. Lombard M, Pastoret PP, Moulin AM. A brief history of vaccines and vaccination. Revue Scientifique et Technique (International Office of Epizootics). 2007; 26(1): p. 29–48.

43. Mitchell PB, Hadzi-Pavlovic D. John Cade and the discovery of lithium treatment for manic depressive illness. Medical Journal of Australia. 1999; 171(5): p. 262–264.

44. Cade JF. John Frederick Joseph Cade: Family Memories on the Occasion of the 50th Anniversary of his Discovery of the Use of Lithium in Mania. Australian and New Zealand Journal of Psychiatry. 1999; 33(5): p. 615–618.

Morality

1. Bekoff M. The Emotional Lives of Animals: New World Library; 2007.

2. Luco A. The Definition of Morality: Threading the Needle. Social Theory and Practice. 2014; 40(3): p. 361–387.

3. Darwin CR. The Descent of Man, and Selection in Relation to Sex. Volume 1. 1st edition London: John Murray; 1871.

4. Joyce R. The evolution of morality (1st ed.): MIT Press; 2006.

5. De Waal FD, Macedo S, Ober J, Primates and Philosophers: How Morality Evolved (Princeton Science Library): Princeton University Press. Kindle Edition.

6. Wiley D, WC, Bocconcelli A, Cholewiak D, Friedlaender A, Thompson M, et al. Underwater components of humpback whale bubble-net feeding behaviour. Behaviour. 2011; 148(5/6): p. 575–602.

7. Manning A, Stamp Dawkins M. Introduction to Animal Behaviour: Cambridge University Press; 2012.

8. RL T. The evolution of reciprocal altruism. Quarterly Review of Biology. 1971; 46: p. 35–57.

9. De Waal FBM. Good natured: the origins of right and wrong in humans and other animals: Harvard University Press; 1996.

10. Carter GG, Wilkinson GS. Food sharing in vampire bats: reciprocal help predicts donations more than relatedness or harassment. Proceedings-Royal Society. Biological Sciences/Proceedings - Royal Society. Biological Sciences. 2013; 280(1753): p. 20122573–20122573.

11. Clutton-Brock T. Cooperation between non-kin in animal societie. Nature (London). 2009; 462(7269): p. 51–57.

12. Cheney DL. Extent and limits of cooperation in animals. Proceedings of the National Academy of Sciences - PNAS. 2011; 108(Supplement 2): p. 10902–10909.

13. Oldroyd B, Beekman M, Brooks R. Origins of altruism: Why Hamilton still rules 50 years on. [Internet]. 2014 [cited 2024 December 15]. Available from: http://theconversation.com/origins-of-altruism-why-hamilton-still-rules-50-years-on-27223

14. Cuff BMP, Brown SJ, Taylor L, Howat DJ. Empathy: A Review of the Concept. Emotion Review. 2016; 8(2): p. 144–153.

15. Panksepp J. Toward a cross-species understanding of empathy. Trends in Neurosciences. 2013; 36(8): p. 489–496.

16. Haidt J. The Happiness Hypothesis: Finding Modern Truth in Ancient Wisdom: Basic Books; 2006.

17. Bartal IBA, DJ, Mason P. Empathy and Pro-Social Behavior in Rats. Science. 2011; 334(6061): p. 1427–1430.

18. De Waal FBM, Preston SD. Mammalian empathy: behavioural manifestations and neural basis. Nature Reviews. Neuroscience. 2017; 18(8): p. 498–509.

19. Zaki J, Wager TD, Singer T, Keysers C, Gazzola V. The Anatomy of Suffering: Understanding the Relationship between Nociceptive and Empathic Pain. Trends in Cognitive Sciences. 2016; 20(4): p. 249–259.

20. Brosnan SF, de Waal FBM. Evolution of responses to (un)fairness. Science. 2014; 346(6207): p. 314–314.

21. Brosnan SF, de Waal FBM. (2003). Monkeys reject unequal pay. Nature. 2003; 425(6955): p. 297–299.

22. Panksepp J. Affective neuroscience: the foundations of human and animal emotions (1st ed.).: Oxford University Press; 1998.

23. Lewis M, Haviland-Jones JM, Barrett LF. Handbook of emotions (3rd ed.): Guilford Press; 2008.

24. Burghardt GM. Defining and Recognizing Play. In The Oxford Handbook of the Development of Play.: Oxford University Press; 2012.

25. Bekoff M, Pierce J. Wild justice the moral lives of animals: The University of Chicago Press; 2009.

26. Palagi E, Burghardt GM, Smuts B, Cordoni G, Dall'Olio S, Fouts HN, et al. Rough-and-tumble play as a window on animal communication. Biological Reviews of the Cambridge Philosophical Society. 2016; 91(2): p. 311–327.

27. Smith PK, StGeorge JM. Play fighting (rough-and-tumble play) in children: developmental and evolutionary perspectives. International Journal of Play. 2023; 12(1): p. 113–126.

28. Marley CL, Pollard TM, Barton RA, Street SE. A systematic review of sex differences in rough and tumble play across non-human mammals. Behavioral Ecology and Sociobiology. 2022; 76(12).

29. Clutton-Brock TH, Parker GA. Punishment in animal societies. Nature (London). 1995; 373(6511): p. 209–216.

Goats

1. Fatet A, Pellicer-Rubio, M.T., Leboeuf B. Reproductive cycle of goats. Animal reproduction science. 2011; 124(3): p. 211-219.

2. Murata K, Tamogami S, Itou M. Identification of an Olfactory Signal Molecule that Activates the Central Regulator of Reproduction in Goats. Current biology. 2014; 24(6): p. 681-686.

3. Ladewig J, Price EO, Hart BL. Flehmen in male goats: Role in sexual behavior. Behavioral and Neural Biology. 1980; 30(3): p. 312–322.

4. Bukhsianidze M, Vekua A. Capra dalii nov. sp. (Caprinae, Bovidae, Mammalia) at the limit of Plio-Pleistocene from Dmanisi (Georgia). CFS Courier Forschungsinstitut Senckenberg. 2006; 256: p. 159–171.

5. Zeder MA, Hesse B. The initial domestication of goats (Capra hircus) in the Zagros mountains 10,000 Years Ago. Science (American Association for the Advancement of Science). 2000; 287(5461): p. 2254–2257.

6. Amills M, Capote J, Tosser-Klopp G. Goat domestication and breeding: a jigsaw of historical, biological and molecular data with missing pieces. Animal Genetics. 2017; 48(6): p. 631–644.

7. Groves M. Goats left for shipwreck survivors on remote island recognised as heritage breed. [Internet]. 2020 [cited 2024 December 12]. Available from: https://www.abc.net.au/news/rural/2020-08-20/percy-island-goats-saved-as-heritage-breed-but-fight-continues/12569548

8. Roser M. Our World in Data. [Internet]. [cited 2024 December 7]. Available from: ourworldindata.org/how-many-animals-get-slaughtered-every-day

9. List of Livestock, Provisions, Plants and Seeds | First Fleet Fellowship Victoria Inc. [Internet]. 2013 [cited 2024 December 13]. Available from: Firstfleetfellowship.Org.Au/. https://firstfleetfellowship.org.au/library/first-fleetlist-livestock-provisions-plants-seeds/

10. Facts and Stats – GICA. [Internet]. 2024. Available from: goatindustrycouncil.com.au/goats-in-australia/goat-facts-and-stats/

11. Bergström A, Frantz L, Schmidt R, Ersmark E, Lebrasseur O, Girdland-Flink L, et al. Origins and genetic legacy of prehistoric dogs. Science (American Association for the Advancement of Science). 2020; 370(6516): p. 557–564.

12. Valenze DM. Milk: a local and global history (1st ed.): Yale University Press; 2011.

13. Galápagos Conservancy. Project Isabela. [Internet]. N.D [cited 2024 December 13]. Available from: galapagos.org/conservation/project-isabela/

14. Carrion V, Donlan CJ, Campbell KJ, Lavoie C, Cruz F, Gratwicke B. Archipelago-wide Island restoration in the galápagos islands: Reducing costs of invasive mammal eradication programs and reinvasion risk. PloS One. 2011; 6(5): p. e18835–e18835.

15. Waite AE. Pictorial Key to the Tarot: Red Wheel Weiser; 1975.

16. Ezzy D. Reassembling religious symbols: the Pagan God Baphomet. Religion (London. 1971). 2015; 45(1): p. 24–41.

17. Hart G. The Routledge dictionary of Egyptian Gods and Goddesses: Taylor & Francis Group; 2005.

18. Redford S, Redford DB. The Cult and Necropolis of the Sacred Ram at Mendes. In Divine Creatures: Animal Mummies in Ancient Egypt.: 2005 American University in Cairo Press; 2005.

19. LacusCurtius • Herodotus—Book II: Chapters 1 98. [Internet]. Available from: penelope.uchicago.edu/Thayer/E/Roman/Texts/Herodotus/2a*.html

20. Gilmour-Bryson A. Sodomy and the Knights Templar. Journal of the History of Sexuality. 1996; 7(2): p. 151–183.

21. Stahuljak Z. Pornographic archaeology. In medicine, medievalism, and the invention of the French nation (1st ed.).: University of Pennsylvania Press; 2013.

22. McIntosh C. Eliphas Lévi and the French Occult Revival. In In Eliphas lévi and the French Occult Revival.: State University of New York Press.; 2011. p. 73-152.

23. Decker R, Demmet M. The History of the Occult Tarot: Duckworth Books; 2013.

24. Pratesi F. In search of Tarot sources-after fifteen years. The Playing-Card. 2012; 41, (2): p. 95-112.

25. Lehrich CI. The occult mind: magic in theory and practice (1st ed.): Cornell University Press; 2007.

26. Gallup GG. Chimpanzees: Self-Recognition. Science (American Association for the Advancement of Science). 1970; 167(3914): p. 86–87.

27. de Waal FBM. Fish, mirrors, and a gradualist perspective on self-awareness. PLoS Biology. 2019; 17(2): p. e3000112–e3000112.

28. Nawroth C, von Borell E, Langbein J. Object permanence in the dwarf goat (Capra aegagrus hircus): Perseveration errors and the tracking of complex movements of hidden objects. Applied Animal Behaviour Science. 2015; 167: p. 20–26.

29. Zobel G, Nawroth C. Current state of knowledge on the cognitive capacities of goats and its potential to inform species-specific enrichment. Small Ruminant Research. 2020; 192: p. 106208.

30. Sankey DWE, O'Bryan LR, Garnier S, Cowlishaw G, Hopkins P, Holton M, et al. (2021). Consensus of travel direction is achieved by simple copying, not voting, in free-ranging goats. Royal Society Open Science. 2021; 8(2): p. 201128.

31. Briefer EF, Haque S, Baciadonna L, McElligott AG. Goats excel at learning and remembering a highly novel cognitive task. Frontiers in Zoology. 2014; 11(1): p. 20.

32. Nawroth C, Baciadonna L, McElligott AG. Goats learn socially from humans in a spatial problem-solving task. Animal Behaviour. 2016; 121: p. 123–129.

33. Briefer EF, Padilla de la Torre M, McElligott AG. Mother goats do not forget their kids' calls. Proceedings of the Royal Society. B, Biological Sciences. 2012; 279(1743): p. 3749–3755.

34. Meyer S, Nürnberg G, Puppe B, Langbein J. The cognitive capabilities of farm animals: categorisation learning in dwarf goats (Capra hircus). Animal Cognition. 2012; 15(4): p. 567–576.

35. Cuaya LV, Hernández-Pérez R, Concha L, Stamatakis EA. Our faces in the dog's brain: Functional imaging reveals temporal cortex activation during perception of human faces. PloS One. 2016; 11(3): p. e0149431–e0149431.

36. Kendrick KM, da Costa AP, Leigh AE., Hinton MR, Peirce JW. Sheep don't forget a face. Nature (London). 2011; 414(6860): p. 165–166.

37. Joassin F, Pesenti M, Maurage P, Verreckt E, Bruyer R, Campanella S. Cross-modal interactions between human faces and voices involved in person recognition. Cortex. 2011; 47(3): p. 367–376.

38. Pitcher BJ, Briefer EF, Baciadonna L, McElligott AG. Cross-modal recognition of familiar conspecifics in goats. Royal Society Open Science. 2017; 4(2): p. 160346–160346.

39. Call J. Inferences by exclusion in the great apes: The effect of age and species. Animal Cognition. 2006; 9(4): p. 393–403.

40. Nawroth C, Brett JM, McElligott AG. Goats display audience-dependent human-directed gazing behaviour in a problem-solving task. Biology Letters. 2016; 12(7): p. 20160283–20160283.

41. Kaminski J, Riedel J, Call J, Tomasello M. Domestic goats, Capra hircus, follow gaze direction and use social cues in an object choice task. Animal Behaviour. 2005; 69(1): p. 11–18.

42. Bellegarde LGA, Haskell MJ, Duvaux-Ponter C, Weiss A, Boissy A, Erhard HW. Face-based perception of emotions in dairy goats. Applied Animal Behaviour Science. 2017; 193: p. 51–59.

43. Leliveld LMC, Langbein J, Puppe B. The emergence of emotional lateralization: Evidence in non-human vertebrates and implications for farm animals. Applied animal behaviour science. 2013; 145(1-2): p. 1-14.

44. Miranda-de la Lama GC, Sepúlveda WS, Montaldo HH, María GA, Galindo F. (2011). Social strategies associated with identity profiles in dairy goats. Applied Animal Behaviour Science. 2011; 134(1): p. 48–55.

45. Sapolsky RM. A Primate's Memoir: Scribner; 2002.

46. Bryant SH. Myotonia in the goat. Annals of the New York Academy of Sciences. 1979; 317(1): p. 314–325.

47. Lush JL. "Nervous" goats. The Journal of Heredity. 1930; 21(6): p. 243–247.

Sheep

1. Rezaei HR, Naderi S, Chintauan-Marquier IC, Taberlet P, Virk AT, Naghash HR, et al. Evolution and taxonomy of the wild species of the genus Ovis (Mammalia, Artiodactyla, Bovidae). Molecular Phylogenetics and Evolution. 2010; 54(2): p. 315–326.

2. Domestic Animal Diversity Information System (DAD-IS). [Internet]. [cited 2025 January 13]. Available from: https://www.fao.org/dad-is/data/en/

3. Okstate.edu. Lincoln Sheep. [Internet]. [cited 2025 January 3]. Available from: https://breeds.okstate.edu/sheep/lincoln-sheep.html

4. BBC. 'Oldest sheep' in the world dies on Lewis in Western Isles. [Internet]. [cited 2025 January 13]. Available from: https://www.bbc.com/news/uk-scotland-highlands-islands-17182541

5. National Museum Australia. World record sheep fleece. [Internet]. [cited 2025 January 13]. Available from: https://www.nma.gov.au/explore/collection/highlights/world-record-sheep-fleece

6. Allais-Bonnet A, Hintermann A, Deloche MC, Cornette R, Bardou P, Naval-Sanchez M, et al. Analysis of Polycerate Mutants Reveals the Evolutionary Co-option of HOXD1 for Horn Patterning in Bovidae. Molecular Biology and Evolution. 2021; 38(6): p. 2260–2272.

7. McKay AL. Allowed to die"? Prison Hulks, Convict Corpses and the Inquiry of 1847. Cultural and Social History. 2021; 18(2): p. 163–181.

8. Flynn M. The Second Fleet: Britain's Grim Convict Armada of 1790: Library of Australian History; 2001.

9. National Museum of Australia. National Museum of Australia—Merino sheep introduced. [Internet]. [cited 2025 January 9]. Available from: nma.gov.au/defining-moments/resources/merino-sheep-introduced

10. Evatt H. Curious corps. In Rum rebellion: a study of the overthrow of Governor Bligh by John Macarthur and the New South Wales Corps. Sydney: Angus and Robertson; 1937. p. 22.

11. Macarthur Onslow S. Some early records of the Macarthurs of Camden Sydney: Angus & Robertson Ltd; 1914.

12. Ciani E, Lasagna E, D'Andrea M, Alloggio I, Marroni F, Ceccobelli S, et al. Merino and Merino-derived sheep breeds: A genome-wide intercontinental study. Genetics Selection Evolution (Paris). 2015; 47(1): p. 64–64.

13. Carter HB. His Majesty's Spanish Flock. Sir Joseph Banks and the Merinos of George III of England: Angus & Robertson; 1964.

14. Smith E. The Life of Sir Joseph Banks: President of the Royal Society, with Some Notices of His Friends and Contemporaries: Cambridge University Press; 2011.

15. Robert Jacob Gordon. [Internet]. [cited 2025 January 9]. Available from: robertjacobgordon.nl/about

16. Massy C. Breaking the sheep's back: the shocking true story of the decline and fall of the Australian wool industry (1st ed.).: University of Queensland Press.; 2011.

17. Chen JK. I only have eye for ewe: the discovery of cyclopamine and development of Hedgehog pathway-targeting drugs. Natural Product Reports. 2016; 33(5): p. 595–61.

18. Lee ST, Welch KD, Panter KE, Gardner DR, Garrossian M, Chang CWT. Cyclopamine: From Cyclops Lambs to Cancer Treatment. Journal of Agricultural and Food Chemistry. 2014; 62(30): p. 7355–7362.

19. Passarge E. Color atlas of genetics (Fifth edition, revised and updated.): Thieme; 2018.

20. Chiang C, Litingtung Y, LE, Young KE, Corden JL, Westphal H, et al. 1996). Cyclopia and defective axial patterning in mice lacking Sonic hedgehog gene function. Nature (London). 1996; 383(6599): p. 407–413.

269

21. Cooper MK, Porter JA, Young KE, Beachy PA. Teratogen-mediated inhibition of target tissue response to Shh signaling. Science (New York, N.Y.). 1998; 280(5369): p. 1603–1607.

22. Kendrick KM. Neurobiological correlates of visual and olfactory recognition in sheep. Behavioural Processes. 1994; 33(1): p. 89–111.

23. KKendrick KM, da Costa AP, Leigh AE, Hinton MR, Peirce JW. Sheep don't forget a face. Nature (London). 2011; 414(6860): p. 165–166.

24. Lue PY, Oliver MH, Neeff M, Thorne PR, Suzuki-Kerr H. Sheep as a large animal model for hearing research: comparison to common laboratory animals and humans. Laboratory Animal Research. 2023; 39(1): p. 31–19.

25. Griffiths SK, Pierson LL, Gerhardt KJ, Abrams RM, Peters AJM. Noise induced hearing loss in fetal sheep. Hearing Research. 1994; 74(1): p. 221–230.

26. Kendrick KM, Atkins K, Hinton MR, Broad KD, Fabre-Nys C, Keverne B. Facial and vocal discrimination in sheep. Animal Behaviour. 1995; 49(6): p. 1665–1676.

27. McBride SD, Perentos N, Morton AJ. Understanding the concept of a reflective surface: Can sheep improve navigational ability through the use of a mirror? Animal Cognition. 2015; 18(1): p. 361–371.

28. Quail MR, Fraser MD. Pulling the wool over their eyes? Object permanence, numerical competence and categorisation in alternative livestock species. Applied Animal Behaviour Science. 2024; 270: p. 106131.

29. Nawroth C, von Borell E, Langbein J. Object permanence in the dwarf goat (Capra aegagrus hircus): Perseveration errors and the tracking of complex movements of hidden objects. Applied Animal Behaviour Science. 2015; 167: p. 20–26.

30. Lowrey B, Proffitt KM, McWhirter DE, White PJ, Courtemanch AB, Dewey SR, et al. Characterizing population and individual migration patterns among native and restored bighorn sheep (Ovis canadensis). Ecology and Evolution. 2019; 9(15): p. 8829–8839.

31. Knolle F, Goncalves RP, Davies EL, Duff AR, Morton JA. Response-Inhibition During Problem Solving in Sheep (Ovis Aries). International Journal of Comparative Psychology. 2019; 32: p. 1–14.

32. Lee C, Colegate S, Fisher AD. Development of a maze test and its application to assess spatial learning and memory in Merino sheep. Applied Animal Behaviour Science. 2006; 96(1): p. 43–51.

33. Eftang S, Vas JB, Holand Ø, Bøe KE, Andersen IL. Sheep's learning ability and behavioural response to a fully automated virtual fencing system. Applied Animal Behaviour Science. 2023; 269: p. 106112.

34. Ozella L, Langford J, Gauvin L, Price E, Cattuto C, Croft DP. The effect of age, environment and management on social contact patterns in sheep. Applied Animal Behaviour Science. 2020; 225: p. 104964.

35. Gómez-Nava L, Bon R, Peruani F. Intermittent collective motion in sheep results from alternating the role of leader and follower. Nature Physics. 2022; 18(12): p. 1494–1501.

36. Monk JE, Belson S, Colditz IG, Lee C. Attention bias test differentiates anxiety and depression in sheep. Frontiers in Behavioral Neuroscience. 2018; 12: p. 246–246.

37. Finkemeier MA, Langbein J, Puppe B. Personality research in mammalian farm animals: Concepts, measures, and relationship to welfare. Frontiers in Veterinary Science. 2018; 5: p. 131–131.

38. Réale D, Reader SM, Sol D, McDougall PT, Dingemanse NJ. Integrating animal temperament within ecology and evolution. Biological Reviews of the Cambridge Philosophical Society. 2007; 82(2): p. 291–318.

39. Miranda-de la Lama GC, Pascual-Alonso M, Aguayo-Ulloa L, Sepúlveda WS, Villarroel M, María GA. Social personality in sheep: Can social strategies predict individual differences in cognitive abilities, morphology features, and reproductive success? Journal of Veterinary Behavior. 2019; 31: p. 82–91.

Chickens

1. Our World in Data. Chicken meat production. (n.d.).. [Internet]. [cited 2025 January 17]. Available from: ourworldindata.org/grapher/chicken-meat-production

2. ABC. From exotic treat to weekly staple, Australians are obsessed with chicken. [Internet]. 2025 [cited 2025 January 28]. Available from: abc.net.au/news/2025-01-27/why-does-australia-eat-so-much-chicken-meat/104588708

3. Pennisi E. Quaillike creatures were the only birds to survive the dinosaur-killing asteroid impact. Science (American Association for the Advancement of Science). 2018.

4. Xiang H, Gao J, Yu B, Zhou H, Cai D, Zhang Y, et al. Early Holocene chicken domestication in northern China. Proceedings of the National Academy of Sciences - PNAS. 2014; 111(49): p. 17564–17569.

5. Miao YW, Peng MS, Wu GS, Ouyang YN, Yang ZY, Yu N, et al. Chicken domestication: An updated perspective based on mitochondrial genomes. Heredity. 2013; 110(3): p. 277–282.

6. Guinness World Records. Search. (n.d.). [Internet]. 2025 [cited 2025 January 19]. Available from: guinnessworldrecords.com/search/index.html

7. Pedrosa MA. Guinness World Records recognizes 'Manok ni Cano Gwapo'. [Internet]. 2024 [cited 2025 January 19]. Available from: sunstar.com.ph/bacolod/guinness-world-records-recognizes-manok-ni-cano-gwapo

8. Prakash A, Singh Y, Chatli M, Sharma A, Acharya P, Singh M. Review of the black meat chicken breeds: Kadaknath, Silkie, and Ayam Cemani. World's Poultry Science Journal. 2023; 79(4): p. 879–891.

9. Mukhtar N, Khan SH. Comb: An important reliable visual ornamental trait for se-lection in chickens. World's Poultry Science Journal. 2012; 68(3): p. 425–434.

10. Herrera AM, Shuster SG, Perriton CL, Cohn MJ. Developmental Basis of Phallus Reduction during Bird Evolution. Current Biology. 2013; 23(12): p. 1065–1074.

11. Rigby S. How the battle of the sexes left the duck with an awkwardly long, corkscrew-shaped penis. [Internet]. 2024 [cited 2025 January 19]. Available from: sciencefocus.com/nature/duck-penis-corkscrew

12. Horner J. Jack Horner. Current Biology. 2014; 24(9): p. R346–R347.

13. Horner J. X. [Internet]. 2023 [cited 2025 January 18]. Available from: x.com/dustydino

14. Bhullar BAS, Morris ZS, Sefton EM, Tok A, Tokita M, Namkoong B, et al. A molecular mechanism for the origin of a key evolutionary innovation, the bird beak and palate, revealed by an integrative approach to major transitions in vertebrate history. Evolution. 2015; 69(7): p. 1665–1677.

15. Harris MP, Hasso SM, Ferguson MWJ, Fallon JF. The Development of Archosaurian First-Generation Teeth in a Chicken Mutant. Current Biology. 2006; 16(4): p. 371–377.

16. Botelho JF, Smith-Paredes D, Soto-Acuña S, O'Connor J, Palma V, Vargas AO. Molecular development of fibular reduction in birds and its evolution from dinosaurs. Evolution. 2016; 70(3): p. 543–554.

17. Life. Mike the Headless Chicken: A Rooster Loses His Head. and Lives. [Internet]. 2013 [cited 2025 January 19]. Available from: life.com/animals/life-with-mike-the-headless-chicken-photos-of-a-famously-tough-fowl/

18. BBC. The chicken that lived for 18 months without a head. [Internet]. 2015 [cited 2025 January 19]. Available from: bbc.com/news/magazine-34198390

19. Schipper M, Ye S, Yin H. China's creation and origin myths: Cross-cultural explorations in oral and written traditions: BRILL; 2011.

20. Leeming DA. A dictionary of Asian mythology (1st ed.) : Oxford University Press; 2001.

21. Foster MD. The Book of Yokai: Mysterious Creatures of Japanese Folklore: University of California Press; 2015.

22. Lagerwey J, Kalinowski M. Early Chinese religion: Brill; 2009.

23. Xing L, Zhang J, Klein H, Mayor A, Chen Y, Dai H, et al. Dinosaur Tracks, Myths and Buildings: The Jin Ji (Golden Chicken) Stones from Zizhou Area, Northern Shaanxi, China.Ichnos (Chur, Switzerland). 2015; 22(3–4): p. 227–234.

24. Marino L. Thinking chickens: a review of cognition, emotion, and behavior in the domestic chicken. Animal Cognition. 2017; 20(2): p. 127–147.

25. Dawkins SM, Woodington A. Distance and the presentation of visual stimuli to birds. Animal Behaviour. 1997; 54(4): p. 1019–1025.

26. Dawkins M. What are birds looking at? Head movements and eye use in chickens. Animal Behaviour. 2022; 63: p. 991–998.

27. McGilchrist I. The master and his emissary: the divided brain and the making of the Western world: Yale University Press; 2009.

28. Jones RB, Roper TJ. Olfaction in the Domestic Fowl: A Critical Review. Physiology & Behavior. 1997; 62(5): p. 1009–1018.

29. Liu HX, Rajapaksha P, Wang Z, Kramer NE, Marshall BJ. An Update on the Sense of Taste in Chickens: A Better Developed System than Previously Appreciated. Journal of Nutrition & Food Sciences. 2018; 8(2).

30. Liu JG, Xia WG, Chen W, Abouelezz KFM, Ruan D, Wang S, et al. Effects of capsaicin on laying performance, follicle development, and ovarian antioxidant capacity in aged laying ducks. Poultry Science. 2021; 100(4): p. 100901–100901.

31. Laurijs KA, Briefer EF, Reimert I, Webb LE. Vocalisations in farm animals: A step towards positive welfare assessment. Applied Animal Behaviour Science. 2021; 236: p. 105264.

32. McGrath N, Phillips CJC, Burman OHP, Dwyer CM, Henning J. Humans can identify reward-related call types of chickens. Royal Society Open Science. 2024; 11(1): p. 231284–231289.

33. Zeyl JN, Ouden O, Köppl C, Assink J, Christensen-Dalsgaard J, Patrick SC, et al. Infrasonic hearing in birds: a review of audiometry and hypothesized structure–function relationships. Biological Reviews of the Cambridge Philosophical Society. 2020; 95(4): p. 1036–1054.

34. Hillemacher S, Tiemann I. Domestic chickens solving mirror-mediated spatial location tasks uncovering their cognitive abilities. Scientific Reports. 2024; 14(1): p. 14164–11.

35. Abeyesinghe SM, Nicol CJ, Hartnell SJ, Wathes CM. Can domestic fowl, Gallus gallus domesticus, show self-control? Animal Behaviour. 2005; 70(1): p. 1–11.

36. Edgar JL, Paul ES, Harris L, Penturn S, Nicol CJ, Chapouthier G. No evidence for emotional empathy in chickens observing familiar adult conspecifics. PloS One. 2012; 7(2): p. e31542–e31542.

37. Lea SEG, Slater AM, Ryan CME. Perception of object unity in chicks: A comparison with the human infant. Infant Behavior & Development. 1996; 19(4): p. 501–504.

38. Wood JN, Ullman TD, Wood BW, Spelke ES, Wood SMW. Object permanence in newborn chicks is robust against opposing evidence. arXiv.Org. 2024.

39. Hall MJ, Martin JM, Burns AL, Hochuli DF. (2024). The decline, fall, and rise of a large urban colonising bird. Wildlife Research (East Melbourne). 2024; 51(7).

40. Schmelz M, Krause ET. Simple but Complex—A Laying Hen Study as Proof of Concept of a Novel Method for Cognitive Enrichment and Research. Frontiers in Animal Science. 2021; 2.

41. Nicol CJ, Pope SJ. Effects of social learning on the acquisition of discriminatory keypecking in hens. Bulletin of the Psychonomic Society. 1992; 30(4): p. 293–296.

42. Nicol C. (2006). How animals learn from each other. Applied Animal Behaviour Science. 2006; 100(1–2): p. 58–63.

43. Hollén LI, Radford AN. The development of alarm call behaviour in mammals and birds. Animal Behaviour. 2009; 78(4): p. 791–800.

44. Potvin DA, Ratnayake CP, Radford AN, & Magrath RD. Birds Learn Socially to Recognize Heterospecific Alarm Calls by Acoustic Association. Current Biology. 2018; 28(16): p. 2632-2637. e4.

45. Freire R, Cheng HW. (2004). Experience-dependent changes in the hippocampus of domestic chicks: a model for spatial memory. The European Journal of Neuroscience. 2004; 20(4): p. 1065–1068.

46. Favati A, Zidar J, Thorpe H, Jensen P, Løvlie H. The ontogeny of personality traits in the red junglefowl, Gallus gallus. Behavioral Ecology. 2016; 27(2): p. 484–493.

47. Oishi S, Graham J, Kesebir S, Galinha IC. Concepts of Happiness Across Time and Cultures. Personality & Social Psychology Bulletin. 2013; 39(5): p. 559–577.

48. Humphrey T. Are happy chickens safer chickens? Poultry welfare and disease susceptibility. British Poultry Science. 2006; 47(4): p. 379–391.

49. Ishikawa A, Takanuma T, Hashimoto N, Goto T, Tsudzuki M. New Behavioral Handling Test Reveals Temperament Differences in Native Japanese Chickens. Animals (Basel). 2023; 13(22): p. 3556.

50. Schütz KE, Jensen P. Effects of Resource Allocation on Behavioural Strategies: A Comparison of Red Junglefowl (Gallus gallus) and Two Domesticated Breeds of Poultry. Ethology. 2001; 107(8): p. 753–765.

Bovines

1. Orr AI. How cows eat grass. [Internet]. 2024 [cited 2025 February 8]. Available from: fda.gov/animal-veterinary/animal-health-literacy/how-cows-eat-grass

2. Habel RE. The Anatomy of the Domestic Animals, ed. Getty, R. : (Saunders, Philadelphia), 5th Ed; 1975.

3. Data OWi. Number of cattle. [Internet]. 2025 [cited 2025 January 30]. Available from: ourworldindata.org/grapher/cattle-livestock-count-heads

4. Food and Agriculture Organization of the United Nations. Browse by country and species | Domestic Animal Diversity Information System (DAD-IS). [Internet]. 2025 [cited 2025 January 31]. Available from: fao.org/dad-is/browse-by-country-and-species/en/

5. Guinness World Records. Search. (n.d).. [Internet]. 2025 [cited 2025 January 19]. Available from: guinnessworldrecords.com/search/index.html

6. Ajmone-Marsan P, Garcia JF, Lenstra JA. On the origin of cattle: How aurochs became cattle and colonized the world. Evolutionary Anthropology. 2010; 19(4): p. 148–157.

7. Zeyland J, Wolko Ł, Lipiński D, Woźniak A, Nowak A, Szalata M, et al. Tracking of wisent–bison–yak mitochondrial evolution. Journal of Applied Genetics. 2012; 53(3): p. 317–322.

8. Stokstad E. Bringing back the aurochs. Science (American Association for the Advancement of Science). 2015; 350(6265): p. 1144–1147.

9. Driessen CPG, Lorimer J. Back-breeding the aurochs: the Heck brothers, National Socialism and imagined geographies for nonhuman Lebensraum. In Hitler's Geographies: The Spatialities of the Third Reich.: The University of Chicago Press; 2016.

10. Bruce G. Through the lion gate: a history of the Berlin Zoo: Oxford University Press; 2017.

11. White HM, Donkin SS, Lucy MC, Grala TM, Roche JR. Short communication Genetic differences between New Zealand and North American dairy cows alter milk production and gluconeogenic enzyme expression. Journal of Dairy Science. 2012; 95(1): p. 455–459.

12. Grandin T, Whiting M. Are we pushing animals to their biological limits? : welfare and ethical implications: CABI; 2018.

13. Bauman DE. Bovine somatotropin and lactation: from basic science to commercial application. Domestic Animal Endocrinology. 1999; 17(2): p. 101–116.

14. Raux A, Bichon E, Benedetto A, Pezzolato M, Bozzetta E, Le Bizec B, et al. The Promise and Challenges of Determining Recombinant Bovine Growth Hormone in Milk. Foods. 2022; 11(3): p. 274–13.

15. FDA. Bovine Somatotropin (bST). [Internet]. 2024 [cited 2025 February 2]. Available from: fda.gov/animal-veterinary/product-safety-information/bovine-somatotropin-bst

16. World Health Organization & Food and Agriculture Organization of the United Nations. Evaluation of certain veterinary drug residues in food. ; 2014.

17. Steinfeld H, Gerber P, Wassenaar T, Castel V, Rosales M, de Haan C. Livestock's long shadow (PDF) (Report). FAO. ; 2006.

18. ICT Leather. Statistics & Sources of Information. [Internet]. 2025 [cited 2025 January 30]. Available from: leather-council.org/information/statistics-sources-of-information/

19. World Health Organization. Obesity and overweight. (n.d.). Retrieved2, 2025, from https://www. [Internet]. 2024 [cited 2025 February 2]. Available from: who.int/news-room/fact-sheets/detail/obesity-and-overweight

20. Otterbach S, Oskorouchi HR, Rogan M, Qaim M. (2021). Using Google data to measure the role of Big Food and fast food in South Africa's obesity epidemic. World Development. 2021; 140: p. 105368.

21. Silva Junior CHL, Pessôa ACM, Carvalho NS, Reis JBC, Anderson LO, Aragão LEOC. The Brazilian Amazon deforestation rate in 2020 is the greatest of the decade. Nature Ecology and Evolution. 2021; 5(2): p. 144–145.

22. Mcdonald's. What countries does McDonald's operate in?. [Internet]. 2018 [cited 2025 February 3]. Available from: mcdonalds.com/gb/en-gb/help/faq/what-countries-does-mcdonald-s-operate-in.html

23. Meat & Livestock Australia. McDonald's visits Australian beef businesses with a focus on sustainability. [Internet]. Available from: mla.com.au/news-and-events/industry-news/mcdonalds-visits-australian-beef-businesses-with-a-focus-on-sustainability/

24. Folbre N. The 300 Billionth Burger, Economix Blog. [Internet]. [cited 2025 January 30]. Available from: archive.nytimes.com/economix.blogs.nytimes.com/2013/07/22/the-300-billionth-burger/

25. Ziegler H. Chicken sustains fast-food chains as cost of beef rises. [Internet]. 2024 [cited 2025 January 30]. Available from: washingtonpost.com/business/2024/12/05/chicken-fast-food/

26. Ruback B, Neil C. The 18 Best Burger Chains In America. [Internet]. 2024. Available from: https://www.eatthis.com/best-burger-chains-in-america/?utm_

27. Lowe M, Gereffi G, Ayee G, Denniston R, Fernandez-Stark K, Kim J, et al. A Value Chain Analysis of the U.S. Beef and Dairy Industries Report. ; 2009.

28. Hu H, Mu T, Ma Y, Wang XP, Ma Y. Analysis of Longevity Traits in Holstein Cattle: A Review. Frontiers in Genetics. 2021; 12: p. 695543–695543.

29. Moreira LC, Rosa GJM, Schaefer DM. Beef production from cull dairy cows: a review from culling to consumption. Journal of Animal Science. 2021; 99(7).

30. Prayson B, McMahon JT, Prayson RA. Fast food hamburgers. what are we really eating. Annals of Diagnostic Pathology. 2008; 12(6): p. 406–409.

31. Moraïs S, Winkler S, Zorea A, Levin L, Nagies FSP, Kapust N, et al. Cryptic diversity of cellulose-degrading gut bacteria in industrialize industrialized humans. Science (American Association for the Advancement of Science). 2024; 383(6688): p. eadj9223–eadj9223.

32. Jazbec M, Salim H, Khara T, Cordell DaWS. Shifting the Menu: Reducing the carbon footprint of fast-food consumption by switching to plant-based options. Report prepared by the Institute for Sustainable Futures. ; 2022.

33. Miller M. How Some Veggie Burgers Have Stood the Test of Time at Fast Food Restaurants. [Internet]. 2025. Available from: https://www.foodandwine.com/do-fast-food-customers-want-veggie-burgers-8702072

34. Zilber A. Not lovin' it McDonald's McPlant burger failed, customers shunned non-meat option. [Internet]. 2024 [cited 2025 February 3]. Available from: nypost.com/2024/06/27/business/mcdonalds-says-mcplant-burger-failed-customers-shunned-non-meat-option/

35. Ronto R, Alves Lopes CV, Bogueva D, Davis B, Bhatti AJ, Navarrete P, et al. Exploring Australian News Media Portrayals of Sustainable and Plant-Based Diets. Nutrients. 2024; 16(7): p. 996.

36. Kirsch M, Morales-Dalmau J, & Lavrentieva A. Cultivated meat manufacturing: Technology, trends, and challenges. Engineering in Life Sciences. 2023; 23(12): p. e2300227-n/a.

37. Stephens N, Sexton AE, Driessen C. Making Sense of Making Meat: Key Moments in the First 20 Years of Tissue Engineering Muscle to Make Food. Frontiers in Sustainable Food Systems. 2019; 3: p. 45–45.

38. Haiwang Y. Becoming a dragon: Forty Chinese proverbs for lifelong learning and classroom study: Berkshire Publishing Group; 2018.

39. Grandin T, Johnson C. Animals in Translation: Using the Mysteries of Autism to Decode Animal Behaviour: Harcourt; 2006.

40. Chandler DL. Temple Grandin: Look at what people can do, not what they can't. [Internet]. 2015 [cited 2025 February 10]. Available from: news.mit.edu/2015/temple-grandin-talk-0318

41. Moran J, Doyle R. Cow talk: understanding dairy cow behaviour to improve their welfare on asian farms: CSIRO Publishing; 2015.

42. Rollin BE, Klingborg DJ, Engle T. The Welfare of Cattle: CRC Press; 2018.

43. Grandin T. Livestock handling and transport (T. Grandin, Ed.; 5th edition.): CABI; 2019.

44. Chamber of Agriculture Lower Saxony. Cow glasses of the Chamber of Agriculture wins digitisation prize of the state of Lower Saxony. [Internet]. N.D. [cited 2025 February 5]. Available from: https://www.lwk-niedersachsen.de/lwk/news/36183_Kuhbrille_der_Landwirtschaftskammer_gewinnt_Digitalisierungspreis_des_Landes_Niedersachsen

45. Heffner RS, & Heffner HE. (1983). Hearing in large mammals: Horses (Equus caballus) and cattle (^IBos taurus^R). Behavioral Neuroscience. 1983; 97(2): p. 299–309.

46. Mota-Rojas D, Whittaker AL, Domínguez-Oliva A, Strappini AC, Álvarez-Macías A, Mora-Medina P, et al. Tactile, Auditory, and Visual Stimulation as Sensory Enrichment for Dairy Cattle. Animals. 2024; 14: p. 1265.

47. Green A, Clark C, Favaro L, Lomax S, Reby D. Vocal individuality of Holstein-Friesian cattle is maintained across putatively positive and negative farming contexts. Scientific Reports. 2019; 9(1): p. 18468–18469.

48. Grandin T, Deesing M . Genetics and the behavior of domestic animals (2nd ed.): Elsevier/AP; 2014.

49. Yousefi-Nooraie R, Mortaz-Hedjri S. Dermatoglyphic asymmetry and hair whorl patterns in schizophrenic and bipolar patients. Psychiatry Research. 2008; 157(1): p. 247–250.

50. Wegrzyn D, Juckel G, Faissner A. Structural and Functional Deviations of the Hippocampus in Schizophrenia and Schizophrenia Animal Models. International Journal of Molecular Sciences. 2022; 23(10): p. 5482.

51. Białoń M, Wąsik A. Advantages and Limitations of Animal Schizophrenia Models. International Journal of Molecular Sciences. 2022; 23(11): p. 5968.

52. Broucek J, Kisac P, Mihina S, Hanus A, Uhrincat M, Tancin V. Hair whorls of Holstein Friesian heifers and affects on growth and behaviour. Archiv Für Tierzucht. 2007; 50(4): p. 374–380.

53. Comstock G, Fenton A, Shriver A, Johnson LSM. Bovine Prospection, the Mesocorticolimbic Pathways, and Neuroethics: Is a Cow's Future Like Ours? In Advances in neuroethics.: Springer International Publishing; 2020. p. 73–97.

54. De Waal FBM. Putting the altruism back into altruism: The evolution of empathy. Annual Review of Psychology. 2008; 59(1): p. 279–300.

55. Boissy A, Terlouw C, Le Neindre P. Presence of Cues from Stressed Conspecifics Increases Reactivity to Aversive Events in Cattle: Evidence for the Existence of Alarm Substances in Urine. Physiology & Behavior. 1998; 63(4): p. 489–495.

56. Marino L, Allen K. The Psychology of Cows. Animal Behavior and Cognition. 2017; 4(4): p. 474–498.

57. Creamer M, Horback K. Consistent individual differences in cattle grazing patterns. Applied Animal Behaviour Science. 2024; 271: p. 106176.

58. Lecorps B, Weary DM, von Keyserlingk MAG. Pessimism and fearfulness in dairy calves. Scientific Reports. 2018; 8(1): p. 1421–1429.

59. Hirata M, Tomita C, Yamada K. Use of a maze test to assess spatial learning and memory in cattle: Can cattle traverse a complex maze? Applied Animal Behaviour Science. 2016; 180: p. 18–25.

60. Katz J. The World's Smartest Cow. [Internet]. 2006 [cited 2025 February 15]. Available from: https://slate.com/news-and-politics/2006/04/elvis-the-world-s-smartest-cow.html

61. de Freslon I, Peralta JM, Strappini AC, Monti G. Understanding Allogrooming Through a Dynamic Social Network Approach: An Example in a Group of Dairy Cows. Frontiers in Veterinary Science. 2020; 7: p. 535–535.

62. Compitus K, Bierbower SM. Cow cuddling: Cognitive considerations in bovine-assisted therapy. Human-Animal Interactions. 2024.

63. Sapolsky R. Behavioral Evolution. [Internet]. 2010 [cited 2025 February 15]. Available from: https://www.youtube.com/watch?v=Y0Oa4Lp5fLE

64. Ksiksi T, Laca EA. Cattle Do Remember Locations of Preferred Food over Extended Periods. Asian-australasian journal of animal sciences. 2002; 15(6): p. 900–904.

65. Gabrieli R, Malkinson D. Grazing beef cattle vegetation preferences and their effects on fitness. Agriculture, Ecosystems & Environment. 2025; 388: p. Article 109650.

66. Coulon M, Deputte BL, Heyman Y, Delatouche L, Richard C, Baudoin C. Visual Discrimination by Heifers (Bos taurus) of Their Own Species. Journal of Comparative Psychology (1983). 2007; 121(2): p. 198–204.

67. Rybarczyk P, Koba Y, Rushen J, Tanida H, de Passillé AM. Can cows discriminate people by their faces? Applied Animal Behaviour Science. 2011; 74(3): p. 175–189.

Pigs

1. Orwell G. Animal farm London: Secker and Warburg; 1945.

2. Fontana D, Firmin H. The secret language of symbols: a visual key to symbols and their meanings: Universal International; 1997.

3. Our World in Data. Live pigs. [Internet]. 2025. Available from: https://ourworldindata.org/explorers/animal-welfare?Metric=Live+animals&Animal=Pigs&Per+capita=false

4. Gonyou HW, Keeling LJ. Social behavior in farm animals (1st ed.): CABI Pub; 2001.

5. Campbell JM, Crenshaw JD, Polo J. The biological stress of early weaned piglets. Journal of Animal Science and Biotechnology. 2013; 4(2): p. Article 19.

6. Weary DM, Appleby MC, Fraser D. Responses of piglets to early separation from the sow. Applied Animal Behaviour Science. 1999; 63(4): p. 289–300.

7. Nelson EE, Panksepp J. Brain Substrates of Infant–Mother Attachment: Contributions of Opioids, Oxytocin, and Norepinephrine. Neuroscience and Biobehavioral Reviews. 1998; 22(3): p. 437–452.

8. Grandin T, Johnson C. Making Animals Happy London: Bloomsbury; 2010.

9. Lander B, Schneider M, Brunson K. A History of Pigs in China: From Curious Omnivores to Industrial Pork. The Journal of Asian Studies. 2020; 79(4): p. 865–889.

10. Our World in Data. Land animals slaughtered for meat, China, 1961 to 2023. [Internet]. 2025. Available from: https://ourworldindata.org/grapher/land-animals-slaughtered-for-meat?country=~CHN

11. Yang Y. High on the hog: skyscraping hi-tech China swine farm produces 1.2 million pigs a year. [Internet]. 2024. Available from: https://www.scmp.com/news/people-culture/article/3268839/high-hog-skyscraping-hi-tech-china-swine-farm-produces-12-million-pigs-year

12. Davison N. Rivers of blood: the dead pigs rotting in China's water supply. [Internet]. 2013. Available from: https://www.theguardian.com/world/2013/mar/29/dead-pigs-china-water-supply

13. Verlini G. In the People's Republic of China, Manure is Being Turned into Money. [Internet]. 2016. Available from: https://www.adb.org/results/people-s-republic-china-manure-being-turned-money

14. Sorvino C. Raw Deal Hidden Corruption, Corporate Greed, and the Fight for the Future of Meat: Atria Books; 2022.

15. Simon DR. Meatonomics: how the rigged economics of meat and dairy make you consume too much-and how to eat better, live longer, and spend smarter San Francisco: Conari Press; 2013.

16. United States Environmental Protection Agency. National Water Quality Inventory Report to Congress. [Internet]. 2024. Available from: https://www.epa.gov/waterdata/national-water-quality-inventory-report-congress

17. Prothero DR, Domning D, Fordyce RE, Foss S, Janis C, Lucas S, et al. On the unnecessary and misleading taxon "Cetartiodactyla.". Journal of Mammalian Evolution. 2022; 29(1): p. 93–97.

18. Gingerich PD. Evolution of whales from land to sea. Proceedings of the American Philosophical Society. 2012; 156(3): p. 309–323.

19. Thewissen JGM, Cooper LN, Clementz MT, Bajpai S, Tiwari BN. Whales originated from aquatic artiodactyls in the Eocene epoch of India. Nature. 2007; 450(7173): p. 1190–1194.

20. Frantz L, Meijaard E, Gongora J, Haile J, Groenen MAM, Larson G, et al. The Evolution of Suidae. Annual Review of Animal Biosciences. 2016; 4(1): p. 61–85.

21. Price M, Hongo H. The archaeology of pig domestication in Eurasia. Journal of Archaeological Research. 2020; 28(4): p. 557–615.

22. Elstein D. Chinese pigs provide insight to U.S. swine reproduction. In Agricultural research (Washington). Agricultural Research. 2002 November: p. 17.

23. Megens HJ, de Visser M, Liu L, Bosse M. Pygmy Hogs. Current Biology. 2021; 31,8: p. R366 - R368.

24. Liu L, Bosse M, Megens H, de Visser M, Groenen M, Madsen O. Genetic consequences of long-term small effective population size in the critically endangered pygmy hog. Evolutionary Applications. 2021; 14(3): p. 710–720.

25. Ke A, Luskin MS. Integrating disparate occurrence reports to map data-poor species ranges and occupancy: a case study of the Vulnerable bearded pig Sus barbatus. Oryx. 2019; 53(2): p. N.P.

26. Lucchini V, Meijaard E, Diong CH, Groves CP, Randi E. New phylogenetic perspectives among species of South-east Asian wild pig (Sus sp.) based on mtDNA sequences and morphometric data. Journal of Zoology (1987). 2005; 266(1): p. 25–35.

27. Blouch RA. Ecology and conservation of the Javan warty pig Sus verrucosus Müller, 1840. Biological Conservation. 1988; 43(4): p. 295–307.

28. Kingdon J. The Kingdon field guide to African mammals (Second edition.): Bloomsbury Academic; 2015.

29. White AM, Cameron EZ. Evidence of helping behaviour in a free-ranging population of communally breeding warthogs. Journal of Ethology. 2011; 29(3): p. 419–425.

30. Berriat-Saint-Prix J. Rapport et recherches sur les procès et jugemens relatifs aux animaux: L'Imprimerie de Selligue; 1829.

31. Gins S. Casting justice before swine: late mediaeval pig trials as instances of human exceptionalism. Sophia. 2023; 62(4): p. 631–663.

32. Evans PE. THE CRIMINAL PROSECUTION London: William Heinemann; 1906.

33. Carver MOH, SA, Semple S, Pluskowski A. Animal Magic. In Signals of belief in early England: Anglo-Saxon paganism revisited.: Oxbow Books; 2010. p. 103-122.

34. Pluskowski A. The zooarchaeology of medieval "Christendom": ideology, the treatment of animals and the making of medieval Europe. World Archaeology. 2010; 42(2).

35. Spencer DC, Fitzgerald A. Criminology and animality: stupidity and the anthropological machine. Contemporary Justice Review: CJR. 2015; 18(4): p. 407–420.

36. Taylor L. Colombia's 'cocaine hippo' population is even bigger than scientists thought. Nature (London). 2023; 618(7965): p. 444–445.

37. Taronga Conservation Society Australia. Australian Shark Incident Database. [Internet]. 2025. Available from: https://taronga.org.au/conservation-and-science/australian-shark-incident-database

38. Mayer JJ, Garabedian JE, Kilgo JC. Human fatalities resulting from wild pig attacks worldwide – 2000-2019. Human-Wildlife Interactions. 2024; 17(1).

39. Grandin T, Johnson C. How animals think. In Grandin T, and Johnson C. Animals in Translation. Using the Mysteries of Autism to Decode Animal Behaviour.: Harcourt; 2006. p. 248-249.

40. ABC News. Canadian serial killer Robert Pickton dies after prison assault aged 74. [Internet]. 2024. Available from: https://www.abc.net.au/news/2024-06-01/robert-pickton-dies-in-prison-from-assault-canada/103923016

41. BBC News. Oregon farmer eaten by his pigs. (2012,).. [Internet]. 2012. Available from: https://www.bbc.com/news/world-us-canada-19796224

42. Paras J. Dismayed buyers surrendering 'teacup' pigs weighing up to 300kg. [Internet]. 2025. Available from: https://www.abc.net.au/news/2025-06-14/teacup-mini-pigs-buyers-shocked-when-fully-grown/105224426

43. Tompkins S. Warthogs invade South Texas. [Internet]. 2015. Available from: https://www.chron.com/sports/outdoors/article/Warthogs-invade-South-Texas-6671689.php

44. Kupferman CA, Snow NP, Vercauteren KC, Melton MH, Gann WJ, Beasley JC. Seasonal changes in occupancy and activity patterns in native Collared Peccary and non-native wild pig and Common Warthog in southern Texas, the United States. Journal of Mammalogy. 2025.

45. Holley P. His Best Friend Was a 250-Pound Warthog. One Day It Decided to Kill Him. [Internet]. 2024. Available from: https://www.texasmonthly.com/news-politics/warthog-attack-texas-exotics/

46. Brunjes PC, Feldman S, Osterberg SK. The pig olfactory brain: a primer. Chemical Senses. 2016; 41(5): p. 415–425.

47. Olender T, LD, Nebert DW. Update on the olfactory receptor (OR) gene superfamily. Human Genomics. 2008; 3: p. 87.

48. Allen K, Bennett JW. Tour of truffles: aromas, aphrodisiacs, adaptogens, and more. Mycobiology. 2021; 49(3): p. 201–212.

49. ABC News. Australia's largest truffle, worth $2,000 a kilo, grown in NSW town of Robertson. [Internet]. 2014. Available from: https://www.abc.net.au/news/2014-06-30/largest-truffle-ever-grown-in-australia-french-black-perigold/5559260

50. Claus R, Hoppen HO, Karg H. secret of truffles: a steroidal pheromone? Experientia. 1981; 37(11): p. 1178–1179.

51. Zonderland JJ, Cornelissen L, Wolthuis-Fillerup M, Spoolder HAM. Visual acuity of pigs at different light intensities. Applied Animal Behaviour Science. 2008; 111(1): p. 28–37.

52. Neitz J, Jacobs GH. Spectral sensitivity of cones in an ungulate. Visual Neuroscience. 1989; 2(2): p. 97–100.

53. Donohue MW, Cohen JH, Cronin TW. Cerebral photoreception in mantis shrimp. Scientific Reports. 2018; 8: p. 9689.

54. Heffner RS, Heffner HE. Hearing in domestic pigs (Sus scrofa) and goats (Capra hircus). Hearing Research. 1990; 48(3): p. 231–240.

55. Held S, Mendl M, Devereux C, Byrne R. Behaviour of domestic pigs in a visual perspective taking task. Behaviour. 2001; 138: p. 11-12.

56. Mendl M, Held S, Byrne RW. Pig cognition. Current Biology. 2010; 20(18): p. R796–R798.

57. Schaffer A, Widdig A, Holland R, Amici F. Evidence of object permanence, short-term spatial memory, causality, understanding of object properties and gravity across five different ungulate species. Scientific Reports. 2024; 14: p. 13718.

58. Quail MR, Fraser MD. (2024). Pulling the wool over their eyes? Object permanence, numerical competence and categorisation in alternative livestock species. Applied Animal Behaviour Science. 2024; 270: p. Article 106131.

59. Broom DM, Sena H, Moynihan KL. Pigs learn what a mirror image represents and use it to obtain information. Animal Behaviour. 2009; 78(5): p. 1037–104.

60. Gieling ET, Mijdam E, van der Staay FJ, Nordquist RE. Lack of mirror use by pigs to locate food. Applied Animal Behaviour Science. 2014; 154: p. 22–29.

61. Croney CC, Adams KM, Washington CG, Stricklin WR. A note on visual, olfactory and spatial cue use in foraging behavior of pigs: indirectly assessing cognitive abilities. Applied Animal Behaviour Science. 2003; 83(4): p. 303–308.

62. Bensoussan S, Tigeot R, Lemasson A, Meunier-Salaün MC, Tallet C. Domestic piglets (Sus scrofa domestica) are attentive to human voice and able to discriminate some prosodic features. Applied Animal Behaviour Science. 2019; 210: p. 38–45.

63. Pérez Fraga P, Gerencsér L, Lovas M, Újváry D, Andics A. Who turns to the human? Companion pigs' and dogs' behaviour in the unsolvable task paradigm. Animal Cognition. 2021; 24(1): p. 33–40.

64. Masilkova M, Ježek M, Silovský V, Faltusová M, Rohla J, Kušta T, et al. Observation of rescue behaviour in wild boar (Sus scrofa). Scientific Reports. 2021; 11(1): p. Article 16217.

65. Moscovice LR, Eggert A, Manteuffel C, Rault JL. Spontaneous helping in pigs is mediated by helper's social attention and distress signals of individuals in need. Proceedings of the Royal Society B. 2023; 290: p. 20230665.

66. Luna D, Calderón-Amor J, González C, Byrd CJ, Palomo R, Huenul E, et al. The protective effect of social support: Can humans reassure pigs during stressful challenges through social learning? Applied Animal Behaviour Science. 2024; 273: p. Article 106221.

67. Arts JWM, van der Staay FJ, Ekkel ED. Working and reference memory of pigs in the spatial holeboard discrimination task. Behavioural Brain Research. 2009; 205(1): p. 303–306.

68. Elizabeth Bolhuis J, Oostindjer M, Hoeks CWF, de Haas EN, Bartels AC, Ooms M, et al. Working and reference memory of pigs (Sus scrofa domesticus) in a holeboard spatial discrimination task. Animal Cognition. 2013; 16(5): p. 845–850.

69. Goursot C, Düpjan S, Kanitz E, Tuchscherer A, Puppe B, Leliveld LMC. Assessing animal individuality: links between personality and laterality in pigs. Current Zoology. 2019; 65(5): p. 541–551.

70. Horback KM, Parsons. TD. Ontogeny of behavioral traits in commercial sows. Animal (Cambridge, England). 2018; 12(11): p. 2365–2372.

What Does it all Mean?

1. Fleagle JG. Primate adaptation and evolution (2nd ed.): Academic Press; 1999.

2. Berger LR (. Brief communication: Predatory bird damage to the Taung type-skull of Australopithecus africanus Dart 1925. American Journal of Physical Anthropology; 131(2): p. 166–168.

3. Mann NJ. A brief history of meat in the human diet and current health implications. Meat Science. 2018; 144: p. 169–179.

4. Wrangham RW. Catching Fire: How Cooking Made Us Human: Basic Books; 2009.

5. Dunbar RIM. The social brain hypothesis and its implications for social evolution. Annals of Human Biology. 2009; 36(5): p. Article 912879712.

6. Burini RC, Leonard WR. The evolutionary roles of nutrition selection and dietary quality in the human brain size and encephalization. Nutrire : Revista de Sociedade Brasileira de Alimentação e Nutrição = Journal of the Brazilian Society of Food and Nutrition. 2018; 43(1): p. 19.

7. Herculano-Houzel S. The human brain in numbers: a linearly scaled-up primate brain. Frontiers in Human Neuroscience. 2009; 3: p. Article 31.

8. Stibel JM. Decreases in brain size and encephalization in anatomically modern humans. Brain, Behavior and Evolution. 2021; 96(2): p. 64–77.

9. Suddendorf T. The Gap, What Separates us from other Animals: Basic Books; 2013.

10. Panksepp J. Affective neuroscience: the foundations of human and animal emotions (1st ed.).: Oxford University Press; 1998.

11. Daeschler EB, Shubin NH, Jenkins FA. A Devonian tetrapod-like fish and the evolution of the tetrapod body plan. Nature. 2006; 440(7085): p. 757–763.

12. Shubin N. Your Inner Fish London: Penguin Books; 2009.

13. Kelly AL, Baugh ME, Oster ME, DiFeliceantonio AG. The impact of caloric availability on eating behavior and ultra-processed food reward. Appetite. 2022; 178: p. Article 106274.

14. Gearhardt AN, Schulte EM, Balling R, Stover P. Is Food Addictive? A Review of the Science. Annual Review of Nutrition. 2021; 41(1): p. 387–410.

15. Our World in Data. Meat Production. [Internet]. 2023. Available from: https://ourworldindata.org/meat-production

16. Avieli N. Dog meat politics in a Vietnamese town. Ethnology. 2011; 50(1): p. 59–78.

17. Mitchell T. Religion and food. [Internet]. 2021. Available from: https://www.pewresearch.org/religion/2021/06/29/religion-and-food/#

18. Ball C. Migration Museum, 'Beef Riot', SA History Hub. [Internet]. 2025. Available from: https://sahistoryhub.history.sa.gov.au/events/beef-riot/

19. Roy Morgan. Rise in vegetarianism not halting the march of obesity. [Internet]. 2019. Available from: https://www.roymorgan.com/findings/rise-in-vegetarianism-not-halting-the-march-of-obesity

20. Manktelow KI. Thinking and reasoning: an introduction to the psychology of reason, judgment and decision making (1st ed.): Psychology Press; 2012.

21. Caviola L, Schubert S, Kahane G, Faber NS. Humans first: Why people value animals less than humans. Cognition. 2022; 225: p. Article 105139.

22. Greer A. Speciesism – the Ism that Isn't. Australian Quarterly (Balmain, N.S.W.). 2015; 86(4): p. 29–33.

23. Miralles A, Raymond M, Lecointre G. Empathy and compassion toward other species decrease with evolutionary divergence time. Scientific Reports. 2019; 9(1): p. Article 19555.

24. Estren MJ. The Neoteny Barrier: Seeking Respect for the Non-Cute. Journal of Animal Ethics. 2012; 2(1): p. 6–11.

25. Festinger L. A theory of cognitive dissonance. Evanston, IL: Row Peterson.; 1957.

26. Loughnan S, Haslam N, Bastian B. The role of meat consumption in the denial of moral status and mind to meat animals. Appetite. 2010; 55(1): p. 156–159.

27. Bastian B, Loughnan S. Resolving the Meat-Paradox: A Motivational Account of Morally Troublesome Behavior and Its Maintenance. Personality and Social Psychology Review. 2017; 21(3): p. 278–299.

28. Rothgerber H, Rosenfeld DL. Meat-related cognitive dissonance: The social psy-chology of eating animals. Social and Personality Psychology Compass. 2021; 15(5): p. Article e12592.

29. Bem DJ. Self-perception: an alternative interpretation of cognitive dissonance phenomena. Psychological Review. 1967; 74(3): p. 183–200.

The True Cost of Meat

1. Our World in Data. Data Insights. [Internet]. 2024. Available from: https://ourworldindata.org/data-insights/every-second-10-cows-47-pigs-and-2400-chickens-are-slaughtered-for-meat

2. Singer P. Animal Liberation Now: Vintage; 2024.

3. Our World in Data. Our World in Data. [Internet]. 2024. Available from: ourworldindata.org/grapher/daily-meat-consumption-per-person

4. Klok MD, Jakobsdottir S, Drent ML. The role of leptin and ghrelin in the regulation of food intake and body weight in humans: a review. Obesity Reviews. 2007; 8(1): p. 21–34.

5. Simon DR. Meatonomics: how the rigged economics of meat and dairy make you consume too much-and how to eat better, live longer, and spend smarter San Francisco: Conari Press; 2013.

6. Dairy Checkoff. Dairy Checkoff Annual Report Offers 2023 Highlights, Financials. [Internet]. 2024. Available from: https://www.dairycheckoff.com/DairyCheckoff/files/1c/1c3abdf5-4b5b-48a8-b81b-a761393693ae.pdf

7. U.S. Department of Agriculture. Industry Insight: Checkoff Programs Empower Business. [Internet]. 2011 [cited 2025 July 17]. Available from: https://www.usda.gov/about-usda/news/blog/industry-insight-checkoff-programs-empower-business

8. Meat and Livestock Australia. How we are funded. [Internet]. [cited 2025 July 17]. Available from: https://www.mla.com.au/about-mla/how-we-are-funded/

9. Beef Australia. Beef2027 Rockhampton. [Internet]. [cited 2025 July 20]. Available from: https://beefaustralia.com.au/

10. Department of Agriculture Fisheries and Forestry. Joint media release: Labor to help deliver a bigger and better Beef2027. [Internet]. 2025. Available from: https://minister.agriculture.gov.au/chisholm/media-releases/beef2027

11. Meat Institute. Sales at record high, Americans view meat as part of a healthy, balanced lifestyle Power of Meat analysis marks 20th anniversary at Annual Meat Conference. [Internet]. 2025 [cited 2025 July 19]. Available from: https://meatinstitute.org/press/sales-record-high-americans-view-meat-part-healthy-balanced-lifestyle-power-meat-analysis

12. Australian Bureau of Statistics. Apparent Consumption of Selected Foodstuffs, Australia. [Internet]. 2025. Available from: https://www.abs.gov.au/statistics/health/health-conditions-and-risks/apparent-consumption-selected-foodstuffs-australia/2023-24

13. Our World in Data. Meat Production. [Internet]. 2023. Available from: https://ourworldindata.org/meat-production

14. McAfee AJ, McSorley EM, Cuskelly GJ, Moss BW, Wallace JMW, Bonham MP, et al. red meat consumption: An overview of the risks and benefits. Meat Science. 2010; 84(1): p. 1–13.

15. International Agency for Research on Cancer. IARC Monographs evaluate consumption of red meat and processed meat. Lyon; 2015.

16. Our World in Data. Prevalence rate of obesity in adults. [Internet]. 2025. Available from: https://ourworldindata.org/grapher/obesity-prevalence-adults-who-gho?time=latest&mapSelect=~VEN

17. Bartlett H, Zanella M, Kaori B, Sabei L, Araujo MS, de Paula TM, et al. Trade-offs in the externalities of pig production are not inevitable. Nature Food. 2024; 5(4): p. 312–322.

18. Scarborough P, Clark M, Cobiac Lea. Vegans, vegetarians, fish-eaters and meat-eaters in the UK show discrepant environmental impacts. Nature Food. 2023; 4: p. 565–574.

19. Ritchie H(-. What are the trade-offs between animal welfare and the environmental impact of meat. [Internet]. 2024. Available from: https://ourworldindata.org/what-are-the-trade-offs-betweenanimal-welfare-and-the-environmental-impact-of-meat

20. Garnett T, Godde C, Muller A, Röös E, Smith P, de Boer IJM, et al. Grazed and Confused? Ruminating on cattle, grazing systems, methane, nitrous oxide, the soil carbon sequestration question – and what it all means for greenhouse gas emissions. ; 2017.

21. Derbyshire EJ. Flexitarian Diets and Health: A Review of the Evidence-Based Literature. Frontiers in Nutrition (Lausanne). 2017; 3: p. Article 55.

22. Mathieu E, Ritchie R. What share of people say they are vegetarian, vegan, or flexitarian? [Internet]. 2022. Available from: https://ourworldindata.org/vegetarian-vegan'

23. Grandin T, Johnson C. Animals in Translation: Harcourt; 2006.

24. Duncan I. Welfare Problems of Poultry. In The Well-Being of Farm Animals.: Wiley; 2008. p. 314-315.

25. Millman ST, Duncan IJH. Strain differences in aggressiveness of male domestic fowl in response to a male model. Applied Animal Behaviour Science. 2000; 66(3): p. 217–233.

26. Kidd B, Mackay S, Vandevijvere S, Swinburn B. Cost and greenhouse gas emissions of current, healthy, flexitarian and vegan diets in Aotearoa (New Zealand). BMJ Nutrition, Prevention & Health. 2021; 4(1): p. 275–284.

27. Herzon I. What can the Dublin Declaration teach us about credible scientific advocacy? [Internet]. 2024. Available from: https://www.tabledebates.org/essays/what-can-dublin-declaration-teach-us-about-credible-scientific-advocacy

28. Declaration TD. The Dublin Declaration of Scientists on the Societal Role of Livestock. Animal Frontiers. 2023; 13(2): p. 10–10.

29. Hutchens G. Ken Henry wants Australia's media to do a better job. [Internet]. 2025. Available from: https://www.abc.net.au/news/2025-07-20/ken-henry-wants-australian-media-to-do-a-better-job/105546186?utm_source=abc_news_app&utm_medium=content_shared&utm_campaign=abc_news_app&utm_content=other

30. Quinn.R. Kind Animal Behaviour Services. [Internet]. 2025. Available from: https://www.kindanimalbehaviourservices.com/

31. Mason GJ, Latham NR. Can't stop, won't stop is stereotypy a reliable animal welfare indicator? Animal Welfare. 2004; 13(1): p. S57–S69.

32. Hampton JO, Hemsworth LM, Hemsworth PH, Hyndman TH, Sandøe P. Re-thinking the utility of the Five Domains model. Animal Welfare. 2023; 32: p. e62.

33. Mellor DJ, Beausoleil NJ, Littlewood KE, McLean AN, McGreevy PD, Jones B, et al. The 2020 Five Domains Model: Including Human–Animal Interactions in Assessments of Animal Welfare. Animals. 2020; 10(10): p. 1870.

34. Project 1882. Sweden becomes cage-free. [Internet]. 2025. Available from: https://www.project1882.org/news/sweden-becomes-cage-free

35. Open Wing Alliance. 2024 Cage-Free Fulfillment Report. [Internet]. 2024. Available from: https://openwingalliance.org/2024-cage-free-fulfillment-report

36. McNaughton j, Long W, Aldridge A. Victorian Farmers Federation calls for pause to caged egg phase-out plan. [Internet]. 2025. Available from: https://www.abc.net.au/news/rural/2025-02-13/caged-egg-farmers-please-pause-phase-out/104931692

37. Windsor M. The Tipping Point: 45.7% of US Hens Are Now Free from Cages. [Internet]. 2025. Available from: https://thehumaneleague.org/article/45-percent-cage-free-in-the-us

38. RSPCA UK. Life of a typical meat chicken. [Internet]. 2020. Available from: https://www.rspca.org.uk/webContent/staticImages/BroilerCampaign/EatSitSufferRepeat.pdf

39. Humane League. UK Court Delivers Groundbreaking Verdict for Farmed Animals. [Internet]. 2025. Available from: https://thehumaneleague.org/article/uk-court-frankenchickens-verdict

40. Hansard. HC Deb vol 768 Animal welfare in farming col 67WH (2025, June 3) [Electronic version]. [Internet]. Available from: https://hansard.parliament.uk/commons/2025-06-03/debates/DC78274F-F44F-40E1-938C-2B64CA6E1FF7/AnimalWelfareInFarming

41. Burton L, Barker E, Prendergast J, Collins A. What would Australia look like without live exports? [Internet]. 2018. Available from: https://www.abc.net.au/news/rural/2018-09-19/impact-on-australia-without-live-export/10254566

42. Ferguson S, Doyle M. VIDEO: A Bloody Business. [Internet]. 2011. Available from: https://www.abc.net.au/news/2011-05-31/4c-full-program-bloody-business/8961434

43. RSPCA Australia. The dark history of Australian live sheep exports to Saudi Arabia. [Internet]. 2024. Available from: https://www.rspca.org.au/latest-news/blog/the-dark-history-of-australian-live-sheep-exports-to-saudi-arabia/

44. Darwin CR. The Descent of Man, and Selection in Relation to Sex. Volume 1. 1st edition London: John Murray; 1871.

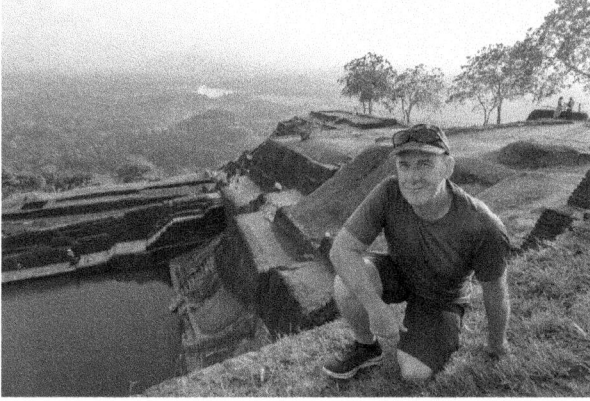

About the Author

Shane Gehlert is an artist, photographer, and filmmaker who found his passion for academia later in life by pursuing a degree in psychology. His love for travel and a deep fascination with animals has taken him all over the world, where he enjoys observing and photographing the incredible creatures with which we share this planet. Shane lives in Queensland, Australia, with his wife, Cristine, and a menagerie of rather spoilt animals.